Preventing Family Violence

Preventing Family Violence

A Multidisciplinary Approach

Edited by
Ko-Ling Chan

香港大學出版社
HONG KONG UNIVERSITY PRESS

Hong Kong University Press
14/F Hing Wai Centre
7 Tin Wan Praya Road
Aberdeen
Hong Kong
www.hkupress.org

ISBN 978-988-8083-78-7

British Library Cataloguing-in-Publication Data
A catalogue record for this book is available from the British Library.

10   9   8   7   6   5   4   3   2   1

Printed and bound by Caritas Printing Training Centre, Hong Kong, China

Contents

Preface

Family violence, including intimate partner violence, elder abuse and child maltreatment, is a serious social problem that has been gaining public concern both in Chinese societies and around the globe over the past few decades. It is such a serious and complicated problem that any single discipline can only portray a small piece of the big picture. Family violence not only influences one's physical and mental health, but it also has profound effects on one's social functioning, welfare, and legal status. Fragmented approaches to the formulation of preventive strategies may only touch on the surface of individual disciplines, and therefore hamper their overall effectiveness. Integrated approaches that involve multiple disciplines appear to be more effective in tackling the problem, although they are sadly lacking to date.

In regard to the lack of comprehensive and integrated approaches to preventing family violence, we, a longstanding team involving experts in law, public health, obstetrics, nursing, paediatrics, emergency medicine, social work, psychology and sociology, have been working together in combating family violence through developing research- and evidence-based intervention for almost a decade. In May 2009, our team organized a symposium in Hong Kong on "Multidisciplinary Approach to the Prevention of Domestic Violence: Social, Legal and Health Perspectives", which brought together social, legal and health professionals to review current research and to promote multidisciplinary collaboration in the prevention of family violence. Speakers at the symposium were experts in health, law, social sciences, policy analysis, and women's and children's advocacy.

This book stems from the synergistic effort in the symposium. Almost all the speakers, as well as some professionals who newly joined in the undertaking, contributed to its chapters. We had the vision of documenting our collaborative effort in this book, with the aim of developing a multidisciplinary approach for the prevention of family violence with an illustrative application in Hong Kong. We shared the vision that one day, professionals from different disciplines will be breaking boundaries and working alongside each other in promoting stable families and a safe society.

The book is now a reality. I am deeply appreciative of the contributions from all my team partners. With the insights of Patrick Ip, CB Chow, Elsie Yan and Daniel Fong, we first address the research findings on intimate partner violence, child abuse and elder mistreatment, as well as the methodological issues of research on family violence. Dennis Ho and Anne Cheung guide us through the recent legal reform in Hong Kong to examine whether the best interests of a child can be served through legal proceedings. Tiwari, Kam, Lau and So address the practical issues in health settings related to the handling of family violence cases. Throughout, we identify effective measures in the screening and treatment of victims in busy clinical settings. WC Leung is in a prime position to review how we came to work together as a team and, more importantly, how we found great satisfaction and support through collaboration. From a more macro perspective, Anna Choi and Margaret Wong examine the multidisciplinary collaboration in social and health services. Services need to be guided by good policy. They will fall short of their optimal effect unless approached with the right perspective. CB Chow and Patrick Ip provide an excellent discussion on the importance of adopting a child's rights perspective in the making of child policy.

This is not a project that could be accomplished by one person's effort alone. It is indeed my great honour to be working alongside all these team partners in the last decade. This book documents the hard work that has gone towards promoting and securing the well-being of families at risk, as well as the synergy of our team. My deepest thanks to all the contributors for their passion and support!

Last but not the least, my heartfelt appreciation to my wife Janice and my kids, Sammie and Dominic, who are the cornerstones of our happy family. They are my angels who bring me endless love!

Ko Ling Chan

Contributors

Ko-Ling Chan

Dr Chan is currently an assistant professor at the Department of Social Work and Social Administration of the University of Hong Kong. He specializes in the research of family violence. He has conducted high-impact, socially relevant research on areas including intimate partner violence; narrative accounts by male batterers; pregnancy and violence; and child abuse, neglect and other forms of victimization.

Anne Shann-Yue Cheung

Dr Cheung is an associate professor at the Department of Law of the University of Hong Kong. She received her legal education at the University of Hong Kong (LL.B), the University of Toronto (JD), the University of London (LL.M) and Stanford University (JSM, JSD). She specializes in media law, internet issues on freedom of expression and privacy, sociolegal studies, the study of domestic violence and feminist legal studies.

Anna Wai-Man Choi

Anna Choi is a fieldwork supervisor and also a Ph.D. candidate at the Department of Social Work and Social Administration of the University of Hong Kong. She has over ten years of experience in family social work, specializing in the assessment and intervention of family violence. Her current research includes spousal violence, in-law conflict and child abuse.

Chun-Bong Chow, BBS, JP

Dr Chow is an Honorary Clinical Professor at the Department of Paediatrics and Adolescent Medicine of the University of Hong Kong. He serves on various boards in the community, as Chairman of the Scientific Committee on Vaccine Preventable Diseases and the Working Group on Injury Prevention, the Department of Health. He is also Chairman of the Hong Kong Committee of Children's Rights and the Hong Kong Playright Children's Play Association, as well as executive member of Against Child Abuse.

Daniel Yee-Tak Fong

Dr Fong is currently an assistant professor at the School of Nursing of the University of Hong Kong. He is a statistician by training with many years of experience in clinical trials and statistical consulting. His research interests are adolescent idiopathic scoliosis, quality-of-life research and biostatistics.

Dennis Chi-Kuen Ho

Dennis Ho has been a solicitor of Hong Kong since 1986. He is a member of the Family Law Committee of the Law Society of Hong Kong, and chairs its Subcommittee on Domestic Violence Ordinance and the Subcommittee on Enforcement of Maintenance Orders. He is also a member of the Legal Aid Committee of the Law Society of Hong Kong. He is a member of the Family Court Users Committee and the Working Group on Children in Family Proceedings of the Judiciary. He was a part-time lecturer on Principles of Family Law for the Juris Doctor Programme of the Chinese University of Hong Kong.

Patrick P. K. Ip

Dr Ip is a clinical associate professor and consultant in paediatrics at the Department of Paediatrics and Adolescent Medicine of the University of Hong Kong. Dr Ip specializes in child neurology and developmental paediatrics. He received his training in both Hong Kong and London, and has been working in the field of hospital paediatrics for more than fifteen years. He has much experience and many publications in child protection and on the care and management of disabled children and disadvantaged families. He is now coordinating the new Community Child Health Programme at the University of Hong Kong.

Chak-Wah Kam

Dr Kam is a consultant at the Accident and Emergency Department of Tuen Mun Hospital in Hong Kong.

Terry Chu-Leung Lau

Dr Lau is an associate consultant at the Accident and Emergency Department of Pok Oi Hospital in Hong Kong.

Wing-Cheong Leung

Dr Leung is currently the chief of service and consultant obstetrician at the Department of Obstetrics and Gynaecology (O & G) of Kwong Wah Hospital; honorary clinical associate professor at the Department of Obstetrics and Gynaecology of the University of Hong Kong; and the honorary secretary of the Hong Kong College of Obstetrics and Gynaecology. He became an accredited subspecialist in Maternal Fetal Medicine of the Royal College of Obstetrics and Gynaecology (UK) in 2003 and of the Hong Kong College of Obstetrics and Gynaecology in 2005.

Agnes Tiwari

Dr Tiwari is a professor at the School of Nursing of the University of Hong Kong. She is internationally recognized for her work on interpersonal violence prevention and intervention, including the validation of the Chinese Abuse Assessment Screen and several clinical trials of violence prevention models at primary, secondary and tertiary levels.

Fung-Ling So

Fung-Ling So is a trauma nurse coordinator on the Cluster Trauma Advisory Committee for the New Territories West Cluster of the Hospital Authority, Hong Kong.

Margaret Fung-Yee Wong

Margaret Wong is the Assistant Community Secretary (Youth and Family) at the Tung Wah Group of Hospitals. She received her social work education in the United States, and has, since then, worked in the social service arena in the US, Canada and Hong Kong for over thirty years. She directs services for addictions including pathological gambling, substance abuse, smoking and alcohol abuse; domestic violence crisis support services; youth services; residential and child care services; and family services.

Elsie Chau-Wai Yan

Dr Yan is currently an assistant professor at the Department of Social Work and Social Administration of the University of Hong Kong.

1
The Public Health Approach to the Prevention of Family Violence in Hong Kong

Ko-Ling Chan

> **Chapter summary**
>
> 1. The public health approach has been adopted by the World Health Organization as a conceptual framework for the prevention of family violence.
> 2. The public health approach has four key steps: (a) problem description/public health surveillance; (b) risk and protective factor research; (c) preventive intervention development and evaluation; and (d) broad implementation of effective prevention programmes.
> 3. Public health intervention can be categorized into three levels of prevention: primary, secondary, and tertiary prevention.
> 4. Preventive strategies can be classified as universal, selective, or indicated.
> 5. The social ecological model of family violence conceptualizes the risk factors at four levels: the individual, relationship, community, and societal levels.

Prevention is the key to combating family violence. The World Health Organization has adopted the public health approach as a conceptual framework in order to identify the essential elements that would contribute to the prevention and intervention of family violence (Krug, Dahlberg, Mercy, Zwi, & Lozaro, 2002). The approach also provides a common framework for professionals from various disciplines—including social scientists, health and legal professionals, psychologists, and social workers—with which to work collaboratively. This chapter introduces the framework and discusses how it can inform a multidisciplinary approach to the prevention of family violence.

The approach

Public health relates to individuals as well as populations. The public health approach, with the building of healthy communities as an end goal, posits that the health of individuals and groups depends upon social policies and programmes, as well as coordinated national, regional, and community services. Historically, the public health approach has attempted to control morbidity and mortality through targeted measures against infectious diseases. The approaches identify and control factors that affect the two rates among men and women across the life span (Arias & Ikeda, 2006). It has been found that behavioural, psychosocial, and sociocultural factors associated with lifestyle choices are major contributors to the leading causes of chronic diseases or death (Schneiderman & Speers, 2001).

Many public health researchers have begun to adopt the public health approach in examining the roots of family violence. In the context of such an approach, family violence is not conceived of as an individual problem; rather, its appearance is seen to reflect a deeper-rooted problem within the society where the violence occurs. The public health approach therefore attempts to promote collaboration between various sectors—legal, health, and social— and diverse disciplines in carrying out preventive actions against violence.

The public health perspective has broadened from one emphasizing the role of government policy to one which includes the "development and dissemination of interventions at the community level" (Arias & Ikeda, 2006, p. 175). Traditionally, the government took the lead in implementing public health interventions, as many such interventions required decision making and the exercise of leadership at the higher level. But the public health model has since expanded and moved beyond its earlier practice to a new and more comprehensive approach. The new approach draws upon knowledge from multiple disciplines including medicine, epidemiology, sociology, psychology, criminology, education, and economics, and involves a greater role of the community (Arias & Ikeda, 2006). This creates greater innovation and versatility in the field of public health, and widens the applicability of the approach to a range of problems around the world.

The four steps

The public health approach to violence adheres to the rigorous process of the scientific method. It comprises four key steps in the progression from problem to solution: (a) surveillance, (b) risk and protective factor research, (c) preventive intervention development and evaluation, and (d) broad implementation of effective prevention programmes (Mercy, Rosenberg, Powell, Broome, & Roper, 1993). Although the model suggests a linear progression from the first to the fourth step, with data obtained from earlier on used to guide and inform the subsequent steps, it should be noted that actions at different stages may occur concurrently.

The first step—problem description—includes those activities that help to define and to delineate the public health problem. This goes beyond simply counting cases or tracking, but also includes monitoring the problem over time. Public health surveillance, which can be defined as the "ongoing systematic collection, analysis, and interpretation of outcome-specific data for use in the planning, implementation, and evaluation of public health practice" (Thacker & Berkelman, 1988, p. 164), falls into this category. Public health surveillance systems are designed to provide data regarding the incidence and prevalence of health problems, the general demographic characteristics of the persons involved, and temporal and geographic characteristics such as regarding the incidence of violence.

The second step involves identifying risk and protective factors associated with the public health problem. This is done through etiologic and epidemiologic research. Factors that might be modifiable via interventions are also examined in this step.

In the third step, interventions and preventions are identified and developed based on the information obtained from the previous steps. The interventions may include treatment programmes, policies, and any other efforts adopted to prevent violence (Hammond, Haegerich, & Saul, 2009). This step also includes evaluating the interventions for both efficiency and effectiveness. Methods for evaluation include prospective randomized controlled trials, controlled comparisons of populations for the occurrence of health outcomes, time-series analyses of trends in multiple areas, and observational studies such as case-control studies.

In the fourth step, effective preventions are advocated on a wide scale. Broad application of effective strategies against violence would decrease its incidence at the population level. Another important component of this step is to determine the cost effectiveness of such programmes: evaluating the cost and benefit can be useful for policymakers in determining optimal public health practices.

Prevention strategies

The first two steps of the public health model provide important information about populations requiring preventive interventions, as well as the risk and protective factors that need to be addressed. A foremost goal of public health is to formulate this knowledge into actionable solutions, in the form of interventions characterized into three levels of prevention: primary, secondary, and tertiary prevention (Krug et al., 2002).

Primary prevention aims to prevent the very occurrence of such health problems as intimate partner violence. Unlike earlier prevention efforts primarily concentrated on victims of abuse, this level of prevention also attempts to address directly the risk and protective factors associated with the perpetration of violence.

Secondary prevention focuses on more immediate responses to public health problems that have already manifested. In the case of violence prevention, for example, secondary prevention may include hospital care, emergency services, and treatment for sexually transmitted diseases following a rape.

Tertiary prevention addresses the long-term impacts of public health problems. It may include rehabilitation and reintegration to lower the likelihood of recurrent violence, therapy to lessen trauma, and attempts to mitigate long-term health effects caused by violence.

The three levels of prevention, forming a critical strategy of the public health approach, are defined by their temporal aspect—whether preventive measures take place prior to an incident, immediately afterwards, or over a period of time in the aftermath. On the other hand, researchers have increasingly characterized preventive strategies in terms of the target group of interest (Tolan & Guerra, 1994). According to the targeted intervention approach, preventive strategies can be universal, selective or indicated (Gordon, 1987).

Universal strategies, which usually aim to function as primary prevention, are targeted at the entire population (i.e., without regard to individual risk). Prevention is implemented on a general, indiscriminate basis through reducing risk and enhancing health. One example would be launching public education campaigns in schools about violence prevention.

Selective strategies, usually aiming to function as primary or secondary prevention, target heightened risk groups and individuals. Prevention is implemented through the reduction of risks. One example would be providing support through home visitation to families dealing with issues related to substance abuse, or to families headed by low-income single parents, and offering them training in parenting skills.

Indicated strategies, usually aiming to function as secondary or tertiary prevention, target symptomatic and high-risk individuals. This may include administering interventions such as targeted treatment and rehabilitation for perpetrators of domestic violence, in order to prevent relapse into undesirable behaviour or reoccurrence of risk factors.

Comprehensive prevention therefore not only protects and supports victims as has been traditionally the case, but also ensures immediate and long-term services are in place in the unfortunate event of an incidence, in addition to guiding persons with violent and abusive behaviour towards healthy ways of interaction, especially within the family.

Study of risk factors using the ecological model

The study of risk factors or markers associated with family violence is one which demands to be grounded on rigorous research. Risk markers of violence are defined as antecedent variables that are significantly correlated with consequent variables, either increasing risk (in which case they are known as risk factors), or decreasing risk of the latter (i.e., protective factors; Barnett, Miller-Perrin, & Perrin, 2005).

Past research has identified potential risk markers for family violence at all levels of the environment in which individuals and families live. The risk markers could be better understood using the ecological model proposed by Bronfenbrenner (1977). The ecological model was initially applied to child abuse (Belsky, 1980, 1993) and subsequently, to youth violence (Garbarino, 1985). More recently over the past decade, researchers have applied it to understanding intimate partner violence (Dutton, 1995; Heise, 1998) and elderly abuse (Carp, 2000; Schiamberg & Gans, 1999). In the respective applications, Bronfenbrenner's framework was modified to suit the subjects of different studies. As Heise (1998) notes, "considerable room exists for interpretation as to exactly where a particular factor most appropriately fits into the framework" (p. 266), so both the nomenclature and the indicators of the systems in the framework vary across these applications (Brownridge, 2006). The strength of the ecological model is that at the same time of distinguishing between the myriad influences leading to violence, it provides a framework for understanding the interactive dynamics between such influences (Bronfenbrenner, 1977). The application of the nested ecological framework to family violence conceptualizes the environment into four contexts: the individual, relationship, community, and societal levels; and explores the linkage between each risk factor and its influence on violence (Krug et al., 2002).

Individual level. The first level of the ecological model seeks to identify the demographic characteristics that influence an individual's behaviour. These characteristics include an individual's personal history, biological factors, and personality traits. With regard to violence prevention, this level of the ecological model examines how these characteristics may increase the likelihood of an individual's being a victim or a perpetrator of violence.

Relationship level. The second level of the model explores how proximal social relationships (e.g., relations with peers, intimate partners, and family members) have an effect on one's risk of being a perpetrator or victim of violence. In the case of intimate partner violence, risk factors at the relationship level are significantly correlated with partner violence (K. L. Chan, 2004; Hicks, 2006; Lau, 2005; Parish, Luo, Laumann, Kew, & Yu, 2007). Daily interactions with perpetrators of violence also increase the risk of repeated victimization among children (Stith et al., 2009). Thus, social relationships are likely to shape an individual's behaviour and experience.

Community level. The third level examines the formal and informal social networks/structures, such as schools, workplaces and the community, in which the family is involved. These networks may influence what takes place in the family setting, and hence, the incidence of violent behaviours. In cases of intimate partner violence, many women who were abused reported that their partners had attempted to socially isolate them from family, friends, and other social support systems (Taillieu & Brownridge, 2010). In addition, poverty is an important variable in predicting family violence in a community (Y. C. Chan, Lam, & Cheng, 2009). The importance of focusing on the community as a primary site of prevention against family violence is also suggested in recent research (Arias & Ikeda, 2006; Slep & Heyman, 2008).

Societal level. The fourth level includes societal factors that foster or perpetuate family violence. These factors include:

1.   cultural norms that support violence as an acceptable way to resolve conflicts;
2.   attitudes that regard suicide as a matter of individual choice instead of a preventable act of violence;
3.   norms that give priority to parental rights over child welfare;
4.   norms that entrench male dominance over women and children;
5.   norms that support the use of excessive force by police against citizens;
6.   norms that support political conflict;
7.   health, educational, economic, and social policies that maintain high levels of economic or social inequality between groups in society.

These factors are conducive to creating a climate in which violence is more likely to be seen as acceptable, and are also likely to reduce inhibitions against perpetration of violence.

The ecological model highlights the multifaceted nature of violence and the different risk factors operating on the individual, family, and broader community and social levels, as well as the entangled interactions between them. Indeed, Bronfenbrenner (1977) emphasizes that "in ecological research, the principal main effects are likely to be interactions" (p. 518). Child abuse and intimate partner violence, for example, are often found within the same nuclear family (Appel & Holden, 1998; Edleson, 1999). Violent home settings resulting in intimate partner violence have also been shown to pose a risk for elderly abuse (Aronson, Thornewell, & Williams, 1995; Deitch, 1997). The links between different types of family violence suggest that addressing risk factors across the various levels of the ecological model may contribute to decreases in more than one type of violence.

Application of the public health approach to the prevention of child abuse and partner violence in Hong Kong

A social ecological model has been applied to categorize the risk factors of child abuse and partner violence in Hong Kong. Based on the household survey commissioned by the Social Welfare Department in 2005 (K. L. Chan, 2005), a number of risk factors were identified, as summarized in Table 1.1.

Table 1.1 Risk factors associated with child abuse and spouse battering in Hong Kong

Individual factors	Relationship factors	Family factors	Societal factors
• Pregnancy • Young age • Exhibiting stalking behaviour • Experienced or witnessed parental violence in childhood • Criminal history • Face need • Low self-esteem • Suicidal ideation • Violence approval • Lack of support • Stressful conditions • Alcohol and drug abuse • Depression • Poor anger management • Low social desirability	• Spousal age difference • Male domination • Jealousy • Relationship distress • Negative attribution • In-law conflict • Influence of extended family	• Unemployment • Disability • New immigrants • Chronic illness • Low income/ poverty (receiving social security) • Indebtedness	• Violence approval (social norms supportive of violence) • Gender inequality (male domination) • Lack of social resources to render support

I have modified the ecological model adopted in the household survey (K. L. Chan, 2005) to categorize risk factors at the individual, relationship, family, and societal levels. Family risk factors are highlighted because family constitutes an important basis for understanding social problems in Chinese culture. Based on the identified risk factors, strategies for violence prevention have been developed following the public health approach (see Table 1.2).

Universal strategies

Several universal strategies of violence prevention have been proposed. These include introducing anti-domestic violence policy, anti-violence education/campaigns, anti-poverty policy, and campaigns for global health and psychological health awareness; building enhanced and coordinated community and legal responses; promoting legal remedies and judicial reforms; and

Table 1.2 Summary table of preventive strategies for domestic violence in Hong Kong

Intervention Approach	Target Populations	Scope	Objectives	Risk Factors	Preventive Strategies	
					Child Abuse	**Spousal Abuse**
Universal Preventive Intervention	General populations or groups regardless of individual risk	Society	Prevent violence through reducing risk and enhancing protective or mitigating factors across broad groups of people	• Violence approval (i.e., social norms supportive of violence) • Gender inequality	• Anti-domestic violence policy and policy in tackling poverty • Global health and psychological health awareness • Enhancing coordinated community and legal responses • Anti-violence education/campaign • Legal remedies and judicial reforms • Research on domestic violence	
		Community		• Pregnancy • Mental illness • Child abuse and neglect	• School programmes on reduction of delinquency, substance and alcohol abuse • Training programmes for healthcare professionals and other related parties to facilitate detection and reporting of abuse • Universal screening for people at risk	
					• Training in parenting • Resources for child care • Encourage reporting of child abuse	• Encourage help-seeking
Selective Preventive Intervention	Identified individuals or subgroups bearing a significantly higher-than-average risk	Community	Prevent violence through addressing population-specific characteristics that place individuals at a higher-than-average risk	• Low income/ poverty • Lack of social resources	• Outreach work • Coordinated community response • Multidisciplinary collaboration in conducting standardized risk assessments	
		Families or individuals at risk		• Receiving social security • Chronic illness • Mental illness • New immigrants • Disability • Spousal age difference • Separation • Indebtedness	• Screening for potential risk and risk assessment • Programmes to contact isolated individuals/families • Home visitation • Family support programmes	
					• Training and support in parenting • Training in child protection procedures	• Referral for drug and alcohol treatment, and gambling, debt, or suicide crisis counselling • Community "gatekeepers" to detect changes in lives of people

(continued on page 10)

Table 1.2 (*continued*)

Intervention Approach	Target Populations	Scope	Objectives	Risk Factors	Preventive Strategies	
					Child Abuse	Spousal Abuse
Indicated Preventive Intervention	Identify high-risk individuals with detectable symptoms	Problematic families/ victims	Treat individuals with symptoms and risk factors to prevent emergence of full-blown disorder and reoffending violence	• Familial conflict • Male dominance • Economic stress	• Family approach of risk assessment • Family support services • Home visitation and referral • Court-mandated batterers intervention programme	
		Perpetrators		• Mental disorders • Criminal and antisocial behaviours • Addiction problems	• Treatment and supervision of mentally ill perpetrators • Treatment for drug and alcohol abuse, gambling, debt, suicidal ideation or suicide attempt	
		Victims	Protect, support, and treat victims of spousal battering, child abuse, and children who have witnessed domestic violence		• Therapy for victims and survivors of domestic violence • Helplines and other resources for victim support • Legal and health support services for victims of domestic violence	
					• Child protective services • Surrogate parents for children being abused	• Women's shelter for the victims

supporting research on domestic violence (K. L. Chan, 2005). Each of these universal strategies aims to reduce risk factors at the societal level (e.g., violence approval, gender inequality). Other universal strategies such as offering school programmes and universal screening in school or health settings, encouraging the reporting of violence, and training professionals in different intervention skills are also directed toward this end.

Selective strategies

Findings from the household survey (K. L. Chan, 2005) showed that families receiving social security and those headed by young couples may have an increased likelihood of using violence as a means of handling conflict. Without the proper conflict resolution skills, these families are more susceptible to intense conflict, which may in turn result in severe violence. Regular monitoring of families in this category can aid early identification of high-risk cases. Several preventive strategies that focus on helping families at risk are recommended; these include outreach work, initiating neighbourhood watch, engaging the public to serve as community "gatekeepers", developing coordinated community response as well as multidisciplinary collaboration in conducting standardized risk assessment. In particular, protocols and tools for screening for potential risk and risk assessment should be promoted to professionals who specialize in family violence. Special preventive strategies for child abuse should include training and support in parenting, as well as training for teachers, health professionals, and social workers on child protection procedures. These selective strategies target at-risk individuals and families to reduce risk factors at family and individual levels (e.g., low income, mental illness).

Indicated strategies

Among high-risk individuals who have demonstrated violent behaviour in the past, it is recommended that a family approach of risk assessment be adopted, in view of the close association of various types of violence, e.g., that between spousal battering and child abuse. The family approach has the merit of extending its investigation into other types of violence (e.g., physical, psychological, and sexual) once incidence of a certain type of family violence is identified. Family support services should encompass counselling, health services, and support for victims and perpetrators. Home visitation and referral of social services, as well as treatment for perpetrators are crucial in reducing recurrent violence and promoting change and rehabilitation. Launching court-mandated batterer intervention programmes can also serve protective and rehabilitative functions through a legal framework.

Multidisciplinary collaboration in violence prevention

The ecological model views violence as the product of a complex interplay of individual, relational, social, cultural, and environmental factors. In light of the multifaceted nature of family violence, we must conceive of prevention strategies not in the form of piecemeal solutions, but under the purview of comprehensive and integrative violence prevention programmes—capable of addressing risk factors at multiple levels—if the strategies are to be at all effective. Multidisciplinary collaboration is thus emphasized as a way to allow social scientists across disciplines (e.g., psychologists, sociologists, anthropologists) and professionals working in health, the judiciary, and social services to pool together their information and expertise. Collaboration with stakeholders representing different sectors in the society (e.g., education, labour, public housing, media, business, hospital, criminal justice) is also warranted. The public health approach also emphasizes the involvement of local communities in policy and programme development, and encourages communities to assume ownership and responsibility in countering problems whose impact have important ramifications for all (Slep & Heyman, 2008).

Multidisciplinary collaboration is to be championed for three reasons. First, it allows us to take advantage of the synergistic benefits of cooperation. Resources can be combined and allocated more effectively and efficiently based on the information obtained from multiple disciplines. Second, we can learn from different prevention efforts and share experiences and lessons. As Mercy et al. (1993) emphasizes, "the more coordinated these disparate initiatives and programmes are, the easier it will be to ensure adequate evaluation and to derive and share prevention knowledge from those activities" (p. 25). Third, since different organizations have their own methods of identifying, preventing, and intervening in cases involving family violence, there is a possibility for confusion and redundancy of services. Thus, there is a need to establish a consistent mechanism (e.g., a centrally-coordinated government committee) to take on the tasks of supervision and regulation. The prevention of violence requires the collaborative work of a broad spectrum of community leaders and organizations, including governmental, business, and grassroots organizations. Each sector has an important role to play in addressing the problem, and collectively, the approaches taken by each have the potential to effect important reductions in violence rates.

The government has now set up two committees, the Committee on Child Abuse (CCA) and the Working Group on Combating Violence (WGCV), to serve facilitating roles within Hong Kong. Both CCA and WGCV are convened by the director of Social Welfare, and are made up of representatives from different policy bureaus, departments, and nongovernmental organizations (NGOs). The two committees are tasked with mapping out strategies and approaches at the government level for the prevention and handling of spouse battering and sexual violence. Procedural guides for handling child abuse and battered spouse cases have since been developed and revised to promote multidisciplinary collaboration, so as to serve the best interests of the victims. More generally, since suspected cases and victims of family violence may come to the attention of different organizations at the same time, be it schools, the police, medical social services, hospitals, clinics, or child centres, it has been recommended that all parties concerned should maintain communication regarding case progress, as they act as advocates on behalf of victims, survivors and other vulnerable individuals.

Conclusion

This review describes the framework of the public health approach, and explores its application to family violence prevention through collaboration across disciplines, organizations and communities. In doing so, it attempts to address the various associated risk factors at different levels. The public health approach and framework can serve as the underpinning framework informing the discussion of violence prevention in this book.

References

Appel, A. E., & Holden, G. W. The co-occurrence of spouse and physical child abuse: a review and appraisal. *Journal of Family Psychology, 12*, 578–599. Retrieved from http://jcsafefamily.org/wp-content/uploads/2009/02/co-ocurrence-of-spouse-and-physical-child-abuse-appel-and-holden.pdf

Arias, I., & Ikeda, R. M. (2006). Etiology and surveillance of intimate partner violence. In J. R. Lutzker (Ed.), *Preventing Violence: Research and Evidence-Based*

Intervention Strategies (pp. 173–194). Washington, DC: American Psychological Association.

Aronson, J., Thornewell, C., & Williams, K. (1995). Wife assault in old age: coming out of obscurity. *Canadian Journal on Aging, 14*, 72–88.

Barnett, O., Miller-Perrin, C. L., & Perrin, R. D. (2005). *Family Violence Across The Lifespan: An Introduction* (2nd ed.). Thousand Oaks, CA: Sage.

Belsky, J. (1980). Child maltreatment: an ecological integration. *American Psychologist, 35*, 320–335. doi: 10.1037/0003-066X.35.4.320

Belsky, J. (1993). Etiology of child maltreatment: a developmental-ecological analysis. *Psychological Bulletin, 114*, 413–434. doi: 10.1037/0033-2909.114.3.413

Bronfenbrenner, U. (1977). Toward an experimental ecology of human development. *American Psychologist, 32*, 513–531. doi: 10.1037/0003-066X.32.7.51

Brownridge, D. A. (2006). Violence against women post-separation. *Aggression and Violence Behavior, 11*, 514–530. doi: 10.1016/j.avb.2006.01.009

Carp, R. M. (2000). *Elder Abuse in the Family: An Interdisciplinary Model for Research*. New York, NY: Springer.

Chan, K. L. (2004). Correlates of wife assault in Hong Kong Chinese families. *Violence and Victims, 19*, 189–201.

Chan, K. L. (2005). *Study on Child Abuse and Spouse Battering: Report on Findings of Household Survey*. Retrieved from Department of Social Work and Social Administration, the University of Hong Kong website: http://www.swd.gov.hk/doc/family/Report%20on%20findings%20of%20Household%20Survey.pdf

Chan, Y. C., Lam, G. L. T., & Cheng, H. C. H. (2009). Community capacity building as a strategy of family violence prevention in a problem-stricken community: a theoretical formulation. *Journal of Family Violence, 24*, 559–568.

Deitch, I. (1997). When golden pond is tainted: domestic violence and the elderly. In I. Dietch & C. W. Howell (Eds.), *Counseling the Aging and Their Families* (pp. 87–101). Alexandria, VA: American Counseling Association.

Dutton, D. G. (1995). *The Domestic Assault of Women: Psychological and Criminal Justice Perspectives* (Revised and expanded ed.). Vancouver, Canada: UBC Press.

Edleson, J. L. (1999). The overlap between child maltreatment and woman battering. *Violence Against Women, 5*, 134–154. doi: 10.1177/107780129952003

Garbarino, J. (1985). *Adolescent Development: An Ecological Perspective*. Columbus, OH: Charles E. Merrill.

Gordon, R. (1987). An operational classification of disease prevention. In J. A. Steinberg & M. M. Silverman (Eds.), *Prevention of Mental Disorders* (pp. 20–26). Rockville, MD: U.S. Department of Health and Human Services.

Hammond, W. R., Haegerich, T. M., & Saul, J. (2009). The public health approach to youth violence and child maltreatment prevention at the Centers for Disease Control and Prevention. *Psychological Services, 6*, 253–263. doi: 10.1037/a0016986

Heise, L. L. (1998). Violence against women: an integrated ecological framework. *Violence Against Women, 4*, 262–290. doi: 10.1177/1077801298004003002

Hicks, M. H. R. (2006). The prevalence and characteristics of intimate partner violence in a community study of Chinese American women. *Journal of Interpersonal Violence, 21*, 1249–1269. doi: 10.1177/0886260506291651

Krug, E. G., Dahlberg, L. L., Mercy, J. A., Zwi, A. B., & Lozaro, R. (2002). *World Report on Violence and Health*. Retrieved from World Health Organization, Geneva website: http://www.who.int/violence_injury_prevention/violence/world_report/en/

Lau, Y. (2005). Does pregnancy provide immunity from intimate partner abuse among Hong Kong Chinese women? *Social Science & Medicine, 61*, 365–377. doi: 10.1016/j.socscimed.2004.12.002

Mercy, J. A., Rosenberg, M. L., Powell, K. E., Broome, C. V., & Roper, W. L. (1993). Public health policy for preventing violence. *Health Affairs, 12*, 7–29. Retrieved from http://content.healthaffairs.org/cgi/reprint/12/4/7

Parish, W. L., Luo, Y., Laumann, E. O., Kew, M., & Yu, Z. (2007). Unwanted sexual activity among married women in urban China. *Journal of Sex Research, 44*, 158–171. doi: 10.1080/00224490701263751

Schiamberg, L. B., & Gans, D. (1999). An ecological framework for contextual risk factors in elder abuse by adult children. *Journal of Elder Abuse and Neglect, 11*, 79–103. doi: 10.1300/J084v11n01_05

Schneiderman, N., & Speers, M. A. (2001). Behavioral science, social science, and public health in the 21st century. In N. Schneiderman, M. A. Speers, J. M. Silva, H. Tomes, & J. H. Gentry (Eds.), *Integrating Behavioral and Social Sciences with Public Health* (pp. 3–28). Washington, DC: American Psychological Association.

Slep, A. M. S., & Heyman, R. E. (2008). Public health approaches to family maltreatment prevention: resetting family psychology's sights from the home to the community. *Journal of Family Psychology, 22*, 518–528. doi: 10.1037/0893-3200.22.3.518

Stith, S. M., Liu, T., Davies, L. C., Boykin, E. L., Alder, M. C., Harris, J. M., Som, A., McPherson, M., & Dees, J. E. M. E. G. (2009). Risk factors in child maltreatment: a meta-analytic review of the literature. *Aggression and Violence Behavior, 14*, 13–29. doi: 10.1016/j.avb.2006.03.006

Taillieu, T. L., & Brownridge, D. A. (2010). Violence against pregnant women: prevalence, patterns, risk factors, theories, and directions for future research. *Aggression and Violent Behavior, 15*, 14–35. doi: 10.1016/j.avb.2009.07.013

Thacker, S. B., & Berkelman, R. L. (1988). Public health surveillance in the United States. *Epidemiologic Reviews, 10*, 164–190.

Tolan, P. H., & Guerra, N. G. (1994). Prevention of juvenile delinquency: current status and issues. *Journal of Applied and Preventive Psychology, 3*, 251–273.

Part 1

Prevalence and Risk Factors

2
Intimate Partner Violence in Hong Kong

Ko-Ling Chan

Chapter summary

1. Underreporting of the prevalence of intimate partner violence (IPV) in Hong Kong is serious. Only 4% of violent cases are reported to social services.
2. A number of IPV risk factors and predictors for various health outcomes have been identified through studies conducted in Hong Kong.
3. Culture-specific factors like face orientation have strong effects on whether or not a person will commit IPV and whether or not victims will seek help.
4. Intervention and preventative strategies should be able to address risk factors on different levels, using the ecological model.

In the last decade, my research team and I have conducted a number of studies on intimate partner violence (IPV) in Hong Kong. It is time to review the studies in order to see what must be done for the future development of research, policy, and services related to domestic violence in Hong Kong. Understanding how to combat domestic violence in Hong Kong provides valuable insight into how this can be done in greater Chinese societies. The Chinese are the largest ethnic group in the world, making up a full one-fifth of the world's total population. Yet little is known about the prevalence, culture-specific risk factors, and health outcomes of IPV among the Chinese. In Hong Kong, significant social changes—the increasing participation of women in the labour force, rising unemployment, and the growing acceptance of gender equality in recent years (K. L. Chan, 2000)—are transforming gender roles, and hence IPV.

This chapter provides a review of IPV studies in Hong Kong. This review focuses on journal articles and book chapters located in databases including Criminal Justice Abstracts, MEDLINE, PsycINFO, Social Services Abstracts, and Sociological Abstracts using the keyword "Hong Kong" and any other terms which consequently indicated in the abstract that violence or abuse was the theme of the study. The search focused mainly on English journals available in the databases, but some book chapters and official reports in both English and Chinese were also reviewed.

The term "intimate partner violence" will be used interchangeably with terms like "wife battering", "domestic violence", and "spousal" or "partner violence" throughout this chapter. The review starts with research on IPV prevalence in Hong Kong, and then synthesizes its universal and culture-specific risk factors. To point out the seriousness of IPV and the need for interventions and treatments for IPV victims in Hong Kong, I will briefly review what research has been done in Hong Kong on the physical and mental health effects of IPV. I then lay out the implications of the data presently available, and suggest directions for future research that can help us grasp the full scope of the issue.

Prevalence of IPV in Hong Kong

The prevalence of partner violence victimization has been found to range from 1.8% (T. W. Leung, Ng, Leung, & Ho, 2003) to 17.9% (W. C. Leung, Leung, Lam, & Ho, 1999), based on clinical samples. When the nature of violence is broken down by type and time of abuse, these widely divergent results become more understandable (see Table 2.1). The details of the studies are listed in Table 2.2.

With regard to physical violence, lifetime prevalence rates for victimization have ranged from 8.1% to 17.9% (based on population or community samples), 94% to 96.7% for victimization (based on clinical samples), and 7.3% to 28.6% for perpetration (population or community samples). Annual prevalence rates for physical victimization have ranged from 3.9% to 27.2% (population or community samples), 4.1% to 91.4% for victimization (clinical samples), and 3.4% to 46% for perpetration (population or community samples).

Table 2.1 Summary of rates reported in studies of the prevalence of spousal violence in Chinese societies (in descending chronological order)

	Population Sampling/Community Sampling				Clinical Sampling			
	Lifetime prevalence (%)		Annual prevalence (%)		Lifetime prevalence (%)		Annual prevalence (%)	
Violence	Perpetration	Victimization	Perpetration	Victimization	Perpetration	Victimization	Perpetration	Victimization
Spousal violence						7.2 (T. W. Leung et al., 2005)		9.0 (K. L. Chan et al., 2009; Tiwari et al., 2008)
						1.8 (T. W. Leung et al., 2003)		11.2 (Y. Lau, 2005; Y. Lau & Chan, 2007)
						17.9 (W. C. Leung et al.,1999)		9.1 (Tiwari, Chan, et al., 2007)
								5.0 (Tiwari et al., 2005)
								15.7 (W. C. Leung et al., 1999)

(continued on page 22)

Table 2.1 (*continued*)

	Population Sampling/Community Sampling				Clinical Sampling			
	Lifetime prevalence (%)		Annual prevalence (%)		Lifetime prevalence (%)		Annual prevalence (%)	
Violence	Perpetration	Victimization	Perpetration	Victimization	Perpetration	Victimization	Perpetration	Victimization
Physical violence	7.3_a (Y. C. Chan, Au, Lam & Chung, 2006)	8.5 (K. L. Chan & Straus, 2008)	35.2 (China); 36.9 (Hong Kong) (K. L. Chan & Straus, 2005; K. L. Chan, Straus, et al., 2008)	4.5 (K. L. Chan, 2005; K. L. Chan & Straus, 2008)		96.7 (K. L. Chan & Brownridge, 2008)		91.4 (K. L. Chan & Brownridge, 2008)
	19.1_b (Y. C. Chan et al., 2006)	8.1_a (Y. C. Chan et al., 2006)	46.0 (K. L. Chan & Straus, 2008)	27.2 (China); 25.6 (Hong Kong) (K. L. Chan & Straus, 2005; K. L. Chan, Straus, et al., 2008)		94.0 (Y. C. Chan, 1997)		4.1 (Y. Lau, 2005; Y. Lau & Chan, 2007)
	10.8 (K. L. Chan, 2005)	17.9_b (Y. C. Chan et al., 2006)	3.4_a (Y. C. Chan et al., 2006)	3.9_a (Y. C. Chan et al., 2006)				27.0 (Tiwari, Chan, et al., 2007)
	28.6 (Straus et al., 2004)	9.6 (K. L. Chan, 2005)	14.2_b (Y. C. Chan et al., 2006)	12.9_b (Y. C. Chan et al., 2006)				
		14.0 (Tang, 1994)	5.5 (K. L. Chan, 2005)	10.0 (Tang, 1999a)				

(continued on page 23)

Table 2.1 *(continued)*

| | Population Sampling/Community Sampling | | | | Clinical Sampling | | | |
| | Lifetime prevalence (%) | | Annual prevalence (%) | | Lifetime prevalence (%) | | Annual prevalence (%) | |
Violence	Perpetration	Victimization	Perpetration	Victimization	Perpetration	Victimization	Perpetration	Victimization
Psychological abuse	39.2_a (Y. C. Chan et al., 2006)	37.3_a (Y. C. Chan et al., 2006)	27.2_a (Y. C. Chan et al., 2006)	27.1_a (Y. C. Chan et al., 2006)		88.1 (K. L. Chan & Brownridge, 2008)		95.2 (K. L. Chan & Brownridge, 2008)
	58.2_b (Y. C. Chan et al., 2006)	47.5_b (Y. C. Chan et al., 2006)	35.4_b (Y. C. Chan et al., 2006)	30.7_b (Y. C. Chan et al., 2006)				8.8 (Y. Lau, 2005; Y. Lau & Chan, 2007)
	61.1 (K. L. Chan, 2005)	57.2 (K. L. Chan, 2005)	43.8 (K. L. Chan, 2005)	40.8 (K. L. Chan, 2005)				73.0 (Tiwari, Chan, et al., 2007)
		75.0 (Tang, 1994)		67.2 (Tang, 1999a)				61.5 (T. W. Leung et al., 2005)

(continued on page 24)

Table 2.1 (*continued*)

Violence	Population Sampling/Community Sampling				Clinical Sampling			
	Lifetime prevalence (%)		Annual prevalence (%)		Lifetime prevalence (%)		Annual prevalence (%)	
	Perpetration	Victimization	Perpetration	Victimization	Perpetration	Victimization	Perpetration	Victimization
Sexual abuse	7.3 (K. L. Chan, 2005)	6.9 (K. L. Chan, 2005)	12.7 (China); 9.5 (Hong Kong) (Chan & Straus, 2005; K. L. Chan, Straus, et al., 2008)	15.4 (China); 13.0 (Hong Kong) (Chan & Straus, 2005; K. L. Chan, Straus, et al., 2008)		62.9 (K. L. Chan & Brownridge, 2008)		56.7 (K. L. Chan & Brownridge, 2008)
			3.5 (K. L. Chan, 2005)	3.2 (K. L. Chan, 2005)				5.5 (Y. Lau, 2005; Y. Lau & Chan, 2007)
								9.4 (W. C. Leung et al., 1999)

Note. *a* = measured by the Revised Conflict Tactics Scales Short Form (CTS2S); *b* = measured by the Conflict Tactics Scales (CTS).

Table 2.2 Studies of the prevalence of spousal violence in Hong Kong by abuse type (in descending chronological order)

Source	Abuse Type	Sample	Sampling	Measure	Prevalence
K. L. Chan & Brownridge (2008)	Spousal Violence	210 women aged 18 or above; residents and ex-residents (left less than one year ago) of a shelter for battered women		Face-to-face interview: Revised Conflict Tactics Scales (CTS2) to measure wife abuse; self-constructed items measuring characteristics of male batterers; partner's use of violence against their children	Lifetime: Physical = 96.7% Injury = 88.1% Psychological = 97.6% Sexual = 62.9% Preceding year: Physical = 91.4% Injury = 80.5% Psychological = 95.2% Sexual = 56.7%
K. L. Chan, Brownridge, et al. (2008)	Spousal violence	1,870 women with complete records on characteristics of their partners within Hong Kong households	Data from the 2003–2004 Hong Kong households survey ($N = 5,049$) Random sampling	The questionnaire used has three main components: demographic questions; the Revised Conflict Tactic Scales (CTS2) for data on spouse violence; and the Family Needs Screener (FNS) from the Personal and Relationship Profile (PRP) for data on etiology.	Lifetime: Physical = 8.5% Severe physical = 3.4% Less severe physical = 8.3% Preceding year: Physical = 4.5% Severe physical = 1.3% Less severe physical = 4.4%

(continued on page 26)

Table 2.2 *(continued)*

Source	Abuse Type	Sample	Sampling	Measure	Prevalence
K. L. Chan (2005)	Spousal violence	5,049 Chinese couples in Hong Kong; 53.6% female (response rate = 70%)	Random sample of Hong Kong households	The questionnaire used has three main components: demographic questions; the Revised Conflict Tactic Scales (CTS2) for data on spouse violence; and the Family Needs Screener (FNS) from the Personal and Relationship Profile (PRP) for data on etiology.	Lifetime: Physical: Perpetration = 10.8% Victimization = 9.6% Sexual: Perpetration = 7.3% Victimization = 6.9% Psychological: Perpetration = 61.1% Victimization = 57.2% Annual: Physical: Perpetration = 5.5% Victimization = 4.5% Sexual: Perpetration = 3.5% Victimization = 3.2% Psychological: Perpetration = 43.8% Victimization = 40.8%
Tang (1999a)	Wife abuse	1,132 Chinese women in Hong Kong, aged 18 or over	Randomly selected from the local telephone directory for 1995	The Conflict Tactic Scales (CTS)	Preceding year: Verbal = 67.2% Physical = 10.0%

(continued on page 27)

Table 2.2 (*continued*)

Source	Abuse Type	Sample	Sampling	Measure	Prevalence
Y. C. Chan et al. (2006)	Intimate partner violence	2,011 married or cohabiting adults (aged 18 or above) in Hong Kong (response rate = 48.4%)	Random sample of Hong Kong household by telephone survey	Revised Conflict Tactics Scales and the Revised Conflict Tactics Scales Short Form	Lifetime: Physical: Perpetration = $7.3\%_a$ / $19.1\%_b$ Victimization = $8.1\%_a$ / $17.9\%_b$ Psychological: Perpetration = $39.2\%_a$ / $58.2\%_b$ Victimization = $37.3\%_a$ / $47.5\%_b$ Injury: Perpetration = $3.8\%_a$ / $4.0\%_b$ Victimization = $3.9\%_a$ / $4.2\%_b$ Annual: Physical: Perpetration = $3.4\%_a$ / $14.3\%_b$ Victimization = $3.9\%_a$ / $12.9\%_b$ Psychological: Perpetration = $27.2\%_a$ / $35.4\%_b$ Victimization = $27.1\%_a$ / 30.7_b Injury: Perpetration = $1.8\%_a$ / $1.6\%_b$ Victimization = $1.8\%_a$ / $2.0\%_b$
K. L. Chan & Straus (2008)	Dating violence	1,736 university students from Hong Kong, China, and New Hampshire, USA, 70% female (response rate = 90%)	Data from International Dating Violence study ($N = 15,927$). Focus only on Hong Kong and US samples	Questionnaire survey Revised Conflict Tactics Scales (CTS2) and the Personal and Relationship Profile (PRP)	Preceding year: 46% of the participants perpetrated violence against a dating partner 8% for injury inflicted against a dating partner

(*continued on page 28*)

Table 2.2 (*continued*)

Source	Abuse Type	Sample	Sampling	Measure	Prevalence
K. L. Chan, Straus, et al. (2008)	Dating violence	University students Hong Kong ($N = 959$), 69.4% female Shanghai and Beijing, China ($N = 2,247$), 62% female	Data from International Dating Violence study ($N = 15,927$). Focus only on China and Hong Kong samples Convenience sampling (students in social science classes at local universities)	Questionnaire survey Revised Conflict Tactics Scales (CTS2) and the Personal and Relationship Profile (PRP)	Annual: Assault perpetration: China: 35.2% Hong Kong: 36.9% Assault victimization: China: 27.2% Hong Kong: 25.6% Sexual perpetration: China: 12.7% Hong Kong: 9.5% Sexual victimization: China: 15.4% Hong Kong: 13.0%
Straus et al. (2004)	Dating violence	University students in Hong Kong ($N = 220$), 60.5% female	Hong Kong data from International Dating Violence study. Convenience sampling	Violence defined by Revised Conflict Tactics Scales (CTS2)	Assault perpetration: Overall = 28.6% Severe = 11.4% Injury perpetration: Overall = 5.5% Severe = 2.3%
K. L. Chan et al. (2009)	Violence against pregnant women	3,245 pregnant women from seven hospitals in Hong Kong	Convenience sampling	Definition of abuse by the Chinese Abuse Assessment Screen	Preceding year: 9% of pregnant women abused by partners 2.5% physically or sexually abuse

(*continued on page 29*)

Table 2.2 (*continued*)

Source	Abuse Type	Sample	Sampling	Measure	Prevalence
Y. Lau, Wong, & Chan (2008)	Violence against pregnant women	1,200 postnatal women from Queen Mary Hospital (response rate = 94.9%)	Community sampling	Definition of abuse by the Abuse Assessment Screen, and Revised Conflict Tactics Scales (CTS2) Medical Outcomes Study Short-Form 36 Health Survey (SF-36) measured the health-related quality of life	Preceding year: 11.2% of pregnant women abused by partners Of these women, Only physical = 20.9% Only psychological = 32.1% Combined psychological & physical = 47.0% More than one type = 53%
Y. Lau & Chan (2007)	Violence against pregnant women	1,200 Chinese mother and infant pairs in a university-affiliated regional hospital in Hong Kong	Randomly selected from the hospital with exclusion criteria: non-Chinese, known cases of family violence before pregnancy, personal or family history of psychiatric problems, complicated medical problems, severe obstetric complications, and abnormal infant deliveries	Three questionnaires (demographic, socioeconomic, and obstetric data) were self-administered in the study. The Abuse Assessment Screen (AAS) and the Revised Conflict Tactics Scales (CTS2) were used to measure intimate partner violence, and the Chinese version of the Edinburgh Postnatal Depression Scale (EPDS) was used to measure postnatal depression	During pregnancy: 11.2% of pregnant women abused by partners Physical = 4.1% Injury = 2.0% Psychological = 8.8% Sexual = 5.5%

(continued on page 30)

Table 2.2 (*continued*)

Source	Abuse Type	Sample	Sampling	Measure	Prevalence
Tiwari, Chan, et al. (2007)	Abuse against pregnant women	3,245 pregnant women attending antenatal clinics, aged over 18 years, between 32–36 weeks into pregnancy	Consecutive sampling; territory-wide survey conducted in the Obstetrics & Gynaecology departments of seven public hospitals across six hospital clusters	The Abuse Assessment Screen (AAS) to identify prevalence and type of IPV; sociodemographics	Preceding year abuse: 9.1% Physical/Sexual = 27% Psychological = 73%
Y. Lau (2005)	Violence against pregnant women	1,200 postnatal women from Queen Mary Hospital (response rate = 94.9%)	Community sampling	Demographic questions Definition of abuse by the Abuse Assessment Screen, Revised Conflict Tactics Scales (CTS2)	Preceding year: 11.2% of pregnant women abused by partners Of these women, Physical = 36.6% Injury = 19.9% Psychological = 74.1% Sexual = 49.3%
Tiwari et al. (2005)	Violence against pregnant women	2,361 women in their first antenatal clinic visit in a public hospital in Hong Kong	Randomized controlled trial	Violence defined by the Conflict Tactic Scales (CTS) and Abuse Assessment Screen (AAS)	Preceding year: 5% reported intimate partner violence

(continued on page 31)

Table 2.2 (*continued*)

Source	Abuse Type	Sample	Sampling	Measure	Prevalence
W. C. Leung et al. (1999)	Violence against pregnant women	631 Chinese pregnant women attending the antenatal clinic of a local teaching hospital in Hong Kong	Convenience sampling	Definition of abuse by the Abuse Assessment Screen	Lifetime: 17.9% had a history of abuse In the last year: 15.7% abused 9.4% sexually abused In current pregnancy: 4.3% abused
Tiwari et al. (2008)	Violence against women	3,245 women in their 32nd–36th gestational week in Hong Kong	Consecutive sampling	Violence defined by the Chinese Abuse Assessment Screen	In the last year: 9.1% abused Since being pregnant: 6.5% abused
T. W. Leung et al. (2003)	Violence against women	500 Chinese female patients	Consecutive patients attending the outpatient infertility clinic of a university teaching hospital in Hong Kong	Definition of abuse by the modified Abused Assessment Screen	Lifetime: Victimization = 1.8%
Y. C. Chan (1997)	Violence against women	300 cases of domestic violence were reported by the newspaper under study	Data from a research project entitled *A Documentation of Newspaper Reports on Family Violence in Hong Kong in the Past Decade* between 1992 and 1994	Any cases of domestic violence reported in the *Wah Kiu Yat Po* newspaper was used in the study	25% of all victims (91/364) of domestic violence in the study and 94% are of physical nature

(*continued on page 32*)

Table 2.2 (*continued*)

Source	Abuse Type	Sample	Sampling	Measure	Prevalence

T. W. Leung et al. (2005)	Violence against women in obstetric/ gynaecological patients (OB/ GYN)	1,614 OB/GYN patients	Consecutive patients attending the Department of Obstetrics and Gynaecology, Queen Mary Hospital in Hong Kong	A structured questionnaire modified from the Abuse Assessment Screen Questionnaire, and the World Health Organization Quality of Life Measure- abbreviated version (Hong Kong) questionnaire was used to measure quality of life	Lifetime:
					  Overall = 7.2%
					  Emotional/Verbal = 61.5%
					12.7% for patients requesting termination of pregnancy
					1.8% for infertility patients
					4.7% for gynaecological patients
					10.9% for obstetric patients

Tang (1994)	Interparental aggression and violence	Chinese college students in Hong Kong: 246 females and 136 males	Convenience sampling	Violence defined by Conflict Tactic Scales (CTS)	75% reported verbal aggression 14% indicated parents' use of physical violence

Note. *a* = measured by the Revised Conflict Tactics Scales Short Form (CTS2S); *b* = measured by the Conflict Tactics Scales (CTS).

With regard to psychological abuse, lifetime prevalence rates for victimization have ranged from 37.3% to 75% (population or community samples), while standing at 88.1% for victimization (clinical sample), and ranging from 39.2% to 61.1% for perpetration (population or community samples). Annual prevalence rates for psychological abuse victimization have ranged from 27.1% to 67.2% (population or community samples), 8.8% to 95.2% for victimization (clinical samples), and 27.2% to 43.8% for perpetration (population or community samples).

With regard to sexual abuse, lifetime prevalence rate is 6.9% for victimization and 7.3% for perpetration (population or community samples), and 62.9% for victimization (clinical sample). Annual prevalence has ranged from 3.2% to 15.4% for victimization, 3.5% to 12.7% for perpetration (population or community samples), and 5.5% to 56.7% for victimization (clinical samples).

Although IPV may include dating partner violence, four of the studies reviewed focused exclusively on dating violence. The rates for overall and severe assault perpetration in Hong Kong were 28.6% and 11.4% respectively (Straus, 2004b). The prevalence rate for Hong Kong was similar to those of two major cities, Shanghai and Beijing, in mainland China (K. L. Chan & Straus, 2005; Chan, Straus, Brownridge, Tiwari, & Leung, 2008). With regard to physical assault, the prevalence rates reported for perpetration were 35.2% (China) and 36.9% (Hong Kong) and, for victimization, 27.2% (China) and 25.6% (Hong Kong). With regard to sexual coercion, 12.7% (China) and 9.5% (Hong Kong) reported having sexually coerced their dating partner, while 15.4% (China) and 13% (Hong Kong) said they had experienced sexual coercion from their dating partner. K. L. Chan and Straus (2008) interviewed university students from Hong Kong, China, and the United States, and found the overall perpetration rate of dating violence to be 46%. Freshmen and individuals in shorter relationships (6–12 months) were more likely to commit dating violence (K. L. Chan & Straus, 2008).

Most studies did not adequately address gender differences, and studies usually assumed that females were the victims of partner violence. Yet in the few studies that investigated abuse in both males and females (K. L. Chan, 2005; Parish, Wang, Laumann, Pan, & Luo, 2004; Wang, Parish, Laumann, & Luo, 2009), males also reported being victims of partner violence. However, these studies also found significant gender differences: females were more likely to be victims, and males more likely to be perpetrators.

Although massive research efforts have been undertaken to understand partner violence, the underreporting of maltreatment is common (Tang, 1999a). In a population-sampling study on spouse battering in Hong Kong, 10% of the respondents reported having battered their partner in the previous 12 months (K. L. Chan, 2005). This means that one in every ten couples has suffered from spouse battery. Calculating from the 2004 population estimate of married couples, an estimated 160,000 citizens aged 15 and over suffer from spouse battery. And this number is likely much higher, since the Hong Kong Census and Statistics Department does not take into account nonmarried couples. However, only 6,843 intimate partner abuse cases were recorded in 2008 by the Central Information System, according to its report on Battered Spouse Cases (Social Welfare Department, 2008). Comparing this number with the prevalence estimate, the reported cases in the government statistics represent only the tip of the iceberg—only about 4% of the actual cases.

The full extent of this hidden domestic violence is alarming. How victims perceive maltreatment is suggested as one of the reasons for underreporting. Studies on public perception and reporting of abuse show quite clearly that people who perceive abuse tend to report it, people who perceive no abuse tend not to report it, and people with an uncertain perception of abuse have an uncertain tendency to report (Y. C. Chan, Chun, & Chung, 2008). This significant correlation between perception of abuse and reporting indicates a need for public education about the nature of abuse so that the public is informed and aware of when and how to report suspected abuse cases.

In addition, cultural factors also play an important role in the reporting of IPV. People with strong traditional Chinese beliefs are likely to underreport because they believe family affairs should be kept away from public scrutiny (Y. C. Chan et al., 2008). The Chinese believe that what happens between a couple is the core of family privacy and that outsiders have no right to intervene in other people's family matters (Chiu, Ho, & Sze, 2009). Thus, researchers and policymakers should be aware of the discrepancy between actual IPV prevalence and the reporting rate. It is also important to identify what factors lead to these discrepancies.

Risk factors for IPV

An increasing number of studies are providing a comprehensive profile of the risk factors associated with IPV. Current models of family violence have adopted a multifactorial ecological approach in explaining the occurrence of IPV. The available research has suggested that Chinese families with IPV may share the same problems (e.g., demographic and socioeconomic risk factors) that are reported in Western studies. The details of the studies of risk factors are listed in Table 2.3.

Chinese abusive partners tend to be unemployed or of a low socioeconomic status (Y. C. Chan, 1997; Y. Lau, 2005; T. W. Leung et al., 2003; W. C. Leung et al., 1999; Tsui, Chan, So, & Kam, 2006; Tsun & Lui-Tsang, 2005); indebted or experiencing financial difficulties (K. L. Chan & Straus, 2008; K. L. Chan et al., 2009; Y. C. Chan, 1997; Tiwari, Chan, et al., 2007; Tiwari et al., 2008; Tiwari, Fong, et al., 2007); abusers of alcohol and drugs (K. L. Chan & Brownridge, 2008; K. L. Chan & Straus, 2008; K. L. Chan et al., 2009; T. W. Leung, Leung, Ng, & Ho, 2005; Tsui et al., 2006); relatively young (K. L. Chan & Straus, 2008; Y. Lau, 2005; Tang, 1999a); insecure, with an aggressive personality, poor anger management, and a lack of empathy (K. L. Chan, 2004; K. L. Chan & Brownridge, 2008; Lee, Chan, & Raine, 2009); suffering from psychological disorders (Y. C. Chan, 1997; T. W. Leung et al., 2003; Tsui et al., 2006) or chronic illness (K. L. Chan et al., 2009); and suffering from hyperresponsivity to stimuli (Lee et al., 2009). Some studies have identified characteristics that victims tend to have, such as unplanned pregnancy (K. L. Chan et al., 2009; Y. Lau, 2005; W. C. Leung et al., 1999; Tiwari, Chan, et al., 2007; Tiwari et al., 2008). A lack of legal and social support also makes women more likely to be victims in an abusive relationship (K. L. Chan et al., 2009; T. W. Leung et al., 2003; Tsun & Lui-Tsang, 2005). Relationship factors significantly correlated with partner violence include relationship length (K. L. Chan & Straus, 2008; Tang, 1999a) and relationship stress and conflict (K. L. Chan, 2004; Y. C. Chan, 1997; Y. Lau, 2005). Extramarital affairs were also found to be a strong predictor of partner violence (Y. C. Chan, 1997; Tsui et al., 2006).

Although these universal risk factors have all been found to apply in Chinese culture, some characteristics specific to Chinese societies have also been investigated. In Hong Kong, a large age difference between spouses was found to be a significant risk factor. Both minor and severe violence are most frequent among couples aged 10 to 20 years apart (K. L. Chan, 2005; Tang, 1999a; Tiwari, Fong, et al., 2007). Such a large age difference is prevalent among new arrival families, in which a husband, usually aged over 50, marries a young woman from mainland China. When these cross-border brides move

Table 2.3 Studies of risk factors of spousal violence in Chinese societies

Source	Abuse Type	Sample	Risk Factors
Y. C. Chan (1997)	Violence against women	300 cases of domestic violence were reported by the newspaper under study	• Dispute • Marital problem: broken marriage • Marital problem: extramarital affair • Psychiatric problem • Financial problem • Unemployment
K. L. Chan (2004)	Spousal violence	107 Hong Kong Chinese battered women aged 5 to 70 years	• Dominance, a sense of insecurity, and conflict had significant positive correlations with minor physical assault • Aggressive personality predicted minor and severe physical assault • Dominance, poor anger management, aggressive personality, sense of insecurity, conflict, and lack of empathy showed a significant correlation with psychological aggression at both minor and severe levels • Relationship stress predicted severe psychological aggression • Conflict showed a positive correlation with severe sexual coercion
K. L. Chan (2005)	Spousal violence	5,049 Chinese couples in Hong Kong, 46.4% male and 53.6% female (response rate = 70%)	Among 30 significant risk factors identified, including: • Face, in-law conflict, and most of the PRP scales. • New arrival family and spousal age difference

(continued on page 37)

Table 2.3 (*continued*)

Source	Abuse Type	Sample	Risk Factors
K. L. Chan (2006)	Spousal violence	18 Hong Kong Chinese male batterers aged 21–55	• Face • In-law conflict • Lose temper in face-losing situations • Conscious of their performance in society and appraisals from others, especially peers • Batterers held a traditional gender role assumption that the man should be the provider and the woman the caregiver; believed that a man must be self-sufficient and competent; believed in the phrase "no income, no power", and felt it was shameful to have to rely on wives' financial support
K. L. Chan (2009)	Spousal violence	17 males aged 21–55; married / cohabiting with female partner > 6 months; involved in > 2 reported IPV; referred by social service agencies	• Protection of face • Avoidance of responsibility • Blame wife or condemn her for not fulfilling the role and expectations of wife and mother • Victimization of self: feeling suffocated, distressed, and unacknowledged in terms of difficulties of fulfilling their masculine roles as husband and father • Externalization of responsibility in an attempt to explain violent behaviour that seems to be out of their control • Privatization of violence: view that IPV is familial and unrelated to legal or social issues

(continued on page 38)

Table 2.3 (*continued*)

Source	Abuse Type	Sample	Risk Factors
K. L. Chan & Brownridge (2008)	Spousal Violence	210 women aged > 18; residents and ex-residents (left less than one year ago) of a shelter for battered women	• Males with poor anger management and approval of the use of violence used more physical assault and caused more injury to their female partners • Males who abused alcohol used more physical assault but didn't cause more injuries • Males with poor anger management, violence approval, alcohol abuse, apathy, jealousy, control, and domination used psychological aggression more frequently • Males with poor anger management, alcohol abuse, jealousy, and dominance used more sexual coercion
K. L. Chan & Straus (2005)	Dating violence	University students Hong Kong ($N = 959$), 69.4% female Shanghai and Beijing, China ($N = 2,247$), 62% female	• Dating physical and sexual violence, both perpetration and victimization, are associated with an increased rate of suicidal ideation • The relationship between dating violence and suicidal ideation is explained by depression
K. L. Chan & Straus (2008)	Dating violence	1,736 university students from Hong Kong, China and New Hampshire, USA, 70% female (response rate = 90%)	Dating violence in the preceding year • Year in college: freshman • Relationship length (6–12 moths)

(continued on page 39)

Table 2.3 (*continued*)

Source	Abuse Type	Sample	Risk Factors
K. L. Chan, Brownridge, et al. (2008)	Spousal violence	1,870 women with complete records on the characteristics of their partners within Hong Kong households	Lifetime IPV and preceding-year IPV • Being young • Indebtedness • Husband's alcohol abuse • Woman's higher income • Woman's in-law conflict
K. L. Chan et al. (2009)	Violence against pregnant women	3,245 pregnant women from seven hospitals in Hong Kong	• In-law conflict • Having chronic illness or having family member with chronic illness • Dependence on social support, indebtedness, low level of education • Unplanned pregnancy • Having more children • Alcoholism
Y. Lau (2005)	Violence against pregnant women	1,200 postnatal women from Queen Mary Hospital (response rate = 94.9%)	• Young age • Single and cohabiting • Born in Hong Kong with high level of acculturation • Low socioeconomic status • Poor relationship • Unplanned pregnancy

(continued on page 40)

Table 2.3 (*continued*)

Source	Abuse Type	Sample	Risk Factors
Lee, Chan, & Raine (2009)	Intimate partner violence	10 male batterers and 13 male matched controls were recruited in Hong Kong	• Higher neural hyperresponsivity to the threat stimuli in the hippocampus, fusiform gyrus, posterior cingulated gyrus, thalamus, and occipital cortex • Increased activation to the aggression against women stimuli • Increased activation to positive affect stimuli in right hemisphere orbitofrontal, anterior cingulated and inferior parietal cortical regions
W. C. Leung et al. (1999)	Violence against pregnant women	631 Chinese pregnant women attending the antenatal clinic of a local teaching hospital in Hong Kong	• Unplanned pregnancy • Husband/partner being unemployed
T. W. Leung et al. (2003)	Intimate partner violence	500 Chinese female patients attending the outpatient infertility clinic of a university teaching hospital in Hong Kong	Compared to the control group, the abused group showed: • Significantly lower scores for the social relationship domain • Tended to score lower in the psychological health domain and the environment domain
T. W. Leung et al. (2005)	Violence against women in obstetric/ gynaecological patients (OBGYN)	1,614 OBGYN patients were interviewed	Compared to the nonabused women, the abused victims tended to be/have: • Unemployed or nonskilled manual workers • Single/separated • Smokers • Drinkers • Lower monthly family income

(continued on page 41)

Table 2.3 (*continued*)

Source	Abuse Type	Sample	Risk Factors
Tang (1994)	Interparental aggression and violence	Chinese college students in Hong Kong: 246 females and 136 males	• Interparental responses to family conflicts did not vary with children's gender • Female subjects observed fathers reasoned less but engaged in more insulting, throwing, smashing, hitting, or kicking things than mothers
Tang (1999a)	Wife abuse	1,132 Chinese women in Hong Kong, aged 18 or over, currently or previously married or cohabiting with the opposite sex for the past year	• Couples' ages and their age differences related to physical but not verbal wife abuse • Minor physical abuse most frequent among couples aged 30 or under • Both minor and severe violence most frequent among couples aged 20+ years apart • The length of marriage and marital satisfaction significantly correlated with wife abuse
Tang (1999b)	Spousal violence	1,270 (518 males and 752 females) married Chinese in Hong Kong who were 18 years or older	• Egalitarian decision making was directly associated with marital satisfaction and inversely related to marital aggression • Severe violence was more prevalent in relationships that were husband-dominant
Tiwari, Chan, et al. (2007)	Abuse against pregnant women	3,245 pregnant women attending antenatal clinics, aged over 18 years, between 32–36 weeks into pregnancy	• Conflict with in-laws influenced IPV among pregnant women • Financial difficulties • Unplanned pregnancy

(*continued on page 42*)

Table 2.3 (*continued*)

Source	Abuse Type	Sample	Risk Factors
Tiwari, Fong, et al. (2007)	Violence against pregnant women	Convenience sampling	• Age differences • In need of financial assistance
Tiwari et al. (2008)	Violence against women	Consecutive sampling	• Being in debt • In need of financial assistance • Unplanned pregnancy • In-law conflict
Tsun & Lui-Tsang (2005)	Violence against women	Four clinical cases in Hong Kong	• Immigration background of the family • Low socioeconomic status • Perceived lack of support • Chinese values of obedience to authority
Tsui, Chan, So, & Kam (2006)	Violence against women	293 married women aged 18–60 years who attended an accident and emergency department for treatment of a domestic violence injury from January 2004 to June 2005, compared to 313 controls	Abused women were more likely to: • Have husband with low educational level • Have presence of extramarital affairs • Have unemployed husband • Have husband who abuses alcohol • Have husband who has mental illness

to Hong Kong after marriage, they often find that their husband's economic circumstances are much worse than they have expected. This leads to frequent marital conflicts which may easily spiral into violence.

The social and cultural legitimacy of female subordination is thought to be an important factor contributing to violence against women (Liu, 1999). Societies that approve of using violence are much more likely to have family violence. Unlike the typical Western domestic violence scenario that usually involves a lone man battering a lone woman, violence against women in Asia is often perpetrated by other members of the husband's family—in particular, senior women, such as the mother-in-law (K. L. Chan et al., 2009). Chinese culture prescribes three widely accepted rules of obedience for a moral, good woman: (a) when young, she must obey her father and elder brother(s); (b) when married, she must obey her husband; (c) when her husband is dead, she must obey her son (Pearson & Leung, 1995). It is very common for a mother-in-law to follow the will of her son by disciplining a wife. Previous research has confirmed the finding that women often suffer IPV at the hands of their in-laws (K. L. Chan, 2005, 2006; K. L. Chan, Brownridge, Tiwari, Fong, & Leung, 2008; K. L. Chan & Straus, 2008; K. L. Chan et al., 2009; Tiwari, Chan, et al., 2007; Tiwari et al., 2008). Thus, conflict with the in-laws is a risk factor for women, although it is not discussed in Western literature.

In addition, research in Hong Kong found significant correlations between partner violence and patriarchal authority and strong beliefs in patriarchal gender relationships (K. L. Chan, 2004, 2006, 2009; Tang, 1999b; Xu, Campbell, & Zhu, 2001). In Chinese culture, male dominance and patriarchal ideology have been seen as core family values and treated as facts of life. And it is not just among men; many women were found to have held on to traditional values and to believe there are good reasons to beat a wife (Jin, Eagle, & Yoshioka, 2007; Xu et al., 2005), especially when the face of the man is tarnished (K. L. Chan, 2005, 2006, 2009). In a large-scale study of 1,270 male and female respondents, male domination in marital relationships was found to be associated with marital aggression and dissatisfaction (Tang, 1999b). K. L. Chan (2006) also found that male abusers tended to hold a traditional gender-role belief that the man should be the provider and the woman the caregiver. Believing in the phrase "no income, no power", they felt it was shameful to have to rely on their wives' financial support. They believed that they had to dominate their wives. Violence became a tool with which to build the patriarchal platform, and thus was normalized on a large-scale cultural basis, legitimizing abusive acts in homes.

Health outcomes

Researchers in Hong Kong have found that battery is a significant risk factor for a variety of physical health problems. In Hong Kong, the physical injury perpetration rate is around 5% overall, with the rate of severe injury perpetration at 2.3%. Men are the dominant perpetrators of injurious assault (K. L. Chan, Straus, et al., 2008; Straus, 2004b). Studies have indicated that IPV leads to different kinds of physical injuries. The head, face, upper limbs, and lower limbs are most commonly injured. In a study assessing 1,695 victims of IPV seeking medical help in the emergency room, approximately 73% of IPV victims had mild physical injuries such as tenderness, hematoma, bruising, abrasion, or erythema. Overall, 10% of injuries were severe and 1% were life-threatening. Life-threatening injuries included lacerations or cuts, nasal bone fractures, limb fractures, and ruptured tympanic membranes (Y. Lau et al., 2008).

Studies also showed that abuse causes significant mental health consequences and leads victims to use healthcare services more often (Y. Lau et al., 2008; T. W. Leung et al., 2005; Tang, 1997). These studies found that depression, anxiety, lower overall psychological health, and higher stress levels correlated strongly with IPV. Domestic violence is even a significant precipitant of homicide suicides in Hong Kong. Domestic killing constitutes the major type of homicide suicides in Hong Kong, and over 60% of these homicides were motivated by spousal conflicts or mercy killing (Yip, Wong, Cheung, Chan, & Beh, 2009). IPV not only increases the rate of homicide, but also correlates with suicidal ideation among the perpetrators and victims of IPV. In studies of dating violence, physical violence and sexual violence, both perpetration and victimization were found to be associated with an increased rate of suicidal ideation (K. L. Chan & Straus, 2005; K. L. Chan, Straus, et al., 2008).

IPV can start at any point in a relationship; it can even happen while a woman is pregnant. The negative health impact of abuse is particularly significant among pregnant women, and it may take its toll directly, or indirectly through the trauma it brings. Women who experience IPV during their pregnancy are at greater risk of postnatal depression, having thoughts about harming themselves, and poorer mental health (Tiwari et al., 2008).

IPV is rarely an isolated event. Most victims experience multiple types of abuse. Compared with women who had suffered only one type of abuse, women who had experienced more than one type of abuse had significantly worse scores in five subscales (bodily pain, general health, vitality, social functioning, and mental health) and in two overall domains (total physical and total mental health; Y. Lau, Wong, & Chan, 2008). The more types of abuse experienced, the more acute was the impairment of health-related quality of life.

IPV during pregnancy also has a tremendous influence on the quality of the care received by newborn children. Women who do not experience IPV during pregnancy are more likely to initiate breastfeeding compared to women who report abuse (Y. Lau & Chan, 2007). Possible explanations for this finding are power and control issues in the abusive relationship, stress from IPV interfering with the production of breast milk, and jealousy from the abusive partner (Y. Lau & Chan, 2007).

Given the severe health problems IPV inflicts upon its victims, healthcare professionals who have the capability to provide aid to women in abusive relationships should consider offering screening services and interventions for IPV. As well as physical forms of aggression, studies of domestic violence prevention or treatment should also extend to nonphysical forms of aggression. Continuous efforts should be made towards increasing IPV knowledge and recognition so that resources can be directed towards implementing prevention strategies that will be most effective.

Culture and help-seeking behaviour

Face orientation has an important effect on self disclosure (Cheung, Leung, & Tsui, 2009). The more an individual associates face with morality, the less willing he/she is to disclose immoral behaviour. Men have been found to have a higher face orientation than women because they are under greater pressure to present themselves as capable (K. L. Chan, 2009). Thus, Chinese men regard help-seeking and disclosure of personal problems as a sign of weakness. Male subjects may be aware of their face needs when presenting their views or disclosing their problems. They would feel a loss of face if they were to reveal their vulnerability and socially undesirable behaviour, such as violence against women, ineffective coping strategies, and angry or destructive activities. In order to avoid loss of face, they may make up stories and use cultural values to justify their behaviour.

An analysis of the accounts of Chinese male batterers demonstrated how Chinese batterers rationalize their violence in order to save face and avoid responsibility (K. L. Chan, 2006, 2009). While recognizing violence as socially unacceptable, they minimized their responsibility for the event and tried to present themselves as responsible and honourable. Their main self-presentation strategy was to construct a self-image of a man of "passion and responsibility", while at the same time blaming their spouses for not fulfilling the duties of wife and mother. Physical violence for them was a way to punish their wives and educate them to be virtuous, dutiful, and obedient. They saw violence as an effective means of resolving conflicts and disciplining spouses. Clearly, these male batterers were not prepared to accept full responsibility for their use of violence.

Face orientation also has a strong effect on female victims of IPV, especially on their help-seeking behaviour. The majority of female victims living in shelters for battered women in Hong Kong had tolerated violence from their husbands for more than five years (K. L. Chan, 2000). They saw family violence as shameful, and the concern to save face prevented them from disclosing their predicament to others. This finding is echoed by other studies which have found that the cultural values of suffering and fatalism interfere with people's desire to seek help with their family problems (Malley-Morrison & Hines, 2004).

To better understand the dynamics of a Chinese woman's decision to remain in or leave an abusive relationship, I have designed a process model.

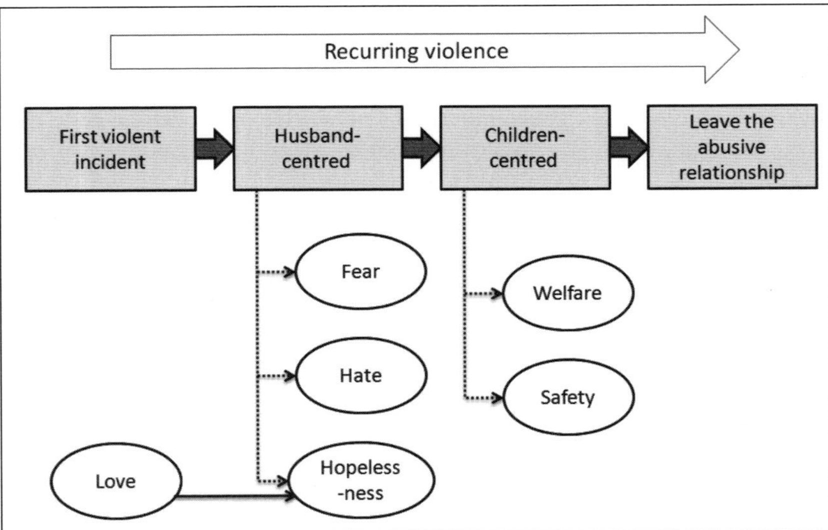

Figure 2.1   Being battered—from staying to leaving: a process model for Chinese women

Most battered women in my sample were willing to forgive and forget after the first incidence (Chan, 2000). It is very unusual for a woman to leave an abusive husband after the first incidence of violence; this is especially true for a woman who has long been subordinate to her husband and has put him at the centre of the family. Women usually make accommodations to maintain harmony, and they often resort to self-blame instead (Cardarelli, 1997). Chinese battered women tend to hold the belief that a woman should be faithful to a sole husband until death (Chiu, 2001). They equate success in marriage to success in life. As Chinese societies associate a broken family with loss of face and family shame, the stigma of divorce can hinder early disclosure of family violence. Battered women may be reluctant to get divorced, which they see as a failure, and thus violence may be tolerated for years. Only when the violence becomes recurring and more severe—and their lives are filled with fear and hatred—will they begin to feel that the relationship is hopeless. Extramarital affairs become increasingly common, with the husband often raising another family with a partner whom he is not wedded to, or with a woman to whom he is illegally married in mainland China. If the second family has children, it is likely to occasion even greater hopelessness in the first wife. However, recurring violence and even extramarital affairs are often not enough to prompt battered wives to leave an abusive relationship. Instead, their concern shifts from being husband-centred to child-centred. Many believe that a family with both parents can provide best for their children, even despite intense spousal conflict. Only when battered women feel that the violence could endanger their children do they think about leaving the abusive relationship.

Intervention

Violence screening measures

In order to prevent IPV in the family, we first need to screen for the existence of violence. Different types of measures have been suggested for screening IPV in healthcare settings. The Revised Conflict Tactics Scales (CTS2), with its well-documented psychometric characteristics (Straus, 1990) and high cross-cultural reliability (Straus, 2004a), has been used as the "gold standard" to identify IPV. It has been modified from the original Conflict Tactics Scales (CTS) with the inclusion of two new subscales to improve its validity (Straus, Hamby, Boney-McCoy, & Sugarman, 1996). In the modified version, five areas of spousal conflicts are assessed: negotiation, physical assault, psychological aggression, physical injury, and sexual coercion. The CTS2 has been translated into Chinese and validated using data collected in Hong Kong (K. L. Chan, 2004).

Although this scale has been used widely, the 39-item tool may not be practical for a busy clinical setting. The Revised Conflict Tactics Scales Short Form (CTS2S) has been developed for testing in Hong Kong. However, results have shown that the CTS2S yields a consistently lower rate in almost all areas of IPV compared to the CTS2. The CTS2 has three to six items to assess each specific type of IPV, but the CTS2S contains only one item to measure each problem, making it a less sensitive screening tool (Y. C. Chan, Au, Lam, & Chung, 2006).

The Abuse Assessment Screen (AAS) has been suggested as a tool for IPV screening. With only five questions, the AAS can be used in many busy healthcare settings. It has been used extensively throughout the United States and internationally (Campbell & Furniss, 2002). Research has also testified to the accuracy of the Chinese version of the AAS in identifying risk factors of IPV in Hong Kong (Tiwari, Fong, et al., 2007). The Chinese AAS has demonstrated a satisfactory level of measurement accuracy with high specificity, positive predictive values, and satisfactory to high negative predictive values in screening IPV (Tiwari, Fong, et al., 2007).

In addition, recent research has attempted to use the Brief Spousal Assault Form for the Evaluation of Risk (B-SAFER) to assess IPV risk factors in Hong Kong (Au et al., 2008). Results have shown that the B-SAFER can differentiate batterers from controls with good concurrent validity with the CTS2. The B-SAFER has been demonstrated to be useful, since it is time-efficient and flexible enough to capture case-specific details and variation in IPV risk factors in Hong Kong (Au et al., 2008). Healthcare professionals can adopt the guided clinical approach with the help of the B-SAFER screening tool to generate management and intervention strategies.

Treatments

Given that a high percentage of IPV perpetrators in Hong Kong are male, male dominance is thought to be a central component to understanding why domestic violence occurs—and a key to finding solutions. Interventions carried out in Hong Kong often target the battered woman rather than the male wife-abuser.

Among services targeted at males, most focus on men as perpetrators and help them find ways to avoid violence, with some services attending to male victims of domestic violence (Cheung et al., 2009).

Current law also targets men as the perpetrators, and uses jail sentences to achieve the two-pronged purpose of punishing abusers and protecting victims. However, the effectiveness of current legal provisions in controlling domestic violence has received criticism. According to Chiu (2001), jailing a wife-abuser does not guarantee the victim's safety, since the victim may not demand divorce out of concern over receiving a poor financial settlement or custody arrangement. Even if the couple does get divorced, they will inadvertently keep contact in the process of raising their children. Furthermore, imprisonment of the abuser—oftentimes the breadwinner—may further aggravate the family's financial problems. If imprisonment fails to elicit changes in the abuser's attitude, releasing him will lead to further violence against the wife for having reported him. Therefore, Chiu (2001) proposed a court-mandated counselling programme for abusers, aimed at restructuring the gender balance and subverting their patriarchal thinking which is thought to be the main cause of IPV in Hong Kong. Counselling programmes using feminist approaches to therapy tend to work towards men's recognition of their rigid and distorted beliefs and expectations, and lead them to acknowledge responsibility for their violence (Chiu, 2001).

On the other hand, some interventions have aimed at helping victims to adjust the situation and protect their physical and mental health. However, systematic reviews of these types of interventions have found insufficient evidence of their effectiveness. Tiwari and her colleagues (2005) used a randomized controlled trial to test the effectiveness of empowerment training proposed for abused pregnant Chinese women in Hong Kong. The intervention was based on an empowerment protocol developed by Parker, McFarlane, and Soeken (1994), which was designed to enhance an abused woman's independence and control by giving advice on safety, choice making, and problem solving. Empathic understanding (Rogers, 1951) was emphasized in the empowerment protocol in addressing perceptions and feelings from a female perspective. This modified intervention was given to the experimental group, whereas the control group received standard care routine: a wallet-sized card with information on community resources for abused women, including hotlines to shelters, law enforcement, social services, and nongovernmental organizations. Results showed that the experimental group had significantly higher physical functioning and improved scores on the role limitation measures for both physical and emotional problems. They also reported significantly less psychological abuse and minor physical violence. Therefore, the empowerment training for abused pregnant Chinese women showed positive results (Tiwari et al., 2005).

However, it should be noted that the abuse experienced by pregnant Chinese women may be predominantly psychological (W. C. Leung et al., 1999). Therefore, interventions aimed at Chinese women in general may be different from those for pregnant women. An empowerment intervention developed by Tiwari and colleagues (2005) was tested for its effectiveness in improving an abused woman's health. Standard care with emergency housing and food, crisis interventions, referrals to welfare, legal advocacy, and other services were provided to both treatment and control groups. The treatment group received an additional empowerment intervention for six hours, delivered over a three-week period. The intervention included:

> (a) cycle of violence recognition, (b) danger assessment, (c) selecting an option, (d) application for legal protection orders and filing criminal charges, (e) development of a safety plan, (f) retention of community resource phone numbers, (g) group counselling on legal advocacy, (h) diagnostic assessment of health (based on concepts of Chinese medicine, teaching on Chinese dietary regimens and group counselling on health risk behaviours), and (i) teaching of parenting skills and group counselling on management of children's behavioural problems (Tiwari, Salili, Chan, Chan, & Tang, 2010).

Results showed that the empowerment intervention was not more effective or better than standard care in improving battered women's psychological health and quality of life. However, it did improve diet planning and parenting skills. Moreover, women in the treatment group had gone further towards divorcing their partners (Tiwari et al., 2010). The empowerment intervention may have provided them with the necessary skills and knowledge to take action to end the abusive relationship.

Prevention of IPV from the ecological perspective

Tsun and Lui-Tsang (2005) have developed a multifaceted and multileveled prevention model to bring wife battery to a halt in Hong Kong.

Microsystem-level prevention

Intervention should be targeted to address perpetrator-related and victim-related risk factors separately. Through treatment, perpetrators of abuse should be educated to unlearn the violent acts and restructure the beliefs and attitudes they use to justify their use of violence. Anger management training, stress management, emotional and behavioural control, and treatment for men with aggressive personalities will be helpful for preventing battery. Hong Kong in particular needs a face-sensitive intervention to address the abusers' face needs and the stress they experience when confronted with challenges to their gender role expectations. It is believed that Chinese abusers with higher acquisitive face orientation will be more willing to talk about their experience in such an intervention (K. L. Chan, 2006). An attitude of open listening and support can also help bring about effective engagement, while at the same time stressing one's personal responsibility in steering clear of violent behaviour (K. L. Chan, 2009).

Victims should be educated about domestic violence, strategies for coping with adversity in life, the development of mutual respect, and human rights, in order to raise their general awareness of violence and to change any distorted perceptions they hold about IPV. Interventions that empower women to take control of their own lives and the provision of social services and resources that support women to leave abusive partners are necessary (Chiu, 2001). At this microsystem level of prevention, services that aim to address perpetrator-related and victim-related risk factors should be used.

Exosystem-level prevention

A supportive neighbourhood or community is also a protective factor for reducing the vulnerability of families under stress. Research has demonstrated that IPV springs from the discordance of the environment in which individuals and families live. Thus, higher rates of IPV are often found in poor neighbourhoods.

Poverty or low socioeconomic status and IPV are often interwoven. In this regard, the socioeconomic status of families is an important variable predicting IPV in a community. One way to prevent violence is to provide the opportunity for every individual to achieve a high level of education and participate in lifelong learning. Collaboration between professionals, the general public, families, and individuals in the community should be fostered to establish an open and well-informed community (Tsun & Lui-Tsang, 2005).

Community-level intervention is encouraged in dealing with a communities that have multiple problems, such as Tin Shui Wai (Y. C. Chan, Lam, & Cheng, 2009). Tin Shui Wai, also known as the "City of Sorrows", is an area which gathers new immigrants from mainland China, low-income individuals, unemployed families living on welfare, and families living and coping with high stress. They are relatively excluded both geographically and socially, which increases their vulnerability to IPV. Y. C. Chan and his colleagues (2009) have suggested a community capacity-building model to rebuild Tin Shui Wai. First, the community needs to develop and nurture a true sense of community—a feeling of connectedness and mutuality among its members so as to connect the strengths of each individual. Second, it is important for the community to be aware of the problem of domestic violence, and to recognize that it is a problem worth its effort and investment to find a collaborative solution. Third, stakeholders of the community need to develop problem-solving skills and arrive at a collective resolution to take action. Lastly, access to different kinds of resources should be improved by increasing multilateral communication and collaboration between different departments. Each individual should contribute to his/her capacity in building a better community to live in.

Macrosystem-level prevention

Of paramount importance when providing intervention for IPV is the availability of legal action and government policies against the perpetrators of IPV. However, the police in Hong Kong are inclined to view the problem of IPV more as a private issue between a couple in which they cannot or should not intervene. Research showed that nearly 40% of the 84 victims of wife abuse interviewed hoped that the police could immediately stop the abuse, but only 15% thought that the police had in fact done so. More surprisingly, 1,270 out of 1,608 police officers interviewed were not clear about the formal procedure for handling cases of domestic violence (Chiu, 2001). Social workers in Hong Kong are also inclined to work at enhancing the harmony of the family rather than to address directly the needs of battered women. Therefore, social workers' preference for counselling may unintentionally lead battered women to overlook their need for protection (Y. C. Chan & Lam, 2005).

Obviously, an important objective of existing policies and social services concerning domestic violence in Hong Kong is to adopt a victim-oriented approach in addressing the problem of IPV, in all seriousness and earnestness. Rather than jeopardizing the safety of abused women, this will work towards serving their best interests.

Conclusion

This chapter has provided a comprehensive review of IPV in Hong Kong by examining prevalence and risk factors. Culture-specific factors should be given due recognition in order to put together a complete picture of IPV in Hong Kong. Given the tremendous health problems IPV inflicts on its victims, IPV screening and interventions should be considered. However, domestic violence is difficult to intervene in when both perpetrators and victims are unwilling to disclose the matter. Furthermore, criminal justice practitioners are often less than willing to tackle the problem. Therefore, public education should be promoted to raise awareness and recognition of IPV.

Using an ecological framework, this review sets out a multifaceted model addressing different levels of IPV. The model views domestic violence as the interaction of personal factors at the microsystem level; risk factors at the exosystem level, such as living in a poor neighbourhood, having low socio-economic status, and living in a socially isolated community; and the actions of authorities at the macrosystem level. Interventions will fall short of effectiveness if they do not take into consideration the roles of factors of domestic violence at different levels. Government support, in terms of appropriate central policies and sufficient resources, is necessary for the development of a comprehensive, multipronged intervention for victims of domestic violence.

References

Au, A., Cheung, G., Kropp, R., Yuk-Chung, C., Lam, G. L. T., & Sung, P. (2008). A preliminary validation of the Brief Spousal Assault Form for the Evaluation of Risk (B-SAFER) in Hong Kong. *Journal of Family Violence*, *23*, 727–735. doi: 10.1007/s10896-008-9198-z

Campbell, J., & Furniss, K. K. (2002). *Violence Against Women: Identification, Screening and Management of Intimate Partner Violence*. Washington, DC: Association of Women's Health, Obstetric and Neonatal Nurses.

Chan, K. L. (2000). *Unraveling the Dynamics of Spousal Abuse Through the Narrative Accounts of Chinese Male Batterers* (Doctoral dissertation, the University of Hong Kong, Hong Kong, China). Retrieved from http://hub.hku.hk/handle/123456789/27602

Chan, K. L. (2004). Correlates of wife assault in Hong Kong Chinese families. *Violence and Victims*, *19*, 189–201.

Chan, K. L. (2005). *Study on Child Abuse and Spouse Battering: Report on Findings of Household Survey*. Retrieved from Department of Social Work and Social

Administration, the University of Hong Kong website: http://www.swd.gov.hk/doc/family/Report%20on%20findings%20of%20Household%20Survey.pdf

Chan, K. L. (2006). The Chinese concept of face and violence against women. *International Social Work, 49*(1), 65–73. doi: 10.1177/0020872806059402

Chan, K. L. (2009). Protection of face and avoidance of responsibility: Chinese men's account of violence against women. *Journal of Social Work Practice, 23*, 93–108. doi: 10.1080/02650530902723340

Chan, K. L., & Brownridge, D. A. (2008). Personality characteristics of Chinese male batterers: an exploratory study of women's reports from a refuge sample of battered women in Hong Kong. *American Journal of Men's Health, 2*, 218–228. doi: 10.1177/1557988307308000

Chan, K. L., Brownridge, D. A., Tiwari, A., Fong, D. Y. T., & Leung, W. C. (2008). Understanding violence against Chinese women in Hong Kong: an analysis of risk factors with a special emphasis on the role of in-law conflict. *Violence Against Women, 14*, 1295–1312. doi: 10.1177/1077801208325088

Chan, K. L., & Straus, M. A. (2005). *Prevalence of Dating Partner Violence and Suicidal Ideation Among Male and Female University Students Worldwide.* Paper presented at the 9th International Family Violence Research Conference, organized by the Family Research Laboratory and Crimes Against Children Research Center, Portsmouth, New Hampshire.

Chan, K. L., & Straus, M. A. (2008). Prevalence and correlates of physical assault on dating partners. *The Open Social Science Journal, 1*, 5–14. Retrieved from http://pubpages.unh.edu/~mas2/ID56-Chan-Straus-Prevalence%20and%20Correlates%20of%20Physical%20Assault%20on%20Dating%20Partners-08.pdf

Chan, K. L., Straus, M. A., Brownridge, D. A., Tiwari, A., & Leung, W. C. (2008). Prevalence of dating partner violence and suicidal ideation among male and female university students worldwide. *Journal of Midwifery & Women's Health, 53*, 529–537. doi: 10.1016/j.jmwh.2008.04.016

Chan, K. L., Tiwari, A., Fong, D. Y. T., Leung, W. C., Brownridge, D. A., & Ho, P. C. (2009). Correlates of in-law conflict and intimate partner violence against Chinese pregnant women in Hong Kong. *Journal of Interpersonal Violence, 24*, 97–110. doi: 10.1177/0886260508315780

Chan, Y. C. (1997). Combating violence against women: hindsight from a decade of news reports on family violence in Hong Kong. *Hong Kong Journal of Social Work, 31*, 83–96.

Chan, Y. C., Au, A., Lam, G. L. T., & Chung, K. W. (2006). Intimate partner violence in Hong Kong: findings from a territory-wide telephone survey. *Journal of Psychology in Chinese Societies, 7*, 307–324.

Chan, Y. C., Chun, P. R., & Chung, K. (2008). Public perception and reporting of different kinds of family abuse in Hong Kong. *Journal of Family Violence, 23*, 253–263. doi: 10.1007/s10896-007-9149-0

Chan, Y. C., & Lam, G. L. T. (2005). Unraveling the rationale for a one-stop service under the Family and Child Protection Services Units in Hong Kong. *International Social Work, 48*, 419–428. doi: 10.1177/0020872805053466

Chan, Y. C., Lam, G. L. T., & Cheng, H. C. H. (2009). Community capacity building as a strategy of family violence prevention in a problem-stricken community: a theoretical formulation. *Journal of Family Violence, 24*, 559–568.

Cheung, M., Leung, P., & Tsui, V. (2009). Asian male domestic violence victims: services exclusive for men. *Journal of Family Violence, 24*, 447–462. doi: 10.1007/s10896-009-9240-9

Chiu, M. C. (2001). Politicising Han-Chinese masculinities: a plea for court-mandated counselling for wife abusers in Hong Kong. *Feminist Legal Studies, 9*, 3–27.

Chiu, M. Y. L., Ho, W. W. N., & Sze, F. S. F. (2009). Mental distress and internal stigma in seeking professional help among women in Tin Shui Wai (TSW), Hong Kong. *Hong Kong Journal of Social Work, 43*(1), 67–76.

Hong Kong Social Welfare Department. (2008). *Statistics on Child Abuse, Battered Spouse and Sexual Violence Cases.* Hong Kong: The Central Information System on Battered Spouse Cases.

Jin, X. C., Eagle, M., & Yoshioka, M. (2007). Early exposure to violence in the family of origin and positive attitudes toward marital violence: Chinese immigrant male batterers vs. controls. *Journal of Family Violence, 22*, 211–222.

Lau, C. L., Ching, W. M., Tong, W. L., Chan, K. L., Tsui, K. L., & Kam, C. W. (2008). 1700 victims of intimate partner violence: characteristics and clinical outcomes. *Hong Kong Medical Journal, 14*, 451–457. Retrieved from http://www.hkmj.org/article_pdfs/hkm0812p451.pdf

Lau, Y. (2005). Does pregnancy provide immunity from intimate partner abuse among Hong Kong Chinese women? *Social Science & Medicine, 61*, 365–377. doi: 10.1016/j.socscimed.2004.12.002

Lau, Y., & Chan, K. S. (2007). Influence of intimate partner violence during pregnancy and early postpartum depressive symptoms on breastfeeding among Chinese women in Hong Kong. *Journal of Midwifery & Women's Health, 52*(2), e15–e20. doi: 10.1016/j.jmwh.2006.09.001

Lau, Y., Wong, D. F., & Chan, K. S. (2008). The impact and cumulative effects of intimate partner abuse during pregnancy on health-related quality of life among Hong Kong Chinese women. *Midwifery, 24*, 22–37. doi: 10.1016/j.midw.2006.06.010

Lee, T. M. C., Chan, S. C., & Raine, A. (2009). Hyperresponsivity to threat stimuli in domestic violence offenders: a functional magnetic resonance imaging study. *Journal of Clinical Psychiatry, 70*, 36–45.

Leung, T. W., Leung, W. C., Ng, E. H. Y., & Ho, P. C. (2005). Quality of life of victims of intimate partner violence. *International Journal of Gynecology & Obstetrics, 90*(3), 258–262. doi: 10.1016/j.ijgo.2005.05.010

Leung, T. W., Ng, E. H. Y., Leung, W. C., & Ho, P. C. (2003). Intimate partner violence among infertile women. *International Journal of Gynecology & Obstetrics*, *83*, 323–324. doi: 10.1016/S0020-7292(03)00298-4

Leung, W. C., Leung, T. W., Lam, Y. Y. J., & Ho, P. C. (1999). The prevalence of domestic violence against pregnant women in a Chinese community. *International Journal of Gynecology & Obstetrics*, *66*, 23–30.

Liu, M. (1999). Enduring violence and staying in marriage: stories of battered women in rural China. *Violence Against Women*, *5*, 1469–1492. doi: 10.1177/10778019922183471

Malley-Morrison, K., & Hines, D. A. (2004). *Family Violence in a Cultural Perspective: Defining, Understanding, and Combating Abuse*. Thousand Oaks, CA: Sage Publications.

Parish, W. L., Wang, T. F., Laumann, E. O., Pan, S. M., & Luo, Y. (2004). Intimate partner violence in China: national prevalence, risk factors and associated health problems. *International Family Planning Perspectives*, *30*(4), 174–181.

Parker, B., McFarlane, J., & Soeken, K. (1994). Abuse during pregnancy: effects on maternal complications and birthweight in adult and teenage women. *Obstetrics & Gynaecology*, *84*, 323–328.

Pearson, V., & Leung, B. K. P. (1995). *Women in Hong Kong*. Hong Kong: Oxford University Press.

Rogers, C. (1951). *Client-centered therapy, its current practice, implications and theory*. Boston, MA: Houghton Mifflin.

Straus, M. A. (1990). The Conflict Tactics Scale and its critics: an evaluation and new data on validity and reliability. In M. A. Straus & R. J. Gelles (Eds.), *Physical Violence in American Families: Risk Factors and Adaptations to Violence in 8,145 Families* (pp. 31–54). New Brunswick, NJ: Transaction Publishers.

Straus, M. A. (2004a). Cross-cultural reliability and validity of the Revised Conflict Tactics Scales: a study of university student dating couples in 17 nations. *Cross-Cultural Research*, *38*, 407–432. doi: 10.1177/1069397104269543

Straus, M. A. (2004b). Prevalence of violence against dating partners by male and female university students worldwide. *Violence Against Women*, *10*, 790–811. doi: 10.1177/1077801204265552

Straus, M. A., Hamby, S. L., Boney-McCoy, S., & Sugarman, D. B. (1996). The Revised Conflict Tactics Scales (CTS2): development and preliminary psychometric data. *Journal of Family Issues*, *17*, 283–316. doi: 10.1177/019251396017003001

Tang, C. S. K. (1997). Psychological impact of wife abuse: experiences of Chinese women and their children. *Journal of Interpersonal Violence*, *12*, 466–478. doi: 10.1177/088626097012003010

Tang, C. S. K. (1999a). Wife abuse in Hong Kong Chinese families: a community survey. *Journal of Family Violence*, *14*, 173–191. doi: 10.1023/A:1022028803208

Tang, C. S. K. (1999b). Marital power and aggression in a community sample of Hong Kong Chinese families. *Journal of Interpersonal Violence*, *14*(6), 586–602. doi: 10.1177/088626099014006002

Tiwari, A., Chan, K. L., Fong, D., Leung, W. C., Brownridge, D. A., Lam, H., Wong, B., Lam, C. M., Chau, F., Chan, A., Cheung, K. B., & Ho, P. C. (2007). A territory-wide survey on intimate partner violence among pregnant women in Hong Kong. *Hong Kong Journal of Gynaecology, Obstetrics and Midwifery, 7,* 7–15.

Tiwari, A., Chan, K. L., Fong, D., Leung, W. C., Brownridge, D. A., Lam, H., Wong, B., Lam, C. M., Chau, F., Chan, A., Cheung, K. B., & Ho, P. C. (2008). The impact of psychological abuse by an intimate partner on the mental health of pregnant women. *BJOG, 115,* 377–384

Tiwari, A., Fong, D. Y. T., Chan, K. L., Leung, W. C., Parker, B., & Hoe, P. C. (2007). Identifying intimate partner violence: comparing the Chinese Abuse Assessment Screen with the Chinese Revised Conflict Tactics Scales. *BJOG, 114,* 1065–1071.

Tiwari, A., Leung, W. C., Leung, T. W., Humphreys, J., Parker, B., & Ho, P. C. (2005). A randomised controlled trial of empowerment training for Chinese abused pregnant women in Hong Kong. *BJOG, 112,* 1249–1256.

Tiwari, A. F. Y., Salili, F., Chan, R. Y. P., Chan, E. K. L., & Tang, D. (2010). Effectiveness of an empowerment intervention in abused Chinese women. *Hong Kong Medical Journal, 16*(Suppl 3), S25–28. Retrieved from http://www.hkmj. org/supplements/article_pdfs/hkm1006sp3p25.pdf

Tsui, K. L., Chan, A. Y., So, F. L., & Kam, C. W. (2006). Risk factors for injury to married women from domestic violence in Hong Kong. *Hong Kong Medical Journal, 12,* 289–293. Retrieved from http://www.hkmj.org/article_pdfs/ hkm0608p289.pdf

Tsun, A. O., & Lui-Tsang, P. S. (2005). Violence against wives and children in Hong Kong. *Journal of Family and Economic Issues, 26*(4), 465–486. doi: 10.1007/ s10834-005-7845-6

Wang, T., Parish, W. L., Laumann, E. O., & Luo, Y. (2009). Partner violence and sexual jealousy in China: a population-based survey. *Violence Against Women, 15,* 774–798. doi: 10.1177/1077801209334271

Xu, X., Campbell, J. C., & Zhu, F. C. (2001). Intimate partner violence against Chinese women: the past, present, and future. *Trauma Violence Abuse, 2,* 296–315. doi: 10.1177/1524838001002004002

Xu, X., Zhu, F., O'Campo, P., Koenig, M. A., Mock, V., & Campbell, J. (2005). Prevalence of and risk factors for intimate partner violence in China. *American Journal of Public Health, 95,* 788–5. Retrieved from http://ajph.aphapublications.org/cgi/reprint/95/1/78.pdf

Yip, P. S. F., Wong, P. W. C., Cheung, Y. T., Chan, K. S., & Beh, S. L. (2009). An empirical study of characteristics and types of homicide-suicides in Hong Kong, 1989–2005. *Journal of Affective Disorders, 112*(1–3), 184–192.

3
Child Abuse and Child Policy

Hong Kong's Situation and Global Experience

Patrick P. K. Ip and Chun-Bong Chow

Chapter summary

1. Evolution of child rights and recognition of child abuse—the problems of child abuse and maltreatment have increasingly gained attention overseas and locally over the past two centuries. It is now better recognized as a critical issue affecting the health and well-being of children and their family.

2. Severity and rising trend of child maltreatment—child maltreatment has been identified as a prevalent problem affecting a large proportion of children worldwide. The prevalence of child abuse in Hong Kong has been increasing in the past decade.

3. Importance of prevention and early intervention—emerging evidence in early child development research forms the basis of primary prevention in child protection and early intervention for child abuse, with the aim of avoiding all adverse long-term complications.

4. A preventive approach is more effective—Hong Kong needs a comprehensive long-term child policy with vision, including a clear policy in child protection, and should also embrace a new concept which emphasizes primary prevention of child maltreatment.

According to the multidisciplinary procedural guidelines developed for handling child abuse cases in Hong Kong, child abuse is defined as any act of commission or omission that endangers or impairs a child's physical or psychological health and development (Working Group on Child Abuse, 1998). Child abuse refers to the physical and emotional mistreatment, sexual abuse, neglect and negligent treatment of children, as well as to their commercial or other exploitation. With its complex dynamics and predisposing factors, child maltreatment is recognized internationally as a serious public health, human rights, legal and social issue.

History of child abuse and cultural change

Child abuse has been described in literature for hundreds of years, but the context of child abuse and the awareness of children's rights have not evolved much over the course of human history. Until the eighteenth century, children were viewed as possessions of their parents, who had the ultimate authority to treat children in any way they wished. Lynch (1985) examined evidence produced throughout the centuries on the recognition of physical abuse, and found that many of the early references were medical and that physicians easily accepted that caring acts for children might injure them. Such cultural values, however, started to change in the past two centuries. Incest became punishable as a crime under church law (De Mause, 1974). And by the early eighteenth century, children were being punished for such things as touching their genitals, a suggestion of "inherent badness" which called for discipline. By the nineteenth century, maltreatment of children was often observed but denied, and more obscure diagnoses were sought to explain away any injuries and lesions. However, even during a time when some physicians were pursuing such "scientific" etiologies, there were publications being put out that demonstrated a continuing acknowledgement of the problem of child abuse (Lynch, 1985). Around the turn of the twentieth century, social denial of abuse continued. Freud's work in which patients reported that they had been sexually abused by their parents was not accepted at the time, and he changed his interpretation to imply that it was fantasy (Reder, Duncan, & Gray, 1993). Sexual abuse of children was still thought to be a rare occurrence; however, incest was made a criminal offence when the Punishment of Incest Act was passed in 1908.

The twentieth century saw the beginnings of an acknowledgement of the problem of child abuse and the recognition that children needed protection, though society was slow to accept that carers could deliberately harm children for whom they were responsible. In 1946, Caffey, a paediatric radiologist in the US, described bone lesions and subdural haematomas resulting from trauma, and Kempe, a paediatrician in the US, described the "battered child syndrome" (Kempe, Silverman, & Steel, 1962). The term "non-accidental injury" (NAI) became the medically accepted label for this syndrome in the United Kingdom, and doctors became increasingly involved with the work of social workers and the police in its diagnosis. Medical evidence was necessary for proof, and the methods of history, examination, investigation and diagnosis in the traditional medical model were gradually adopted for this initial stage of child protection development (Polnay, 2001).

In the 1980s, many articles began appearing in the medical press on child sexual abuse. Mrazek et al. (1983) showed that professional recognition of child sexual abuse was at a similar stage as that of physical abuse twenty years ago. Sexual abuse of children was seldom if at all mentioned, resulting in a lack of diagnosis and inadequate treatment. Thus, in society and in the medical profession, the problem of child sexual abuse was beginning to be seriously highlighted only in the mid-1980s. The actual confirmation of sexual abuse was still seen to be based on the medical model, with the doctor retaining a principal role in diagnosis. At the same time, society's level of acknowledgement lagged behind that of professionals, whether in Western or oriental societies.

Despite the progress made on recognizing child abuse, defining what constitutes child abuse has remained a matter of debate in the past decades. Many countries for a long time deemed corporal punishment at school as acceptable; yet nowadays, such practices as caning of school children, which used to be widely accepted and almost universally practised, have been incorporated within the widening spectrum of child abuse. Even today, the debate continues as to the appropriateness of smacking or spanking children by parents who seek to enforce discipline.

Definitions and types of abuse

Child abuse is defined as actions or different forms of physical, emotional or psychological ill-treatment, sexual abuse, neglect or negligent treatment that result in actual or potential harm to the child's health, survival, development or dignity in the context of a relationship of responsibility, trust or power. It can be classified into five categories: physical abuse, child neglect, sexual abuse, psychological abuse and a combination of any of the above types (Department of Health, UK Government, 2006).

Physical child abuse, which usually occurs in the context of non-accidental injuries, is an intentional use of physical force against a child that results in harm to the child. Common examples include hitting, beating, shaking, biting, kicking, scalding, burning, poisoning, strangling and suffocating. Important and alarming clinical features include multiple bruises of different age, bite or cigarette burn marks; unexplained fractures such as complex skull fracture after a short fall (<1.2 m), posterior rib fracture, metaphyseal long-bone or femur fracture in an infant, multiple fractures in various stages of healing, torn frenulum and unexplained dental injury. Physical abuse also includes fabricated or induced illness (Munchausen syndrome by proxy) when a child suffers from unnecessary procedures, tests and operations. Common examples include fabricated illnesses like false haematuria, false fever, induced vomiting and improper use of parent's drug, e.g., diuretic.

Child neglect is a condition in which a parent or caretaker either deliberately or by extraordinary inattentiveness allows a child to experience avoidable suffering, and fails to provide basic ingredients essential for developing a person's physical, emotional and intellectual capacities. It can be defined as the persistent failure to meet a child's basic needs, resulting in or likely to result in impairment of the child's health and development. Common examples of neglect include substance abuse by mother during pregnancy, a parent or carer failing to provide adequate food, clothing, and/or shelter including exclusion from home or abandonment, failing to protect a child from physical and emotional harm or danger, failing to ensure adequate supervision including the use of inadequate caregivers, and failing to ensure access to appropriate medical care or education. Clinically, the child appears dull, apathetic and emotionally indifferent. He/she may present with nonspecific symptoms including multiple hospitalizations related to hygiene issues, failure to thrive with ill-defined feeding problem, developmental delay especially in language and social skills. There is ongoing environmental and emotional deprivation and limited parent-child interactions.

Sexual abuse is defined as the involvement of a child in sexual activity that he/she does not fully comprehend or is unable to give informed consent to, or that violates the laws or social taboos of the society. Sexual abuse involves forcing or enticing a child or young person to take part in sexual activities, whether or not the child is aware of what is happening. The activities may involve physical contact, including penetrative (for example, rape, buggery or oral sex) or nonpenetrative (for example, fondling) acts. They may also include noncontact activities, such as involving children in looking at, or in the production of, pornographic material or sexual activities, or encouraging children to behave in sexually inappropriate ways. Sexual child abuse may be detected by self-disclosure of the child victim. Most of the time, the child presents with nonspecific symptoms including enuresis, encopresis, school avoidance, change in behaviour or personality. There may be physical complications including genital injuries, sexually transmitted diseases (for example, gonorrhoea, syphilis, HIV) and pregnancy. However, absence of medical findings on physical examination does not exclude sexual abuse.

Psychological or emotional abuse is defined as the persistent emotional maltreatment of a child such as to cause severe and persistent adverse effects on the child's emotional development. It may involve conveying to children that they are worthless, flawed, unloved, endangered, inadequate, or only valuable in meeting the needs of another person. It may feature age or developmentally inappropriate expectations being imposed on children. These may include interactions that are beyond the child's developmental capability, as well as overprotection and preventing the child from performing normal social interactions. Examples include hostile rejection, degrading, shaming, threatening to physically hurt, abandoning or placing in dangerous situations, and imposing unreasonable restrictions on movement. It may involve serious bullying causing children to feel frightened or in danger, or the exploitation or corruption of children. Some level of emotional abuse is involved in all types of maltreatment of a child, though it may occur alone.

Prevalence of child abuse

Child abuse has been recognized as a major social and public health issue worldwide, including among high income countries. Around 4% to 16% of children are physically abused, and one in ten is neglected or psychologically abused every year. During childhood, between 5% to 10% of girls and up to 5% of boys are exposed to penetrative sexual abuse, and up to three times this number are exposed to any type of sexual abuse (Gilbert et al., 2009). However, official rates for substantiated child maltreatment indicate less than a tenth of this burden.

Prevalence of child abuse varies among countries, cities and communities, and the true incidence of child abuse is difficult to ascertain. The perception as to what constitutes child abuse varies not only according to the society, but also from family to family. Severe physical chastisement that is family-based but not known to others may not be accounted for in figures for physical abuse. It has been well recognized that child abuse is globally underdiagnosed, and local official statistics regarding the extent of child abuse cannot be directly extended to community samples. Hence it is important to explore the issue at the community and household levels and to work together among stakeholders across social work, medical, legal and education sectors in order to get a clear picture and establish a reliable surveillance system.

The case overseas

The main sources of data on the extent of child maltreatment in many Western countries, for example, the United Kingdom, are official statistics such as the child protection register (which is a confidential list of names of children within every local authority of the UK who are at risk of child abuse) (Department of Health, UK, 2000), lists of children referred to child protection services (Department of Health, UK, 2001) or statistics on offenses against children (Kilsby, 2001). With the exception of the few UK prevalence studies conducted on specific forms of maltreatment, which were either sexual (Baker & Duncan, 1985; Kelly, Regan, & Burton, 1991), physical (Smith, Bee, Heverin, & Nobes, 1995), or both (Creighton & Russell, 1995), very little is known about other forms of maltreatment that are not reported to the authorities. The British study conducted by Cawson, Wattam, Brooker, and Kelly (2000) was the first national survey of all types of abuse and neglect, and one of the few worldwide to have addressed the issue of child maltreatment comprehensively in a large random probability sample of the general population (May-Chahal and Cawson, 2005). Between September 1998 and February 1999, by using a computer-assisted personal and self-interviewing method, Cawson et al. interviewed 2,869 young adults aged between 18 and 24 years, and assessed the prevalence of abuse (physical, sexual, and emotional) and neglect, which were collectively described as maltreatment. Maltreatment (both intra and extrafamilial) was experienced by 16% of the sample. The prevalence of serious physical abuse (violence used regularly over the years, or which had caused physical injury or frequently led to physical effects) was 7%, of serious absence of physical care (behaviours which carried a high risk of injury or long-term harmful effects) was 6%, of serious absence of parental supervision (staying home alone without supervision overnight under 10 years of age or staying out overnight without parents knowing their whereabouts under 14 years of age) was 5%, of serious emotional maltreatment (control and domination, humiliation, withdrawal, antipathy, terrorizing and proxy attacks) was

6%, of sexual abuse (contact and noncontact—against their wishes or under the age of 13 years) was 16%. Prevalence data reveal that children are most at risk in the home for physical and emotional abuse and neglect. They are at greater risk of sexual abuse outside the home, particularly in dating relationships (Cawson, Wattam, Brooker, & Kelly, 2000).

Extent of physical abuse

Assessing the prevalence of physical abuse is challenging as attitudes towards the use of physical punishment vary between countries and even within the same culture. Attitudes, perceptions, and self-reporting are likely to be related to one's experience of child maltreatment. Steele (1997) found that many people do not perceive childhood experiences such as "being whipped or beaten to the point of laceration" as abuse because there is a tendency to believe that the discipline they experienced was deserved and accepted as normal (Bower & Knutson, 1996). Subjective and objective definitions of maltreatment will result in variable prevalence rates (Carlin et al., 1994). Personal experience of physical abuse had been found to have an impact on one's attitudes regarding the appropriateness of physical punishment. People reporting histories of physical abuse, who rated their own experiences as deserved or normal, tended to rate physical punishment as more appropriate than those who had not been so treated (Kelder, McNamara, Carlson, & Lynn, 1991), and a direct relationship has been established between childhood experience and disciplinary attitudes (Bower & Knutson, 1996).

In the United Kingdom, there have been only a few studies that explored physical punishment, including the two normative studies reported by Nobes and Smith (Nobes & Smith, 1997; Nobes, Smith, Upton, & Heverin, 1999). Nobes and colleagues found that 16% of children had received a beating over the leg or bottom, while 10% of children had been hit on the head. In 2002, Lane reported that serious physical abuse was often more frequently diagnosed in minority groups in the United States, however, there was also a possibility that the diagnosis was more likely to be considered and explored in these children (Lane, Rubin, Monteith, & Christian, 2002).

Studies in the UK, the US, New Zealand, Finland, Italy and Portugal reported that 3.7% to 16.3% (5% to 35% cumulative) of children per year experienced severe parental violence (Woodman, 2008; Machado, 2007). The yearly prevalence of physical abuse for Macedonia, Moldova, Latvia, and Lithuania was 12.2% to 29.7% (Sebre et al., 2004), while the cumulative prevalence of physical abuse for Siberia, Russia and Romania was 24.0% to 29.0% (Browne, 2002; Berrien, Aprelkov, Ivanova, Zhmurov, & Buzhicheeva, 1995).

Extent of sexual abuse

The wide scope of definitions poses major problems in comparing the prevalence of child sexual abuse reported in different studies. With the most restrictive definition, 4% of females and 2% of males had been sexually abused (Kelly et al., 1991). In fact, definitions aside, the calculated incidence depends on what is perceived to be abusive. The covert and mostly hidden nature of sexual abuse also leads to underestimation in all official figures (Fleming, 1997).

According to the findings of the population-based studies in developed countries including Australia, New Zealand, the US and Canada, the cumulative prevalence of any type of sexual abuse was 15% to 30% for girls and 5% to 15% for boys, while prevalence of penetrative sexual abuse was 5% to 10% for girls and 1% to 5% for boys (Fergusson & Mullen, 1999; Nelson et al., 2002). The estimates of childhood prevalence rates according to the meta-analysis by Andrews and colleagues (Andrews, Corry, Slade, Issakidis, & Swanston, 2004) were: 3.1% (boys) and 6.8% (girls) for noncontact sexual abuse; 3.7% (boys) and 13.2% (girls) for contact sexual abuse; 1.9% (boys) and 5.3% (girls) for penetrative sexual abuse; and 8.7% (boys) and 25.3% (girls) for any type of sexual abuse.

Extent of child neglect

Child neglect is the commonest category of child abuse. It has been estimated to account for two-thirds of all child abuse cases (Polnay et al., 2007). Quantifying the number of children exposed to child neglect is difficult as the signs are subtle and not as overt as physical injury. This is influenced by a doctor's own values in deciding when a parent's or caregiver's attitude or level of care falls below the threshold that requires intervention.

The incidence of persistent absence of care or placing a child at risk of harm has been reported to be between 1.4% to 15.4% (Finkelhor, Ormrod, Turner, & Hamby, 2005; Theodore, Chang, & Runyan, 2007). For example, there were reports of lacking sufficient food, medical care when needed, a safe place to stay (Finkelhor et al., 2005), sufficient care (May-Chahal & Cawson, 2005), and supervision (Theodore et al., 2007).

Extent of psychological abuse

Studies in Sweden, the US and the UK reported a cumulative prevalence of 4% to 9% based on categories consistent with severe emotional abuse (Edwards, Holden, Felitti, & Anda, 2003; May-Chahal & Cawson, 2005; Janson, Langberg, & Svensson, 2007). A yearly prevalence of 10.3% was reported in a US study on verbal abuse by adults (Finkelhor et al., 2005), and a range of 12.5% to 33.3% was reported as the yearly prevalence of severe or moderate psychological abuse for four eastern European countries including Latvia, Lithuania, Moldova and Macedonia (Sebre et al., 2004).

Agency reports in different developed countries

United States: A national survey on child abuse conducted in 1995 estimated that the rate of child physical abuse in the US was 49 per 1,000 children (Straus et al., 1998). According to the official data reported in 2006, 4.78% of children in the US were investigated for child abuse while 1.21% were substantiated. A total of 60% of all cases were neglect, 10% were physical abuse, 11% were psychological abuse, 7% were sexual abuse and 12% were multiple abuse (US Department of Health and Human Services, 2006).

Canada: An estimated 9.71 per 1,000 children were substantiated as experiencing child maltreatment in 1998 (Trocmé & Wolfe, 2001). In the Canadian Incidence Study of Reported Child Abuse and Neglect in 2003, 2.15% of children were investigated for child abuse, 0.47% remained suspicious and 0.97% were substantiated. Of all identified cases, 38% were neglect, 23% were physical abuse, 23% were psychological abuse, 9% were sexual abuse (Trocmé, MacMillan, Fallon, & Marco, 2003).

Australia: According to official data under the Australian Institute of Health and Welfare, the number of substantiated reports of child neglect or abuse in Australia increased from 24,732 in the years 1999–2000 to 40,416 in 2002–2003. The rates of children aged 0 to 16 years who were the subjects of child protection substantiations in 2002–2003 ranged from 1.8 per 1,000 in Tasmania to 10.1 per 1,000 in Queensland. In 2002–2003, 3.34% of children were referred for investigation of child abuse, and 0.68% of children were substantiated. Of all cases, 34% were neglect, 28% were physical abuse, 34% were psychological abuse, 10% were sexual abuse (Australian Institute of Health and Welfare, 2004).

United Kingdom: There were around 26,600 children on the child protection registers in England, which represented 24 children per 10,000 of the population under the age of 18 (Department for Education and Skills, 2004). 1.5% of children in the UK were estimated to have been referred to social services for abuse issues (Cleaver & Walker, 2004). 4.96% of children younger than 18 have been referred to social welfare services in 2007 (Department for Children, Schools and Families, 2008). Of all social welfare referrals, 0.84% were estimated to have been investigated for abuse (Cleaver & Walker, 2004). In 2007, 2.77% of children were investigated, and 0.30% started on a child protection plan. Of all abuse cases, 44% were neglect, 15% were physical abuse, 23% were psychological abuse, 7% were sexual abuse and 10% were multiple abuse (Department for Children, Schools and Families, 2008).

Hong Kong's experience

Local studies conducted more than a quarter of a century ago have shown that child abuse tended to occur at a later age in childhood in Hong Kong than in the West (Lieh-Mak, Chung, & Liu, 1983). Some professionals believed that infants are usually treated with attention and loving care in Chinese culture, hence the prevalence of abuse among infants and toddlers seemed to be lower than that reported in the West. However, strict discipline after the age of four or five is a common practice in Chinese society in order to ensure filial piety, and thus, the risk of abuse would be much higher beginning from there (Tang & Davis, 1996).

The extent to which abuse continues in adolescence has not been widely explored in the Asian context. Tang's study (1996) of the experience of 375 university students in Hong Kong estimated the prevalence of respondents who had experienced minor or severe physical violence from their parents in the past year. Of the sample, 62.2% had been verbally abused by their parents, 13.2% experienced minor physical violence, and 8.5% reported severe physical violence. However, these figures were based on a selected sample of university students, and could not be generalized to the larger community. Tang (1998) conducted another telephone survey of 1,019 households randomly selected in Hong Kong, where 359 fathers and 660 mothers of a child at or under the age of 16 participated in the study. By using the Chinese version of the Conflict Tactics Scale, the base rate of physical child abuse was found to be 526 per 1,000 children for minor violence and 461 per 1,000 children for severe violence. Minor violence was most likely directed at children aged 3 to 6 years or children without siblings in the family, and tended to be committed by mothers, parents aged 19 to 37 years, or housewives/unemployed fathers. The highest rate of severe violence occurred among boys or children aged 3 to 6 years, and were also committed by mothers, parents aged 19 to 37 years, or housewives/unemployed fathers. When compared to families in the US, Chinese families showed slightly lower rates of minor violence but higher rates of severe violence towards children. Children aged 3 to 6 years were the most vulnerable victims and female caregivers the most likely abusers in both US and Chinese families.

Based on a cross-sectional survey of over 3,000 students from 12 secondary schools in Kwai Tsing District, one of the most underprivileged districts in Hong Kong, Lau, Liu, and Cheung (1999) reported that the prevalence rates of corporal punishment, being beaten by parents for no apparent reason, and being beaten to injury by family members in the past three months were 4.9%, 2.0% and 1.1% respectively.

In a local study commissioned by the Social Welfare Department in 1997 on the incidence of child abuse in Hong Kong which interviewed over 1,600 Chinese parents aged 18 or above, 68% of the parents had at least one incident of psychological child abusive behaviour in the surveyed year, 52% had used minor violent behaviour toward their children, and 40% had used severe violent behaviour (Social Welfare Department, 1999).

Chan (2005) reported the prevalence and incidence of child abuse based on a territory-wide household survey conducted during the period from December 2003 to August 2004. Key findings were as follows: *physical assault*—around 45% of child respondents indicated they had ever encountered physical assault by either of or both their parents. The ever prevalence rate for very severe physical assault was about 9%. Around 23% of child respondents indicated they had encountered physical assault by either of or both their parents during the 12 months prior to enumeration. The annual prevalence rate for very severe physical assault was about 4%. *Psychological aggression*—around 72% of child respondents indicated they had ever encountered psychological aggression by either of or both their parents. About 58% indicated they had encountered psychological aggression during the 12 months prior to enumeration. *Child neglect*—around 36% of child respondents indicated they had ever encountered neglect by either of or both their parents. About 27% indicated they had encountered neglect during the 12 months prior to enumeration.

Through the joint efforts of the Social Welfare Department, nongovernmental organizations and the Hong Kong Council of Social Service, a computerized record system for maintaining the Child Protection Registry has been devised, which carries the functions of case registration, case checking as well as facilitating statistical research under the administration of the Family and Child Welfare Branch of the Social Welfare Department.

According to the Child Protection Registry captured by the Social Welfare Department in Hong Kong, the number of newly reported child abuse cases was 993 in 2009, as compared to the numbers of 481 in 2003 and 622 in 2004. Physical abuse was the major type of abuse (503 cases), comprising 50.7% of the cases. There were 331 sexual abuse cases, comprising one-third of all reported cases in 2009. Child neglect (102 cases), psychological abuse (15 cases) and multiple abuses (42 cases) accounted for 10.3%, 1.5% and 4.2% respectively (Social Welfare Department, 2009). Yuen Long (14.6%), Tuen Mun (11.8%), Shatin (8%), Kwun Tong (7.9%) and Kwai Tsing (6.3%) were found to be the most prevalent areas of child abuse in 2009.

In 2001, the committee of Medical Coordinators on Child Abuse (MCCA) under the Hospital Authority published the first set of valuable data on child abuse cases admitted into paediatric departments of public hospitals in Hong Kong between June 1997 and August 1999 (Medical Coordinators on Child Abuse, 2001). Within the two-year study period, 494 cases of suspected child abuse were reported from 12 public hospitals in Hong Kong. Three hospitals contributed more than 50 patients each, accounting for 60% of the reported cases, and were arbitrarily designated as busy units. The suspected victims included 230 (47%) boys and 264 (53%) girls at a mean age of 7.5 (range 0–17.2) years. Children of suspected sexual abuse were more likely to be girls (94% vs. 48%, $p<0.001$) and younger in age (5.7 years vs. 7.7 years, $p<0.001$) when compared with the nonsexual abuse cases. Among the whole group of patients, 288 (58%) were diagnosed for child abuse. The forms of maltreatment included physical abuse ($n=211$), neglect ($n=8$), psychological abuse ($n=3$), sexual abuse ($n=22$), and multiple abuses ($n=44$). Physical abuse, alone or in combination with other forms of abuse, accounted for the majority of cases (251/288, 87%). Either or both biological parents constituted 71% of the perpetrators. Concerning subsequent placement of the child victim, 67% cases were restored home, while the others required special placement. Five (1%) patients died as a result of serious head injury. Of the 452 cases where a multidisciplinary case conference was held, abuse was established in 254 (56%) (Medical Coordinators on Child Abuse, 2001).

An analysis of the admission data on child abuse cases from 2001 to 2008 available in the computerized Clinical Management System of the Hong Kong Hospital Authority conducted by this chapter's author (Ip, 2010) showed a significant increasing trend in the year prevalence of child abuse admissions throughout the study period. The yearly prevalence rate of child abuse admissions increased from 3.3 per 10,000 population aged less than 19 in 2000 to 7.3 per 10,000 population aged less than 19 in 2008. Tuen Mun, Yuen Long, Sham Shui Po, Kwai Tsing, Mong Kok and Kwun Tong were the most prevalent areas, in descending order. There were a total number of over 5,400 admissions into public hospitals in Hong Kong because of child abuse in the eight-year period. Among the admissions, 37.1% of them were due to physical child abuse, 9.1% were due to sexual abuse, 1.2% due to psychological abuse, 3.2% due to child neglect, 0.9% due to shaken baby syndrome and around 48.5% due to nonspecific child abuse. The perpetrators were the child's father (48%), mother (36.4%), other carer (e.g., domestic helper) (6.1%), sibling (3.9%), father and mother (2.4%), other relative (1.8%), and grandparent (1.4%). Around 5.6% of the cases had been readmitted because of child abuse within the studied period. The most useful predictors of readmission due to child abuse included age of first admission, and living district related to socioeconomic status.

Prevalence data vary across different countries and nations, but have similarly shown child abuse to be an important public health issue affecting both developed and developing countries. The statistics reported officially in national or government registries tend to underestimate the true incidence, as many abused cases are probably left unreported. In general, there has been an increasing trend of child abuse prevalence in the past few decades according to both official and self-reported data. This may reflect a true increase in incidence of abuse cases or an increased reporting rate due to increased alertness, coverage in media and publicity of child abuse prevention and help-seeking, or lower thresholds for reporting maltreatment.

Risk factors

Clinical experiences and previous findings have established the importance of certain personal, social and family attributes which predispose children to child abuse and neglect. Identification of these risk factors is clinically important as children at risk of harm can be identified so that early intervention could be offered. This would certainly involve enquiries and collaboration from other professionals to gather information about a particular family and to provide extra assistance to prevent further abuse and neglect.

Child abuse and neglect usually occur in circumstances where there are several risk factors. Studies and reviews on the etiologies of child abuse have emphasized that child maltreatment has multifactorial origins. Family violence is found to be a product of poor relationships, with dysfunctional family relationships and poor parent-child interactions both contributing to and maintaining child abuse and neglect (Burrell, Thompson, & Sexton, 1994; Crittenden 1985; Wolfe, 1991, 1993). Based on that perspective, good family relationships and parent-child interactions carry the potential to act as protective factors and provide some resilience to social and environmental stress impinging on the family (Browne & Herbert, 1997).

The Child Protection Registry captured by the Social Welfare Department is the major official database for registration of child abuse and neglect cases in Hong Kong. Social workers from the government, nongovernmental organizations and hospitals report established cases and cases at risk of child abuse to the registry by returning a standard report form containing information on essential demographics and contributing factors of abuse. The factors include: (a) child-related factors (e.g., school performance, behaviour, emotional or psychological problem, mental illness, mental retardation or developmental delay, chronic illness, physical disability, unwanted pregnancy, long period of separation from parents in early infancy); (b) abuser- (parent- or other perpetrator-) related factors (e.g., marital problems, in-law relationship problems, emotional or psychological problems, mental illness or mental retardation, chronic illness, physical disability, lack of parenting skills, false expectation on child-in-question, risk behaviours such as gambling, indulgence in alcohol, substance abuse); and (c) environmental or social circumstances (e.g., financial difficulty, unemployment, housing problem, family crisis or stress not coped with by abuser, lack of support system or community resources) (Child Protection Registry, 2007).

Factors predisposing a child to the risk of being abused

Vulnerable children are easily subject to abuse by people close to them, ranging from family members to friends, acquaintances in the community and even staff in institutions. The most important risk factors can be categorized into child factors, parental factors, and community or environmental factors (Browne & Herbert, 1997) (Table 3.1):

Table 3.1 Predisposing factors to being abused

I) Child factors	
Early attachment	Prematurity, low birth weight, early illness, and situations resulting in separation from their parents at birth may disrupt the formation of attachment between parent and child, which would make children vulnerable.
Behavioural problems	Children with hyperactivity, aggressive behaviour, difficult temperament, and/or inconsolable crying have been reported in increasing risk of being abused.
Chronic physical illness	The demanding care makes a child more vulnerable and less ready to protect themselves.
Mental retardation or developmental delay	Children with unexpected soiling or wetting, uncontrolled behaviour and poor self-caring make child care more demanding and child carer more irritable.
Unwanted child	Children born from unwanted pregnancy, of unexpected gender or who failed to meet their parents' expectations were at risk of being neglected or abused.
II) Parental factors	
High-risk behaviours	Parents with alcoholism or substance abuse are found to have higher risk of abusing their children; these factors are often associated with parents having multiple stress and trauma.
Teenage pregnancy	Immature parents are more likely to neglect the needs of a young and growing child.
Multiple pregnancies and rapid repeat pregnancy	Parents having twins or another child before weaning a child's older sibling or having the duty to look after many children within the same period were found to experience greater stress on their capacity, and suffer from a higher chance of child abuse and neglect.
Single-parent	Living in a single-parent family increases the probability of child abuse due to lack of social support and backup network, extra parental stress, social isolation and economic problems.
Domestic violence	There is a higher risk to children living in a household where there is a violent adult. Co-occurrence of multiple abuses within the same family have been widely reported.

(continued on page 74)

Table 3.1 *(continued)*

Mental health problems	Parents with active psychiatric disorders such as neurosis, psychosis, or psychopathology may carry a higher risk of abusing and neglecting their children, if proper intervention is not provided.
Personality problems	Parents with antisocial and/or rigid personalities may be impulsive and aggressive, and lack empathic responses to the child's needs and necessities.
Step parent	Parents not biologically related to the child may be more reluctant to show care and affection.
Parent having been abused in childhood	Parents who have experienced abuse in their own childhood are often characterized by attachment disorders which affect their relationships as an adult and their ability to show affection and care towards their own children (Morton & Browne, 1998).
Disabled parents	Parents with special needs may unwittingly abuse and neglect their children due to lack of social support and more demanding parenting required, as a result of their limited mobility or mental capacity.
III) Community or environmental factors	
Marital conflicts	Parents with poor relationship or extramarital affairs lead to chaotic family dynamics, resulting in increased risk of child abuse and neglect.
Poverty and unemployment	Financial difficulties increase the chances of child abuse and neglect due to parents' stressful circumstances and adversely affected relationships in the family.
Poor housing conditions	Overcrowding, inadequate housing conditions, unhealthy living arrangements and lack of sanitation increases the risk of child abuse.
Social isolation	Families with a lack of social support and in detachment from the community have been found to be at risk of child abuse.
Family violence and dysfunctional family interaction	Children who grow up in a violent family are more likely to show aggression and violence to others. Dysfunctional relationships and violence in the family are harmful to children, even if the violence is directed toward the mother or other siblings (Gelles, 1997). Previous studies showed a high correlation between elder abuse, intimate partner violence and child abuse in families. Parents who hit each other or their elderly relatives were found to be more likely to abuse or neglect their children (Browne & Hamilton, 1998, 1999).

(continued on page 75)

Table 3.1 *(continued)*

Violence towards pets	Cruelty to pets in the family has been found to have linkage with different kinds of family violence including child abuse and intimate partner violence. Animal abuse is probably part of a continuum of violence within the family (Becker & French, 2004).
Cultural factors	Societies or communities with gender or social inequality and the existence of child labour and child prostitution were found to have a higher risk of abuse and neglect.

Recognizing risk factors and ways to reduce child abuse

Understanding risk factors is clearly relevant when assessing child abuse and neglect. A knowledge of risk factors can help identify vulnerable families and children, and children at risk can be safeguarded by appropriate intervention to mitigate adverse circumstances. This is a challenging task, as any effective intervention needs to be highly specialized, intensive and long-term.

In a study on risk factors in families with child abuse, Dixon, Browne, and Hamilton-Giachristis (2005) found that having a parent who was abused as a child increased the likelihood of that parent abusing their children by a factor of four, when compared with nonabused parents. Three significant risk factors, including (a) being a parent under 21, (b) having a history of mental illness, and (c) living with a violent adult, made abused parents 17 times more likely than nonabused parents to abuse their children. From these findings, it can be speculated that parents who recognize themselves as having been maltreated as children, can conceivably reduce their own risk to abuse by having children at an older age, not living with violent partners and seeking early intervention for any mental illness. These parents can certainly be prioritized for preventive work.

In addition, findings from randomized controlled trials as reported by Olds et al. (1995, 1997) showed that when vulnerable families had a programme of nurse home visits over a prolonged period of time during the antenatal period and the first two years of childhood, there was a reduction in incidence of child abuse and neglect and subsequent pregnancies. Meanwhile, improvement in maternal circumstances was also shown. The nurse-partnership home visitation programme is an organized intervention programme focused on families in greater need of services (e.g., low-income, unmarried teens, with a history of substance abuse), offering regular home visitation by a trained nurse to promote positive health-related behaviours and quality infant caregiving following a strict protocol beginning in pregnancy and continuing through the first two years of life (American Academy of Pediatrics, 1998). It may serve as a promising model of early intervention targeted at vulnerable families, although it is a demanding programme with its success relying on expertise training and programme fidelity.

Critical issue: impact of child abuse and damage to the developing brain

Emerging evidence from research on early brain development[*]

In recent years, there has been an upsurge of research into early brain development, including the effects of maltreatment on the developing brain during infancy and early childhood. The early years of life (from 0 to 5 years) are the most critical years of development as they mark the most rapid phase of brain growth, when the cerebral cortex is adding an astounding 40,000 synaptic connections every second. It has been well recognized worldwide since the past decade how development in the early years of life is crucial in the setting of the stage for later life, and how it builds the base for future development. There is encouraging evidence that good nutrition, nurturing and responsive caregiving in the first years of life, linked with good early child development programmes, improve the outcomes for all children's learning, behaviour, and mental and physical health throughout life (Shonkoff & Phillips, 2000).

Child Abuse and Toxic Stress

Stress is a part of life. Whether it is the stress of meeting new people, learning to walk, or dealing with problems, learning how to cope with it is an important part of a child's healthy development. Three levels of stress: (a) positive stress, (b) tolerable stress, and (c) toxic stress may occur at any period of human life.

---

[*]   Early brain development is usually referred to the fastest growth period of the human brain from in-utero period to the first five years of life, when environment and life experience affect the development of important sensing pathways determining a child's outcome.

There is a range of physiological responses to stress, including increased heart rate and fluctuations in stress hormone levels, such as cortisol. In case of mild and positive stress, when stress occurs to a young child within an environment of supportive relationships with adults, these physiological effects are buffered and brought back down to baseline. The result is a healthy stress response system. For tolerable stress due to larger stressors, such as the death or serious illness of a loved one, a frightening injury, the divorce of one's parents, or a natural disaster, these physiological responses are sustained for a longer period of time. The buffering effects of supportive adult relationships would still allow the brain to recover from what might otherwise be damaging effects. When situations of extreme stress are prolonged and unrelenting, in the absence of supportive adults, a child becomes affected by toxic stress. These situations can include physical or emotional abuse, chronic neglect, severe maternal depression, substance abuse, family violence or extreme poverty. Without the support of a caring network of adults, toxic stress can disrupt brain architecture and lead to stress management systems that respond at relatively lower thresholds, thereby increasing the risk of stress-related physical and mental illnesses.

Early brain growth and stress

The science of early childhood development serves as a new lens for health promotion and disease prevention. There has been greater focus on studying causal links between toxic stress in the early years and susceptibility to physical and mental health impairments in later adulthood, which has led to a shift to addressing the early childhood roots of disparities rather than trying to change adult behaviours associated with poor health. Emerging evidence from new research is giving clear indications that the brain's development can be physiologically altered by prolonged, severe or unpredictable stress—including maltreatment—during a child's early years. Such an alteration in the brain's development can in turn negatively affect the child's physical, cognitive, emotional and social growth. With the advancement in new technology, early experience from conception to age five was found to affect the learning and subsequent behaviour of a child. The rates of synapse formation in sensing pathways (e.g., vision and hearing), language and higher cognitive function vary in early years, but all of the peak rates lie within the first few years of life (Tsujimoto, 2008). Any damage or exposure to risks in this early critical period of life would result in more significant long-term impairment. Development of different parts of the brain depends on the stimulation received in early life that provokes activity in that region. By the age of three, the human brain grows larger and denser, reaching nearly 90% of its adult size.

Impact of child abuse on the growing brain

If child maltreatment occurs in early years of life resulting in a lack of stimulation and nurture—for example, if the parents or caregivers are hostile to or uninterested in the child—the development of the child's brain would be at risk of impairment. Since the brain adapts to its environment, it will adapt to a negative environment just as readily as it will to a positive one. When a child is being abused and brought up in a neglected environment, chronic stress sensitizes neural pathways and overdevelops those regions of the brain involved in responses to anxiety and fear. It also often results in the underdevelopment of other neural pathways and other regions of the brain. The brains of children who experience the stress, in the form of physical or sexual abuse or chronic neglect, will focus their resources on survival and responding to threats in the environment. This chronic stimulation of the brain's response to fear leads to frequent activation of particular regions of the brain, which would therefore be likely to be overdeveloped at the expense of other regions that cannot be activated at the same time, such as those involved in the important function of complex thought. For instance, children being abused and neglected in early years may live in a persistent state of hyperarousal or dissociation, anticipating threats from every direction. This would result in an impairment of their ability to benefit from social, emotional and cognitive experiences. In order to learn and incorporate new information, whether from teachers, parents or a new social experience, the child's brain must be in a state of "attentive calm"— one that a traumatized child rarely achieves. Children without healthy attachments with their parents or caregivers, and whose early emotional experiences, through their impact on the brain, have not laid the necessary ground for positive emotional development, may suffer from a limited capacity for empathy as the ability to feel remorse and empathy are built on experience. In the extreme case, if a child feels no emotional attachment to anyone, that child cannot be expected to feel remorse for hurting or even killing another person (National Clearinghouse on Child Abuse and Neglect, 2001). As a result, a child who experiences abuse or neglect in early life grows at an unequal starting point, and is at risk of developmental delay and developing morbidities affecting his/ her mental and physical health in later adulthood. The effects of experiences during infancy and early childhood on brain development create the basis for the expression of intelligence, emotions and personality. When these early experiences are primarily negative, children may develop emotional, behavioural and learning problems that persist throughout their lifetime, especially if targeted interventions are lacking (WHO & ISCAN, 2006).

Adversity in early childhood and roots of impairment

Biology tells us that early life experiences are built into our bodies. Recent scientific studies confirmed the linkage between the biology of adversity and the early childhood roots of impairments in health, learning and behaviour (Shonkoff, Boyce, & McEwen, 2009).

Significant early adversity impairs development in the first three years. Children aged 18 to 36 months who have been maltreated are at substantial risk of experiencing subsequent developmental problems. Specific risk factors that were examined included child maltreatment, longstanding poverty, caregiver mental health problem, low caregiver education, and biomedical risk condition; the chance of being developmentally delayed increased with the existence of more risk factors (Scarborough, Lloyd, & Barth, 2009). In order to study how physical health and social-emotional behaviours could be affected by adverse early experiences, Dong and his team (2004) investigated adults with a history of early adverse childhood experiences including abuse, neglect and domestic violence, to determine whether these experiences increased the odds that they would experience alcoholism, drug abuse, and a range of unhealthy behaviours later in life. They found that all of these behaviours increased dramatically in adults who had higher numbers and prevalence of adverse childhood experiences in their early years. These experiences also led to dramatically increased odds (i.e., the risk) of having a range of physical health problems as adults—for example, cardiovascular disease (Danese et al., 2008). Similar trends also appeared for diabetes, hypertension, stroke, obesity, and cancer.

Brain resilience and benefits of early intervention

Besides the evidence shown on the adverse effects of child abuse on subsequent health and development, new evidence from research on influences on children's vulnerability and resilience has also provided a scientific base for the significance and effectiveness of early life intervention programmes in reducing the risk of child abuse and improving long-term outcomes in health and behaviour. Where maltreatment has already occurred, there is some evidence that intensive, early intervention can help minimize the long-term effects of this trauma on the brain's development. Early intervention in life could have significant long-term impacts on crimes and other social problems like substance abuse. Adverse outcomes including school failure, mental health problems, drug use and criminality could be predisposed by identified risk factors incorporating genetic and biological characteristics of the child, family characteristics, stressful life events, and community or cultural factors. In addition, protective or resilience factors, including the availability of social support, and connectedness to schools and family are associated with positive outcomes (Chapman & Scott, 2001). However, while early intervention with maltreated children can minimize the effects of abuse and neglect, it is considerably more beneficial to prevent maltreatment before it occurs. The costs, both in human and economic terms, of trying to heal these children are much greater than the costs of preventing maltreatment and thereby promoting healthy development of the brain during the first few years of life (Cunha, Heckman, Lochner, & Masterov, 2005).

Child health policy and policy on child protection in Hong Kong

There has been a significant change in the population structure in the past four decades along with the rapid development in Hong Kong. In the 60s, over 43% of the population was under 16 years of age, and that was the time when Hong Kong was once regarded as the "City of Children". In 1980, around 27% of the population was under 15 years of age. At present, there are more than 1.3 million children aged under 18 years, accounting for around 20% of the total local population. The vital statistics of children have improved dramatically over the past three decades, and the infant mortality rate of 1.8 per 1000 live births was the second lowest in the world in 2006.

On the other hand, services provided for children and support for families with children in Hong Kong are scattered among different government bureaus, departments and divisions, and nongovernmental organizations with a lack of coordination and little integration. The services involve aspects of child health, child care, education and social support networking. Some of the services are overlapping and even competing with each other, while important gaps are identified in different important domains. Children have been regarded as a family's own business, and child health issues have been considered as a minor part of the healthcare system, drawing much less attention as it is usually set as one of the lowest priorities. Children are "invisible" in many policy areas in Hong Kong.

In spite of the increasing demand from our young population and the request of local professionals, there is still a lack of child policy and a high-level official body to be responsible for child health and development issues in Hong Kong (Ip, 2000; Chow, 2009). A holistic approach to the development of a coherent policy agenda on child and family well-being remains to be established, but raising awareness and assessing the policies affecting this demographic would be vital if we are to improve the well-being of children and their families.

In contribution to the International Year of the Child, a Hong Kong International Year of the Child (IYC) Commission was formed in 1979 with representatives from social, medical, educational, legal and Christian bodies. The commission produced a comprehensive evaluation report on *The Child in Hong Kong* (Hong Kong International Year of the Child Commission, 1980). However, the Hong Kong government did not adopt their recommendation in developing a child policy and setting up a child commission.

In order to safeguard our future generation, the Convention on the Rights of the Child (UNCRC) was endorsed by the United Nations in 1989. At present, all countries have ratified the convention except for the United States and Somalia. In 1994, the British government ratified the UNCRC on Hong Kong's behalf with two reservations. After ratification of the convention, Hong Kong should be obliged to fully implement the articles in the convention, and to make a progress report to the United Nations Committee on the Rights of the Child (UNCCR) every five years. The first report was submitted to UNCCR in 1996. In the concluding observation, Hong Kong was recommended to establish an independent mechanism specifically to monitor the implementation of government polices consistent with the UNCRC. A second comprehensive report, *Hong Kong's Children: Our Past, Their Future*, published in 1999 by the Centre of Asian Studies, again concluded the need for a comprehensive child policy and child commission in Hong Kong (Pryde & Tsoi, 1999).

A third Hong Kong report was submitted to the UN Committee on Children's Rights in 2005, and again, the Hong Kong government still considered that "existing arrangements were effective, enabling us to make flexible and quick responses to address concerns of the public on children". The

UNCRC in the concluding observation recommended again that Hong Kong should establish an independent child commission to implement and monitor the implementation of the UNCCR.

The American Academy of Pediatrics (AAP) endorsed the UNCRC in 1989 and used it as a framework for the provision of healthcare services to children. A training module was also developed to educate resident doctors on the convention, emphasizing that the articles characterize the fundamental pre-requisites for child health, paediatrics in general and community paediatrics. Community paediatricians in particular must expand their professional skills to engage in advocacy, policy development and social science research as essential elements of the practice of paediatrics. Meanwhile, the Royal College of Paediatics and Child Health (RCPCH) in the United Kingdom adopted an overall aim "to advocate the rights of children and young people in society and to promote their health needs and services", promoting implementation of the UN Convention on the Rights of the Child throughout the College and in all areas of society and institutions. The RCPCH expects all members to act within the framework of this convention when undertaking any form of advocacy for children (RCPCH, 2008).

In 2006, the Alliance for Children's Commission was formed in Hong Kong, composing of 23 NGOs with representatives from the social, health, education and legal professions to advocate and lobby the government in the setting up of a children's commission to safeguard and promote the rights and well-being of children. Aided by the work of two legislators, a motion was moved and passed on 8 June 2007 in the Legislative Council "that this Council urges the Government to set up a Commission on Children to fulfill the obligations under the United Nations Convention on the Rights of the Child, safeguard the well-being of children, and ensure that children's perspectives are fully taken into account in the process of formulating government policies" (Alliance for Children's Commission, 2007).

Children of poor and underprivileged families in Hong Kong are provided with social protection by means of the Comprehensive Social Security Allowance (CSSA) provision to their parents. However, as the cash transfer of CSSA is targeted at a low level cash assistance benefit for the poor who have a limited capacity to work, or for traditional social risks of old age, disability and sickness, the measures are inadequate for the protection and healthy development of children from low-income families. In order to enhance early child development in underprivileged or at-risk families, Comprehensive

Child Development Service (CCDS), a community-based multidisciplinary programme using Maternal and Child Health Centres as a platform to provide early intervention to families in need was launched in pilot areas in Hong Kong in 2005–2006. The new interdisciplinary and intersectoral model has successfully identified and provided useful services to young children from families at risk (Family Health Service, 2007). In addition, the Pre-Primary Education Voucher Scheme was implemented in 2007 to support early childhood education. The voucher scheme provides fee subsidy for parents to meet towards school fees for pre-primary education of eligible children in the form of pre school education vouchers. Furthermore, the Child Development Fund implemented in 2008 is another innovative government policy towards development of adolescents in underprivileged districts. However, implementation of these different programmes is usually in a fragmentary manner and not as a coherent package. Long-term effectiveness in improving the outcome of children and their families are yet to be examined.

Healthcare delivery and child abuse recognition

The bulk of curative primary healthcare in Hong Kong is delivered by the private sector, and preventive care by the Department of Health. More complicated and difficult cases are referred to specialists in the Hospital Authority and the private sectors. It is obvious that services for children are fragmented and compartmentalized. A comprehensive range of services is available, but parents often need to shop around or approach several organizations for the services they need. Communications, not to mention collaborations, that span across all sectors (social, healthcare and education) are lacking. Continued emphasis has been put on hospital paediatric specialist care with little planning on preventive, protective and promotive services. The system is nonresponsive, and is unable to meet the changing trends of society and total needs of children.

In view of the rising trend of child abuse cases in society, the primary healthcare system in Hong Kong fails to serve the role of a gatekeeper in safeguarding children. The majority of children receive acute medical care, such as the management of minor injuries and growth issues, at clinics of private family practitioners or private paediatricians. However, there are only a very limited number of child abuse cases being reported by these doctors, and it is common practice to avoid touching on social and welfare issues of children in the private sector. Under the peculiar medical care system with the provision of primary care and acute services mainly by the private doctor, one would conjecture that the majority of child abuse cases presented to primary healthcare providers may have been overlooked and not properly assessed and referred.

The majority of child abuse cases appearing in the child health system in Hong Kong are cases reported to paediatric units in public hospitals scattered throughout the territory. Children suspected of abuse are usually admitted through the Accident and Emergency Department of public hospitals, or through enquiry and request of a case social worker, or direct admission arranged by a medical child abuse coordinator, who is an experienced paediatrician in the respective unit.

Multidisciplinary model in the management of child abuse cases

In Hong Kong, child health and child care professionals in the medical, social and legal fields are working closely together in child protection to provide multidisciplinary intervention to victims and their families. Each party has its specific role and is complementary to the other disciplines, all working together in order to safeguard the rights and interests of children. The multidisciplinary approach allows the professionals to evaluate a situation from different perspectives in order to gain a complete clinical picture, and to provide holistic care and interventions with expertise from different disciplines.

The procedures for handling child abuse cases issued by the Social Welfare Department in 2007 (Social Welfare Department, 2007) list the guidelines of procedures for identifying child abuse cases, involving appropriate parties, organizing multidisciplinary case conferences, determining case nature, formulating welfare plans and subsequent follow-up, applying the Care and Protection Order (C&P) and reporting to the Child Protection Registry if necessary. The decision of applying the C&P Order or reporting to the CPR is usually made at the Multidisciplinary Case Conference (MDCC), but the Child Protection Registry order could also be applied through the court by a social worker or the police during emergency situations needing immediate child protection.

Role of professionals in child protection

The multidisciplinary model usually involves the following parties: (a) medical—paediatricians, psychiatrists, clinical psychologists, nurses, paediatric surgeons/orthopaedic surgeons/neurosurgeons/ophthalmologists, Accident and Emergency doctors, family doctors and primary care physicians; (b) social workers—medical social workers, school social workers, IFSC or NGO workers, FCPSU workers; (c) school teachers and principals; and (d) the police—the Child Abuse Investigation Unit (CAIU), the Criminal Investigation Division (CID), and forensic pathologists.

The role of various professionals is defined and discussed below in order to facilitate understanding of the current system, job delineation and collaborative network.

<u>Paediatricians</u>—In 1996, designated paediatricians in ten paediatric departments of public hospitals under the Hospital Authority started to play the role of medical coordinators in taking care of child sexual abuse cases. Since 1997, experienced and dedicated paediatricians from all Hospital Authority paediatric departments have formed the committee of Medical Coordinators of Child Abuse (MCCA), which coordinates and facilitates the child protection process to minimize trauma to victims, and meets regularly to review and share experience on child abuse issues. Paediatricians play the key role of identifying child maltreatment in daily practice, conducting assessments, medical evaluation and laboratory investigations of cases, providing medical documentation of information and evidence, and making referrals to relevant parties for necessary intervention. As a significant proportion of child abuse cases are referred for admission into paediatric wards in public hospitals under the current system, paediatricians also play a key role in coordinating the multidisciplinary team to formulate a comprehensive child care plan, and in providing training to other parties on the medical aspects of child abuse. They are usually advocates of child protection in the community, providing education to professionals and the public, and supporting children and families by providing them with information and resources. Experienced paediatricians sometimes also play the role of expert or factual witness testimony in court.

<u>Mental health professionals</u> (e.g., psychiatrists, clinical psychologists)— They provide expert assessment and clinical intervention for the psychological needs of children and families of abuse. Professionals specializing in mental health problems assist the investigative interview, evaluate a victim's emotional state, facilitate the psychological recovery of the child victim and his/ her family, and provide counselling and treatment for the abuser. Sometimes, psychiatrists also provide expert testimony on the psychological impact of child abuse in court.

<u>Nurses</u>—Nurses working in paediatric departments provide nursing care to child victims, and usually are involved in the assessment and counselling of the families of abuse. They support the victim and his/her family, and observe the behaviour of a child victim in the ward, such as his/her interactions with other people or staff and with his/her family, prepare assessment reports for case conferences, and offer their expert opinion in formulation of child care plans.

<u>Other health disciplines</u> (e.g., orthopaedic surgeons, neurosurgeons, ophthamologists)—Other specialists provide expert management of the child's physical conditions relevant to their own expertise, refer suspected cases to paediatric units or child protection services for further investigation and management, and attend case conferences to provide expert opinion related to their specialties. They also sometimes provide expert testimony in court.

<u>Accident & Emergency doctors</u>—A&E doctors help conduct the initial assessments, stabilize a child victim's medical condition, provide initial treatment of injuries, and refer suspected cases to paediatric units or child protection for further investigation and management.

<u>Social workers</u>—Case social workers play the role of case manager and chairperson of the Multidisciplinary Case Conference (MDCC). They are the key persons in charge of the assessment, investigation and welfare plan formulation, and are responsible for coordinating the work of different parties involved in the initial assessment and subsequent follow-up of the child victim and the family. They help provide additional information on social enquiry and risk assessment; short-term crisis and therapeutic intervention, such as arranging for emergency shelter and financial assistance for the child and the family; long-term rehabilitative services and follow-up, including the options of preventive services, foster care, and protective custody. Furthermore, social workers work closely with their colleagues in social and educational sectors to arrange counselling, therapy, training courses, and parent aid services for parents, and are usually the ones to monitor family dynamics and progress. If necessary, the case social workers would be responsible for applying the Care & Protection Order, reporting to the Child Protection Registry, and providing testimony in court.

However, it is interesting to note the adverse impact brought about by the practice of routine rotation of social workers in different posts under government employment, and the drawbacks of such a peculiar arrangement on the social support system. The traditional practice of rotating social workers every few years in the name of broadening staff experience and avoiding burnout is a waste of staff training and expertise, and potentially disrupts the valuable rapport built up between an experienced social worker and a family at risk.

<u>Family and Child Protection Service Unit (FCPSU)</u>—The previous Child Protection Service Unit (CPSU) was established under the Social Welfare Department in 1983 for handling child abuse cases. In 2000, the unit was expanded and renamed as the Family and Child Protection Service Unit (FCPSU), and took up responsibility in the work of child protection, domestic violence, child custody and guardianship.

<u>Police</u>—The police are involved in the handling, investigation and management of severe physical abuse, sexual child abuse and other child abuse cases on an individual basis. They help locate victims or suspected abusers, determine whether there is sufficient evidence to arrest a suspect, refer cases to the attorney general's chambers to decide whether to prosecute, and provide evidence for prosecution, such as witness statements, forensic and crime scene evidence. The police also facilitate video interviews of the abused victim, apply for protective custody if necessary, and protect family members and child protection workers during the intervention process.

<u>Child Abuse Investigation Unit (CAIU)</u>—Established in 1995 and comprised of specially trained police staff, the CAIU is responsible for handling severe child abuse or sexual abuse cases, and for conducting video interviews of child abuse victims.

<u>Forensic pathologists</u>—Forensic pathologists perform forensic examinations for child victims of sexual abuse upon request of the police, and also act as expert witnesses in court.

<u>Schools</u>—As children spend most of their time participating in various activities in school, schoolteachers play an important role as a gatekeeper to safeguard children. Teachers are usually one of the first professionals to become aware of an occurrence of child abuse. They help detect any suspected child abuse cases, refer to appropriate services for intervention, and provide information on the child's behaviour at school and on family dynamics. The schoolteacher-in-charge, and sometimes, the school principal, would be invited to attend the Multidisciplinary Case Conference to give their expert opinion and to participate in the welfare plan to support the child and family, and to monitor the progress of the child as part of the long-term management.

One can easily tell that child protection work in Hong Kong is mainly targeted at providing remedial service rather than preventing the occurrence of child abuse. It is not mandatory in Hong Kong to report a case of child abuse, not even for professionals working in child care and child health service. There are no official statistics of mortality due to child abuse in Hong Kong, and the official database of the Child Protection Registry under the Social Welfare Department does not even capture child death cases. In order to safeguard children, Hong Kong should seriously consider mandatory reporting by professionals. Conducting regular child death reviews is a means to identifying preventable causes of unnatural deaths. Focus should be put not only on remedial measures, but also on prevention.

Conclusion

Child abuse is a prevalent issue both overseas and in Hong Kong. Numerous studies in the field have provided emerging evidence on the long-term adverse impact of early life maltreatment on a growing child. Many risk factors that have been recognized as contributing to child abuse are avoidable, hence early recognition and prompt intervention can make a big difference on the situation. In Hong Kong, in spite of the recognition of children as the future of the society, there is no independent policy for children with particular reference to child protection or with particular concern over the prevention of child abuse and neglect. There should be a child protection policy in order to safeguard the welfare of children in Hong Kong.

References

Alliance for Children's Commission. (2007). Our views on the Family Council: Submission to Welfare Services Panel of the Legislative Council. LC Paper No. CB(2)1037/07-08(03).

American Academy of Pediatrics. (1998). The role of home-visitation programs in improving health outcomes for children and families. *Pediatrics*, 101(3): 486–489.

Andrews, G., Corry, J., Slade, T., Issakidis, C., & Swanston, H. (2004). *Child Sexual Abuse: Comparative Quantification of Health Risks*. Geneva: WHO.

Australian Institute of Health and Welfare. (2004). *Child Protection Australia, 2002–03* (AIHW Cat. No. CWS 22). Canberra, Australia: AIHW.

Baker, A. W., & Duncan, S. P. (1985). Child sexual abuse: a study of prevalence in Great Britain. *Child Abuse & Neglect, 9*, 457–467. doi: 10.1016/0145-2134(85)90054-7

Becker, F., & French, L. (2004). Making the links: child abuse, animal cruelty and domestic violence. *Child Abuse Review, 13*, 399–414. doi: 10.1002/car.878

Berrien, F. B., Aprelkov, G., Ivanova, T., Zhmurov, V., & Buzhicheeva, V. (1995). Child abuse prevalence in Russian urban population: a preliminary report. *Child Abuse & Neglect, 19,* 261–264. doi: 10.1016/0145-2134(94)00124-D

Bower, M. E., & Knutson, J. F. (1996). Attitudes toward physical discipline as a function of disciplinary history and self-labeling as physical abuse. *Child Abuse & Neglect, 20,* 689–699. doi: 10.1016/0145-2134(96)00057-9

Browne, K. D. (2002). *National Prevalence Study of Child Abuse and Neglect in Romanian Families.* Copenhagen: WHO Regional Office for Europe.

Browne, K. D., & Hamilton, C. E. (1998). Physical violence between young adults and their parents: associations with a history of child maltreatment. *Journal of Family Violence, 13,* 59–79. doi: 10.1023/A:1022812816957

Browne, K. D., & Hamilton, C. E. (1999). Police recognition of links between spouse abuse and child abuse. *Child Maltreatment, 4,* 136–147. doi: 10.1177/1077559599004002006

Browne, K. D., & Herbert, M. (1997). *Preventing Family Violence.* Chichester, England: Wiley.

Burrell, B., Thompson, B., & Sexton, D. (1994). Predicting child abuse potential across family types. *Child Abuse & Neglect, 18,* 1039–1050. doi: 10.1016/0145-2134(94)90130-9

Carlin, A. S., Kemper, K., Ward, N. G., Sowell, H., Gustafson, B., & Stevens, N. (1994). The effect of differences in objective and subjective definitions of childhood physical abuse on estimates of its incidence and relationship to psychopathology. *Child Abuse & Neglect, 18,* 393–399. doi: 10.1016/0145-2134(94)90024-8

Cawson, P., Wattam, C., Brooker, S., & Kelly, G. (2000). *Child Maltreatment in the United Kingdom: A Study of the Prevalence of Child Abuse and Neglect.* London, England: NSPCC.

Chan, K. L. (2005). *Study on Child Abuse and Spouse Battering: Report on Findings of Household Survey.* Hong Kong: Department of Social Work and Social Administration, the University of Hong Kong.

Chapman, D. A., & Scott, K. G. (2001). The impact of maternal intergenerational risk factors on adverse developmental outcomes. *Developmental Review, 21,* 305–325. doi: 10.1006/drev.2000.0523

Chow, C. B. (2009). Asia's world city deserves a child commission. *Hong Kong Journal of Paediatrics, 14,* 70–73. Retrieved from http://hkjpaed.org/pdf/2009;14;70-73.pdf

Cleaver, H., & Walker, S. (2004). *Assessing Children's Needs and Circumstances.* London, England: Jessica Kingsley Publishers.

Creighton, S., & Russell, N. (1995). *Voices from Childhood: A Survey of Childhood Experiences and Attitudes to Child Rearing among Adults in the United Kingdom.* London, England: NSPCC.

Crittenden, P. M. (1985). Maltreated infants: vulnerability and resilience. *Journal of Child Psychology and Psychiatry, 26,* 85–96. doi: 10.1111/j.1469-7610.1985.tb01630.x

Cunha, F., Heckman, J. J., Lochner, L., & Masterov, D. V. (2005). *Interpreting the Evidence on Life Cycle Skill Formation* (IZA Discussion Paper No. 1675). Retrieved from http://www.iza.org/publications/dps

Danese, A., Moffitt, T. E., Pariante, C. M. Ambler, A., Poulton, R., & Caspi, A. (2008). Elevated inflammation levels in depressed adults with a history of childhood maltreatment. *Archives of General Psychiatry, 65*(4), 409–415.

De Mause, L. (1974). *The History of Childhood*. London, England: Bellew Publishing.

Department for Children, Schools and Families. (2008). *Referrals, Assessments and Children and Young People who are the Subject of a Child Protection Plan or are on Child Protection Registers: Year Ending 31 March 2007*. London, England: Department for Children, Schools and Families.

Department for Education and Skills. (2004). *Statistics of Education: Referrals, Assessments, and Children and Young People on Child Protection Registers, England: Year Ending 31 March 2003*. London, England: National Statistics.

Department of Health, United Kingdom (2000). *Children and Young People on Child Protection Registers: Year Ending 31 March 2000, England*. London, England: Department of Health.

Department of Health, United Kingdom. (2001). Children in need (CIN) census. Retrieved from http://www.doh.gov.uk/cin

Department of Health, United Kingdom (2006). *Working Together to Safeguard Children*. London: The Stationery Office.

Dixon, L., Browne, K., & Hamilton-Giachristis, C. (2005). Risk factors of parents abused as children: a mediational analysis of the intergenerational continuity of child maltreatment (part 1). *Journal of Child Psychology and Psychiatry, 46*, 47–57. doi: 10.1111/j.1469-7610.2004.00339.x

Dong, M., Giles, W. H., Felitti, V. J., Dube, S. R., Williams, J. E., Chapman, D. P., & Anda, R. F. (2004). Insights into causal pathways for ischemic heart disease: adverse childhood experiences study. *Circulation, 100*, 1761–1766. doi: 10.1161/01.CIR.0000143074.54995.7F

Edwards, V. J., Holden, G. W., Felitti, V. J., & Anda, R. F. (2003). Relationship between multiple forms of childhood maltreatment and adult mental health in community respondents: results from the adverse childhood experiences study. *The American Journal of Psychiatry, 160*, 1453–1460.

Family Health Service. (2007). Evaluation report of the Comprehensive Child Development Service (CCDS). Retrieved from the Family Health Service, Department of Health, Hong Kong website: http://www.fhs.gov.hk/english/reports/reports.html

Fergusson, D. M., & Mullen, P. E. (1999). *Childhood Sexual Abuse: An Evidence Based Perspective*. Thousand Oaks, CA: Sage.

Finkelhor, D., Ormrod, R., Turner, H., & Hamby, S. L. (2005). The victimization of children and youth: a comprehensive, national study. *Child Maltreatment, 10*, 5–25. doi: 10.1177/1077559504271287

Fleming, J.M. (1997). Prevalence of childhood sexual abuse in a community sample of Australian women. *The Medical Journal of Australia, 166*, 65–68.Gelles, R. J. (1997). *Intimate Violence in Families*. Thousands Oaks, CA: Sage.

Gilbert, R., Widom, C. S., Browne, K., Fergusson, D., Webb, E., & Janson, S. (2009). Child maltreatment: burden and consequences of child maltreatment in high-income countries. *Lancet, 373*, 68–81. doi: 10.1016/S0140-6736(08)61706-7

Hong Kong International Year of the Child Commission. (1980). *The Child in Hong Kong: Evaluation Report for International Year of the Child*, 1979.

Ip, P. (2010). Child abuse admissions in Hong Kong public hospitals from 2001 to 2008. Unpublished data.

Ip, P. L. S. (2000). Child abuse and neglect in Hong Kong. *Hong Kong Journal of Paediatrics, 5*, 61–64.

Janson, S., Langberg, B., & Svensson, B. (2007). *Violence Against Children in Sweden. A National Survey 2006–2007*. Stockholm: Allmanna Barnhuset and Karlstad University.

Kelder, L. R., McNamara, J. R., Carlson, B., & Lynn, S. J. (1991). Perceptions of physical punishment: the relation to childhood and adolescent experiences. *Journal of Interpersonal Violence, 6*, 432–445. doi: 10.1177/088626091006004003

Kelly, L., Regan, L., & Burton, S. (1991). *An Exploratory Study of the Prevalence of Sexual Abuse in a Sample of 16–21 Year Olds*. London, England: Child Abuse Studies Unit, Polytechnic of North London.

Kempe, C. H., Silverman, F. N., & Steel, B. F. (1962). The battered child syndrome. *Journal of the American Medical Association, 18*(1), 17–24.

Kilsby, P. (2001). *Aspects of Crime: Children as Victims*. London, England: Crime and Criminal Justice Research Unit.

Lane, W. G., Rubin, D. M., Monteith, R., & Christian, C. W. (2002). Racial differences in the evaluation of paediatric fractures for physical abuse. *Journal of the American Medical Association, 288*, 603–695. doi: 10.1001/jama.288.13.1603

Lau, J. T. F., Liu, J. L. Y., & Cheung, J. C. K. (1999). Prevalence and correlates of physical abuse in Hong Kong Chinese adolescents: a population-based approach. *Child Abuse & Neglect, 23*, 549–557. doi: 10.1016/S0145-2134(99)00029-0

Lieh-Mak, F., Chung, S. Y., & Liu, Y. W. (1983). Characteristics of child battering in Hong Kong: a controlled study. *British Journal of Psychiatry, 142*, 89–94.

Lynch, M. A. (1985). Child abuse before Kempe: an historical literature review. *Child Abuse & Neglect, 9*, 7–15. doi: 10.1016/0145-2134(85)90086-9

Machado, C., Goncalves, M., Matos, M., & Dias, A. R. (2007). Child and partner abuse: self-reported prevalence and attitudes in the north of Portugal. *Child Abuse & Neglect, 31*, 657–670. doi: 10.1016/j.chiabu.2006.11.002

May-Chahal, C., & Cawson, P. (2005). Measuring child maltreatment in the United Kingdom: a study of the prevalence of child abuse and neglect. *Child Abuse & Neglect, 29*, 969–984. doi: 10.1016/j.chiabu.2004.05.009

Medical Coordinators on Child Abuse. (2001). Suspected child abuse cases in public hospitals: an interim analysis of 494 cases. *Hong Kong Journal of Paediatrics (new series), 6*, 3–56.

Morton, N., & Browne, K. D. (1998). Theory and observation of attachment and its relation to child maltreatment: a review. *Child Abuse & Neglect, 22*, 1093–1104. doi: 10.1016/S0145-2134(98)00088-X

Mrazek, P. J., Lynch, M. A., & Bentovim, A. (1983). Sexual abuse of children in the United Kingdom. *Child Abuse & Neglect, 7*, 147–151. doi: 10.1016/0145-2134(83)90066-2

National Clearinghouse on Child Abuse and Neglect Information. (2001). *In Focus: Understanding the Effects of Maltreatment on Early Brain Development*. Retrieved from http://nccanch.acf.hhs.gov/pubs/focus/earlybrain/index.cfm

Nelson, E. C., Heath, A. C., Madden, P. A. F., Cooper, M. L., Dinwiddle, S. H., Bucholz, K. K., Glowinski, A., MacLaughlin, T., Dunne, M. P., Statham, D. J., & Martin, M. G. (2002). Association between self-reported childhood sexual abuse and adverse psychosocial outcomes: results from a twin study. *Archives of General Psychiatry, 59*(2), 139–145.

Nobes, G., & Smith, M. (1997). Physical punishment of children in two-parent families. *Journal of Clinical Child Psychology and Psychiatry, 2*, 271–281. doi: 10.1177/1359104597022007

Nobes, G., Smith, M., Bee, P., & Heverin, A. (1999). Physical punishment by mothers and fathers in British homes. *Journal of Interpersonal Violence, 14*, 887–902. doi: 10.1177/088626099014008006

Olds, D., Eckenrode, J., Henderson, C. R., Kitzman, H., Powers, J., Cole, R., Sidora, K., Morris, P., Pettitt, L. M., & Luckey, D. (1997). Long-term effects of home visitation on maternal life course and child abuse and neglect: fifteen year follow up of a randomized trial. *Journal of the American Medical Association, 278*(8), 637–643.

Olds, D. L., Henderson, C. R., Kitzman, H., Cole, R. (1995). Effects of prenatal and infancy nurse home visitation on surveillance of child maltreatment. *Paediatrics, 95*(3), 365–372.

Polnay, J., (Ed.) (2001). *Child Protection in Primary Care*. Oxford: Radcliffe Medical Press.

Pryde, N. A., & Tsoi, M. M. (Eds.) (1999). *Hong Kong's Children: Our Past Their Future*. Hong Kong: Centre of Asian Studies, the University of Hong Kong.

RCPCH. (2008). Advocating for children. London, England: Advocacy Commission, Royal College of Paediatrics and Child Health.

Reder, P., Duncan, S., & Gray, M. (1993). *Beyond Blame*. London, England: Routledge.

Scarborough, A. A., Lloyd, E. C., Barth, R. P. (2009). Maltreated infants and toddlers: predictors of developmental delay. *Journal of Developmental and Behavioural Pediatrics, 30*(6), 489–498.

Sebre, S., Sprugevica, I., Novotni, A., Bonevski, D., Pakalniskiene, V., Popescu, D., Turchina, T., Friedrich, W., & Lewis, O. (2004). Cross-cultural comparisons of child-reported emotional and physical abuse: rates, risk factors and psychosocial symptoms. *Child Abuse & Neglect, 28*, 113–127. doi: 10.1016/j.chiabu.2003.06.004

Shonkoff, J. P., Boyce, W. T., & McEwen, B. S. (2009). Neuroscience, molecular biology, and the childhood roots of health disparities: building a new framework for health promotion and disease prevention. *Journal of the American Medical Association, 301*(21), 2252–2259.

Shonkoff, J. P., Phillips, D. A. (2000). From neurons to neighbourhoods: the science of early childhood development. Washington, DC: National Academy Press.

Smith, M., Bee, P., Heverin, A., & Nobes, G. (1995). Parental control within the family: the nature and extent of parental violence to children. In Department of Health (Ed.), *Child Protection: Message from Research* (pp. 83–85). London, England: HMSO.

Social Welfare Department. (1999). Studies on child abuse: associative factors and district differences.

Social Welfare Department. (2007). *Information Sheet for the Child Protection Registry.* Retrieved from the Social Welfare Department, Hong Kong website: http://www.swd.gov.hk/doc/en/08Appendix VI.pdf

Social Welfare Department. (2007). *Procedure for Handling Child Abuse Cases.* Retrieved from the Social Welfare Department, Hong Kong website: http://www.swd.gov.hk/en/index/site_pubsvc/page_family/sub_fcwprocedure/

Social Welfare Department. (2009). Statistics on child abuse, battered spouse and sexual violence cases. Retrieved from Social Welfare Department, Hong Kong website: http://www.swd.gov.hk/vs/english/stat.html

Steele, B. F. (1997). Psychodynamic and biological factors in child maltreatment. In M. E. Helfer, R. S. Kempe, & R. D. Krugman (Eds.), *The Battered Child* (5th ed.) (pp. 566–576). Chicago, IL: University of Chicago Press.

Straus, M. A., Hamby, S. L., Finkelhor, D., Moore, D. W., & Runyan, D. (1998). Identification of child maltreatment with the Parent-Child Conflict Tactics Scales: development and psychometric data for a national sample of American parents. *Child Abuse & Neglect, 22,* 249–270. doi: 10.1016/S0145-2134(97)00174-9

Tang, C. S. K. (1996). Adolescent abuse in Hong Kong Chinese families. *Child Abuse & Neglect, 20,* 873–878. doi: 10.1016/0145-2134(96)00075-0

Tang, C. S. K. (1998). The rate of physical child abuse in Chinese families: a community survey in Hong Kong. *Child Abuse & Neglect, 22,* 381–391. doi: 10.1016/S0145-2134(98)00010-6

Tang, C. S. K., & Davis, C. (1996). Child abuse in Hong Kong revisited after 15 years: characteristics of victims and abusers. *Child Abuse & Neglect, 20,* 1213–1218. doi: 10.1016/S0145-2134(96)00116-0

Theodore, A., Chang, J. J., & Runyan, D. (2007). Measuring the risk of physical neglect in a population-based sample. *Child Maltreatment, 12,* 96–105. doi: 10.1177/1077559506296904

Trocmé, N., & Wolfe, D. (2001). *Child Maltreatment in Canada: Selected Results from the Canadian Incidence Study of Reported Child Abuse and Neglect.* Ottawa, Ontario: Minister of Public Works and Government Services Canada.

Trocmé N., MacMillan, H., Fallon, B., & Marco, R. D. (2003). Nature and severity of physical harm caused by child abuse and neglect: results from the Canadian Incidence Study. *Canadian Medical Association Journal, 169*(9), 911–915.

Tsujimoto, S. (2008). The prefrontal cortex: functional neural development during early childhood. *Neuroscientist, 14*, 345–358. doi: 10.1177/1073858408316002

U.S. Department of Health and Human Services. (2006). *Child Maltreatment*. Washington, DC: U.S. Government Printing Office.

Wolfe, D. (1991). *Preventing Physical and Emotional Abuse of Children*. New York, NY: Guildford Press.

Wolfe, D. (1993). Child abuse prevention: blending research and practice. *Child Abuse Review, 2*, 153–165. doi: 10.1002/car.2380020305

Woodman, J., Pitt, M., Wentz, R., Taylor, B., Hodes, D., & Gilbert, R. E. (2008). Performance of screening tests for child physical abuse in Accident and Emergency Departments. *Health Technology Assessment, 12*(33), 1–118.

Working Group on Child Abuse. (1998). Procedures for handling child abuse cases Revised 1998. Hong Kong: Social Welfare Department.

World Health Organization (WHO), & International Society for Prevention of Child Abuse and Neglect (ISPCAN). (2006). Preventing child maltreatment: a guide to taking action and generating evidence. Retrieved from World Health Organization website: http://whqlibdoc.who.int/publications/2006/9241594365_eng.pdf

4
Research on Elder Mistreatment in Chinese Society

An Update

Elsie Chau-Wai Yan

Chapter summary

1. While much of the literature on elder mistreatment is developed in non-Chinese cultures, it remains unclear as to whether the present definition accurately reflects the meaning of "elder mistreatment" in the Chinese lens. It is essential to develop a culturally relevant definition for elder mistreatment.

2. Elder mistreatment is prevalent in Chinese societies as it is in other parts of the world.

3. Compared with older Chinese who are intact, those who were subjected to verbal or physical abuse reported higher levels of somatic complaints, anxiety, depressive symptoms, and social dysfunctions.

4. There is some preliminary evidence for the applicability of various theoretical models developed in non-Chinese populations on the Chinese population, including the caregiver stress model, the social exchange theory, and the social learning theory. It would be desirable to incorporate Chinese cultural values into existing theoretical frameworks.

5. Research on elder abuse in Chinese societies is complicated by the lack of valid and reliable instruments in the Chinese language.

What is elder mistreatment?

In research on this subject, one always comes across different terminology such as elder abuse, elder neglect, elder mistreatment, and so on. What exactly is elder mistreatment? The Action on Elder Abuse (1995) defines elder mistreatment as "a single, or repeated act, or lack of appropriate action, occurring within any relationship where there is an expectation of trust which causes harm or distress to an older person". The National Research Council (NRC) proposes a similar definition for research purposes. According to the NRC (2003), elder mistreatment is "(a) intentional actions that cause harm or create a serious risk of harm, whether or not intended, to a vulnerable elder by a caregiver or other person who stands in a trust relationship to the elder, or (b) failure by a caregiver to satisfy the elder's basic needs or to protect the elder from harm" (p. 40). Two important elements in these definitions are: (a) the presence of a trust relationship between the older person and the abuser, and (b) the older person's diminished capacity for self-care or self-protection. Based on these definitions, mistreatment committed by strangers does not constitute elder mistreatment. Similarly, intimate partner violence that persists into old age should not be considered elder mistreatment.

Based on the above definitions, different types of mistreatment may include (a) *physical abuse*, meaning the use of physical force that may result in injury, physical pain, or impairment; (b) *sexual abuse*, involving nonconsensual sexual contact; (c) *emotional abuse*, referring to the infliction of anguish, pain, or distress through verbal or nonverbal acts; (d) *financial abuse or material exploitation*, which is the illegal or improper use of an older person's funds, property, or assets; (e) *neglect*, being a caregiver's refusal or failure to fulfill his or her obligations to an older person; (f) *abandonment*, which is the desertion of an older person by an individual who has assumed responsibility for providing care to the older person; and (g) *self-neglect*, behaviours of an older person that threaten his/her health or safety (National Center on Elder Abuse, 2007).

Elder mistreatment is nothing new. Since the reporting of the first case of "granny battering", which appeared in the British Medical Journal (Burston, 1975), elder mistreatment has attracted considerable attention from researchers worldwide. This topic, however, is understudied in the Chinese population. The world's most populous country, China, makes up one-fifth of the world's population (US Census Bureau, 2007). People aged 60 years or older currently account for 11% of the total Chinese population, and the figure is expected to rise to at least 31% by 2050 (US Census Bureau, 2007). Despite this growing elderly demographic, there is a paucity of studies on elder mistreatment in the Chinese population. Indeed, research on elder abuse in Chinese societies has only begun in the past decade and is still underdeveloped. The aim of this chapter is to update readers with the current knowledge and to highlight some of the obstacles for research on elder mistreatment in the Chinese society. In the following sections, cultural values relevant for intergenerational relationship and elder care in Chinese societies will first be introduced, followed by a discussion on the challenges faced by families. Research on elder mistreatment that was conducted in Chinese populations will then be reviewed in detail. Finally, problems and issues in studying elder mistreatment in Chinese populations will be highlighted.

Aging and intergenerational relationships in Chinese society

In China, the cultural patterns of aging and intergenerational relationships are rooted in the time-honoured tradition of filial responsibility. Elderly persons have always been held in reverence and their children expected to pay them unconditional respect and to fulfil the duties of filial responsibility (Cowgill, 1986; Piovesana, 1979). Filial piety refers to the respect for one's parents and ancestors, and is a virtue held above all else in Confucian teachings. It also demands that one should provide for the material and mental well-being of one's aged parents (Ho, 1997). Adult children are expected to take care of their parents once their parents become aged and frail. Moreover, the eldest son has the obligation to live with his parents after he gets married.

Filial piety has served as the guiding principle governing intergenerational socialization of the Chinese family for centuries, and yet, being exposed to the alternative Western model of the family, the dynamics have been changing (Goodwin & Tang, 1997). Social changes brought about by urbanization and Western influences have posed challenges to traditional Chinese family relationships, and Chinese families now find themselves situated at the crossroads of modernism and traditionalism (Chan & Lee, 1995). There is evidence that traditional filial piety in the younger generation is on the decline (Ho, Hong, & Chi, 1989; Yue & Ng, 1999). Exposed to a diversity of value systems in addition to traditional Chinese values, younger Chinese may favour seeking individual development over fulfilling their prescribed social and familial obligations. Indeed, an increasing number of young Chinese couples choose to cohabit or delay their marriage, remain childless or have fewer children, and prefer not to live with their parents. Older people, however, have become increasingly dependent on their adult offspring because of their longer life expectancy. Moreover, a majority of the elderly Chinese are not beneficiaries of pensions or retirement funds, and their only way to maintain their living is to rely on their meagre savings or the support of their adult offspring (Chow & Chi, 1997). The changing personal and family values of the two generations may lead to different expectations and may, as a consequence, give rise to intergenerational conflicts.

Prevalence of elder mistreatment

Elder mistreatment is a prevalent phenomenon across the world. In the US, between 0.5% and 10% of those aged 65 or older have been mistreated by someone on whom they depended for care or protection (Administration for Children and Families and Administration on Aging, 1998; Fulmer, Paveza, & Guadagno, 2002; NRC, 2003). In Canada, prevalence rates of 1.1% for verbal abuse, 0.5% for physical abuse, 2.5% for material abuse, and 0.4% for neglect have been reported (Podnieks, 1990). Depending on the sampling method, much higher rates of elder mistreatment have also been reported. Pittaway and Westhues (1993) interviewed older persons attending various health and social service agencies in Canada and reported prevalence rates of 14% for verbal abuse, 14.3% for physical abuse, 20% for financial abuse, and 14% for neglect. In Britain, the prevalence rates of elder mistreatment were 5.4% for verbal abuse, 1.5% for physical abuse, and 1.5% for financial abuse (Bennett & Kingston, 1993).

Elder mistreatment is prevalent in Chinese societies as it is in other parts of the world. In a study of 276 older Chinese in Hong Kong (Yan & Tang, 2004), 27.5% of the sample reported having experienced at least one abusive behaviour committed against them by their family caregivers during the surveyed year. Verbal abuse (26.8%) was more commonly reported than physical abuse (2.5%) and violation of personal rights (5.1%). In a separate study on proclivity to elder mistreatment in Hong Kong (Yan & Tang, 2003), a convenient sample of 464 Chinese residing in Hong Kong were asked to indicate whether they would abuse an older person provided there is no legal or social punishment for the behaviour. Results indicated that a whole 20% would use verbal abuse, and 2.4% physical abuse, on an older person.

In a study of 92 family caregivers providing care to an older person in the community in Taiwan, participants reported the degree to which they exhibited each of the 20 depicted psychologically abusive behaviours in carrying out caring activities in the past six months (Wang, Lin, & Lee, 2006). It was found that only 6 out of the 92 caregivers reported that he/she did not engage in any psychologically abusive behaviour in the past six months.

In a convenient sample of 412 older Chinese attending a major urban medical centre in Nanjing, the People's Republic of China (PRC), 145 persons (35%) were screened positive for elder abuse and neglect (Dong, Simon, & Gorbien, 2007). Caregiver neglect was the most common form of abuse and was reported by 16.9% of the respondents. This was followed by financial exploitation (13.6%), emotional abuse (11.4%), physical abuse (5.8%), sexual abuse (1.2%), and abandonment (0.7%). Among those who reported abuse, 36% suffered multiple forms of abuse (Dong, Simon, & Gorbien, 2007).

Previous studies suggested that older adults with cognitive or physical impairments are more likely to be abused by their caregivers than other older adults (Choi & Mayer, 2000). While mistreatment of relatively healthy older Chinese residing in the community is alarmingly common, elder mistreatment is even more prevalent among older Chinese with dementia. In a study of mistreatment of older persons with dementia in Hong Kong (Yan & Kwok, 2010), a convenient sample of 122 family caregivers were asked to indicate whether they had directed any abusive behaviours at the care recipients in the past month. A whole 62.3% ($n = 76$) admitted to at least one incident of verbal abuse against the older care recipient, and 18% ($n = 22$) reported physical abuse in the past month.

Previous studies have also examined elder mistreatment in hospitals and institutions. A recent study showed that nurses reported extensive use of physical restraint in dementia care in Hong Kong (Yan, Kwok, Lee, & Tang, 2009). In a study of 114 caregivers working in nursing homes in Taiwan, participants reported the degree to which they exhibited each of the 20 psychologically abusive behaviours in carrying out the caring activities in the past six months (Wang, 2005). It was found that only one out of the 114 caregivers reported that he or she did not engage in any psychologically abusive behaviour in the caring activities. More common abusive behaviours were "accusing patient verbally", "ignoring patient's request", and "insulting patient by calling his/her full name".

It is commonly observed that elder mistreatment is frequently underreported in official records. In the US, data from the National Center on Elder Abuse report showed that only 19% of all "suspected cases" were reported to agencies (Administration for Children and Families and Administration on Aging, 1998). This pattern of underreporting is also observed in Chinese populations. Although there is yet to be any centralized reporting system in the PRC and Taiwan, according to the Central Information System on Elder Abuse Cases in Hong Kong, only 522, 612, 647 and 465 elder mistreatment cases were reported in the years 2006, 2007, 2008 and 2009 respectively. However, it is possible that many elder mistreatment cases were undetected or unreported.

Impact of Elder Mistreatment

The impact of elder abuse on its victims may be particularly serious and detrimental compared to other forms of family violence, as abusers are most frequently the victims' adult offspring, whom the victims raised themselves (Korbin, Anetzberger, Thomasson, & Austin, 1995). Apart from the bodily injuries resulting from physical assaults, victims may also suffer considerable emotional distress. Elevated levels of depressive symptoms have been observed among mistreated elders relative to intact elders (Harris, 1996). In a case-controlled study of older patients referred for abuse and neglect to a geriatric assessment clinic, Dyer, Pavlik, Murphy, and Hyman (2000) found a higher prevalence of depression in victims of abuse compared with patients referred for other reasons. A thirteen-year prospective study of 2,812 individuals even found that mistreated elders had a greater mortality risk than their intact counterparts even after adjusting for demographic characteristics, chronic diseases, functional status, social networks, cognitive status, and depressive symptomatology (Lachs, Williams, O'Brien, Pillemer, & Charlson, 1998).

Elder mistreatment is not only devastating for victims and their families, but also has significant effects on our healthcare, social welfare, justice and financial systems. A study of urban emergency room utilization in the US found that mistreated elders identified through adult protective service programmes were more likely to go to emergency room for assessment and treatment (Lachs, Williams, & O'Brien, 1997). Elder mistreatment in cases referred to adult protective services is also a compelling predictor of nursing home placement (Lachs, Williams, O'Brien, & Pillemer, 2002).

To date, there has not been any study conducted in the Chinese population examining the relationship between the use of medical and social services, or nursing home, and elder mistreatment. Similar to their Western counterparts, however, abused older Chinese reported deteriorated mental health (Yan & Tang, 2001). Compared to older Chinese who are intact, those who were subjected to verbal or physical abuse reported higher levels of somatic complaints, anxiety, depressive symptoms, and social dysfunctions (Yan & Tang, 2001).

Theories on elder abuse and their application to the Chinese population

Various theories from diverse perspectives have been proposed to explain the occurrence of elder mistreatment. There is some preliminary evidence for the applicability of various theoretical models developed in non-Chinese populations in the local setting. Prominent models include the caregiver stress model, the social exchange theory, and the social learning theory. Each of these models, and their applications to the Chinese population, will be discussed in the following section.

Caregiver Stress Model

The caregiver stress model sees abuse as the result of stress associated with caring for an elderly patient. It has been found that individuals who are frequently assigned the responsibility to care for a frail elder are always unemployed members of the workforce who suffer high levels of stress and even depression (Eckley & Vilakazi, 1995). A caregiver's stress and emotional distress are also related to mistreatment and abuse (McGuire & Fulmer, 1997; Parks & Novielli, 2000). In support of the model, Yan and Kwok (2010) found that being the major caregiver, perception of a high level of caregiver burden, lack of assistance from a domestic helper, and care recipients exhibiting a large number of problem behaviours were related to caregivers' self-reported abusive behaviours directed towards older persons with dementia. In a study of 92 family caregivers in Taiwan, high level of caregiver burden was positively associated with abusive behaviours by family caregivers (Wang, Lin, & Lee, 2006). In a similar study of 183 professional caregivers in Taiwan, caregivers who reported higher levels of work stress showed higher levels of psychological abusive behaviours in caring for the elderly patients (Wang, Lin, Tseng, & Chang, 2009).

Social Exchange Theory

The social exchange theory addresses how unfair social exchange between a caregiver and an older person may result in abuse. According to the theory, the person who is less dependent on the social exchange relationship will enjoy a power advantage. He/she may use this power advantage to effect compliance from the other partner, sometimes in the form of abuse or violence against the other partner. Previous studies found that abuse occurred in cases where the elder victim was dependent on the abuser (Bennet & Kingston, 1993; Harris, 1996; Lachs et al., 1997); where the abusers depended on the elder victims interpersonally and emotionally (Murphy, 1994); or where the abusers depended on the elder victims instrumentally in terms of child care, financial assistance, household repairs, transportation, and housing (Pillemer & Finkelhor, 1989). In support of the social exchange theory, Yan and Tang (2001) found that abused elders, as compared to their intact counterparts, were more dependent on the abusers emotionally, and that they perceived their caregivers as being more emotionally dependent on them.

Social Learning Theory

The social learning theory, sometimes known as the hypothesis of intergenerational transmission of violence, sees violence as a learned behaviour and proposes that individuals exposed to harsh parenting during their childhood are more likely to engage in domestic violence (Simons, Wu, Johnson, & Conger, 1995). In support of this view, it has been found that adult children who reported higher levels of childhood experience of domestic violence also reported higher levels of proclivity to elder mistreatment (Yan & Tang, 2003).

Other situational variables

Apart from the risk factors proposed by elder mistreatment theories, previous research has demonstrated that various situational variables are important determinants for elder mistreatment. For instance, *shared living environment* and *social isolation* have been identified as two telling predictors for the occurrence of elder mistreatment (Dyer et al., 2000; Harisberry, Chen, & Gorbien, 2005; Shugarman, Fries, Wolf, & Morris, 2003). Previous studies found a shared living arrangement to be a risk factor for elder mistreatment among older persons with Alzheimer's disease (Paveza et al., 1992; Pillemer & Suitor, 1992). Similar findings have also been observed in Hong Kong, where a large number of co-residing days was a salient predictor for verbal and physical abuse of older persons with dementia by their family caregivers (Yan & Kwok, 2010).

Social isolation has also been demonstrated to be an important factor for elder mistreatment. In a prospective community-based study, Lachs, Berkman, Fulmer, and Horwitz (1994) found that having a poor social network significantly increased the risk for elder mistreatment. Comptom, Flanagan, & Gregg (1997) also found low levels of social support to be associated with verbal and physical abuse by caregivers. Similarly, Grafstrom, Nordberg, & Winblad (1993) found both caregivers and care recipients to be more socially isolated in families in which abuse occurred. Dong, Simon, and Gorbien (2007), in their study conducted in the PRC, found that a feeling of loneliness reported by the older person was associated with an increased risk for elder abuse—specifically, even after adjusting for confounding factors, the feeling of lacking companionship and of sometimes being left out in life, as well as the overall loneliness scores. Similarly, reports of feeling bored, often feeling hopeless, feeling worthless, as well as the overall feeling of depression, were associated with increased risk of elder abuse and neglect (Dong, Simon, Odwazny, & Gorcien, 2008). In a study of professional caregivers in Taiwan, caregivers who lacked social resources reported more psychological abusive behaviours (Wang, Lin, Tseng, & Chang, 2009).

Protective Factors

Despite the fact that caregiving is generally perceived as stressful, not all caregivers end up abusing their older care recipients. Resilience refers to the ability to maintain relatively stable, healthy levels of functioning in the face of an isolated and potentially disruptive event (Bonanno, 2004). It is recognized to be one of the most important factors in successful adaptation to life adversities across the life span (Agaibi & Wilson, 2005; Bonanno, 2004; Luthar, Cicchetti, & Becker, 2000; Masten, 2001). Among the many possible determinants of resilience, social support is an important factor moderating the dynamics between various caregiver characteristics and elder mistreatment. In fact, it has been found that greater social support, as in "having someone to listen to or talk to", "having someone to get advice from", "having someone to show love and affection", or "having someone to help with daily chores", was associated with a 59% lower risk for elder mistreatment in the PRC (Dong & Simon, 2008).

Assessing elder abuse in the Chinese population

Research on elder abuse in Chinese societies is further complicated by the lack of valid and reliable instruments in the Chinese language. In the past decades, a large number of screening instruments for elder abuse have been developed. These include the Hwalek-Sengstock Elder Abuse Screening Test (Sengstock & Hwalek, 1987), a 15-item screening instrument administered to persons who may be at risk of abuse for use in health and social service agencies; the Caregiver Abuse Screen (CASE; Reis-Nahmiash, 1995), an 8-item screening tool for caregivers to self appraise personal risks for abusive caregiving situations; and the Elder Assessment instrument (Fulmer, Etreet, & Carr, 1984), a 41-item comprehensive assessment of all aspects of abuse of an older person. Due to the problem of cultural sensitivity and translation issues, however, very few available studies in Chinese populations employed these instruments. This section reviews the psychometric properties as well as the strengths and weaknesses of some of the measures used in previous studies of elder mistreatment in Chinese societies.

The Revised Conflict Tactic Scales (CTS2; Straus et al., 1996)

The two subscales of "psychological aggression" and "physical assault" of the Revised Conflict Tactic Scales (CTS2; Straus, Hamby, Boney-McCoy, & Sugarman, 1996) have been used to assess the extent and nature of elder abuse in various studies in Hong Kong. The CTS2 scale has good reliability (alpha = .79 for Psychological Aggression, and .86 for Physical Assault) and satisfactory construct validity (correlation among the 3 subscales ranged from .25 to .90). Physical abuse means at least one act of physical violence against an elder individual in the preceding year. The 12 items from the physical abuse subscale of the CTS2 cover a wide range of violent behaviours, from being slapped, grabbed, or choked, to being assaulted with a knife. Verbal abuse is defined as insulting or threatening an elder person at least 10 times in the preceding year. Typically, older care recipients or their caregivers will be asked whether the caregiver displayed such behaviours in the past 12 months on a four-point scale depicting occurrence from "never", "seldom", "sometimes" to "always".

A major strength of the CTS2 is that, being a widely used measure for intrafamilial violence, it allows for comparison between different types of violence occurring in the same family. The fact that it is widely used in various populations also makes it a convenient measure for studies involving cross-cultural comparisons. A downside of using CTS2 in researching elder abuse in Chinese population, however, is the potential lack of cultural sensitivity of the instrument.

The Elder's Psychological Abuse Scale (EPAS)

Having reviewed the various abuse indicators from the literature, and based on the results from a focus group study, Wang and her colleagues (2007) developed the Elder's Psychological Abuse Scale (EPAS). The EPAS consists of 32 "yes/no" questions depicting different behavioural indicators for psychological abuse. In a study testing the psychometric properties of the EPAS in a sample of 195 older Taiwanese residing in a variety of institutional care settings and private homes, Wang (2007) showed that the EPAS had a significant inverse relationship with both the Short Portable Mental State Questionnaire and the Barthel's Index ($r = .32$ & $-.36$ respectively, $p < .001$), thereby demonstrating that older people with poorer cognitive and physical functioning experienced more psychological abuse. Sample items for the EPAS include an older person "being left alone involuntarily", "having personal belongings being used without permission" or "taking of improper medication for unknown reason". Wang and her colleagues suggested that the instrument could be administered by asking an older person directly, by active observation, or by asking an elderly person's caregiver(s).

The strengths of the EPAS are that it is culturally sensitive and is easily administered. The instrument is also comprehensive, and assesses both behavioural indicators such as "privacy not respected", as well as symptoms, e.g., "nightmares" and "low self-esteem", associated with psychological abuse. However, the construct of psychological abuse is unclear, lumping together concepts such as neglect and abandonment, e.g., "left alone involuntarily"; social abuse, e.g., "expectation to see relatives unfulfilled"; and possible financial exploitation, e.g., "personal belongings used without permission". Moreover, other important dimensions of elder abuse, including physical and sexual abuse, are overlooked.

Other locally developed measures

On the basis of their definition of elder abuse and neglect, Dong, Simon, and Gorbien (2007) developed for the purposes of study their own measure, which consists of a list of 12 specific questions depicting each type of mistreatment. Physical abuse is defined as the wilful infliction of injury or cruel punishment resulting in physical harm or pain, and is assessed by the item, "Does anyone close to you hit, kick, slap, push, or throw things at you?" Neglect is defined as the failure to provide or have provided the goods or services necessary to avoid physical harm and/or mental anguish, or the failure of the caretaker to provide such goods and services. It is assessed by the question, "Does anyone in your family make you stay in bed or tell you that you are sick when you know you are not?" Psychological and emotional abuse are assessed by asking, "Is there anyone who called you names or put you down or made you feel bad recently?" Financial exploitation is assessed by asking, "Is there anyone who has taken your money without your OK or stopped you from getting your money or knowing about it?", "Has anyone taken your house or apartment away from you?", and "Has anyone taken your assets without your permission, misused your money, transferred money from your account; intentionally prevented you from using your money, or sold, appropriated, or transferred your property without your authorization?" The item on sexual abuse enquires, "Have you had any nonconsenting sexual contact of any kind?" Lastly, abandonment is assessed by asking, "Has any family member ever abandoned you in a clinic, hospital, or any other public places?"

While similar to the EPAS in demonstrating cultural sensitivity, Dong's instrument has the advantage of detailing specific behavioural indicators for different forms of elder abuse. The weakness, however, is that a number of items assessed several behaviours concurrently.

Conclusion

Future directions for elder mistreatment research in Chinese societies

Although elder mistreatment has been a concern around the globe in the past three decades, research and understanding of elder mistreatment are still relatively green in the Chinese society. Given the tremendous impact on its victims, the victim's families and the society as a whole, with the added prospect of a rapidly aging Chinese population, addressing elder mistreatment should be on the top of our research agenda. On this front, we need to address several issues.

While much of the literature on elder mistreatment is developed in non-Chinese cultures, it remains unclear as to whether the present definition accurately reflects the meaning of elder mistreatment in the Chinese lens. It is thus essential to develop a culturally relevant definition for elder mistreatment. For instance, it has been suggested that older Chinese considered disrespect (Tam & Neysmith, 2006), being refrained from seeing their relatives (Wang, 2006), or being treated by family members as if they were transparent (Hong Kong Christian Service, 2002) as elder mistreatment. Further studies need to be done to examine these facets.

It is also important to revisit the various theories on elder mistreatment. While previous studies have demonstrated that a number of theoretical frameworks developed in non-Chinese societies are also applicable to the Chinese population, it would be desirable to incorporate Chinese cultural values into the existing frameworks. In doing so, one should note that there may be subtle differences in the cultural values among Chinese residing in the PRC, Hong Kong, Taiwan, and other countries.

It would also be desirable to explore potential similarities and differences in issues related to elder abuse across cultural contexts. Therefore, as we develop assessment tools sensitive for measuring elder mistreatment in the local setting, we should ensure that the new tools are constructed with some degree of comparability for the purpose of cross-cultural analyses.

References

Action on Elder Abuse. (1995). *What is Elder Abuse?* London, England: Action on Elder Abuse.

Agaibi, C. E., & Wilson, J. P. (2005). Trauma, PTSD, and resilience: a review of the literature. *Trauma, Violence, & Abuse, 6,* 195–216. doi: 10.1177/1524838005277438

Bennett, G. & Kingston, P. (1993). *Elder Abuse. Concepts, Theories and Interventions.* London, England: Chapman & Hall.

Bonanno, G. A. (2004). Loss, trauma, and human resilience: have we underestimated the human capacity to thrive after extremely aversive events? *American Psychologist, 59,* 20–28. doi: 10.1013/0003-066X.59.1.20

Burston, G. W. (1975). Granny battering. *British Medical Journal, 3,* 592. doi: 10.1136/bmj.3.5983.592-a

Chan, H., & Lee, R. (1995). Hong Kong families: at the crossroad of modernism and traditionalism. *Journal of Comparative Family Studies*, *26*, 83–99.

Choi, N. G., & Mayer, J. (2000). Elder abuse, neglect and exploitation: risk factors and prevention strategies. *Journal of Gerontological Social Work*, *33*, 5–25. doi: 10.1300/J083v33n02_02

Chow, W. S., & Chi, I. (1997). Aging in Hong Kong. In S.K. Lam (Ed.), *The Health of the Elderly in Hong Kong* (pp. 173–193). Hong Kong: Hong Kong University Press.

Compton, S. A., Flanagan, P., & Gregg, W. (1997). Elder abuse in people with dementia in Northern Ireland: prevalence and predictors in cases referred to a psychiatry of old age service. *International Journal of Geriatric Psychiatry, 12*, 632–635. doi: 10.1002/(SICI)1099-1166(199706)12:6<632::AID-GPS570>3.0.CO;2-9

Cowgill, D.O. (1986). *Aging around the world*. Belmont, CA: Wadsworth Publishing Co.

Dong, X., Simon, M. A., Odwazny, R., & Gorbien, M. (2008). Depression and elder abuse and neglect among a community-dwelling Chinese elderly population. *Journal of Elder Abuse and Neglect*, *20*, 25–41. doi: 10.1300/J084v20n01_02

Dong, X., & Simon, M. (2008). Is greater social support a protective factor against elder mistreatment? *Gerontology*, *54*, 381–388. doi: 10.1159/000143228

Dong, X., Simon, M. A. & Gorbien, M. (2007) Elder abuse and neglect in an urban Chinese population. *Journal of Elder Abuse and Neglect, 19*, 79–96. doi: 10.1300/J084v19n03_05

Dyer, C. B., Pavlik, V. N., Murphy, K. P., & Hyman, D. J. (2000). The high prevalence of depression and dementia in elder abuse or neglect. *Journal of American Geriatric Society*, *48*, 205–208.

Eckley, S., & Vilakazi, P. (1995). Elder abuse in South Africa. In J. Kosberg & J. Garcia (Eds.), *Elder Abuse: International and Cross Cultural Perspective* (pp. 171–182). Binghamton, NY: The Haworth Press, Inc.

Fulmer, T., Paveza, G., & Quadagno, L. (2002). Elder abuse and neglect: policy issues for two very different problems. *Public Policy and Aging Report*, *12*, 15–18.

Fulmer, T., Street, S., & Carr, K. (1984). Abuse of the elderly: screening and detection. *Journal of Emergency Nursing*, *10*, 131–140.

Goodwin, R., & Tang, C. (1998). The transition to uncertainty? The impacts of Hong Kong 1997 on personal relationships. *Personal Relationships*, *5*, 183–190. doi: 10.1111/j.1475-6811.1998.tb00166.x

Grafstrom, M., Nordberg, A., & Winblad, B. (1993). Abuse is in the eye of the beholder: reports by family members about abuse of demented persons in home care: a population study. *Scandinavian Journal of Social Medicine, 21*, 247–255. doi: 10.1177/140349489302100404

Hansberry, M. R., Chen, E., & Gorbien, M. J. (2005). Dementia and elder abuse. *Clinical Geriatric Medicine, 21*, 315–332. doi: 10.1016/j.cger.2004.11.002

Harris, S. (1996). For better or for worse: spouse abuse grown old. *Journal of Elder Abuse & Neglect, 8*, 1–33. doi: 10.1300/J084v08n01_01

Ho, D. Y. F., Hong, Y. Y., & Chiu, C. Y. (1989). *Filial Piety and Family-Matrimonial Traditionalism in Chinese Societies.* Paper presented at the International Conference on Moral Values and Moral Reasoning in Chinese Societies, Taipei, Taiwan.

Ho, D. Y. F. (1997). Interpersonal relationship and relationship dominance: an analysis based on methodological relationalism. *Asian Journal of Social Psychology, 1,* 1–16. doi: 10.1111/1467-839X.00002

Hong Kong Christian Service. (2002). *Elder Abuse Research and Protocol.* Hong Kong: Hong Kong Christian Service.

Korbin, J. E., Anetzberger, Y. J., & Austin, C. (1995). The intergenerational cycle of violence in child and elder abuse. *Journal of Elder Abuse and Neglect, 7,* 1–15. doi: 10.1300/J084v07n01_01

Lachs, M. S., Berkman, L., Fulmer, T., & Horwitz, R. I. (1994). A prospective community-based pilot study of risk factors for the investigation of elder mistreatment. *Journal of the American Geriatrics Society, 42,* 169–173. doi: 10.1093/geront/37.4.469

Lachs, M. S., Williams, C., & O'Brien, S. (1997). Risk factors for reported elder abuse and neglect: a nine-year observational cohort study. *The Gerontologist, 37,* 469–74. doi: 10.1093/geront/37.4.469

Lachs, M. S., Williams, C. S., O'Brien, S. & Pillemer, K., & Charlson, M. E. (1998). The mortality of elder mistreatment. *The Journal of American Medical Association, 280,* 428–432. doi: 10.1001/jama.280.5.428

Lachs, M. S., Williams, C. S., O'Brien, S. & Pillemer, K. (2002) Adult protective service use and nursing home placement. *The Gerontologist, 42,* 734–739. doi: 10.1093/geront/42.6.734

Luthar, S. S., Cicchetti, D., & Becker, B. (2000). The construct of resilience: a critical evaluation and guidelines for future work. *Child Development, 71,* 543–562. doi: 10.1111/1467-8624.00164

Masten, A. S. (2001). Ordinary magic: resilience processes in development. *American Psychologist, 56,* 227–238. doi: 10.1037/0003-066X.56.3.227

McGuire, P., & Fulmer, T., (1997). Elder Abuse. In C. K. Cassel (Ed.), *Geriatric Medicine* (3rd ed., pp. 855–864). New York, NY: Springer-Verlag.

Murphy, N. (1994). *Resource and Training Kit for Service Providers: Abuse and Neglect of Older Adults.* Ottawa, Ontario: Minister of Supply and Services Canada.

National Center on Elder Abuse. (2007). *Preventing Elder Abuse by Family Caregivers.* Retrieved from the National Catholic Educational Association website: http://www.ncea.aoa.gov/ncearoot/main_site/pdf/family/caregiver.pdf

National Research Council. (2003). *Elder Mistreatment: Abuse, Neglect, and Exploitation on Aging America.* Washington, DC: The National Academies Press.

Parks, M. S., & Novielli, K. D. (2000). A practical guide to caring for caregivers. *American Family Physican, 15,* 2215–2219.

Paveza G. J., Cohen, D., Eisdorfer, C., Freels, S., Semla, T., Ashford, W., Gorelick, P., Hirschman, R., Luchins, D., & Levy, P. (1992) Severe family violence and Alzheimer's disease: prevalence and risk factors. *The Gerontologist, 32*, 493–497. doi: 10.1093/geront/32.4.493

Pillemer, K., & Finkelhor, D. (1989). Causes of elder abuse: caregiver stress versus problem relatives. *American Journal of Orthopsychiatry. 59*, 179–187. doi: 10.1111/j.1939-0025.1989.tb01649.x

Pillemer, K., & Suitor, J. J. (1992). Violence and violent feelings: what causes them among family givers? *Journal of Gerontology, 47*, S165–S172.

Piovesana, G. K. (1979). The aged in Chinese and Japanese cultures. In J. Hendricks, & C. D. Hendricks (Eds.), *Dimensions of Aging: Readings* (pp. 13–20). Cambridge, MA: Winthrop Publishers.

Pittaway, E., & Westhues, A. (1993). The prevalence of elder abuse and neglect of older adults who access health and social services in London, Ontario, Canada. *Journal of Elder Abuse and Neglect, 5*, 77–93. doi: 10.1300/J084v05n04_06

Podnieks, E., Pillemer, K., Nicholson, J. P., Shillington, T., & Frizzell, A. F. (1990). *National Survey on Abuse of the Elderly in Canada*. Toronto, Ontario: Ryerson Polytechnical Institute.

Sengstock, M. C., & Hwalek, M. A. (1987). A review and analysis of measures for the identification of elder abuse. *Journal of Gerontological Social Work, 10*, 21–35.

Shugarman, L., Fries, B. E., Wolfe, R. S., & Morris, J. N. (2003). Identifying older people at risk of abuse during routine screening. *Journal of American Geriatric Society, 51*, 24–31. Retrieved from http://deepblue.lib.umich.edu/bitstream/2027.42/65922/1/j.1601-5215.2002.51005.x.pdf

Simons, R. L., Wu, C., Johnson, D., & Conger, R. D. (1995). A test of various perspectives on the intergenerational transmission of domestic violence. *Criminology, 33*, 141–171. doi: 10.1111/j.1745-9125.1995.tb01174.x

Straus, M. A., Hamby, S. L., Boney-McCoy, S., & Sugarman, D. B. (1996). The Revised Conflict Tactics Scales (CTS2): development and preliminary psychometric data. *Journal of Family Issues, 17*, 283–316. doi: 10.1177/019251396017003001

Tam, S., & Neysmith, S. (2006). Disrespect and isolation: elder abuse in Chinese communities. *Canadian Journal on Aging, 25*, 141–151. doi: 10.1353/cja.2006.0043

The National Center on Elder Abuse, & Westat, Inc. (1998). *The National Elder Abuse Incidence Study: Final Report*. Retrieved from http://permanent.access.gpo.gov/lps104188/ABuseReport_Full.pdf

US Census Bureau. (2007). *World Population Data Sheet*. Washington, DC: Population Reference Bureau.

Wang, J. J. (2005). Psychological abuse behaviour exhibited by caregivers in the care of the elderly and correlated factors in long-term care facilities in Taiwan. *Journal of Nursing Research, 13*, 271–80. doi: 10.1097/01.JNR.0000387550.50458.bc

Wang, J. J. (2006). Psychological abuse and its characteristic correlates among elderly Taiwanese. *Archives of Gerontology and Geriatrics, 42*, 307–318. doi: 10.1016/j.archger.2005.08.006

Wang, J. J., Lin, M., Tseng, H., & Chang, W. (2009). Caregiver factors contributing to psychological elder abuse behaviour in Taiwan: a structural equation model approach. *International Psychogeriatrics, 21*, 314–320. doi: 10.1017/S1041610208008211

Wang, J. J., Tseng, H. F., & Chen, K. M. (2007). Development and testing of screening indicators of psychological abuse of older people. *Archives of Psychiatric Nursing, 21*, 40–47. doi: 10.1016/j.apnu.2006.09.004

Yan, E., & Tang, C. (2001). Prevalence and psychological impact of elder abuse. *Journal of Interpersonal Violence, 16*, 1158–1174. doi: 10.1177/088626001016011004

Yan, E., & Tang, C. (2003). The role of individual, interpersonal and organizational factors in mitigating burnout among elderly Chinese volunteers. *International Journal of Geriatric Psychiatry, 18*, 795–802. doi: 10.1002/gps.922

Yan, E., & Tang, C. (2004). Elder abuse by caregivers: a study of prevalence and risk factors in Hong Kong Chinese families. *Journal of Family Violence, 19*, 269–277. doi: 10.1023/B:JOFV.0000042077.95692.71

Yan, E., & Kwok, T. (2010). Abuse of older Chinese with dementia by their family caregivers: an inquiry into the role of caregiver burden. *International Journal of Geriatric Psychiatry*, in press.

Yan, E., Kwok, T., Lee, D. T. F. & Tang, C. (2009). The prevalence and correlates of the use of restraint and force in older hospital patients: a study of nurses and nursing assistants in Hong Kong. *Journal of Nursing and Healthcare of Chronic Illness, 1*, 147–155. doi: 10.1111/j.1752-9824.2009.01015.x

Yue, X. D., & Ng, S. H. (1999). Filial obligations and expectations in China: current views from young and old people in Beijing. *Asian Journal of Social Psychology, 2*, 215–226. doi: 10.1111/1467-839X.00035

5
Research Instruments for Domestic Violence Studies in Hong Kong

Daniel Yee-Tak Fong

> ### Chapter summary
>
> 1. Research instruments should have their intended purposes first determined before their relevance for adoption in a research study can be confirmed.
> 2. Research instruments should be adequately evaluated before they are adopted in a research study. The evaluation methods for different types of instruments vary substantially. For assessment instruments, evaluation other than the Cronbach's alpha is desirable. For screening instruments, it is preferable to report sensitivity, specificity and the likelihood ratios.
> 3. Consistency of administration mode of a research instrument should be maintained in view of the potential differences across different administration methods.

Types of research instruments

Research studies on domestic violence (DV) frequently employ instruments that identify or assess constructs associated with health-related problems and/ or the well-being of an individual. These problems can be of a physical or a psychological nature, which may not be directly measurable. These underlying constructs may, however, be assessed by using the responses of a number of items that are associated with the constructs. Responses to these items are then scored and used to form a scale score for assessment. A compendium of Chinese instruments available for DV studies is provided in the final section of this chapter. In general, these instruments can be categorized according to the purpose for which they are developed, or the target group of individuals to which they apply.

Assessment versus screening instruments

Assessment instruments are developed to assess one or more underlying constructs of an individual. For example, the Revised Conflict Tactics Scales (CTS2) is a popular instrument used to measure the frequency of different types of violence suffered by an individual, including physical assault, psychological aggression and sexual coercion (Chan, 2005; Straus, Hamby, BoneyMcCoy, & Sugarman, 1996). A score can be computed based on the item responses from an individual, with a higher score indicating greater severity. The score may serve as an outcome indicator in studies which examine the efficacy of an intervention for domestic violence.

Screening instruments identify individuals with experience of a specific condition. For example, the Abuse Assessment Screen (AAS) was developed to identify individuals who have experienced violence (Tiwari et al., 2007). It consists of three anchor items to identify individuals who have experienced physical, psychological or sexual abuse. Such instruments serve the purposes of identifying abused individuals for subject recruitment in intervention studies, and more generally, of examining the prevalence of a problem in the community or a clinical setting.

It is worth noting that an instrument originally developed for assessment may also be used as a screening tool, or may eventually evolve into one. Indeed, the CTS2 may also be used as a screening tool to identify individuals who have been victims of some form of violence (Straus et al., 1996).

Generic versus specific instruments

Generic instruments are applicable to the general population across age, gender, disease and other parameters. An example is the SF-12 Health Survey (SF-12), which can be administered to all individuals, irrespective of their conditions of health and disease. In contrast, *specific instruments* are restricted in use only among individuals in a particular category. For example, in the diabetic foot ulcer scale (Hui, Fong, Yam, & Ip, 2008), the item—"Because of your foot ulcer problems, how often have you felt drained?"—is relevant only to patients suffering from a foot ulcer, but not to others without the condition.

In researching specific diseases or conditions, specific instruments may show greater sensitivity in differentiating individuals at different severity levels (Velanovich, 2000), higher responsiveness to changes over time (Angst, Verra, Lehmann, & Aeschlimann, 2008), and greater relevance to the individuals being surveyed (Velanovich, 1998). On the other hand, generic instruments may cover general aspects such as social functioning and general health that may not be considered in specific instruments. It is, therefore, sometimes advisable for studies to combine a use of both types of instruments (Angst et al., 2008).

Developing and evaluating research instruments

New research instruments can be developed where there are no relevant instruments available, or adapted from an existing one developed in another cultural group. The process of development and evaluation is depicted in Figure 5.1.

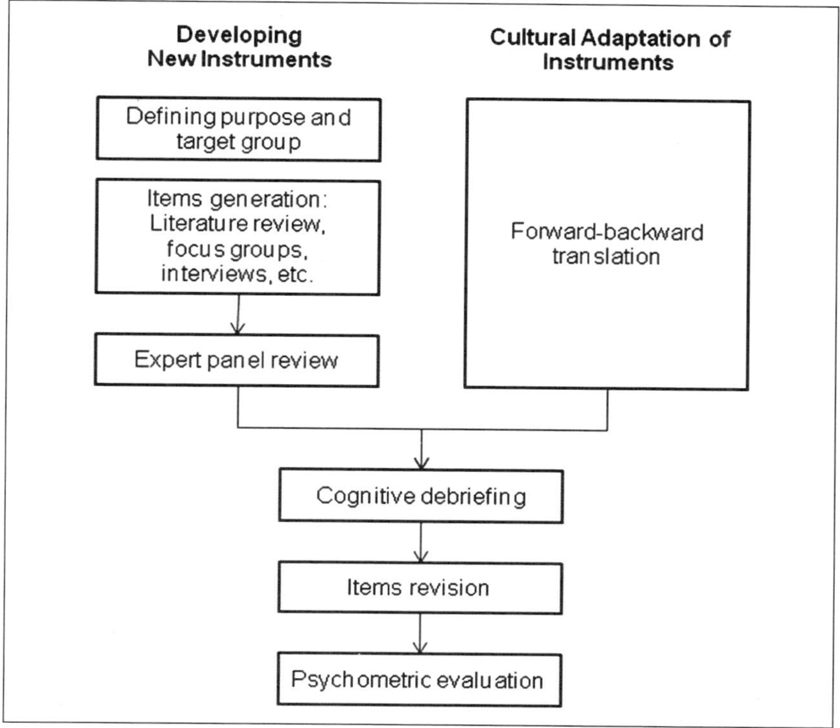

Figure 5.1 Developing and evaluating a research instrument.

Items generation

First and foremost in developing a new research instrument, the purpose and target group should be clearly defined. A review of the literature is inevitable in determining if relevant items can be derived from existing instruments. This review is often followed by interviews to generate themes and further items.

Interviews may be conducted individually to facilitate in-depth understanding of the individuals. However, it may take a long time before a saturation of themes and topics is achieved. Focus group interviews are also sometimes used to interview an entire group at once (Streiner & Norman, 2008). Each focus group often consists of 6–12 individuals, but its size may vary depending on the complexity of the instrument. Participating members should demonstrate willingness to engage themselves fully in the discussion; and to foster a congenial atmosphere for such, they would preferably be in the same peer group and have similar clinical characteristics.

There are different variants of focus group interviews, differentiated according to their interview method and the type of participant. In a structured interview, participants are asked a number of questions predesigned in order to solicit focused information. A semi-structured interview similarly poses predesigned questions, but offers participants the chance to propose topics for further group discussions. Unstructured interviews may also be used as a quick means to solicit new themes and relevant topics. Apart from the above methods, exploratory cognitive interviews that utilize think-aloud interviewing and verbal probing techniques may be conducted. Think-aloud observes a participant's ability to talk through the thinking process from comprehension of an item to completion, while verbal probing involves posing questions to the participant to assess his/her understanding of an item. This method aims to gain understanding of participants' thought processes in order to generate new hypotheses and inform item design (Rat et al., 2007). Also varying across interview designs is the type of participant. Participants may be individuals from the target group under study, healthcare professionals or researchers, including clinicians, epidemiologists, nurses, psychologists, social workers, and so on.

The use of different interviewing approaches has recently been reviewed and compared in the development of a quality-of-life instrument (Rat et al., 2007). Individual interviews with patients appeared to be the best method for formulating items, while none of the other methods appeared to contribute any other substantial information.

In generating items, it is preferable to invite a panel of experts to assess the relevance and clarity of additional items, as well as the need for such, so as to establish the content validity of an instrument. Content validity can be measured by several indices, such as the percentage of experts rating an item as relevant (Aiken, 1985). Face validity—whether an instrument appears to be valid to participants—can also be assessed by asking individuals from the target group about the acceptability of the generated items (Nevo, 1985).

Linguistic validation

When an instrument is available in a foreign language, it must undergo a linguistic validation process before a locally relevant version can be obtained for further evaluation (Acquadro, Conway, Girourdet, & Mear, 2004). Linguistic validation consists of two steps: (1) forward-backward translation, and (2) cognitive debriefing.

The forward-backward translation aims to produce a local version of an instrument that is equivalent to the original version in terms of its content, after possible modifications due to cultural differences. This process involves a forward translation of the instrument into the local language. To ensure the quality of the translation, it is desirable to have two translators independently perform the translation; thereby, two local versions are produced. A reconciliation meeting is then held with the two translators and a person preferably with prior experience in the cultural adaptation of research instruments and a good understanding of the original instrument. During the meeting, the two local versions are discussed in order to generate a consensus version. In order to ensure translational equivalence, the consensus version is then back-translated into the original language to cross-check with the original version. Modifications to the consensus version can be made according to the observed discrepancies between the back-translated version and the source. A second consensus version is then obtained for cognitive debriefing.

Cognitive debriefing ensures the clarity and relevance of the locally translated instrument to the target group. The process involves the administration of the final consensus version to around three to five individuals from the target group. For each individual, we record the time it takes to complete the instrument and ask for the individual's personal understanding of each item in order to check for the items' relevance and clarity. Suggestions for improving item wording are also solicited. As a result of the cognitive debriefing, modifications may be made, and the first local version is obtained and ready for subsequent psychometric evaluation.

Psychometric evaluation

Psychometric evaluation of an instrument, designed for the assessment of one or multiple constructs, involves the assessment of reliability, validity, sensitivity and responsiveness (Fayers & Machin, 2007).

Reliability may be subdivided into different types, and each type may be assessed by a different approach.

Test-retest reliability

This measure assesses the stability of an instrument over a time period within which no change is expected in the underlying constructs. It is often assessed by the intraclass correlation coefficient (ICC) or by weighted kappa, depending on whether the assessment is made by a continuous or a categorical score. It is worth noting that test-retest reliability assesses the degree of agreement between the scores obtained from the first test and retest, and two perfectly associated scores may not necessarily agree. Thus, test-retest reliability should not be assessed by the Pearson or Spearman rank correlation coefficient, which measure association but not agreement. Caution should be taken to ensure proper assessment of the test-retest reliability.

Internal reliability

This parameter is sometimes also known as internal consistency. It is an attribute of a multi-item scale that refers to the extent to which the items of a scale are related (Cronbach, 1951). It is often assessed by Cronbach's alpha, a value between 0 and 1, with a higher alpha value indicating a higher internal reliability. An alpha value above 0.7 is often considered satisfactory (Nunnally, 1978). An alpha value higher than 0.9 indicates potential redundancy of some items, and item reduction may be worth exploring. It is also noteworthy that the alpha value of a scale generally increases with the number of items in the scale. Thus, it is unfair to compare the alpha values between scales consisting of different numbers of items. In addition, care should also be taken when there are inconsistent responses which may inflate or reduce the alpha value depending on their type, and adjustments may be made to correct for their effects (Fong, Ho, & Lam, 2010).

Inter-rater and intra-rater reliability

When an instrument is administered by interview, there is potential for inconsistency between raters or observers, known as inter-rater reliability, and within a single rater or observer, known as intrarater reliability. It is certainly desirable to have high inter- and intra-rater reliability, where a rater or different raters give scores on a consistent and comparable basis. This reliability can be assessed by the ICC or weighted kappa, depending again on the measurement scale of the scores.

Validity refers to whether or not a scale is measuring what it intends to measure. There are many different types of validity, but we will only discuss the most common ones here.

Criterion validity

This measure assesses the association between a scale score and a more direct measurement or a well-established tool that may be taken as the gold standard. These measurements are expected to have an association with the test scale. When both measurements are taken concurrently, the validity is subclassified as concurrent validity. However, when the scale score is measured prior to the other measurement, their association describes predictive validity. In either type of validity, the association can be assessed by a correlation coefficient or multiple regression analysis when adjustment for potential confounding factors is desirable. An example can be found in the assessment of the SF-12v2 (HK) in Chinese adolescents, in which the criterion validity was taken as clinical validity as different clinical measures were used as the criteria (Fong et al., 2010).

Construct validity

This measure assesses the theoretical relationships of the items to each other and to the hypothesized constructs. It checks for dimensionality in terms of whether items in a multi-item scale can be broken down into subscales; homogeneity in terms of whether all items are equally strongly associated with their hypothesized scale; and overlap between scales. For these measures, we may subclassify construct validity as known-group, convergent, or discriminant validity. Known-group validity examines whether or not the test instrument can discriminate between specific groups of individuals which are known to be different in the scale scores. The identification of these groups may be determined from the literature or by general consensus. Convergent validity examines if the scale scores of the test instrument are associated with established scales that are expected to be associated with the constructs of the test instrument. In contrast, discriminant validity assesses if the scale scores of the test instrument are not associated with established scales that are expected to not be associated with the constructs of the test instrument. The discriminant validity was assessed for the CTS2 by hypothesizing that the two pairs of scales—Negotiation versus Sexual Coercion and Negotiation versus Injury—should not be correlated, and for the Parent-Child Conflict Tactics Scales (CTSPC) by hypothesizing that Nonviolent Discipline is not associated with Severe Assault or Sexual Abuse (Straus et al., 1996; Straus, Hamby, Finkelhor, Moore, & Runyan, 1998). Both convergent and discriminant validity may be assessed by a correlation coefficient.

Item-scale and scale-scale correlations may also be performed to assess if items are more associated with the scale they belong to than any others. In particular, item-scale correlation may be obtained, preferably after correction for overlap (Fong, Lam et al., 2010). That is, the corrected item-scale correlation for an item is the correlation between the item and the score from the scale it belongs to, and is obtained without involving the particular item. This method avoids the unnecessary inflation of the correlation due to the intrinsic association observed when the scale score is also computed from the item response.

Factor analysis is a common statistical method used to examine construct validity. It may be performed in two forms, namely, exploratory factor analysis (EFA) and confirmatory factor analysis (CFA). EFA is used to explore plausible groups of items with items driven by the underlying constructs. Thus, new scales of items may be formed. In contrast, CFA is used to confirm the "fitness" of a hypothesized scale structure. The fitness is examined by checking if a collection of fit indices falls within its respective range. Although there have been several different recommendations regarding the choice of fit indices, the actual collection often depends on the software used for the analysis. The difference between EFA and CFA depends on whether we start from a hypothesized scale structure. EFA is useful for developing new scale structures, whereas CFA is useful for validating a hypothesized scale structure. Hence, the two factor analyses may complement each other for a newly developed instrument when the scale structure is still obscure. To pursue this strategy, we may randomly split a sample of data into two halves, with one half as the development set and the other as the validation set. EFA is applied to the development set to identify a scale structure, which can then be confirmed by a CFA using the validation set.

However, in practice, one may be surprised to find that EFA has its limitations. The format of an instrument may not allow EFA to be used to identify a scale structure that is driven by the underlying constructs. For example, an EFA of the SF-12 in a sample of Chinese adolescents identified only three factors, and two of them clearly did not resemble any underlying constructs. One consisted of only negatively worded items, and the other only included items using a three-point Likert scale response (Fong, Lam et al., 2010). In such cases where EFA does not help guide the development of a scale structure, we have to rely on CFA with modifications of a scale structure in searching for one that fits the data well.

Sensitivity

Sensitivity examines whether the scale scores of the test instrument can discriminate between individuals of small but discernible differences within the constructs. Sensitivity is, indeed, similar but not identical to known-group validity, which aims to determine if the test instrument can pick up large differences. The establishment of sensitivity is desirable before an instrument is used to assess differences across individuals. Sensitivity is determined most often in cross-sectional studies, in which there is an exploration of factors associated with the constructs of interest.

Responsiveness

Responsiveness assesses the longitudinal change of the scale scores of the test instrument when there is an expected change in the measuring constructs over time. This measure is similar to but also different from test-retest reliability. Responsiveness is concerned with whether or not the scale scores change with the underlying constructs over time, whereas test-retest reliability determines if the scale scores would remain stable when there is no noticeable change in the underlying constructs. Nevertheless, both of these measures are essential when one aims to assess change over time. Responsiveness is often measured in longitudinal studies including cohort studies and randomized controlled studies, when temporal or even causal relationships are examined.

In practice, psychometric evaluation of an assessment instrument is a never-ending process, unless a gold standard exists by which we can directly compare it with the test instrument. Otherwise, there can be different criteria or established scales that may be used to assess the criterion or convergent/ discriminant validity. Hence, psychometric evaluation mostly assesses if an instrument is ill-behaved, rather than actually proving its validity.

For instruments that aim to screen for the presence of a certain condition, a different class of evaluation tools is required. An instrument used for screening should be able to make a categorical statement about the presence of the condition. This statement could be a direct consequence of the responses to the instrument or there could be an actual cutoff value. In either case, when the instrument indicates the presence of the condition, we take it as a positive result; otherwise, the result is negative. Figure 5.2 shows plausible results from screening. To assess if an instrument can accurately pick up individuals with the condition of interest, we may use statistical measures including sensitivity, specificity, positive predictive value (PPV), negative predictive value (NPV), positive likelihood ratio (PLR) and negative likelihood ratio (NLR) (Zhou, Obuchowski, & McClish, 2002).

| | | Screening result | |
		Positive	Negative
Bearing the	Yes	a	b
condition?	No	c	d

Figure 5.2 Notation for the results after using a screening instrument.

Sensitivity is the proportion of individuals with the condition who are correctly picked up by the instrument, i.e., a/(a+d). Specificity is the proportion of individuals without the condition who are correctly picked up by the instrument, i.e., d/(c+d). These values range from 0 to 100%, with a higher value indicating greater accuracy.

PPV is the proportion of screened positive individuals who possess the condition, i.e., a/(a+c). NPV is the proportion of screened negative individuals who do not possess the condition, i.e., d/(b+d). Both of these values range from 0 to 100%, with a higher value indicating a better screening performance. These measures are intuitively more acceptable to most people, as they directly assess whether those screened as positive or negative are truly positive and truly negative. Hence, these measures are also known as utility measures.

It is noteworthy that both the PPV and the NPV are dependent on the prevalence of the condition. When the prevalence decreases, the PPV will become lower and the NPV will become higher. Hence, they should not be used to compare the screening accuracy of an instrument in two populations with different prevalences of the condition. In contrast, sensitivity and specificity are not prevalence-dependent and, thus, can be generically used across different populations.

The PLR assesses how much more likely individuals with the condition would be screened positive than individuals without the condition. It is the ratio of the probability of screening positive among individuals with the condition to the probability of screening positive among individuals without the condition, which can be computed as sensitivity/(1-specificity). On the other hand, the NLR assesses how much more likely individuals with the condition would be screened negative than individuals without the condition. It is the ratio of the probability of screening negative among individuals with the condition to the probability of screening negative among individuals without the condition, which can be calculated as (1-sensitivity)/specificity. By the definitions of the PLR and the NLR, an instrument is considered an accurate screening tool when the PLR is sufficiently larger than 1 and the NLR is sufficiently smaller than 1. The PLR should be at least 2 before an instrument is considered slightly useful, at least 5 to be considered moderately useful, and at least 10 to be considered definitely useful (Jaeschke, Guyatt, & Sackett, 1994). Similarly, the NLR should be 0.5 or less for a slightly useful instrument, 0.2 or less for a moderately useful instrument, and 0.1 or less for a definitely useful instrument.

Likelihood ratios enable the calculation of pre- and post-test probabilities. Pre-test probability is the chance of having the condition prior to knowing the screening result. This value is often estimated by professionals or based on the prevalence of the condition. Post-test probability is the chance of having the condition after knowing the screening result. It can be calculated based on the screening result. When an individual is screened positive, post-test odds = (pre-test odds x PLR). Note that odds is related to probability by the equation: odds = probability/(1-probability), and odds and probability can be computed from each other. Since the PLR is greater than 1 in this case, the post-test probability is larger than the pre-test probability. On the other hand, an individual with a negative screening result would have post-test odds = (pre-test odds x NLR) and, thus, the resulting post-test probability would be smaller than the pre-test probability.

A useful screening instrument should substantially alter the chance of one's having the condition. Otherwise, there is no point in knowing the screening result. The post-test probability is indeed useful to healthcare professionals to inform their decision of whether any form of treatment should be administered. Thus, PLR and NLR are also utility measures, and have been gaining interest as measures for assessing screening accuracy. They are not dependent on the prevalence of the condition, a property not shared by the predictive values. Moreover, likelihood ratios enable the calculation of post-test probabilities, a property not shared by the sensitivity and specificity.

The Chinese AAS has been assessed for its accuracy in screening women suffering from intimate partner violence (IPV) (Tiwari et al., 2007). Based on the responses of an individual, the tool may signify if the individual has experienced IPV. In a sample of 357 Chinese women, the AAS was compared with the Chinese CTS2, which is taken as the gold standard for diagnosing different types of IPV. For the screening of psychological abuse, the Chinese AAS has a PPV and a NPV of 89% (95% CI = 81% to 94%) and 66% (95% CI = 58% to 73%) respectively. The sensitivity and specificity are 66% (95% CI = 58% to 73%) and 89% (95% CI = 81% to 94%) respectively. The PLR and NLR are 5.92 (95% CI = 3.43 to 10.2) and 0.39 (95% CI = 0.31 to 0.49) respectively. All of these measures reflect the Chinese AAS as an accurate instrument to screen for individuals with psychological abuse.

Administering instruments

After an instrument is properly evaluated, it may be used in practice for assessment or screening. In general, instruments may be administered in different modes by: self-completion, computer, or interview.

Self-completion is the most popular form of administration by which we can efficiently administer an instrument to a large group of individuals all at the same time. Thus, a large volume of data can be collected within a short time period. Moreover, it allows individuals to complete the instrument anonymously, an advantage often welcomed by respondents.

Computer-based administration requires the development of a decent screen input form so that study individuals may respond to the items in front of a computer terminal even if they do not have any prior experience with using a computer. Responses are then directly entered into a computerized database, thus avoiding the costs and time required for data entry. However, although the completion time of computer-based administration may be shorter with a nicely designed screen input form (Lenert & Hornberger, 1996), the efficiency would depend on the availability of computer terminals. Study individuals may also utilize their personal computers at home and complete a screen input form via the internet. This format may, however, require more effort in ensuring data security when confidentiality is a concern.

Both self-completion and computer-based administration share the common assumption that the study individuals are sufficiently literate and possess the required physical capabilities. In the case of individuals who are illiterate or have problems reading, there could be many missing responses or responses of questionable quality. Hence, sometimes an instrument would preferably be administered through interview, during which an interviewer reads off the items for the individuals. The rate and quality of the response rate could be higher when responses are solicited through interview. However, several issues should be considered. It often takes more time to interview an individual, which means greater cost and effort. Moreover, participants may be concerned with confidentiality when responding to items on a sensitive topic, and this may thus lead to inaccurate responses. Besides, completion by interview may also raise the concern of inter- and intra-rater reliability. To alleviate this concern, it is often desirable, if possible, to have only one single interviewer throughout the study. Nevertheless, the potential differences across studies that have used different interviewers remain a concern.

The different modes of administration have been reviewed and compared to determine if they would have any influences on the reliability, validity and scale scores. There have been mixed results regarding these potential influences. To play it safe, it is often advisable to keep consistent in the administration mode of a given study. Any deviations from this mode should be properly documented.

A compendium of Chinese instruments in domestic violence

Medical Outcomes Study (MOS) Short-Form 36-item Health Survey (Hong Kong)—SF-36 (HK)

* Purpose and details

The SF-36 is an assessment tool with 36 items. It measures eight scales: Physical Functioning (PF), Role Physical (RP), Bodily Pain (BP), General Health (GH), Vitality (VT), Social Functioning (SF), Role Emotional (RE), and Mental Health (MH), as well as the Physical Component Summary (PCS) and the Mental Component Summary (MCS). The eight scales are scored between 0–100, whereas the two component summary scales are often scored based on the standard US norm and a range roughly between 0–100. For all scales and components, a higher score indicates a better quality of life (Saris-Baglama, Dewey, Chisholm, Bjorner, & Ware, 2004). The MOS SF-36 is a generic and popular health-related quality-of-life instrument. The latest version of the SF-36 is version 2.

* Tested group(s)

Adults.

* Evaluation details

The SF-36 has undergone proper forward and backward translation (C. L. Lam, Gandek, Ren, & Chan, 1998). The validity of the eight scales was examined in a sample of 236 HK Chinese (C. L. Lam et al., 1998). The Cronbach's alpha of the eight scales ranged from 0.65 to 0.87. Item convergent/discriminant validity was assessed and demonstrated. An EFA identified two factors that resembled the two component summary scales. In another study with 2,410 HK Chinese adults, the internal reliability coefficients of the standard PCS and MCS scales were 0.85 and 0.86 respectively (C. L. Lam, Tse, Gandek, & Fong, 2005). A one week test-retest reliability was also assessed in 500 primary care patients, with ICC for the eight scales ranging from 0.70 to 0.88, except for SF which had an ICC of only 0.44 (C. L. K. Lam, 2003).

- Normative data

Normative data have been reported from 2,410 subjects (C. L. K. Lam, Lauder, Lam, & Gandek, 1999).

SF-12 Health Survey (HK)

- Purpose and details

The SF-12 is a 12-item assessment tool which resembles the SF-36 in the constructs and interpretation of scores (Saris-Baglama et al., 2004). The latest version of the SF-12 is SF-12v2. It is a shortened version of the MOS SF-36. The first version of the SF-12 reproduced SF-36 summary scores only, but the SF-12v2 also includes the eight scale scores. The brevity of the SF-12 makes it an appealing tool for assessing health-related quality of life, especially in large-scale studies.

- Tested group(s)

Adolescents; adults.

- Evaluation details

In a group of 2,410 HK Chinese adults, the SF-12 has demonstrated criterion validity when compared with the SF-36 (C. L. Lam, Tse, & Gandek, 2005). Moreover, the standard SF-12 PCS and MCS, respectively, explained 82% and 89% of the total variance of the corresponding component summary scales of the SF-36. For adolescents, the standard SF-12v2 was evaluated in a group of 31,357 HK Chinese students (Fong, Lam et al., 2010). The instrument has demonstrated criterion validity by comparison with previously hypothesized associations on the SF-12 or SF-36. Its scale structure was also confirmed by a CFA.

- Normative data

Normative data for adolescents have been reported from 28,981 Chinese students (Mak, Ho et al., 2011).

Chinese Assessment Abuse Screen (AAS)

- Purpose and details

The Chinese AAS is a screening tool comprised of three items for a recall period. It identifies women suffering from psychological, physical or sexual abuse.

- Recall period(s)

Lifetime, preceding 12 months, and during pregnancy.

- Tested group(s)

Women in the community.

- Evaluation details

The Chinese AAS has demonstrated sensitivity, specificity, positive and negative predictive values, as well as positive and negative likelihood ratios in a sample of 257 HK Chinese women (Tiwari et al., 2007).

- Normative data

Not applicable.

Chinese Revised Conflict Tactics Scales (CTS2)

- Purpose and details

The CTS2 is both a screening and an assessment tool for spousal battering. It is comprised of 39 items in five scales: Negotiation, Psychological Aggression, Physical Assault, Sexual Coercion, and Injury. The instrument can indicate the presence and severity of the five types of spousal violence, and assess their frequency. The minimum scale score is 0, with a higher score indicating a higher frequency of the type of violence (Chan, 2005).

- Recall period(s)

Lifetime, preceding 12 months.

- Tested group(s)

Couples.

- Evaluation details

In a sample of 5,049 HK Chinese adult couples, the Cronbach's alpha was high and ranged from 0.88 to 0.96 (Chan, 2005). Moreover, convergent validity was also examined by demonstrating the previously identified association between the instrument and risk factor measures, including Anger Management, Couple Conflicts, Negative Attributions and Violence Approval (Chan, 2005; Straus et al., 1996).

- Normative data

Not available.

Chinese Parent-Child Conflict Tactics Scales (CTSPC)

- Purpose and details

This scale is both a screening and an assessment tool for assessing psychological and physical maltreatment and neglect of children by parents, as well as nonviolent modes of discipline. It has 27 items covering seven scales, including Nonviolent Discipline, Psychological Aggression, Minor Physical Assault (Corporal Punishment), Severe Assault (Physical Maltreatment), Very Severe Assault (Severe Physical Maltreatment), Neglect, and Weekly Discipline. As in the CTS2, the Chinese CTSPC also indicates the presence and severity of the different scales and assesses their frequency (Chan, 2005). The score of a scale starts from 0, and a higher score indicates greater severity.

- Recall period(s)

Lifetime, preceding 12 months.

- Tested group(s)

Children aged between 12 to 17 years.

- Evaluation details

Using a sample of 1,484 children in Hong Kong, the internal reliability has been established by a Cronbach's alpha ranging from 0.60 to 0.87 (Chan, 2005). Criterion validity was found by demonstrating the expected relation that more younger children experienced physical maltreatment (Chan, 2005; Straus et al., 1998). Moreover, convergent validity was found from the expected association of physical maltreatment with negative attribution, perceived threat and self-blame scales from a questionnaire that assesses children's attitudes towards discipline by their parents.

- Normative data

Not available.

Chinese Juvenile Victimization Questionnaire (JVQ)

- Purpose and details

It is both a screening and an assessment tool to assess the presence and frequency of different types of victimization during childhood, covering five types: Conventional Crime, Child Maltreatment, Peer and Sibling Victimization, Sexual Victimization, and Witnessing and Indirect Victimization. It has 34 items, with a higher scale score indicating a higher frequency of the type of victimization (Chan, 2009). The original version is in English (Finkelhor, Hamby, Ormrod, & Turner, 2005).

- Recall period(s)

Lifetime, preceding 12 months.

- Tested group(s)

Children between 15 to 17 years old, parents of children aged between 0 to 14 years.

- Evaluation details

In 152 parents of Chinese children aged between 0 to 14 years and 41 children between 15 to 17 years old, the Cronbach's alpha was at least 0.69 (Chan, 2009).

* Normative data

Not available.

Conclusion

The use of research instruments in DV studies is gaining popularity and importance. Therefore, it is very important for one to choose reliable and valid instruments. This chapter describes the basic skills for developing, adopting, and administering a research instrument in practice.

The development of a new research instrument requires significant effort and resources. Fortunately, substantial work has already been invested, and properly tested instruments are available. A compendium of Chinese instruments in DV has been compiled to facilitate the use of these research instruments.

The choice of an instrument to be used in research first requires a determination of whether the instrument would be used for assessment or screening. This determination informs what evaluation should be performed before an instrument can be considered ready for clinical use. The sufficiency of the Cronbach's alpha in demonstrating reliability and validity has been overestimated. Indeed, more comprehensive evaluation is required before an instrument can be considered appropriate for a specific purpose.

The use of a proper instrument does not guarantee the success of a research study. The administration mode should also be carefully considered to ensure a good response rate as well as the quality of responses. No matter which mode of administration is chosen, it should be kept consistent throughout the study, and any deviations should be properly documented in order to assess the potential bias of the results.

References

Acquadro, C., Conway, K., Girourdet, C., & Mear, I. (2004). *Linguistic Validation Manual for Patient-Reported Outcomes (PRO) Instruments*. Lyon: MAPI Research Trust.

Aiken, L. R. (1985). Three coefficients for analyzing the reliability and validity of ratings. *Educational and Psychological Measurement, 45*, 131–142. doi: 10.1177/0013164485451012

Angst, F., Verra, M. L., Lehmann, S., & Aeschlimann, A. (2008). Responsiveness of five condition-specific and generic outcome assessment instruments for chronic pain. *BMC Medical Research Methodology, 8*, 26. doi: 10.1186/1471-2288-8-26

Chan, K. L. (2005). *Study on Child Abuse and Spouse Battering: Report on Findings of Household Survey*. Retrieved from Social Work Department, Hong Kong SAR Government website: http://www.swd.gov.hk/doc/family/Report%20on%20 findings%20of%20Household%20Survey.pdf

Chan, K. L. (2009). *Optimus Study on Child Protection in China: Report on the Feasibility Study*. Hong Kong: Department of Social Work & Social Administration, the University of Hong Kong

Cronbach, L. J. (1951). Coefficient alpha and the internal structure of tests. *Psychometrika, 16*, 297–334. doi: 10.1007/BF02310555

Fayers, P. M., & Machin, D. (2007). *Quality of Life : The Assessment, Analysis, and Interpretation of Patient-Reported Outcomes* (2nd ed.). Hoboken, NJ: John Wiley & Sons, Inc.

Finkelhor, D., Hamby, S. L., Ormrod, R., & Turner, H. (2005). The juvenile victimization questionnaire: reliability, validity, and national norms. *Child Abuse & Neglect, 29*, 383–412. doi: 10.1016/j.chiabu.2004.11.001

Fong, D. Y., Ho, S. Y., & Lam, T. H. (2010). Evaluation of internal reliability in the presence of inconsistent responses. *Healthy and Quality of Life Outcomes, 8*, 27. doi: 10.1186/1477-7525-8-27

Fong, D. Y., Lam, C. L. K., Mak, K. K., Lo, W. S., Lai, Y. K., Ho, S. Y., & Lam, T. H. (2010). The Short Form-12 Health Survey was a valid instrument in Chinese adolescents. *Journal of Clinical Epidemiology*. doi: 10.1016/j.jclinepi.2009.11.011

Hui, L. F., Fong, D. Y. T., Yam, M., & Ip, W. Y. (2008). Translation and validation of the Chinese Diabetic Foot Ulcer Scale—Short Form. *The Patient, 1*, 137–145.

Jaeschke, R., Guyatt, G., & Sackett, D. L. (1994). Users' guides to the medical literature. III. How to use an article about a diagnostic test. A. Are the results of the study valid? Evidence-Based Medicine Working Group. *Journal of the American Medical Association, 271*, 389–391. Retrieved from http //www.thoracic.org/ global-health/mecor-courses/resources/level2/DiagnosisA.pdf

Lam, C. L. K., Gandek, B., Ren, X. S., & Chan, M. S. (1998). Tests of scaling assumptions and construct validity of the Chinese (HK) version of the SF-36 Health Survey. *Journal of Clinical Epidemiology, 51*, 1139–1147. doi: 10.1016/ S0895-4356(98)00105-X

Lam, C. L. K., Tse, E. Y., & Gandek, B. (2005). Is the standard SF-12 health survey valid and equivalent for a Chinese population? *Quality of Life Research, 14*, 539–547. doi: 10.1007/s11136-004-0704-3

Lam, C. L. K., Tse, E. Y., Gandek, B., & Fong, D. Y. (2005). The SF-36 summary scales were valid, reliable, and equivalent in a Chinese population. *Journal of Clinical Epidemiology, 58*, 815–822. doi: 10.1016/j.jclinepi.2004.12.008

Lam, C. L. K. (2003). Reliability and construct validity of the Chinese (Hong Kong) SF-36 for patients in primary care. *Hong Kong Practitioner, 25*, 468–475.

Lam, C. L. K., Lauder, I. J., Lam, T. P., & Gandek, B. (1999). Population based norming of the Chinese (HK) version of the SF-36 health survey. *Hong Kong Practitioner, 21*, 460–470.

Lenert, L. A., & Hornberger, J. C. (1996). Computer-assisted quality of life assessment for clinical trials. *Proceedings: A Conference of the American Medical Informatics Association Annual Fall Symposium*, 992–996.

Mak, K. K., Ho, S. Y., Fong, D. Y., Lo, W. S., Lai, Y. K., Lam, T. H. (2011). Norms and demographic differences of the Short Form-12 Health Survey version 2 in Chinese adolescents. *Journal of Paediatrics and Child Health, 47*, 173–182.

Nevo, B. (1985). Face validity revisited. *Journal of Educational Measurement, 22*, 287–293. doi: 10.1111/j.1745-3984.1985.tb01065.x

Nunnally, J. C. (1978). *Psychometric theory* (2d ed.). New York, NY: McGraw-Hill.

Rat, A. C., Pouchot, J., Guillemin, F., Baumann, M., Retel-Rude, N., Spitz, E., & Coste, J. (2007). Content of quality-of-life instruments is affected by item-generation methods. *International Journal for Quality in Health Care, 19*, 390–398. doi: 10.1093/intqhc/mzm040

Saris-Baglama, R. N., Dewey, C. J., Chisholm, G. B., Bjorner, J. B., & Ware, J. E., Jr. (2004). *SF Health Outcomes Scoring Software: User's Guide*. Lincoln, NE: QualityMetric, Incorporated.

Straus, M. A., Hamby, S. L., Boney-McCoy, S., & Sugarman, D. B. (1996). The revised Conflict Tactics Scales (CTS2)—development and preliminary psychometric data. *Journal of Family Issues, 17*, 283–316. doi: 10.1177/019251396017003001

Straus, M. A., Hamby, S. L., Finkelhor, D., Moore, D. W., & Runyan, D. (1998). Identification of child maltreatment with the Parent-Child Conflict Tactics Scales: development and psychometric data for a national sample of American parents. *Child Abuse & Neglect, 22*, 249–270. doi: 10.1016/S0145-2134(97)00174-9

Streiner, D. L., & Norman, G. R. (2008). *Health Measurement Scales: A Practical Guide to Their Development and Use* (4th ed.). Oxford, England: Oxford University Press.

Tiwari, A., Fong, D. Y., Chan, K. L., Leung, W. C., Parker, B., & Ho, P. C. (2007). Identifying intimate partner violence: comparing the Chinese Abuse Assessment Screen with the Chinese Revised Conflict Tactics Scales. *BJOG, 114*, 1065–1071. doi: 10.1111/j.1471-0528.2007.01441.x.

Velanovich, V. (1998). Comparison of generic (SF-36) vs. disease-specific (GERD-HRQL) quality-of-life scales for gastroesophageal reflux disease. *Journal of Gastrointestinal Surgery, 2*, 141–145. doi: 10.1016/S1091-255X(98)80004-8

Velanovich, V. (2000). Experience with a generic quality of life instrument in a general surgical practice. *International Journal of Surgical Investigation, 1*, 447–452.

Zhou, X. H., Obuchowski, N. A., & McClish, D. K. (2002). *Statistical Methods in Diagnostic Medicine*. New York, NY: Wiley-Interscience.

Part 2

Legal Perspective

6
The Laws Against Domestic Violence and Their Reform, 2010

Dennis Chi-Kuen Ho

> **Chapter summary**
>
> 1. Recognizing domestic violence as a serious issue, Hong Kong society has adopted a zero-tolerance policy.
> 2. Sentencing for offences committed in the context of domestic violence is difficult.
> 3. In a recent evaluation of the introduction of criminalization of domestic violence, the UK showed a drop in applications for injunction.
> 4. The process of reform is never smooth, and the government's policy on certain issues is revealed during the process.
> 5. The present law for non-molestation injunctions has now been expanded to provide protection to people who were not previously protected, and this has led to the change of the title of the legislation to cover same-sex cohabitants.
> 6. Victim support has been recognized as part of the holistic approach in tackling domestic violence.
> 7. More training, education and provision of legal aid should be made readily available to those in need of protection.

On 5 November 2009, under the headline "Wife punched 10 times after she refused to have sex, court told", Loretta Fong (2009) reported in the *South China Morning Post* that "the court was told of four other alleged assaults by . . . [the husband] against his wife between October 1 last year and April 1 this year, . . . [the husband], 46, has a record of 13 convictions, of which

11 were related to violence." This type of report on domestic violence is in fact very common nowadays. Statistics on cases involving child abuse and spouse battering captured by the Child Protection Registry (CPR) and the Central Information System on Battered Spouse Cases and Sexual Violence Cases (CISBSSV) provided the staggering figures of 993 cases in child abuse and 4,807 cases in spouse battering for the year 2009 (Social Welfare Department, 2009).

Domestic violence is a daily occurrence in all parts of the world. It can devastate a person in a domestic relationship and bring about lasting and grave consequences. Different countries are now finding ways to tackle the widespread problem on multiple fronts. The legal redress in dealing with this issue is by way of criminal prosecution and civil redress through protection under the relevant legislation and the common law.

Criminal prosecution and criminalization of domestic violence

In Hong Kong, there is no specific criminal offence of domestic violence. Recommendations have been put forth to the Hong Kong government by different sectors of society for criminalization of domestic violence, especially following the Tin Shui Wai incident in 2004, in the aftermath of which the public called for an immediate revamp of the antiquated Domestic Violence Ordinance (Cap. 189) (1986 DVO). The incident caught the public's attention when on 12 April 2004, Madam Jin and her twin daughters were stabbed to death by her husband, who then committed suicide. Chan, Chiu, and Chiu (2005) in their report, *Peace at Home*, suggested criminalization of domestic violence, saying, "… we should consider making breach of a nonmolestation order and exclusion order a criminal offence" (para. 8.54 and Recommendation 17(b)). "Domestic violence can be treated seriously after a criminal remedy is inserted in the ordinance. The public will understand it clearly, including the police. The whole mindset can therefore be changed," said Margaret Ng, a barrister and lawmaker (Lau & Wong, 2006).

In the Preliminary Proposed Amendments to the 1986 DVO prepared in May 2006, the Health, Welfare and Food Bureau of the Hong Kong government rejected the call for criminalization of domestic violence, and explained that the 1986 DVO was there to provide for civil remedy for the protection of victims of domestic violence. If the act of domestic violence involved a criminal element, it would be dealt with under other legislation, such as the Crimes Ordinance (Cap. 200) and the Offences Against the Person Ordinance (Cap. 212). Another piece of legislation called the Protection of Children and Juveniles Ordinance (Cap. 213) provided the necessary protection for children and young persons under the age of 18. The bureau explained that domestic violence was in essence just another form of violence, whereas the present criminal law in the area is structured on criminal acts, regardless of whether such acts take place at home or in the public. The bureau therefore concluded by saying that "to include in the DVO legal provisions dealing with identical criminal acts may give rise to unnecessary duplication and complication in our current law. We therefore consider the proposal undesirable and result [*sic*] in no practical advantages" (Health, Welfare and Food Bureau, 2006).

While the government introduced proposals for amendments to the 1986 DVO in 2007, there was no suggestion for the criminalization of domestic violence. The bureau reiterated their previous position on the issue, that criminalization of domestic violence would complicate the existing legislation, and was a suggestion fraught with legal difficulties. They argued that it would be a deviation from existing practice (Health, Welfare and Food Bureau, 2006). While there may have been other well-founded reasons not to criminalize domestic violence or to include criminal provisions against acts of violence, the reasoning given by the bureau was an oversimplification on their part. There was, after all, other legislation such as the Employment Ordinance (Cap. 57), which mainly governed the legal relationship of employers and employees in a civil context, and that did not stop numerous criminal offences from being created under this ordinance. Besides, it has already been made possible in other countries, such as Canada, England and Wales, as discussed below.

The government in a later proposal repeated its commitment to continue strengthening multidisciplinary collaboration, promote family education and the building of community support networks, and reach out to vulnerable families to help address their problems early on. However, in dealing with criminal sanctions for domestic violence, there was no proposal to introduce any changes. The government remained satisfied to rely on existing frameworks including the Offences Against the Person Ordinance (Cap. 212), which dealt with criminal acts such as murder, manslaughter, attempts to murder, wounding or inflicting grievous bodily harm, exposing a child whereby his/her life is endangered, ill-treatment or neglect by those in charge of a child or young person, assaults occasioning actual bodily harm and common assaults;

and the Crimes Ordinance (Cap. 200), dealing with acts of intimidation, arson, destroying or damaging property, and sexual offences such as rape, incest, and indecent assaults (Health, Welfare and Food Bureau, 2007). In their final proposal for amendments, although the bureau did allow for a drastic change in its position on other issues, it maintained its stance against introducing criminal sanction of domestic violence under the DVO.

In England and Wales, the Domestic Violence, Crime and Victims Act 2004 (DVCVA) came into force on 1 July 2007. In an effort to improve protective measures for victims of domestic violence, the administration in England and Wales made significant changes to existing legislation, in particular, by criminalizing the breach of a non-molestation order. The new offence would be subject to a maximum of five years in prison. Section 1 of DVCVA inserted a new section 42A into the Family Law Act 1996, which provides:

(1) A person who without reasonable excuse does anything that he is prohibited from doing by a non-molestation order is guilty of an offence.

(2) In the case of a non-molestation order made by virtue of section 45(1) (ex-parte order), a person can be guilty of an offence under this section only in respect of conduct engaged in at a time when he was aware of the existence of the order.

(3) Where a person is convicted of an offence under this section in respect of any conduct, that conduct is not punishable as a contempt of court.

(4) A person cannot be convicted of an offence under this section in respect of any conduct which has been punished as a contempt of court.

The amendment to the law sent out a very clear message to perpetrators that further molestation is a breach of the non-molestation order, and will have serious ramifications. Soon after the new law took effect, a legal practitioner reminded the public that:

> the disadvantages, however, of having the matter dealt with as a criminal offence cannot be overlooked. One of the main problems is that the applicant's sense of autonomy and choice are removed. The applicant becomes a passive bystander in the whole process with little sense of control. As a practitioner, under the old regime I found it immensely satisfying to obtain non-molestation orders for an applicant. The applicant (normally female) would attend court on an ex-parte basis and seek injunctive relief against a partner who would often have perpetrated serious violence against her. Once an order had been made and the applicant had in her possession the power of arrest, she had a palpable, almost physical, sense

of relief. The power of arrest meant that the applicant had received an almost immediate remedy, and she left court confident in the knowledge that if the respondent attempted to breach the injunction she could call the police and he would be arrested (Soni, 2007).

Soni concluded that before the new law was introduced, the victim was able to obtain an adequate remedy by way of injunction in the family courts, without the matter being criminalized. This is no longer the case, and there is no longer such an option. Besides, with the criminal proceedings taking place in open court (unless a special measures application is made with success), this may deter women, especially ethnic minorities, from reporting to the police as this means the matter will go public. It is considered as absolutely vital for an applicant from an ethnic minority community to have his/her problems dealt with in a closed-door family court, which provides privacy and anonymity. These people may be concerned with issues of "shame" and bringing "dishonour" to their family (Soni, 2007). Resulting in the victim's loss of control and choice, the legal amendment is now being considered as having backfired and deterred victims from seeking help.

It was reported in April 2008 that judges in England claimed that, since the introduction of criminalization of domestic abuse, at least 5,000 fewer women have reported their violent partners (Gibb & Ford, 2008). The same report revealed that Judge John Platt, a circuit judge with over twenty years' experience in handling domestic violence cases, reported to Sir Mark Potter, the president of the Family Division, on the views of the judges and told *The Times* that there was a fall of 25% to 30% in applications for non-molestation orders since July 2007.[1] David Hanson, MP, of the Ministry of Justice wrote to *The Times* a few days later denying there was such a decrease in applications. He countered, "Figures show an increase in the number of reports of domestic violence. This testifies to the growing confidence of victims that they will be listened to and that their reports will be effectively investigated."[2]

In another article in *The Independent* of the UK, it was reported that the government's own evaluation of the new legislation accepted that it might have

---

1.   Frances Gibb and Richard Ford, *The Times*, 14 April 2008, "Women at risk of assault failed by new law, say judges".

2.   David Hanson, MP, *The Times*, 17 April 2008, "The Domestic Violence, Crime and Victims Act 2004 is the biggest overhaul of such legislation for 30 years".

deterred some women from pursuing their complaints against their abusers.[3] It made reference to a report commissioned by the Ministry of Justice, which said that convictions for domestic violence have actually fallen to a three-year low in Croydon and South Tyneside, England.[4] There were 247 reports of domestic violence, of which only eight ended in a conviction for the year 2007 in South Tyneside. The report pointed out that the concern was over a marked fall across the country in the number of requests for non-molestation orders after the criminalization of domestic violence and the introduction of the five-year prison sentence. There have been arguments against the granting of a non-molestation order as being based on the civil standard of proof as opposed to the criminal standard. There was a reduction of applications and orders after July 2007, but the reduction was more pronounced for orders issued than it was for applications. It was suggested that a longer time period would be needed to see if this was the direct result of the change in law (Hester et al., 2008). Lawyers, refuge centre workers and others thought that one reason for the fall in orders was the potentially draconian five-year prison sentence for breaching an order. It may indeed be too early to come to a conclusion on whether there is a link between criminalization of domestic violence and the drop in applications for non-molestation orders. But one cannot ignore the fact that there are victims who are reluctant to use the measure because it may lead to partners having a criminal record or a "stigma of conviction", or who might withdraw their complaint to the police in fear that any prosecution, whether successful or not, may increase hatred in their partners.

In Hong Kong, despite two major changes to the Domestic Violence Ordinance (Cap. 189) recently, the government remains sceptical and very cautious about the criminalization of domestic violence. The government is not yet prepared to make domestic violence a crime. The existing law dealing with domestic violence as a crime still remains unchanged. But, in all circumstances, when it comes to dealing with perpetrators charged with the offence of an act of violence in a domestic context, the sentence can range from one

---

3.   Robert Verkaik and Law Editor in *The Independent* (Saturday, 16 August 2008), "Domestic violence laws fail to increase convictions".

4.   Marianne Hester, Nicole Westmarland, Julia Pearce and Emma Williamson, Ministry of Justice Research Series 14/08 August 2008, "Early Evaluation of the Domestic Violence, Crime and Victims Act 2004".

year's imprisonment for common assault to life imprisonment for murder. Depending on the aggravating factors, a perpetrator could receive a sentence of fine, probation order, community service order or bind over order. Factors that the court will take into account in sentencing a perpetrator include background of the perpetrator, the relationship with the victim, the reason for the violent acts, any past history of similar violence, previous convictions of a similar nature, the extent of the injuries suffered as a result of the violent act, any involvement of children, whether they are injured and other circumstances of the case.

Patrick Li (2006), then chief magistrate of Hong Kong, shared his view on the dilemmas courts face in sentencing domestic violence offenders, noting in his article,

> For most cases of domestic violence, imprisonment is not the most appropriate choice. To put a parent or spouse in prison would probably add further tension to the family. Imprisonment sometimes worsens the situation and creates hostility in the family. Having said that, we do acknowledge that a domestic setting for violence should not make it a lesser offence. Where there are circumstances that warrant imprisonment, a court will have no hesitation in making the order.[5]

He believed that the sentence in this sort of cases must reflect the culpability of the offender as well as send the right message to the public. Yet, the personal problems and individual circumstances of the defendant and family cannot be ignored. In addition, imposing an inappropriate sentence may mislead potential offenders and cause grievance to the victims or even serious consequences. Li agreed with Judge LJ of the Court of Appeal in England, who commented on the case of *R v Hegarty* [2004] EWCA Crime 1693, saying that:

> The fact that violence occurs in a domestic situation may require the court to examine with as much sensitivity as it can a good deal of background material. That may provide mitigation: it may aggravate the offence. It should be clearly understood—and sentencing judges up and down the country do fully understand—that the fact that there is a domestic background to violence does not of itself begin to diminish or reduce, let alone extinguish, its criminality, and on some occasions indeed the background may itself accentuate the criminality.[6]

---

5.   *Ibid*, p. 59.
6.   *Ibid*, p. 60.

Civil actions

Apart from charging a perpetrator with a criminal offence, the only other way
to stop a perpetrator from committing another act of violence against the victim
is for the victim to take legal action through civil proceedings. This is entirely
in the hands of the victim, and it is for the victim to decide whether or not to
proceed with such an application. On an application for protection, the court
may grant the necessary injunctions provided that it has the jurisdiction to make
the orders. The court derives its powers to grant the injunctions from its inherent jurisdiction and the Domestic and Cohabitation Relationships Violence
Ordinance (Cap. 189) (DCRVO), which was previously the 1986 DVO.

Inherent jurisdiction

The inherent jurisdiction for the courts to grant the necessary injunctive reliefs
can be found in the High Court Ordinance (Cap. 4) and the District Court
Ordinance (Cap. 336). Under section 21L(1) of the High Court Ordinance
(Cap. 4), the court is vested with the power to grant an injunction " . . . in all
cases which it appears to the Court of First Instance to be just or convenient to
do so". Section 48(1) of the District Court Ordinance provides that, "(1) The
Court has the same power of the Court of First Instance in any proceedings
before it (a) to grant the relief, redress or remedy or combination of remedies,
either absolute or conditional." It can be found from the wordings of these
two provisions that the court would only grant an injunction to redress any
grievances ancillary and incidental to an existing proceedings. In other words,
the applicant has to have a cause of action against the respondent before there
can be an application for injunction relief. An applicant will have to invoke
the inherent jurisdiction of the court if the court cannot find its jurisdiction
from the specific piece of legislation (i.e., DCRVO) dealing with domestic
violence. Prior to the amendments to the 1986 DVO in 2008, an ex-spouse
would have had to rely on the inherent jurisdiction of the court for protection.[7]
If the applicant required protection by excluding the perpetrator from a place,

---

7.   Sections 2 and 3 of the DVO provide that only "parties to the marriage" and het-
      erosexual cohabitants can apply for protection excluding parties after divorce,
      also see Robinson v Robinson [1965] P 39 and *Lucas v Lucas* [1992] 2 FLR 53.

the applicant had to establish his/her proprietary rights to the place, otherwise the court did not possess jurisdiction to exclude someone who had a better right than the applicant to the place. Similarly, any person who fell outside the protection of the 1986 DVO prior to its amendments had to rely on the court's inherent jurisdiction for injunctive relief. This would include anyone who has a familial relationship with the perpetrator other than the spouse, dating couples and same-sex couples[8] who may have to rely on inherent jurisdiction.

In England, the court is prepared to exercise its inherent powers to grant injunction for the protection of those victims who are not covered under the specific piece of legislation against domestic violence. In *Patel v Patel*,[9] the court was ready to grant an injunction to restrain an ex-boyfriend from entering into the plaintiff's house. However, the Court of Appeal in England considered that the court had no jurisdiction to exclude the ex-boyfriend from a zone of 50 yards of the plaintiff's house. The situation changed when the Court of Appeal had to deal with an appeal from a martial arts instructor in *Burris v Azadani*[10] in 1995. Mr Azadani sought a close and intimate relationship with Miss Burris, a divorcee with two young children, despite her resistance. Mr Azadani did not respect her wishes. Without invitation, he made several visits to Miss Burris's house, often in the middle of the night, and refused to leave. There were numerous nuisance telephone calls to her, and he also threatened to commit suicide. Miss Burris was very worried about the safety of her children and herself. Eventually, she applied for and obtained an ex-parte interlocutory injunction (i.e., an interim application on the part of the applicant before the court in the absence of the intended defendant) from the county court against molestation of her and her two children by Mr Azadani. He was restrained from assaulting, molesting, harassing, threatening, pestering or otherwise interfering with the plaintiff or her children, and in particular, from coming or remaining within 250 yards of the plaintiff's home address. Mr Azadani was eventually sent to prison for his breach of the order when he repeatedly visited the plaintiff's house, put notes through her letterbox and left messages on her answering machine. Later on, acting in breach of the orders again on

---

8.   Same-sex couple is protected under section 3B of the DCRVO, which took effect
     from 1 January 2010.
9.   Patel v Patel [1988] 2 FLR 179.
10. *Burris v Azadani* [1995] 4 All ER 802.

two occasions, he cycled past Miss Burris's house. Mr Azadani was sentenced to prison for concurrent terms of four weeks for each of the two breaches, and in addition, received a suspended sentence of eight weeks. In his appeal, he contended that the county court had no jurisdiction to impose an exclusion zone when making a non-molestation order granted under the inherent jurisdiction. Sir Thomas Bingham MR, delivering judgment for the Court of Appeal, refused to accept that the jurisdiction of the High Court under section 37(1) of the Supreme Court Act 1981 and section 38(1) of the County Court Act 1984 were restricted to restraining conduct which was itself tortious or otherwise unlawful, and pointed out that an exclusion zone order could be made if the commission of a tort (such as trespass or assault) was reasonably apprehended and the order could reasonably be judged necessary for the protection of the plaintiff's legitimate interests.[11]

Reforms to the Domestic Violence Ordinance

The 1986 DVO was the first piece of specific legislation to deal with domestic violence in Hong Kong. It came into effect on 19 December 1986. The attorney general at the time, Mr Michael D. Thomas Q.C., in his speech in the second reading of the bill for the 1986 DVO, acknowledged the contribution of the Hong Kong Family Welfare Society, the Hong Kong Women's Council, the Hong Kong Federation of Women Lawyers, Against Child Abuse and the Family Law Association in drawing the government's attention to the problem of domestic violence.[12] This piece of legislation was largely based on the Domestic Violence and Matrimonial Proceedings Act 1976 in England. The 1986 DVO was considered to have effectively resolved the problems in the act at the time. However, its inadequacies soon became apparent.

It had become obvious that the protection given to the people the DVO had intended to protect was insufficient. Sections 2 and 3 of the 1986 DVO gave protection to the parties in a marriage and to cohabitants of the opposite sex, but it did not cover ex-spouses and ex-cohabitants, nor did it extend to other

---

11.   *Ibid* pp. 807–808.
12.   Official Report of Proceedings in the Legislative Council on the second reading of the bill for DVO on 9 July 1986.

members in a familial relationship except the child living with the applicant.[13] Although the child living with the applicant was protected, a child of the marriage who was not living with the applicant was not covered, and in any event, a child under protection had no right of his/her own to make the application for any protection under the 1986 DVO.

Another major attack against the 1986 DVO was the limited protection period given in the exclusion order, the entry order and the power of arrest attached to the injunction orders. These orders were to be granted for three months on first application and were allowed to have one extension of another three months.[14] A total of six months was in fact not sufficient. It could mean a battered spouse had only this short period of six months to decide on how to proceed next. In most cases if divorce proceedings are commenced, it is perfectly possible for the proceedings to take a longer time beyond the six-month period. One example can be found in a judgment delivered shortly before the first major amendment was introduced to the 1986 DVO in 2008.[15] In *YLS v TL* (FCMC 8396/2007), the wife obtained the first nonmolestation order with the ouster order on 13 July 2007. Both orders were extended after a hearing on 3 October 2007. The injunction orders expired on 2 January 2008 after the full

---

13. Sections 2 and 3 of the 1986 DVO: section 2(2) "Subject to section 6(3) this Ordinance shall apply to the cohabitation of a man and a woman as it applies to marriage and references in this Ordinance to 'marriage' and 'matrimonial home' shall be construed accordingly"; and section 3(1) "On an application by a party to a marriage the District Court, if it is satisfied that the applicant or a child living with the applicant has been molested by the other party to the marriage. . . ."

14. Sections 6 and 7 of the 1986 DVO: section 6 "(1) A provision mentioned in section 3(1)(c) or (d) contained in an injunction granted under this Ordinance shall have effect for such period, not exceeding 3 months, as the court considers necessary. (2) A power of arrest attached under section 5(1) to an injunction shall, (a) be granted for such period, not exceeding 3 months, as the court considers necessary; and (b) lapse on the expiry of the period for which the injunction was granted"; and section 7 "A court may extend: (a) an injunction granted under this Ordinance containing a provision mentioned in section 3(1)(c) or (d); or (b) a power of arrest attached to an injunction under section 5(1), prior to the expiry of the period thereof for a further period so that the total period thereof does not exceed 6 months from the date when that injunction was granted or that power of arrest attached."

15. 1986 DVO had major amendments, and the amendments took effect on 1 August 2008. See below.

six-month period, and the wife had to make a fresh application on 23 May 2008. Judge Melloy heard evidence from the parties and the social worker. She was made aware of the fact that following the hearing on 15 October 2007, the husband apparently made some reference to the Tin Shui Wai incident. Judge Melloy wrote in her judgment that:

> He allegedly said that he had learnt something from it. However on the last occasion that the social welfare officer saw the husband and they were discussing the custody issue, the husband allegedly said to him, "If the court granted the custody of the children to the Petitioner which meant the court sentenced her to death." He would do harm to the Petitioner and then he committed suicide, letting the children be orphans.

In the witness box, the social welfare officer confirmed that the threat was made on 25 March 2008. When asked if he considered the threat to be serious, he said "to a certain degree." Judge Melloy recognized that "the non-molestation orders are not time sensitive and continue unabated. The wife now seeks a new order and she does so on the basis of the threat made to the social welfare officer. This is a new threat and as I have said above, I treat it seriously." An ouster order was granted against the husband again.[16]

If the applicant needed the protection with an order of power of arrest, the condition for granting the order of power of arrest was for the court to satisfy that the applicant had sustained actual bodily harm.[17] In other words, a perpetrator may escape arrest if there was only harassment or molestation of the victim without physical violence.

Another deficiency in the 1986 DVO was its failure to address the situation where a perpetrator obtained the orders for custody or access right to the children at the time of the divorce proceedings. The perpetrator would be able to get hold of the address of the victim on the basis of his rights to see the children. The court would not deny such access rights just because there was a possibility of harassment against the other parent.

---

16.   *YLS v TL* (FCMC 8396/2007) paras. 37–40 and paras. 43–44.

17.   Section 5 of the 1986 DVO, "the Court of First Instance or the District Court, as the case may be, if it is satisfied that the other party has caused actual bodily harm to the applicant or, as the case may be, to the child concerned, may, subject to section 6, at the same time as it grants the injunction or at any time during the period for which the injunction is granted, attach to the injunction a power of arrest in the prescribed form."

While the English legislation had already been amended and later repealed with new laws to tackle the problem of the multifaceted nature of domestic violence, in the Family Law Act 1996 and later the Domestic Violence, Crime and Victims Act 2004, nothing was done to change the 1986 DVO in Hong Kong. In fact, little attention was given to this piece of legislation until the public was all of a sudden faced with the tragically violent incident in Tin Shui Wai on 12 April 2004.

As a result of public outcry over this tragedy, a Subcommittee on Strategy and Measures to Tackle Family Violence was formed by the Legco Panel on Welfare Services. In the 2005/06 Policy Address unveiled on 12 October 2005, the Chief Executive announced the government's stance on domestic violence to be zero tolerance. Meanwhile, there was a study commissioned by the Social Welfare Department (SWD) in April 2003 and conducted by a group of consultants from the Department of Social Work and Social Administration of the University of Hong Kong. The consultants completed a report on the Study on Child Abuse and Spouse Battering in June 2005 (Chan et al., 2005). The results were presented to the subcommittee at its meeting held on 5 July 2005. The consultants made a total of 21 recommendations on the social and legal measures for prevention and intervention of domestic violence in Hong Kong.

The Health, Welfare and Food Bureau representing the government made its preliminary responses to the report and presented it to the subcommittee for discussion on 3 November 2005. In its preliminary responses, the bureau took a cautious stance on the batterer intervention programmes (BIPs), the setting up of domestic violence courts,[18] and the need for more study and legal advices as recommended by Chan et al. (2005). However, it quickly pointed out that the SWD planned to launch two pilot projects of BIP from January 2006 to March 2008, which would be run by the SWD and an NGO respectively.[19] Recommendations were also made regarding the need for education for professionals, and for clear policy and practice guidelines on making arrests for the crime of domestic violence.[20] In response, the bureau said that the SWD had been providing ongoing training to related professionals, that public

---

18. *Ibid*—Chan K L; Chiu, M.C. & Chiu, L.S.(2005). *Peace at Home*, see Recommendations 1–6 and Recommendation 11.

19. *Ibid*, and see Annex to LC Paper for Discussion on 3 November 2005 paras. 1–7.

20. *Ibid*—Chan K L; Chiu, M.C. & Chiu, L.S. (2005). *Peace at Home*, see Recommendations 8–10.

education had been a key area of governmental work in preventing domestic violence, and that there were existing publicity campaigns to strengthen
families and combat violence.[21] It also made reference to the 2005/06 Policy
Address, which announced the launch of a Family Support Programme to
proactively identify families who are either socially isolated or unwilling to
contact welfare units. The bureau claimed that, "it is already the current Police
practice for all domestic violence reports to be comprehensively recorded and
properly investigated. Clear guidelines, as well as the required training provided and updated as necessary, are given to the officers concerned on the
handling of domestic violence cases."[22]

In regard to the changes to be made to the 1986 DVO, the consultants suggested a definition should be given to the term "domestic violence", and said
in the report that:

> (a) Violence, defined in the DVO (Cap. 189), includes physical assault,
> sexual violence, psychological abuse, neglect (for children and elderly),
> stalking and exposing a child to domestic violence; (b) Psychological
> abuse involves psychological harm or trauma, caused by physical or
> sexual violence, or the threat of physical or sexual violence, or coercive
> tactics; (c) Neglect should be included as a type of violence under the
> DVO (Cap. 189). For the definition of neglect in legal terms, it should be
> carefully studied and publicly consulted; (d) Stalking in domestic rela-
> tionships should be criminalized, as recommended by the Law Reform
> Commission; and (e) The making of a child witnessing domestic violence
> by a perpetrator of domestic violence should be regarded as a form of
> criminal child abuse.[23]

The bureau accepted the fact that molestation was not defined in the 1986
DVO; however, it suggested that the term used in the 1986 DVO might include
physical and psychological abuse and harassment. It claimed that:

> whilst we are in support of adding clarity to the law, we are concerned that
> the term "psychological abuse" may not be easily defined in precision, a
> problem also recognized by the Consultants (para. 8.17–8.21), and may
> add ambiguity rather than clarity to the law. As the existing DVO already

---

21.   *Ibid*, and see Annex to LC Paper for Discussion on 3 November 2005 paras. 8
      and 13.

22.   *Ibid*, and see Annex to LC Paper for Discussion on 3 November 2005 para. 9.

23.   *Ibid*—Chan K L; Chiu, M.C. & Chiu, L.S.(2005). *Peace at Home*, see
      Recommendation 15.

> applies to psychological abuse, we consider it desirable to maintain the status quo.[24]

In the fight against domestic violence, it has been recognized in other countries that protection is necessary for other members in the familial relationship. Countries like England and Wales,[25] Australia,[26] New Zealand,[27] Canada,[28] Taiwan[29] and Singapore[30] do provide protection for persons in a domestic relationship other than just spouses and cohabitants under their domestic violence law. The consultants contended that:

> (a) The scope of provision of the protection of the DVO (Cap 189) should include an applicant who is "associated with" the respondent/defendant if:—(1) They are or have been married to each other; (including married or divorced couple) (2) They are cohabitants or former cohabitants; (including heterosexual and same-sex couples); (3) They live or have lived in the same household, otherwise than merely by reason of one of them being the other's employee, tenant, lodger or boarder; (4) They are relatives; (5) They have agreed to marry one another; (6) They are parents in relation to any child; or have or have had parental responsibility for the child; (7) They are parties to the same family proceedings; and (8) Relevant child; (b) A child should have the right to apply for an order on his or her own with the Court's permission. If the child finds it difficult to work on his or her own, he or she can be represented by the SWD, with his or her consent, to apply for the restraining orders; and (c) "Cohabiting" in the same household could be used as one of the criteria to identify intimate relationships. However, it should not be the prerequisite of defining relationships (Chan et al., 2005, recommendation 16).

The bureau recognized that overseas legislation could provide useful reference, but in rejecting the idea, they argued that they had to take into account the local context and cultural background in determining whether, and if so, how, the local legislation should be amended. However, they did not accept that the dynamics of other familial relationships are identical to those in

---

24. *Ibid*, and see Annex to LC Paper for Discussion on 3 November 2005, para.15.
25. Section 62 Family Law Act 1996.
26. Sections 5,15, 16, 18 and 19 Crimes (Domestic and Personal Violence) Act 2007.
27. Sections 4 and 7 Domestic Violence Act 1995.
28. Sections 3 and 4 Domestic Violence Protection Act 2000.
29. Act 3 Domestic Violence Prevention Act.
30. Part VII Women's Charter.

spousal or cohabitual relationships, and they did not see a strong case for providing protection to these people by way of a civil injunction under the DVO (Health, Welfare and Food Bureau, 2005, para. 16). They accepted that changes should be made to include a former spouse or former cohabitant, yet it had to be subject to clear definition in the law. Regarding coverage for same-sex couples, the bureau found it premature to consider the proposal before consensus on the social acceptability of this approach had been built up. The suggestion to allow same-sex couples to bring applications was also rejected at the time. The bureau claimed this might give rise to the possibility of abuse of the process of the court, and that any such proposal would be out of place with our existing regime, and hence was not supported.

In proposing changes to the 1986 DVO, the terms of the power of arrest and the duration for the exclusion order, the entry order and the power of arrest had to be dealt with. The consultants made no hesitation in pointing out deficiencies in those respects and in recommending changes (Chan et al., 2005). The bureau, in their early response to the suggestion, agreed to look into it with a view to amending the 1986 DVO (Health, Welfare and Food Bureau, 2005).

The subcommittee involved various stakeholders so as to collect their views and information related to their expertise for the reform against the problems of domestic violence. They included the Law Society of Hong Kong (the Law Society), the Bar Association, Harmony House, the Hong Kong Council of Social Service, Caritas Hong Kong—Family Services, Amnesty International Hong Kong, Hong Kong Alliance for Family, Hong Kong Federation of Women's Centres, Hong Kong Association for the Survivors of Women Abuse (Kwan Fook) and other NGOs which had been lobbying the government to take action.[31] After the bureau had initially tabled their proposals, the battle

---

31.   Amnesty International Hong Kong Section, [LC Paper No. CB(2)2739/06-07(02)]; Association for Concern for Legal Rights of Victims of Domestic Violence, [LC Paper No. CB(2)2769/06-07(09)]; Caritas Hong Kong—Family Service, [LC Paper No. CB(2)2769/06-07(06)]; Hong Kong Alliance for Family, [LC Paper No.CB(2)2769/06-07(07)]; Hong Kong Council of Social Service, [LC Paper No. CB(2)2769/06-07(05)]; Parents for the Family Association, [LC Paper No. CB(2)2456/06-07(04)]; Zonta Club, [LC Paper No. CB(2)2739/06-07(03)]; Civil Rights for Sexual Diversities; Hong Kong Women Christian Council, [LC Paper No.CB(2)2769/06-07(08)]; Hong Kong Women's Coalition on Equal Opportunities, [LC Paper No. CB(2)2769/06-07(02)]; Hong Kong Chinese

for more amendments went under way. A working group with representatives from the aforementioned organizations and other NGOs was formed, calling for a comprehensive reform in line with the laws in other jurisdictions, in particular, for the extension of protection coverage to persons of a familial relationship other than a spousal relationship.

The Law Society, in a Report on Domestic Violence Ordinance released in December 2005 (the Law Society Report), summed up the situation in the conclusion as requiring urgent attention from the government, and called for immediate reform of the 1986 DVO, noting the following:

> The family is the foundation of our society. The government has a duty to implement comprehensive and enlightened policies to tackle social problems. It should acknowledge its current policies, and the legislation underpinning the policies on domestic violence are outdated and in urgent need of reform. Since the tragic events in April 2004, the administration's policy appears to have evolved from one of a "three-pronged approach" to one of "zero tolerance". The administration has recently stated its policies in a comprehensive policy report which will enable much needed reforms to be introduced. The 1986 DVO is outdated and amendments to this piece of legislation should be a top priority for the administration. There is a wealth of material available in other jurisdictions and successful policies and programmes can be adopted and adapted to suit Hong Kong's domestic requirements. In particular, the administration should review the measures taken by the British government to tackle domestic violence in the Home Office report *Domestic Violence: A National Report*. [32]

The Law Society Report cited the experiences and the laws in place in several other jurisdictions, and made a total of 39 recommendations. The recommendations were very similar to those by the consultants insofar as they related to the outdated ordinance. They differed from the consultants' report and other recommendations in the suggestion of criminalization of domestic violence. The Law Society's view in this respect agreed with that of the bureau.

Civil Servants' Association, Social Work Officer Grade Branch, [LC Paper No. CB(2)2769/06-07(03)]; Harmony House, [LC Paper No. CB(2)2739/06-07(04)]; The Law Society of Hong Kong, [LC Paper No. CB(2)2769/06-07(05)]; Against Elderly Abuse of Hong Kong, [LC Paper No. CB(2)2769/06-07(01)].

32. The Law Society of Hong Kong, Report on Domestic Violence Ordinance, December 2005, p. 103.

In a report on child custody and access prepared by the Hong Kong Law Reform Commission (LRC), the commission set out a list of significant short-comings of the 1986 DVO, which were also similar to the other studies (Hong Kong Law Reform Commission, 2005, para. 11.48). The LRC also called on the government to take serious action toward reform, saying:

> We consider the deficiencies in the protections afforded by the current domestic violence legislation in Hong Kong to be serious. We note that these deficiencies were drawn to the Administration's attention in 2000 in the Law Reform Commission's *Report on Stalking*. The first recommendation of that report was that *"the Administration should give consideration to reforming the law relating to domestic violence"* (Hong Kong Law Reform Commission, 2000, para. 4.50). We strongly endorse this view, particularly in light of the successive reforms that have been and are being made to the English legislation on which our ordinance is based. We therefore take the opportunity to note our concern and to make a further recommendation calling for reform of the law in this area (Hong Kong Law Reform Commission, 2005, para. 11.51).

After much negotiation between the bureau and the stakeholders, the bureau produced a paper for discussion at the Legco Panel on Welfare Services on 8 January 2007 (Health, Welfare and Food Bureau, 2006). It acknowledged domestic violence as a subject of public concern and that the number of domestic violence cases over the past years had been on the increase. It also accepted the areas that called for improvements and proposed amendments to the 1986 DVO to (Health, Welfare and Food Bureau, 2006, para. 12):

(a) enable the former spouses and former cohabitants to apply for injunction order;

(b) remove the requirement that the child has to be living with the applicant;

(c) extend protection to a child of either parties whether biological, adopted or step child;

(d) enable a next friend to apply for a child for the injunction order;

(e) enable the court to vary any existing custody/access order in respect of the child;

(f) empower the court to also attach a power of arrest if it reasonably believe that it is likely to cause bodily harm;

(g) remove the 3-month cap on the validity of the injunction order and allow extension of up to a maximum period of 24 months; and

(h) remove the 3-month cap on the validity of the power of arrest and allow extension of up to a maximum of 24 months.

In June 2007, the bureau in its Legislative Council Brief finally took the big step to introduce amendments to include the long awaited changes. The bill was annexed in the Legislative Council Brief submitted by the bureau, and this was the Domestic Violence (Amendment) Bill 2007 (amendment bill) (Health, Welfare and Food Bureau, 2007).

Substantial changes were brought about by the amendment bill. Apart from those set out in the LC Paper for Discussion on 8 January 2007, it also extended protection coverage to familial relationships other than spousal or cohabitant relationships, i.e., to parent-son/daughter, parent-son/daughter-in-law, and grandparent-grandson/granddaughter relationships; and to other extended familial relationships including between a person and his/her brother, sister, brother-in-law, sister-in-law, uncle, aunt, nephew, niece and cousin (Health, Welfare and Food Bureau, 2007, para. 4). In addition to this, the bureau also proposed that the court may, in granting a non-molestation order under the DVO, require the abuser to attend an anti-violence programme as approved by the director of the SWD, seeking to change his/her attitude and behaviour that first led to the granting of the injunction order.

However, the amendment bill came short of responding to other major recommendations from stakeholders such as the Law Society and the consultants. It did not include protection coverage for same-sex couples, laying down a definition for "domestic violence", or setting up a domestic violence court.

At the request of the bills committee on the Domestic Violence (Amendment) Bill 2007, the bureau in its papers gave their reasons for not including same-sex couples, stating:

> in Hong Kong, a marriage contracted under the Marriage Ordinance (Cap. 181) is, in law, the voluntary union for life of one man and one woman to the exclusion of all others. Our law, which reflects the government's policy position, does not recognize same-sex marriage, civil partnership, or any same-sex relationship. Recognizing same-sex relationship is an issue concerning ethics and morality of the society. Any change to this policy stance would have substantial implications on the society and should not be introduced unless consensus or a majority view is reached by the society. [33]

---

33.   The bureau changed its name from Health, Welfare and Food Bureau to Labour and Welfare Bureau with effect from 1 July 2007.

The bureau also called to the attention of the bills committee that any act of violence is liable to criminal sanction under the relevant ordinances, irrespective of the relationship between the abuser and the victim. Same-sex couples have the same level of protection as those in a heterosexual relationship under the existing criminal legislative framework. If they need civil remedies, they also have protection under the law of tort or inherent jurisdiction of the court.

In about the same period, a young man took to the court seeking a declaration that homosexual men have been unjustifiably discriminated against by certain provisions contained in the Crimes Ordinance (Cap. 200) relating to buggery.[34] The Court of Appeal granted the declaration. In another case which occurred at about the same time, the Court of Final Appeal found that section 118F(1) of the Crimes Ordinance, which criminalizes homosexual buggery committed otherwise than in private, was unconstitutional on the ground that it was discriminatory and infringed on the constitutional right to equality.[35] Both cases came to the attention of the bills committee, which subsequently requested more information. The Equal Opportunities Commission was invited to give their view on the issue of giving protection to same-sex couples. Mr Herman L. H. Poon, chief legal counsel of the commission, noting the case of Yau Yuk Lung,[36] wrote in a letter of response to the bills committee,

> However, it is not at all clear that maintaining a difference between same-sex couples and other couples in the context of domestic violence protection is in itself a legitimate aim. It is difficult to see any genuine need to make such a difference in the context of domestic violence. Given that nonmarried heterosexual couples whose relationship is not legally recognized are still given the same protection as legally married couples, it is difficult to argue that the lack of legal status makes it legitimate to deny equal protection (p. 2).

This was very direct to the point, and made a legitimate argument that one could not ignore. Obviously, the view cast doubt on the argument put forward by the bureau in asserting that denying the same protection on the grounds of sexual orientation is hardly justified. Poon concluded his opinion in saying:

---

34.   *T C William Roy v Secretary For Justice* [2006]4 HKLRD 211.
35.   *Secretary For Justice v Yau Yuk Lung Zigo and Another* [2007]3 HKLRD 903.
36.   *Ibid.*

> Although sexual orientation discrimination is not strictly within the remit
> of the Equal Opportunities Commission, equality on this ground is con-
> ducive to equality on grounds which are within our remit. We urge the
> administration to carefully consider whether legislative proposals are
> consistent with the constitutional principles of equality (Poon, 2007, pp.
> 2–3).

At a meeting of the bills committee held on 13 November 2007, the bureau was asked to respond in writing to address the legal point raised by the Equal Opportunities Commission, particularly on the applicability of the case of Yau Yuk Lung, and to give reasoning for the genuine lack of need for including same-sex couples under the DVO.[37] In light of the two rulings by the judiciary which confirmed discrimination based on sexual orientation as unconstitutional and the view given by the chief legal counsel of the Equal Opportunities Commission, the pressure for further extension to cover same-sex couples remained on the bureau.

In dealing with the need for the establishment of a definition for "domestic violence", the bureau explained their position and insisted that the present use of the word "molest" already applied to psychological abuse, and that there were both UK and Hong Kong cases to support this. The bureau referred to a number of cases to demonstrate that whether it is acts such as harassing a pet or a child of the victim, or bombarding the victim with telephone calls or emails to request reconciliation, these could all be regarded as psychological abuse. It further claimed that the term "molest" is a broad term, extending to abuse beyond the more typical instances of physical assaults to include any form of physical, sexual or psychological molestation or harassment, or any related threat, which has a serious detrimental effect upon the health and well-being of the victim. One of the arguments for identifying the range of violent acts to be covered by the legislation is to make clear to the general public what types of behaviours are considered as domestic violence, from which victims are given protection. For those legally trained, it is easy to understand and appreciate the benefit and the need to maintain flexibility on the interpretation of the word "molest", rather than to put it within the constraints of a rigid definition. The English legislation adopted and maintained this approach after several changes to their law on domestic violence. The benefit of using the term "molest" in

---

37.   Minutes of the fourth meeting of the bills committee held on 13 November 2007, LC Paper No CB(2)633.07-08 para. 10.

the UK instead of adopting a statutory definition for "domestic violence" has been seen as a good thing. It was said that "reflecting the response to the Law Commission's proposals that any attempt at a statutory definition of 'molestation' might reduce the level of protection afforded by the former law, the term is deliberately not defined in the 1996 Act. Instead its meaning has been left to case law" (N. Lowe et al., 1991, Law Com No. 207, para. 3.1).

A number of NGOs advocated and supported the consultants' proposal for the establishment of a specialized domestic violence court. It was suggested that a specialized domestic violence court should handle both criminal and civil cases relating to domestic violence. The Law Society was going for a truly dedicated Family Court with exclusive jurisdiction to handle all family disputes, including the making of care or protection orders (The Law Society of Hong Kong, 2005, Chapter 9). It also suggested that a specialized unit should be established within the Family Court to handle all domestic violence crime cases. The Law Society relied on the observations by the English Court of Appeal in the judgment of *Lomas v Parle*,[38] which clearly identified not only the areas of dissatisfaction but also the level of waste of judicial resources within the existing system. In the report, the Law Society made reference to the judgment delivered by Thorpe LJ in the case, which said:

> the unsatisfactory nature of the present interface between the criminal and family courts…is expensive, wasteful of resources and time-consuming. It is stressful for the victim to move from court to court in order to obtain redress and protection from the perpetrator. Other jurisdictions are attempting to solve this problem. The State of New York is setting up integrated courts to hear both criminal and civil proceedings before one tribunal. The publication of the Domestic Violence Crime and Victims Bill is an opportunity, we would suggest, for a reconsideration of the present dual system and an opportunity to look into the possibility of integrated courts to see if they might avoid the problems which we now raise.

In England, the Ministry of Justice announced in March 2010 that there were a total of 141 specialist domestic violence courts (SDVCs), which met and exceeded the government target of having a total of 128 SDVC systems by 2011 a year early.[39] Ms Bridget Prentice, justice minister, said:

---

38.   *Lomas v Parle* [2004]1 FLR 812.
39.   http://www.justice.gov.uk/news.htm

> Specialist domestic violence courts are a key part of our fight against domestic violence and part of a wider government commitment to putting victims at the heart of the criminal justice system, helping the victim and family, and stopping them from ending back in the court. . . . SDVCs are a real testament to the skills and expertise of the people behind them.

In the US, there had been SDVCs in some states since the early 1980s, with considerable variation in their procedures and functions. The Law Society of Hong Kong pointed out that the Brooklyn Felony Domestic Violence Court was one of the first of these courts to be established as a "problem-solving court". In Florida, there was an integrated model of SDVCs dealing with both the criminal and civil aspects of a single domestic violence case. The qualitative evaluation for the Dade County Specialist Domestic Violence Court revealed that both judges and prosecutors felt that the integrated system improved administrative efficiency and helped to reduce recidivism.

At the time of the consideration of the amendment bill, the bureau had looked into the possibility of establishing SDVCs in Hong Kong. In a paper prepared by the bureau for the bills committee in November 2007, the bureau reported that they had already raised with the judiciary the feasibility of modelling on the UK experience in dealing with domestic violence cases in a specialized way, including clustering and fast-tracking cases in the court, in which pre-trial hearings of domestic violence-related criminal cases were grouped in one court session.[40] The judiciary responded to the bills committee on this matter, noting that the implementation of these administrative measures would involve legal and practical issues which have to be carefully considered. It also drew attention to the fact that to set up a specialized court to handle both civil and criminal cases relating to domestic violence would involve a host of complicated legal issues as to how the proposed set-up would fit in with the existing legal framework.[41]

The amendment bill was finally passed, and this first major amendment to the 1986 DVO took effect on 1 August 2008 (2008 DVO).[42] Most of the proposed changes by the stakeholders were taken up in the amendments with the

---

40. Bureau's Summary of Views/Suggestions Given by Deputations, LC Paper No. CB(2)330/07-08(01), para. 3.

41. Judiciary's Response (November 2007), LC Paper No. CB(2)347/07-08(01).

42. Domestic Violence (Amendment) Ordinance 2008 (17 of 2008) Commencement Notice L.N. 184 of 2008, 20 June 2008.

exceptions of extending coverage to same-sex couples, making provisions for a definition for "domestic violence" and setting up specialized courts to deal with domestic violence.

The bureau had correctly decided to press ahead with the changes to be made to the 1986 DVO, and to leave other issues to be dealt with later. The 2008 DVO was well received by stakeholders and the public, despite having taken three to four years for its expansion to suit the changes in society.

The bureau charged a number of Legislative Council members in the bills committee with the task of further amending the ordinance for the extension of coverage to same-sex couples in the 2008–09 legislative session. Mr Cheung Kin Chung, the secretary of the bureau, announced the government's proposal to amend the ordinance for this purpose on 10 January 2009. However, Mr Cheung stressed that the amendment was aimed at providing civil remedies to victims concerned, while upholding the government's policy of not recognizing any same-sex relationship as a matter of legal status, and that they should not be regarded as equivalent to giving legal recognition to same-sex relationships, or providing legal entitlements to persons in such relationships. The secretary was reported to have said that,

> The administration does not recognize same-sex marriage. civil partnership or any same-sex relationship as a matter of legal status and policy stance. It is noteworthy that the proposed amendments have no relevance to the legal definition of marriage. . . .I heard both supporting and opposing views put forward today on the proposed amendments. However, there appears to be a consensus among different groups and Legislative Council members that individuals in specific relationships should be protected from threats of violence from molestation. We will thoroughly consider the views put forward by all sectors. I hope that the community, the Legislative Council and the administration can discuss the subject and resolve the differences in a spirit of understanding.

After the decision to introduce the amendment, a number of members within the Legislative Council took a dramatically opposite view, as a result of which, the Legco Panel on Welfare Services set aside two special sessions to invite representations of different views. In the end, nearly 100 deputations and 45 individuals attended. Out of these attendees, about two-thirds, mostly from religious and parent groups, objected strongly to the proposal, arguing that this would cause ambiguity in the interpretation of "family" and "marriage", and hence, undermine the morality of society. Their arguments lay in the Chinese title of the DVO—"家庭暴力條例"—which contained the Chinese word for "family". They said it was clear from the title that the DVO catered for "family" violence. They believed "family" is constituted of marriage between a man and a woman, and the proposed amendment would distort this sacred concept by suggesting that a family could comprise same-sex cohabitants. They were concerned that the proposal could lead to successful legal challenges by those pushing for the recognition of same-sex marriages under the Marriage Ordinance. Those in favour of the proposal made suggestions to deal with the concerns, such as: changing the Chinese title of the DVO to read as "家居暴力條例" (i.e., Domestic Households Violence Ordinance) or "居所暴力條例" (i.e., Households Violence Ordinance) to encompass all acts of molestation that occur in a domestic setting, while staying clear of any association in its wording with same-sex couples and the concept of "marriage"; enacting separate legislation to deal with same-sex couples while leaving the DVO intact; and extending the existing DVO to cover all persons living under the same roof and ignoring any specific relationships.

The bureau dealt with the situation by introducing a new definition which would not have any effect of equating or linking, in any way, same-sex cohabitation with the concepts of "marriage", "spouse" or "husband and wife". It suggested using the definition of a "cohabitation relationship", which is devoid of any such references. A "cohabitation relationship" would be understood as a "relationship between two persons who live together as a couple in an intimate relationship". The court was to have regard to all the circumstances of the case, including but not limited to a number of factors set out in the ordinance, in determining such relationship for the purpose of the ordinance. To avoid the perceived concern over the Chinese title of the ordinance, it also proposed changing the name of the legislation to read as "Domestic and Cohabitation Relationships Violence Ordinance" ("家庭及同居關係暴力條例" in Chinese) to highlight that the amended DVO is also applicable to persons in cohabitation relationships. The bureau claimed that there was no policy justification for enacting a separate legislation to provide protection against molestation for same-sex couples, and that it was not the established practice where legal provisions addressing the same or similar policy were to be tackled in separate legislation. The preference was to amend the existing legislation, as it was more expedient to enable early protection to same-sex couples. The bureau presented the Domestic Violence (Amendment) Bill 2009 in the Legislative Council Brief in June 2009, setting out the proposed amendments (Labour and Welfare Bureau, 2009).

On 31 December 2009, the Secretary for Labour and Welfare announced to the public that the Legislative Council passed the Domestic Violence (Amendment) Bill 2009 after its third reading on 16 December to further extend the coverage of the ordinance to same-sex cohabitants, former cohabitants and their children. In the press release made on 31 December 2009, he said:

> Currently, heterosexual cohabitants are protected by the DVO. The amendments to the DVO are made in light of the fact that similar special power interface, dynamics and risk factors between heterosexual cohabitants might also exist between same-sex cohabitants in intimate relationships and render the victims reluctant to report to the police the abusers' acts of violence.[43]

The secretary informed the public that the amendments were made in response to the calls of Legislative Council members and the community, fully taking into account the views of religious bodies and parent groups. He emphasized that the amendments would not affect other existing legislation, and should not be regarded as equivalent to giving legal recognition to same-sex relationships. This second amendment, which took effect on 1 January 2010, marked the completion of the course of updating the civil legislation against domestic violence.

The Domestic and Cohabitation Relationships Violence Ordinance (Cap. 189) (DCRVO)

Persons to be protected under the DCRVO

The present civil redress against domestic violence under the DCRVO provides protection to four categories of people in a domestic relationship. They are: (1) spouses and former spouses,[44] (2) relatives,[45] (3) cohabitants and former cohabitants (including both opposite-sex and same-sex couples),[46] and (4) minors.[47]

---

43.   Bureau Press Release, 31 December 2009, "The Domestic Violence (Amendment) Ordinance 2009 to take effect tomorrow".
44.   Section 3(1) DCRVO.
45.   Section 3A(1) and (2) DCRVO.
46.   Section 3B(1) DCRVO.
47.   Sections 3A(1), (2) and (3) DCRVO.

Spouses and former spouses

There is no provision in the DCRVO stipulating any restriction on the period of separation after the divorce or cohabitation for a former spouse or a former cohabitant after which he/she can no longer apply for protection. However, an application should be made within a reasonable time frame of the occurrence of the incident complained of. In *O'Neill v Williams*,[48] a woman complained of violent acts which had happened six months prior after she had left the man. The court refused the application.

Relatives

If a victim of domestic violence is applying against a relative, the relationship has to be the one as defined in section 3A(1) of the DCRVO. There is no stipulation in the DCRVO requiring the parties to be in the same household or having previously lived together at the time of the application. However, if the parties are living together under the same roof and the victim intends to obtain an injunction to oust the relative, the ordinance requires the court to give regard to certain factors in exercising the discretion to oust a relative who has proprietary interests in the property.[49] Section 3A(1) provides a long list of familial relationships covered by the ordinance:

(a) the applicant's father, mother, grandfather or grandmother (whether natural or adoptive);

(b) the applicant's step-father, step-mother, step-grandfather or step-grandmother;

(c) the applicant's father-in-law or mother-in-law who is the natural parent, adoptive parent or step-parent of the applicant's spouse;

(d) the applicant's grandfather-in-law or grandmother-in-law who is the natural grandparent, adoptive grandparent or step-grandparent of the applicant's spouse;

(e) the applicant's son, daughter, grandson or granddaughter (whether natural or adoptive);

(f) the applicant's step-son, step-daughter, step-grandson or step-granddaughter;

(g) the applicant's son-in-law or daughter-in-law who is the spouse of the applicant's natural child, adoptive child or step-child;

---

48.   *O'Neill v Williams* [1984] FLR 1.

49.   Section 3A(6) DCRVO.

(h) the applicant's grandson-in-law or granddaughter-in-law who is the spouse of the applicant's natural grandchild, adoptive grandchild or step-grandchild;

(i) the applicant's brother or sister (whether of full or half blood or by virtue of adoption);

(j) the brother or sister (whether of full or half blood or by virtue of adoption) of the applicant's spouse;

(k) the applicant's step-brother or step-sister;

(l) the step-brother or step-sister of the applicant's spouse;

(m) the applicant's uncle, aunt, nephew, niece or cousin (whether of full or half blood or by virtue of adoption);

(n) the uncle, aunt, nephew, niece or cousin (whether of full or half blood or by virtue of adoption) of the applicant's spouse; or

(o) the spouse of any person mentioned in paragraphs (i), (j), (k), (l), (m) or (n).[50]

Cohabitants or former cohabitants

On an application by a party in a cohabitation relationship, the court may grant an injunction if it is established that the applicant or a specified minor had been molested by the other party in the cohabitation relationship. Section 2 of the DCRVO provides a definition for "cohabitation relationship" (同居關係), which refers to, "(a) ... a relationship between two persons (whether of the same sex or of the opposite sex) who live together as a couple in an intimate relationship; and (b) includes such a relationship that has come to an end."

The ordinance further provides that in determining whether the parties are in a cohabitation relationship, the court shall have regard to all the circumstances of the relationship, including but not limited to any of the following factors that may be relevant in the particular case:

(a) whether the parties are living together in the same household;

(b) whether the parties share the tasks and duties of their daily lives;

(c) whether there is stability and permanence in the relationship;

(d) the arrangement of sharing of expenses or financial support, and the degree of financial dependence or interdependence, between the parties;

(e) whether there is a sexual relationship between the parties;

(f) whether the parties share the care and support of a specified minor;

---

50.   Section 3A(2) DCRVO.

(g) the parties' reasons for living together, and the degree of mutual commitment to a shared life;

(h) whether the parties conduct themselves towards friends, relatives or other persons as parties to a cohabitation relationship, and whether the parties are so treated by their friends and relatives or other persons.[51]

This provision is to assist the court in determining whether a cohabitation relationship should come under the protection of the DCRVO. These eight factors are not to be taken as the only factors to be considered by the court, but other equally important factors can be placed before the court for its consideration. There is no similar provision to be found in English legislation, and since this is a new provision within the ordinance—taking effect only at the beginning of 2010—there is no decided case from any of the Hong Kong courts on any of the factors set out in the provision. Nor should the court consider any one factor as more important than another. Parties having a casual or even a steady sexual relationship are not necessarily considered to have satisfied the requirement under this provision. The court will have to give regard to all the circumstances of a particular case.

Nevertheless, there is English authority suggesting that the definition of cohabitation should not be construed too narrowly to exclude borderline cases and that it should be given a purposive construction.[52] In this case, the justices refused the application because they did not consider the applicant and the respondent as living in the same household, although the respondent would often stay over for two or three nights during the week and the applicant would go to his flat at weekends. On appeal by the applicant, Wall J. in the Family Division found that the court should have taken into account three "admirable signposts": (1) there was a sexual relationship; (2) the parties operated a joint account into which the proceeds of the sale of the respondent's property was paid; and (3) that money was spent on the applicant's property. Wall J. concluded in saying, "In my judgment, the message of this case to justices is that where domestic violence is concerned, they should give the statute a purposive construction and not decline jurisdiction, unless the facts of the case before them are plainly incapable of being brought within the statute."[53]

---

51. Section 3B(2) DCRVO.

52. G v F (Non-Molestation: Jurisdiction) [2000] 2 FLR 533

53. *Ibid.*

Although one of the factors in section 3B(2) of the DCRVO requires the parties to be living in the same household, parties leading separate lives from each other and yet who are living under the same roof are still regarded as living in the same household. In *Adeoso (otherwise Ametepe) v Adeoso*, the Court of Appeal in England had to determine if the parties involved "were living together in the same household as husband and wife" within section 1(2) of the Domestic Violence and Matrimonial Proceedings Act 1976. The applicant and the respondent had lived together since 1976 as man and wife. Although they were not married, the applicant took the respondent's name. Eventually, they became joint tenants of a council flat consisting of one bedroom, a sitting room, a kitchen and a bathroom. In the next few years, their relationship soured, which might have been due to the fact that the applicant could not have children. From 1979 onwards, they slept in separate rooms, the respondent on the floor in the sitting room and the applicant in the bedroom. Later, the applicant even stopped cooking and washing for the respondent. Communication between the parties was by notes; however, they still shared the expenses for electricity, gas and rent. The Court of Appeal considered that in ordinary human terms, the relationship was exactly comparable to a marriage in the last stages of break-up, and concluded that the parties were living in the same household as man and wife for the purpose of section 1(2) of the Act. In one of the cohabitation cases, the court found that the man and the woman had lived together for three months, and the woman

> did not want to continue her association with the respondent but he found out without difficulty where she was and forced his way in. He treated her with some violence. He forced her to have intercourse, she says against her will, from time to time. He began staying at her bed and breakfast accommodation about three times a week, ignored her requests to go away and in October 1978 he moved into her accommodation permanently, she says in spite of her protests.[54]

The English courts have from time to time considered the question of whether the parties had lived in the same household as husband and wife, such as for the purpose of the Inheritance (Provision for Family and Dependants) Act 1975, an act empowering the court to give provision for the spouse, former spouse and children of the deceased. It is suggested that consideration of that

---

54. *Mclean v Nugent* [1980] FLR 26, p. 28.

question should not ignore the multifarious nature of marital relationships, and should take into account the circumstances of the case, the nature and character of the relationship including the assumption of responsibility for the other party, and the fact that they had lived together.[55]

Finally, one should bear in mind that apart from the factors set out above, if the court is to grant an ouster/entry order and to attach an authorization of arrest, the court has to give regard to the permanence of the cohabitation relationship, and consider it as appropriate in all circumstances to grant that injunction or attach that authorization of arrest.

Minors

A minor who has suffered domestic violence from a relative of his or her own may apply through a next friend for protection under the DCRVO.[56] Section 2 defines "minor" to mean any person who is under the age of 18 years. However, a minor may also get protection through an adult applicant who is applying for protection under the DCRVO for herself or himself against the perpetrator with whom he/she has or once had a spousal relationship or a cohabitation relationship.[57] In this case, this minor has to be "the specified minor" for the purpose of the application under the ordinance. As a specified minor, the minor can be a child (whether a natural child, adoptive child or stepchild) of the applicant or respondent concerned, or a child who is living with the applicant concerned. The phrase "living with" should not be interpreted to mean custody of the child; it should be construed in its ordinary meaning. Since the amendment to the ordinance in 2008, the protection for the child is much more satisfactory and wider in scope. A child under the age of 18 is under the protection of the DCRVO in most circumstances.

What kinds of orders are there to offer protection?

There are three types of injunctions in a domestic violence case that a court may consider granting for the protection of the applicant and the specified minor, if the court is satisfied that the applicant and the specified minor have

---

55.   Re Watson [1999] 1 FLR 878.
56.   Section 3A(3) DCRVO.
57.   Sections 3(1) and 3B(1) DCRVO.

been molested by the respondent. These three orders are: (1) a non-molestation order,[58] which is an order to restrain the respondent from molesting the applicant who could be the spouse, a former spouse, a cohabitant, a former cohabitant, a relative or a minor. The usual terms of the restraint order would be that the respondent, whether by himself or herself, his or her servants or agents or otherwise, be strictly enjoined and restrained from assaulting, molesting, annoying, or otherwise causing nuisance, disturbing or interfering with the applicant; (2) an ouster order,[59] which prohibits the respondent from entering or remaining in the residence, a specified part or area, whether or not the residence is the common residence or matrimonial home of the applicant/the specified minor and the respondent; and (3) an entry order,[60] which is an order to the respondent to permit the applicant with the minor, if applicable, to enter and remain in the common residence or matrimonial home of the applicant and the respondent, or in a specified part of such common residence or matrimonial home.

Non-molestation order

There is no definition given to "domestic violence" in the DCRVO. The only word that has reference to violence in the entire ordinance is the word "molest". However, there is also no definition given to this term. As discussed above, the legislation deliberately avoids giving a definition to any particular conduct in domestic violence. The purpose of the legislation is to give the court a wider discretion in considering what kind of conduct or act constitutes "molestation".

In England, Viscount Dilhorne said in his judgment delivered in the House of Lords in the case of Davis and Johnson that "violence is a form of molestation but molestation may take place without the threat or use of physical violence and still be serious and inimical to mental and physical health."[61] Therefore, molestation does not imply necessarily either the threat or use of violence. It includes any conduct that can cause harm to mental and physical health. In *Horner v Horner*,[62] the husband stopped being violent to the wife after the wife obtained an injunction against him prohibiting further use

---

58.   Sections 3(1)(a)(b), 3A (4)(a) and 3B (1)(a)(b) DCRVO.
59.   Sections 3(1)(c), 3A(4)(b) and 3B(1)(c) DCRVO.
60.   Sections 3(1)(d), 3A(4)(c) and 3B(1)(d) DCRVO.
61.   *Davis v Johnson* [1979] AC 264, p. 334.
62.   *Horner v Horner* [1983] 4 FLR 50.

or threat of violence against her. But he started to harass the wife in ways which did not involve the use or threat of violence, including accosting her in public, sending her threatening letters and postcards, repeatedly telephoning the school where the wife taught with disparaging remarks, and intercepting her on her way to work. The Court of Appeal granted an injunction in favour of the wife for such harassment. Ormrod LJ said, "for my part I have no doubt that the word 'molesting' does not imply necessarily either violence or threats of violence. It applies to any conduct which can properly be regarded as such a degree of harassment as to call for the intervention of the court." Molestation definitely does not have to be physical molestation. It includes conduct such as sending letters in extremely abusive terms, or shouting obscenities.[63] The Court of Appeal also accepted the conduct of looking through the wife's handbag as molestation in breach of a previous injunction granted against the husband.[64] Making a nuisance of oneself to the other party, amounting to pestering, is considered as molestation. In the case, the husband kept pestering the wife to go out with him, to see him and speak to him. He also called on her at her house early in the morning and late at night, and also at her place of work. There was evidence from the wife's doctor that the husband's pestering had affected the wife's health. Stephenson LJ concluded that, "Molest is a wide, plain word which I would be reluctant to define or paraphrase. If I had to find one synonym for it, I would select 'pester'."[65]

Molestation does not include invasion of privacy, and conduct that is merely irritating or embarrassing may not be molestation. In *C v C* (Nonmolestation Order: Jurisdiction),[66] the wife gave details of the husband's misbehaviours in their marriage to the media, and articles were published in *People* and *Daily Mail*. The husband tried to prevent the wife from further disclosing such information. The court found that there is a limitation to the term "molestation". Sir Stephen Brown P. considered that this term "implies some quite deliberate conduct which is aimed at a high degree of harassment of the other party, so as to justify the intervention of the court." The wife's disclosure of the husband's misbehaviour might have embarrassed the husband or even damaged his reputation. However, this was no more than an invasion of his privacy, which is different

---

63.　*George v George* [1986] 2 FLR 347.
64.　*Spencer v Camacho* [1983] 4 FLR 662.
65.　*Vaughan v Vaughan* [1973] 2 All ER 449.
66.　*C v C* (Nonmolestation Order: Jurisdiction) [1998] 1 FLR 554.

from molestation. The court said that "the husband's concern was not molestation as such, but damage to his reputation, which, if the information published were untrue, could be dealt with by proceedings for defamation."[67] However, when there is an intention to cause distress, the court will not hesitate to intervene. In *Johnson v Walton*,[68] regarding the husband's giving of an account of the relationship of the parties and including photographs of his wife in a semi-nude state to the national press, the Court of Appeal intervened and said:

> The word "molesting", whether or not used in proceedings under the Domestic Violence and Matrimonial Proceedings Act 1976, applied to any conduct which could properly be regarded as of such a degree of intentional harassment as to call for the intervention of the court. Accordingly, if the offending material had been sent to the press by the defendant with the intent of causing distress to the plaintiff, the defendant's conduct would have amounted to a breach of his undertaking not to molest her, or to urge others to molest her.

Lord Donaldson in his judgment said, "Harassment . . . includes within it an element of intent, intent to cause distress or harm."

In Hong Kong, the Court of Appeal approved the grant of injunction against non-molestation on the basis of the wife's verbal abuse and her conduct in relation to the husband, his parents and brother, and in particular, to the child of the marriage.[69] A threat uttered through a third party has been considered by the court as a sufficient threat of violence.[70] When a husband went beyond scolding, although not to the point of committing actual physical violence, one judge granted the order for non-molestation for the high degree of harassment and intimidation deliberately perpetrated by the husband.[71]

Ouster order/entry order

An ouster order is a draconian order and should only be granted in extreme circumstances.[72] This is a kind of order which requires a party to leave the property in which he/she may have a proprietary interest, and may subsequently

---

67.   *C v C* (Non-molestation Order: Jurisdiction) [1998]1 FLR 554.
68.   *Johnson v Walton* [1990] 1 FLR 350.
69.   *Chan Chun Hon v Chan Lam Lai Bing Shirley* [1994] 3 HKC 196.
70.   *YLS v TL* (FCMC 8396/2007).
71.   *P v C* (Ouster and Domestic Violence) [2007] HKFLR 195.
72.   *Chan Chun Hon v Chan Lam Lai Bing Shirley* [1994] 3 HKC 196.

render this party homeless. The court always has to be extremely careful in granting such an order, in particular when the applicant does not have any interest in the property. Where an application for an ouster order/entry order is made by a spouse or a cohabitant, or after a couple's divorce or separation, as the case may be, the court does not have to give regard to the proprietary rights over the property in question.[73] However, if an application is made by a party against a relative, the court will have to give regard to the one who has the legal or beneficial interest in, or a contractual or legal right to occupy, the common residence of the parties.[74] Despite this discretionary power of the court, the DCRVO provides certain criteria for the court's consideration in making such orders. In the case of an application coming from a spousal or cohabitant relationship, the court has to consider the following factors:

(a) the conduct of the parties;

(b) their respective needs and financial resources;

(c) the needs of any specified minor; and

(d) all the circumstances of the case.[75]

If it is an application for an ouster/entry order against a relative, the factors for the court's consideration are different, and they are:

(a) who has the legal or beneficial interest in, or a contractual or legal right to occupy, the common residence of the applicant and the respondent;

(b) the impact of the injunction on the relationship between the applicant, the respondent and their other family members who reside with them;

(c) the conduct of the applicant and the respondent, both in relation to each other and otherwise;

(d) the respective needs and financial resources of the applicant and the respondent; and

(e) all the circumstances of the case.[76]

---

73.   Sections 3 and 3B DCRVO.
74.   Section 3A DCRVO.
75.   Sections 3 and 3B DCRVO.
76.   Section 3A DCRVO.

It should be noted that the court may order the ouster/entry orders to apply to a specified part or area, whether or not the residence is the common residence or matrimonial home of the applicant/the specified minor and the respondent. It would be possible based on the above wording for a respondent to be excluded from a specified part within the home such as the master bedroom, or an area which could be the applicant's workplace. In *E v E*,[77] the husband was ordered to let the wife have exclusive use of the front bedroom, which the husband was restrained from entering. In another case, a husband who had been violent to his wife made a proposal stating that the wife should return to the matrimonial home, where there were two bedrooms, and that they should live there independently, his occupation being restricted to the smaller bedroom while the kitchen and the bathroom were to be shared. However, the Court of Appeal rejected his proposal on the grounds that it had to take all the circumstances into account and assess the risks to the family. The court said that the judge below had not given proper weight to the complications and difficulties which would arise if the limited accommodation was shared, and that he had not taken into account the repeated breakdowns in the past.[78]

The conduct of the parties

It is a well-established principle in England that there is no prerequisite of actual physical danger or violence for orders made under section 1 of the Domestic Violence and Matrimonial Proceedings Act 1976.[79] The Court of Appeal considers it its duty to examine the conduct of the parties and determine relative culpability to justify making an ouster order.[80] A court refused to grant an ouster order against a husband who had broken down the door to the master bedroom, as the judge considered that "the wife's actions were wholly inappropriate and inciting. Given the circumstances of their relationship at the material time, the wife should have dealt with the matter more sensitively and diplomatically. Instead she went in callously and antagonistically."[81] Where the conduct of the husband endangered the health of the wife and the child,

---

77.   *E v E* [1995] 1 FLR 224.
78.   *Anderson v Anderson* [1984] FLR 566.
79.   *G v J* (ouster order) [1993] 1 FLR 1008.
80.   Blackstock v Blackstock [1991] 2 FLR 308.
81.   *P v L* (Non-molestation and Ouster Order) [2007] HKFLR 1.

the court should make the ouster order. The Court of Appeal, in this case, concluded that:

> an injunction excluding from the former matrimonial home a divorced husband who was lawfully entitled to be there would only be made where the circumstances clearly demonstrated that such an order was both imperative and necessary in that the conditions in the home made it intolerable for the wife and any children of the marriage to continue to share the accommodation with the husband. Thus an order would be granted where it was necessary for the protection of the health, physical or mental, of the wife or child.[82]

Even if the situation at home is one of unpleasantness and inconvenience, or tension pending a divorce, it is not sufficient grounds for ordering a spouse out of the matrimonial home.[83] The Court of Appeal in England dealt with one case in which the matrimonial home was a big house with six bedrooms. The husband in this case left home to work in the morning and returned in the evening. The wife worked as a model and she would look after the children when they were home. There was no evidence of violence. The wife applied for an exclusion order which was granted by the lower court. On appeal by the husband, the injunction was discharged. The Court of Appeal considered that:

> an order excluding a spouse from the matrimonial home was a drastic order and ought not to be made unless it was proved to be impossible for the spouses to live together, the essence of the matter (per Sachs LJ) being whether the order was necessary for the protection of a spouse, though (per Lord Denning MR and Sachs LJ) the interests of the children were also an important consideration.[84]

The question to ask is, is the conduct sufficiently serious to justify the making of an ouster order? When a husband's conduct in seeking to prevail on the wife to effect reconciliation is a breach of his undertaking of non-molestation, the court is justified in concluding that the parties are to be kept apart with an order to prohibit the husband from exercising his right to occupy the matrimonial home.[85]

---

82.   *Phillips v Phillips* [1973] 2 All ER 423.

83.   *Hall v Hall* [1971] 1 All ER 762.

84.   Ibid.

85.   *Scott v Scott* [1992] 1 FLR 529.

Their respective needs and financial resources

The court will have to consider the needs of the parties, but this should not be regarded simply as a housing matter. Ralph Gibson LJ said in *Wiseman v Simpson*,

> The decision which the judge made would appear to most people to be fair and sensible if the task of the court was to decide who, in fairness, between the man who is going to work and the woman who has the care of the child, should have the flat to live in. As a matter of housing policy the judge's answer may well be right. But the court has no power to decide such a case simply as a matter of housing policy. The jurisdiction is given by the Domestic Violence and Matrimonial Proceedings Act 1976 and the question is whether the order can be sustained under the provisions of that Act.[86]

Availability of alternative accommodation for the party would be a consideration for the court. It has been suggested that if the party can find somewhere else to live, and having had regard to the threats of violence, the court would be correct to order an ouster order requiring this party to leave the premises.[87] In *Chan Chun Hon v Chan Lam Lai Bing Shirley*, the court noted that "adequate arrangements have been made for [the wife] to live in a good hotel, at the husband's expense, with access to the daughter. Complaint is made of such behaviour in the home, at the husband's medical clinic and at the Royal Hong Kong Jockey Club." The Court of Appeal approved the lower court's judgment in granting an ouster order against the wife.[88]

The need of any specified minor

The need of any minor is a factor which the court will have to give regard to when considering granting an ouster/entry order; however, the welfare principle in which the interest of the child is the first and paramount consideration will have no application when the court has to consider the exercise of the discretion in granting the ouster/entry order. Lord Hailsham of St. Marylebone L.C. in *Richards v Richards* wrote in his judgment that,

---

86.   *Wiseman v Simpson* [1988] 1 FLR 490.

87.   *Baggott v Baggott* [1986] 1 FLR 377.

88.   *Chan Chun Hon v Chan Lam Lai Bing Shirley* [1994] 3 HKC 196.

> I do not believe that an application for ouster is "a proceeding" in which "the legal custody or upbringing of a minor is in question", although of course "the needs of the children" are expressly required by s 1 of the 1967 Act to be taken into account in an application under that section, and may of course prevail in any given case where it is "just and reasonable" that they should. In the Matrimonial Homes Act 1967, the "needs of the children" are an important and specified, but not in every case first or paramount, consideration to be applied. In the Guardianship of Minors Act 1971, the "welfare" of the children is the "first and paramount" consideration. In my view, the Guardianship of Minors Act criterion is to be applied only in the proceedings of the type specified in the section, i.e., proceedings in which custody, upbringing, or the proprietary jurisdiction implied by section 1(b) fall to be decided as a matter directly in issue, and not in cases to which s 1(3) of the Matrimonial Homes Act 1967 is to be applied so as to produce a just and reasonable result, even though in these cases the interests of the children are directly or indirectly affected, when the various considerations must be balanced in the light of the particular facts.[89]

Therefore, none of the factors which the court has to give regard to carries more weight than the other, unless required by the circumstances of the case. In *Chan Chun Hon v Chan Lam Lai Bing Shirley*, the court took into account the mother's conduct towards the child of the marriage together with other factors, and on that basis, granted the exclusion order against the mother. The Hong Kong Court of Appeal considered the needs of the child and agreed that "the effect on the welfare of the child which must loom large in these considerations".[90]

If it is in the interest of the child to be with the custodial parent, even if the other has no other readily available accommodation, the court may grant an exclusion order against the other party. In a case where a girl of twelve years old from a former marriage made an allegation of indecency against her by the respondent while the natural mother was in hospital, the mother removed the girl and her half brother to live in overcrowded conditions. On the application for ouster/entry order against the respondent, the Court of Appeal found that:

> this involved considering the conduct of the parties, their needs and financial resources, the needs of the children, and all the circumstances of the case. The relationship had been a stormy one owing to the temperaments

---

89. *Richards v Richards* [1983] 2 All ER 807, pp. 815–816.
90. *Ibid*, p. 199.

of both parties so little weight could be attached to conduct. Both parties were in receipt of State benefits. The applicant needed a home for herself and the children whereas the respondent had only himself to provide for. The needs of the children indicated that they should be together in suitable accommodation and that the girl should be reunited with the applicant. Having regard to all the circumstances, including the attitude of the local authority, the needs of the children to be re-established in the family home carried the greatest weight. Therefore an exclusion order would be made against the respondent.[91]

All the circumstances of the case

The court always has to examine the matter from all respects, and no one factor should necessarily carry more weight than the other. The court has also to consider any other situation of which the circumstances should be taken into account. In *Baggott v Baggott*, the court took into account in granting an ouster that the respondent was able to live somewhere else; on appeal, it was concluded that the court can exercise a wide statutory discretion in considering "all the circumstances of the case" having regard to the threats of violence to make an ouster order. However, the ability to find alternative accommodation is not the major consideration in making an ouster order. In another case, the Court of Appeal in Hong Kong emphasized that one should look at the circumstances of each particular case. On hearing the appeal, the Court of Appeal could not agree with the trial judge and concluded that the judge

> concentrated only on the husband's ability to pay for other accommodation and the length of time he had already stayed. It is possible he had in mind as well that the husband would eventually be excluded. This is, of course, a proper factor for consideration: *Bassett* default at p 82H. But it was, in our view, an error of principle to take so narrow a view of the situation and one which also led the judge to a plainly wrong conclusion. What was fair, just and reasonable in the circumstances was the ensuring of reasonable peace and quiet in the flat during normal sleeping hours until such time as a permanent decision could be made. That situation could readily have been obtained, without the drastic act of excluding the husband, by means of appropriate undertakings which, both parties having declined an opportunity which may have enabled a permanent

---

91.   *Lee v Lee* [1984] FLR 243.

> solution to have been found within a few days of our decision, we thought proper to obtain from him then.[92]

Relatives: proprietary rights in the common residence

When the court exercises the discretion to make an ouster/entry order against a relative who has proprietary rights over the residence, the court has to be extremely careful and give regard to the two factors specified in section 3A of the DCRVO. Since this is a relatively new provision in the ordinance, the Hong Kong courts have yet to give an interpretation to the provision. However, in some earlier cases in England, it has been held that where the parties are in a cohabitation relationship, each has an equal legal right to occupy the property as the joint tenants of the council house, but neither has a right to occupy the property to the exclusion of the other.[93] It was held by Wall J, that

> the powers of the court to exclude a person from property in which he had a proprietary interest should be exercised with extreme caution and only where the court was satisfied that if the jurisdiction was not exercised the child was likely to suffer significant harm; and the court must look to all the circumstances of the case and make finding of fact upon which the assessment of future harm could be made. Although there was jurisdiction to make such an exclusion order without limitation of time, the court could not by those means vary a proprietary interest and must in every case consider whether an indefinite order was required to protect the child from harm and to achieve a result which was just.[94]

Definition of "matrimonial home"

Section 2(1) defines "matrimonial home" to include a home in which the parties to a marriage ordinarily reside together, whether or not it is occupied at the same time by other persons. The court tends to adopt a flexible approach for the protection of victims. In *Kinzler v Kinzler*,[95] the Court of Appeal issued a ruling regarding the occupancy of a hotel with 22 rooms, owned by two

---

92. *Lee Cheng Mei Ying v Lee Chow Hung* [1991] 1 HKC 172, at 176.

93. *Ainsbury v Millington* [1986] 1 FLR 331.

94. *C v K* (Ouster Order: Non-Parent) [1996] 3 FCR 488.

95. *Kinzler v Kinzler* [1985] Fam. Law 26.

couples in equal shares, with each couple occupying self-contained accommodation and sharing the only kitchen for the hotel. The lower court granted an ouster order against the husband in question from the hotel, including the establishment's public areas. The reason given was that the wife and the son "had to be able to access parts of the hotel outside their self-contained accommodation in order to carry out functions ordinarily associated with being at home such as cooking, bathing, . . ." On appeal, the husband argued that the court had no jurisdiction to exclude him from the public area of the hotel. The court dismissed his appeal and concluded that "whilst it was a question of fact and degree the whole hotel, in the instant case, was the matrimonial home since there was only one entrance and one kitchen and a child of the family slept in the private part."

In another case, while the wife was away in Bangkok, the husband moved away and terminated the lease of the matrimonial home where the parties had agreed to remain until the separation agreement was reached. The Court of Appeal decided that the new premises where the husband had moved to would become the "matrimonial home". The Court of Appeal held that the wife's right to reside in the matrimonial home could not be defeated simply by the husband's terminating of the lease on the premises in which the parties were residing and moving to another flat. In the light of the sparse evidence of the respondent's ability to afford the petitioner's room and other charges at a hotel, and the fact that suitable accommodation in the form of a service flat was available at much lesser cost, the judge was not justified in ordering that the respondent be responsible for those charges until further order.[96]

In *Chan Chun Hon v Chan Lam Lai Bing Shirley*, the court accepted a premises as falling within the definition of "matrimonial home" where the wife had only resided there for about one month and even though neither party had any propriety rights nor interest in the premises. In this case, the wife had left the husband for several years for certain reasons, and on her return, the husband and daughter were living with his parents and brother. She stayed at this flat for just one month, and the Court of Appeal approved the lower court's decision to grant an ouster order against the wife.

---

96.   *Earl of Cromer v Countess of Cromer* [1992] 2 HKC 54.

Authorization of arrest

On granting a non-molestation order or an ouster/entry order, if the court finds that actual bodily harm has been caused to the applicant or that the court "reasonably believes that the actual bodily harm will be caused", it can order to attach an authorization of arrest to the injunction order.[97] No definition is provided in the DCRVO on the meaning of "actual bodily harm"; but this would include any hurt or injury calculated to interfere with the health or comfort of the victim,[98] and it can include psychiatric injury but not mere emotions, such as fear, distress or panic.[99]

If an authorization of arrest is expressly attached to an injunction, a police officer may arrest the respondent upon his/her breach of the order without warrant.[100] The respondent shall be brought to the court before the expiry of the day after the day of his/her arrest, and he/she shall not be released before he/she is brought before the court except on the direction of the court.[101]

Duration of an ouster/entry or authorization of arrest order

An ouster/entry order shall have effect for no more than 24 months.[102] An authorization of arrest shall have effect for no more than 24 months, and would expire at the end of the period for which the injunction is granted.[103] These orders may be extended so that the total period of the particular order does not exceed 24 months.[104]

Variation and suspension of existing custody or access order

When an ouster order is granted and if there is a custody or access order in force concerning a minor in favour of the respondent, the court may vary or

---

97.   Sections 5(1) and 5(1A) DCRVO.
98.   *R v Donovan* [1934] 2 KB 498.
99.   *R v Chan-Fook* 99 Cr App 147 CA.
100. Section 5(2) DCRVO.
101. Section 5(3) DCRVO.
102. Section 6(1) DCRVO.
103. Section 6(2) DCRVO.
104. Sections 7(1)(a) and (b) DCRVO.

suspend the court order for giving effect to the injunction. However, when considering such variation/suspension of the custody/access order, the court shall have regard to the welfare of the minor as its first and paramount consideration, and give due consideration to the wishes of the minor as well as any material information including any social welfare report. The duration of the variation/suspension shall not exceed the expiry of the validity period of the injunction.[105]

Batterer Intervention Programme (BIP)

On granting the injunction under sections 3, 3A or 3B, the court may include a provision requiring the respondent to participate in any programme to change the attitude and behaviour that led to the granting of the injunction.[106]

Breach of an injunction order

A breach of an injunction order may be dealt with by the court as contempt of court, which may be punishable by a fine or prison sentence.[107]

Victim support

The Law Society of Hong Kong in its report (p. 102) recommended introducing victim support programmes by adopting the English model that employs Independent Domestic Violence Advisors (IDVA).[108] IDVAs have proved to be cost-effective in improving the implementation of the policy initiatives introduced by the British government.

On 30 March 2010, the director of the Social Welfare Department said, "The government is committed to combating domestic violence and has been continuously providing new resources to enhance the preventive, supportive and follow-up services for victims of domestic violence and families in need." It was announced that the SWD will allocate about HK$5 million to the Po Leung Kuk to operate a "Victim Support Programme for Victims of Family

---

105.   Section 7A DCRVO.
106.   Sections 3(1A), 3A(5) or 3B(3) DCRVO.
107.   *H v O* (Contempt of Court: Sentencing).
108.   The Law Society Report on Domestic Violence Ordinance p.102.

Violence". The purpose of the programme is to enhance the support services for victims of domestic violence, particular those undergoing judicial proceedings. The director of the SWD also claimed that "in 2010–11, the total provision earmarked for various services in relation to family and child welfare, including those for victims of domestic violence and families in need, is about $1.792 billion, representing an increase of 4.5% against 2009–10." It stated that the programme aimed to "strengthen protection, alleviate [victims'] fear and feelings of helplessness, and help them return to normal life as early as possible". The following services have commenced in June 2010:

(1) Provision of information: this covers information about civil and criminal proceedings, especially on divorce proceedings, custody issues, and how to apply for injunction orders; and information on community resources such as application for legal aid, child care support, housing support, medical services and psychological treatment.

(2) Provision of support: this covers assistance for victims going to the police station in giving statements, and for those going to the court as witnesses in subsequent civil and/or criminal proceedings; assisting victims to apply for and receive different available community services such as legal service, medical assessment or treatment, and schooling for children; providing necessary temporary child support during legal proceedings, guidance and training to victims on basic skills in personal care, care of family members and household management, as well as providing the necessary emotional support.

(3) Training and development of volunteers: this aims to recruit, develop and mobilize volunteers who may be former service users of the programme.

Although there are no provisions in Hong Kong legislation providing support programmes for victims of domestic violence, the government has shown willingness to take a firm stance in combating domestic violence (Social Welfare Department, 2004). There are many local support programmes for victims of domestic violence, to name but a few: Harmony House's "Third Path Man's Services", and the Family Crisis Support Centre. Similar programmes are available to victims of domestic violence in other jurisdictions.

In England and Wales, the government's stance on providing better-coordinated multidisciplinary support for victims of family violence has been put into clear wording in its statutes. Section 48 of the Domestic Violence, Crime and Victims Act 2004, i.e., the DVCVA, provides that there should be a Commissioner for Victims and Witnesses.[109] One of the services which provides support to victims of domestic violence in the UK is called the Independent Domestic Violence Advisor (IDVA). IDVA services consist of a more structured process of information sharing between agencies. There is recognition of the need for victims to have access to a dedicated, independent source of advice and assistance to help them recognize if they are at risk, make decisions about their future and access the range of services they may need (T. Lowe, 2009). IDVAs are trained support workers who provide assistance and advice in these areas. They work closely with criminal justice and statutory partners, and may be based in many different settings. There has been considerable expansion of IDVA services in recent years, as they are linked to other government initiatives such as Specialist Domestic Violence Courts (SDVCs) and Multi-Agency Risk Assessment Conferences (Robinson, 2009).

Studies have been conducted to evaluate the effect of support provided by IDVAs, and the outcome has been satisfactory (Lowe, 2009). There is a consensus among front-line practitioners of support programmes in the UK that the pilot provision of IDVA services has been successfully implemented. It is expected that such pilot provision has provided empirical evidence to support a wider roll-out of a dedicated, victim-focused IDVA provision in the near future.

New Zealand has made advanced progress in terms of legislation which provides protection to victims of domestic violence. In the Domestic Violence Act 1995, the Act includes as its object, among other things, to provide appropriate programmes for persons who are victims of domestic violence.[110] Furthermore, the 1995 Act provides that where the court makes a protection order, "the applicant may request a Registrar to authorize the provision of a programme to all or any of the following person: (a) the applicant; (b) a child of the applicant's family; (c) a specified person", and "where a request is made . . . the Registrar must arrange for the matter to be referred to a programme provider without delay."[111]

The New Zealand Family Court has in place the Free Protection Order Support Programmes. If one is protected by a protection order made under the

---

109.   Section 48, Chapter 3, Domestic Violence, Crime and Victims Act 2004 (DVCVA 2004).
110.   Section 5, Domestic Violence Act 1995 (NZ).
111.   Subsections 29(1), (2) and (3), Domestic Violence Act 1995 (NZ).

1995 Act, he/she can attend a free support programme to help deal with his/her situation (Family Court of New Zealand, 2009). These support programmes are run by practitioners who are well-informed about family violence and its effects, and who have been approved by the Ministry of Justice. In addition, similar to the recent trend in the UK of providing IDVA services to victims, the support programmes under the New Zealand Family Court system are operated by practitioners who are sensitive to people's different experiences based on age, gender, culture, sexual orientation or disability.

The case in Australia is similar to that in Hong Kong. There is no expressed statutory provision about how support should be provided to victims or their family; however, there are many practical support services in place for such victims.[112] For example, NGOs in Australia provide services including:

(a)   the facilitation and coordination of high-security domestic violence refuge and shelter placements across the state;

(b)   crisis counselling and the assessment and development of safety plans which address the immediate and contingent safety needs of women and their children;

(c)   liaison with related services including regional domestic violence services, the police, the Department of Communities (child protection), health services, hospitals, legal services, migrant and indigenous agencies;

(d)   the coordination of emergency evacuations via taxis, buses, trains and extending to chartering flights from remote areas to take women and children to safety;

(e)   the provision of safe emergency accommodation where refuges are not immediately available;

(f)   the provision of funds for food, baby provisions, fuel and arrangements for medical treatment where required; and

(g)   the coordination of services for women in emergency accommodation en route to refuge placement to ensure that they are supported and given appropriate practical assistance.

Canada has integrated most forms of domestic violence into its criminal justice system; at the same time, the Canadian government has in place many

---

112.   DV Connection: http://www.dvconnect.org/about/dvconnect.asp#Services.

kinds of support to victims other than charging perpetrators. Measures have been put in place to prevent victims from being revictimized by the system.

For example, in Ontario, there are women's shelters and victim support groups which offer victims a whole range of services (The Law Society of Hong Kong, 2005):

(a)   emergency shelters for women and children;

(b)   support programmes to help abused women prepare for life after leaving the shelters;

(c)   helplines providing referrals to services;

(d)   victims can register to receive automatic notification regarding any change in the status of provisionally sentenced perpetrators;

(e)   Victim/Witness Assistance Programmes to help them understand and participate in the criminal justice system;

(f)   Victim Crisis Assistance and Referral Services to provide crisis intervention to victims of crime and disaster through referrals from police; and

(g)   The Partner Assault Response Programme which is an integral part of the Domestic Violence Court Programme, providing 16 weeks of counselling and education for abusers.

Victim support services can be hugely effective, in particular for those who have few close friends or relatives to help them in times of difficulties. The scope of services proposed in the victim support programme in Hong Kong can bring about much help and relief to those really in need. Much more support for this programme is required as it is still in the incipient stage, and is likely to meet many challenges as it develops and expands. But most encouragingly, all signs suggest that the fight against domestic violence is proceeding in the right direction.

Conclusion

The civil law reform against domestic violence has taken over four years to mature to its present form. At the time of the reform, all stakeholders were advocating a better piece of legislation. Although the present DCRVO may not be the fully satisfactory statute hoped for by stakeholders, it has indisputably taken a big step forward. Civil redress is certainly a better alternative to criminalization of domestic violence from the standpoint of certain victims. The recent English experience of the drop in applications for non-molestation orders after the criminalization of domestic acts of violence has yet to be confirmed and consolidated. However, the low utilization rate of civil redress as discovered by Chan et al. (2005) in the consultants' report appears to have remained unchanged despite the reform. There is all the more reason to review the reasons for this phenomenon now, especially when stakeholders concur that the use of civil redress is a better way to address domestic violence. Perhaps some of the reasons set out in paragraph 4.61 of the consultants' report (Chan et al., 2005) may still be valid. These include queries regarding the effectiveness of the injunction order and the difficulty in obtaining legal aid assistance. Further work is waiting to be done, such as further training and education for professionals as well as for victims, if a holistic approach to resolving the problem of domestic violence is to be adopted.

A common remark on the success of any system nowadays makes reference to a computer system: the hardware has been installed, but the overall performance of the system yet depends on the readiness of the software. This is a fitting analogy for the current legal environment concerning domestic violence. Progress in legislation has opened up new possibilities and horizons for services and interventions, but it remains to be seen whether multidisciplinary expertise will be able to make use of this framework to its fullest extent.

References

Chan, K. L., Chiu, M. C., & Chiu, L. S. (2005). *Peace at Home: Report on the Review of the Social and Legal Measures in the Prevention and Intervention of Domestic Violence in Hong Kong*. Retrieved from Legislative Council, Hong Kong website: http://www.legco.gov.hk/yr04-05/english/panels/ws/ws_fvi/papers/ws_ fvi0705cb2-2158-3e.pdf

Family Court of New Zealand. (2009). Domestic violence—free protection order support programmes. Retrieved from Family Court of New Zealand website: http://www.justice.govt.nz/courts/family-court/publications/pamphlets/ domestic-violence-free-protection-order-support-programmes

Fong, L. (November, 2009). *South China Morning Post*.

Gibb, F., & Ford, R. (April, 2008). Women at risk of assault failed by new law, say judges. *The Times*.

Hanson, D., MP. (April, 2008). The Domestic Violence, Crime and Victims Act 2004 is the biggest overhaul of such legislation for 30 years. *The Times*.

Health, Welfare and Food Bureau. (October 2005). LC Paper for Discussion on 3 November 2005.

Health, Welfare and Food Bureau. (2006). *The Administration's Review on Domestic Violence Ordinance—Preliminary Proposed Amendments* (LC Paper No. CB(2)2132/05-06(01)). Retrieved from Legislative Council, Hong Kong website: http://www.legco.gov.hk/yr05-06/english/panels/ws/ws_fvi/papers/ws_fvicb2-2132-1e.pdf

Health, Welfare and Food Bureau. (2007). *Legislative Council Brief: Domestic Violence (Amendment) Bill 2007* (File Ref No. HWF/CR 1/3281/01). Retrieved from Legislative Council, Hong Kong website: http://sc.legco.gov.hk/sc/library.legco.gov.hk/search/.b1052154/.b1052154/1,1,1,B/l962~b1052154&FF=&1,0,,0,0

Health, Welfare and Food Bureau. (December 2006). LC Paper for Discussion on 8 January 2007.

Hester, M., Westmarland, N., Pearce, J., & Williamson, E. (2008). *Early Evaluation of the Domestic Violence, Crime and Victims Act 2004*. Retrieved from Ministry of Justice, England website: http://www.justice.gov.uk/publications/docs/domestic-violence-report-2004.pdf

Hong Kong Law Reform Commission. (2005). *Report on Child Custody and Access*. Hong Kong: Hong Kong Law Reform Commission.

Hong Kong Law Reform Commission. (2000). *Report on Stalking*. Hong Kong: Hong Kong Law Reform Commission.

Labour and Welfare Bureau. (2009). *Legislative Council Brief: Domestic Violence (Amendment) Bill 2009* (File Ref. No. LW/CR 1/3281/01). Retrieved from Legislative Council, Hong Kong website: http://www.legco.gov.hk/yr08-09/english/bills/brief/b16_brf.pdf

Lau, M., & Wong, A. (January, 2006). Crime push over domestic violence. *The Standard*.

Li, P. (2006). *Sentencing in Cases of Domestic Violence*. Retrieved from Hong Kong Lawyer website: http://www.hk-lawyer.com/InnerPages_features/0/1765/2006/2

Lowe, N., Tyre, C., Cobb, S., Angela, N., Nield, A., & Maidment, S. (1991). *Clarke, Hall and Morrison on Children*. London, England: Butterworths Law.

Lowe, T. (2009). *Integrating the Independent Domestic Violence Advisor and Flying Start: A Process and Outcome Evaluation*. Retrieved from Universities' Police Science Institute, Cardiff University website: http://www.upsi.org.uk/resources/IDVA.pdf

Poon, H. L. H. (2007). *Letter to the Bills Committee on Domestic Violence (Amendment) Bill*. Hong Kong: Legislative Council.

Robinson, A. L. (2009). Independent domestic violence advisors: a process evaluation. Retrieved from School of Social Sciences, Cardiff University website: http://www.cardiff.ac.uk/socsi/resources/idvareport.pdf

Social Welfare Department. (December 2004). No tolerance of domestic violence. Retrieved from Social Welfare Department, Hong Kong website: http://www.swd.gov.hk/en/index/site_pubpress/page_press/sub_fullpress/topic_9/

Social Welfare Department. (2009). *Statistics on Child Abuse, Battered Spouse and Sexual Violence Cases*. Retrieved from Social Welfare Department, Hong Kong website: http://www.swd.gov.hk/vs/english/stat.html

Soni, B. (2007). *Domestic Violence and Family Law: A New Era*. Retrieved from Family Law Week website: http://www.familylawweek.co.uk/site.aspx?i=ed725

The Law Society of Hong Kong. (2005). *Report on Domestic Violence Ordinance*. Hong Kong: The Law Society of Hong Kong.

Verkaik, R., & Law Editor in *The Independent*. (2008). Domestic laws fail to increase convictions. *The Independent*.

7
Best Interests of the Child

Justification and Limitation of Corporal Punishment by Parents Before the Hong Kong Courts

Anne Shann-Yue Cheung

Chapter summary

1. There is an urgent need to ban corporal punishment by parents in Hong Kong.

2. Corporal punishment at home is legally condoned and socially accepted in Hong Kong society. An overwhelming majority of parents do not see physical punishment as remotely related to abuse, but as part of their duty of acting in accordance with the cultural norm. Only when the use of force becomes excessive and when tragedy happens, the law then intervenes.

3. This explains partly why parent defendants often resort to using their motivation or best intention as a mitigating factor in their defence before courts. Given the widely shared paternalistic sentiment in Hong Kong society that parents are in the best position to act in the interests of their children, a review of court judgment sadly reveals that the court has showed a distinct sympathy toward parents' benevolent intentions, rather than a desire to protect children's interests or welfare.

4. This chapter argues that the best interests of the child, rather than the motivations of parents or caretakers, should be the focus in judicial reasoning.

5. It is time for statutory intervention to protect children's interests and to prevent further tragedies from happening in Hong Kong society.

Introduction

The saying, "I know what is best for you", is probably a familiar echo to many of us from our childhood days. To promote a happy childhood, the United Nations Declaration of the Rights of the Child stipulated in 1989 that "the best interests of the child shall be the paramount consideration" in providing "special protection . . . opportunities and facilities, by law and by other means" to a child "to enable him to develop physically, mentally, morally, spiritually and socially in a healthy and normal manner and in conditions of freedom and dignity" (United Nations, 2010). The doctrine of best interests is now enshrined in article 3(1) of the United Nations Convention on the Rights of the Child, which states clearly that the best interests of the child shall be a primary consideration in all actions concerning children, whether undertaken by public or private institutions, including courts and legislative bodies.

Yet this doctrine begs the very questions of how to decide and who should decide what the best interests for a child should be. The power play between parental decision, children's wishes and state intervention has been the subject of a universal and perennial discourse. This problem is exemplified in the Hong Kong context of child rearing and discipline, where parents' use of corporal punishment has been legally condoned to the extent that it is not expressly prohibited by the law. Only when the use of force becomes excessive, resulting in injury or even death does the law intervene, which is often too late.

This legal stance is, to a large extent, a reflection of the widely shared paternalistic sentiment in Hong Kong society that parents are in the best position to act and to decide for the interests of their children. An overwhelming majority of parents do not see physical punishment as remotely related to abuse, but as part of their duty of acting in accordance with the cultural tradition of responsible parenting. To examine the ramifications of such views, this chapter studies court decisions relating to corporal punishment of children between 1997 and 2007.[1] There are in total four recorded decisions from the District Court and High Court. Three other cases reported in the media and

---

1. This study on children's interest is part of a larger project on studying court decisions relating to domestic violence in Hong Kong during the decade from 1997 to 2007. The project is funded by The University of Hong Kong CRCG Small Project Funding and the Outstanding Young Researcher Award. The author is grateful for the research assistance of Eric Chiyeung Ip and Michael Mankit Cheung.

in an academic journal will also be analysed in this chapter. Since corporal punishment is not defined in Hong Kong law, this chapter has adopted the broad definition of corporal punishment at home to be any form of physical punishment inflicted by parents (including anyone acting in loco parentis) to discipline a child. The aims of this study are to investigate (1) how the Hong Kong courts have been dealing with cases of serious injury or death in the course of parents punishing or disciplining their children; (2) how relevant parents' motivation has been for judges in deciding the term of sentencing; and (3) whether children's interests or welfare has been taken into account in judicial reasoning. A review of the court decisions sadly reveals that the court has shown a distinct sympathy towards parents' benevolent intentions, rather than a desire to protect children's interests or welfare. What has preoccupied the judicial mind is why parents are punishing their children. As long as the courts are persuaded that parents are motivated by goodwill, they tend to be lenient in sentencing. The pain and suffering that children have to put up with are often blithely glossed over in court reasoning and decisions. This judicial attitude is hardly helpful for the protection of children's interests. Instead of relying on the interpretation and discretion of judges to protect children's welfare, a long-term solution is to ban corporal punishment by parents in Hong Kong.

The law: the liberty to punish one's child

Though there is no universal definition on child abuse, it is generally accepted that "hitting, shaking, throwing, poisoning, burning or scalding, drowning, suffocating or otherwise causing physical harm to a child" constitute physical abuse (Bainham, 2005, p. 496). The particular dilemma confronting one in the disciplining of a child is whether corporal punishment is also a form of physical abuse, when hitting is commonly involved. When we consider the definition of corporal punishment by Donnelly and Straus (2005) to be "the use of physical force with the intention of causing a child to experience pain, but not injury, for the purpose of correction or control of the child's behaviour" (p. 14), the line between corporal punishment and abusive behaviour seems to rest on whether the form of physical chastisement is mild enough only to cause pain but not injury, and is carried out for the benefit of the child. Yet, the boundary drawn is, as admitted by Donnelly and Straus, ambiguous and difficult to apply in reality. Further, different scholars have warned us that corporal punishment, which is prone to escalation, has a tendency to slip into the zone of abuse (McGillivray, 2004), and much abuse of children is the result of corporal punishment gone awfully wrong (Freeman, 1983, p. 113). Much literature has also been written on the harm and long-term negative effects of corporal punishment on the growth of children (Pollard, 2003). Hence, different countries have adopted various approaches to address the need and obligation of disciplining children, but doing so without causing them harm. It ranges from a complete ban on corporal punishment to regulation of it.

Supporters for a total ban of corporal punishment on children include the United Nations. Article 19 of the United Nations Convention on the Rights of Children stipulates that States Parties should take all appropriate legislative, administrative, social and educational measures to protect children from all forms of physical injury or abuse while in the care of their parents or legal guardians. Freeman (2007, p. 43) has pointed out that corporal punishment is clearly incompatible with article 19 and all forms of parental physical punishment should be outlawed. His stance is consistent with that of the United Nations Committee on the Rights of the Child (2006), which requires the prohibition of all forms of violence against children, including corporal punishment at home or family settings. Furthermore, in 2006, the Secretary-General of the United Nations set the year 2009 as the target deadline for all countries to ban all forms of corporal punishment against children (United Nations, 2006). However, as at November 2009, only 25 countries had completely banned corporal punishment at home (End Corporal Punishment, 2010). In contrast, over 70 countries have opted for the model of allowing "reasonable" or "moderate" chastisement of children (Pinheiro, 2006). They have attempted to draw a line between physical abuse and corporal punishment by invoking the concepts of reasonable chastisement (the approach in England and Wales); reasonable force (the approach in Canada); or justifiable assault (the approach in Scotland). This second approach is rife with controversies in terms of interpretation and implementation (Fortin, 2003), but nothing compares with the other extreme end of the spectrum, which essentially allows parents to control and discipline their children as they think fit. Regrettably, the last approach is the current position of the Hong Kong ruling regime.

Although Hong Kong has been a signatory to the United Nations Convention on the Rights of the Child since 1994, it has no explicit law prohibiting corporal punishment by parents. In fact, corporal punishment at home is not defined anywhere in the law. The current laws in Hong Kong only prohibit teachers from administering corporal punishment to pupils,[2] and prohibit anyone, including parents, from administering corporal punishment to a child at any child care centre.[3] While corporal punishment is no longer a sentencing option[4] or a disciplinary measure in penal institutions,[5] corporal punishment by parents remains perfectly lawful and is widely practised.

The prevalence of corporal punishment at home in Hong Kong

In a study carried out by Chan in 2008, it was found that out of 5,841 children aged 9 to 18, 58% had been given corporal punishment by their parents. When analysed by age groups, it was found that an increasingly higher proportion of children experienced corporal punishment when they were younger. Within the age group of 9 to 11 years, 36.7% had been given corporal punishment, while in the 18 years or above group, 6.8% had experienced such. In another study by Chan (2005) conducted in 2004, it was revealed that 44% of the 5,049 adult respondents in Hong Kong admitted they had given corporal punishment to their children. Chan further pointed out that 10% of the adult respondents confessed that they had caused severe injury by means such as hitting with fists or burning. In Chan's study, corporal punishment included spanking on the bottom with bare hand; hitting on the bottom with implement like a belt, hairbrush, a stick or some other hard object; slapping on the hand, arm or leg; pinching or shaking, while physical maltreatment included slapping on the face or head or ears; hitting on some other part of the body besides the bottom with implement

---

2. Since 1992, this has been under Regulation 58 of the Education Regulations (Cap. 279A), Laws of Hong Kong.

3. Since 1976, this has been under Regulation 15 and Regulation 45R of the Child Care Services Regulations (Cap. 243A), Laws of Hong Kong.

4. Since 2003, this has been under section 15 of the Juvenile Offenders Ordinance (Cap. 226), Laws of Hong Kong.

5. For example, since 1997, corporal punishment has not been included in the list of permitted disciplinary measures under Rule 63 of the Prison Rules (Cap. 234A), Laws of Hong Kong. Rule 37 of the Probation of Offender Rules (Cap. 298A, Laws of Hong Kong) states that "(2) (a) No corporal punishment of any kind shall be inflicted on a probationer in an approved institution. (b) For the purpose of this rule the term "corporal punishment" includes striking, cuffing or shaking or the intentional infliction of any form of physical pain as a means of punishment.

like a belt, hairbrush, a stick or some other hard object; throwing or knocking down a child; hitting with a fist or kicking a child (Chan, 2005, p. 118). The statistics not only reveal the widespread practice of corporal punishment in Hong Kong, but also the high-risk abusive nature of corporal punishment.

A brief review of other studies on corporal punishment in Hong Kong in earlier periods further supports that corporal punishment has been commonly and consistently practised, and widely accepted in the local community for decades. A 1983 study showed that 81% of respondents spanked their children more than once a week and 51% considered that as the most effective mode of punishment (Lieh-Mak, Chung, & Liu, 1983). In 1988, a study on 100 university students showed that 95% of the respondents had experienced corporal punishment at home. And one-third of the respondents approved of the spanking of children less than three years old (Samuda, 1988). In another public opinion survey in 1996, it was reported that 79% of adults believed parents had the right to use corporal punishment on their children and 45% considered that to be an effective means of discipline (Lau & Liu, 1999). In sum, Hong Kong parents have the belief that they have the right to punish their children physically.

Yet the boundary between corporal punishment and physical abuse may be easily crossed. Statistics on child abuse showed that out of 944 reported cases to the Social Welfare Department in 2007, 47% were related to physical abuse (Hong Kong SAR Government Secretariat [HKSARGS], 2008). During the same period, 1,550 cases of child abuse were reported to the police, of which 677 (44%) were related to physical abuse including murder and manslaughter (HKSARGS, 2008). In the first six months of 2007, 202 defendants were prosecuted, 168 (83%) were convicted, and 85 (51%) of the defendants were given probation. But Chan's first household study on domestic violence in 2005 estimated that only 1% of child abuse cases were known to police, health or social services.

Since the law does not prohibit corporal punishment by parents, and has failed to clarify what constitutes legitimate corporal punishment, children are only protected from physical punishment at the hands of their parents or caretakers if the violence reaches the level of wounding, assault, manslaughter or murder. The legislation commonly invoked in this type of cases is the Offences Against the Person Ordinance (OAPO, Cap. 212, Laws of Hong Kong). Under section 27(1) of the OAPO, it is unlawful for a person aged 16 or above, including a parent, who has the custody, charge or care of a child or young person under that age, to wilfully assault, ill-treat, neglect, abandon or expose such child or young person in a manner likely to cause unnecessary suffering or injury to his/her health. The maximum penalty is ten years' imprisonment. Under section 39 and section 40 of the same ordinance, a person may be convicted of assault occasioning actual bodily harm or common assault respectively, and this is subject to a maximum penalty of three years' imprisonment.

Judicial attitudes: in the name of best intentions

Between 1997 and 2007, there were 15 reported court decisions on physical child abuse, out of which, four involved corporal punishment, and three ended in death. Sentences handed out by the courts ranged from two to nine years of imprisonment in those three cases. In reading the judgments, it is not hard to detect that the concerns of the parents were child rearing and discipline; and in those cases, obedience to parents was "enforced with brutality" (Freeman, 1983, p. 13). What is even more worrying is that the courts never mentioned any notion or concept of children's interests, let alone the best interests of the child, in the reasoning of their decisions. The dominant theme was the motive and intention of the parents. Even when children died at the hands of their parents due to extreme forms of punishment, as long as the courts were convinced that the defendant parents were motivated by benevolent intentions which had gone awry, the courts tended to view the cases to be incidents of folly or tragedy. Thus, parents were only held partly accountable for their wrongs.

Case 1. HKSAR v Takahashi Koyo and Chu Wing Hon

This is exemplified in the case of *HKSAR v Takahashi Koyo and Chu Wing Hon* (unreported, HCCC 113/2006, 18 October 2006), concerning a family with two young boys. The elder boy was a ten year old who died of suffocation after his parents chose to discipline him for misbehaving by locking him in a suitcase for nearly two hours. The deceased allegedly was hyperactive, had lied repeatedly to his parents and had refused to do his homework. The father left home shortly after his son was forced to go inside the suitcase. While both defendant parents pleaded guilty to manslaughter, the father was sentenced to eighteen months of imprisonment and the mother to two years by the Court.

Defence counsel argued that the parents lacked malice in relation to the death of their son. In the words of the defence counsel, while the form of punishment was "misguided in manner", "the motive of the conduct was to discipline" (*Ibid.*, p. 2). To the above defence, the Court replied that it was "well made" and the force of such argument was to be "appreciated" (*Ibid.*). In the three-page judgment, the judge emphasized no less than four times that the death was "unintended" by the parents. In explaining the term of sentence, the judge even stressed that the mother was receiving a harsher punishment not because "her intentional wrong was greater than her husband", but for the extent of her negligence.

This reasoning is hardly convincing. First, this almost amounts to saying that it was largely a case of reckless negligence in not letting the victim child out of the suitcase in time, whereas the method of punishment was never condemned. Second, the father defendant, in leaving home and not caring for the welfare of his son who was locked in the suitcase, was given a lighter sentence. Essentially, this shifted the burden of blame onto the mother based on the mere fact that she was the one who continued to stay at home. In the facts given, the father should be equally, if not more, culpable than the mother defendant both in terms of negligence and the intentional wrong of forcing the child to go into the suitcase. It is deeply ironic for the Court to remark that a lighter sentence on the father was appropriate so that he could return to his younger son quicker in circumstances where a father's "important support and sense of security [offered] to the young child" (*Ibid.*, p. 3) were essential. Underlying this reasoning is the myth that a child should stay with his biological parent, regardless of whether the parent is suitable or not for parenting, and whether it is in the best interests of the child to be taken care of by his father who had caused the death of his other sibling.

Case 2. *HKSAR v Lam Lui Yin and Yim Ching-ting*

In another case, *HKSAR v Lam Lui Yin and Yim Ching-ting* (transcript of the reasons for verdict, unreported, DCCC850/2005, 6 April 2005), we notice once again that the focus of the Court was on the motive of the parents and the difficulty faced by the parents in enforcing discipline and obedience of a child, sidelining the interests and welfare of the victim child.

The defendant parents were charged under section 27 of the OAPO for wilfully ill-treating and neglecting a child in a manner likely to cause him unnecessary suffering or injury to his health. The deceased child was two years and four months old, one of a triplet, who was born prematurely with various health problems. He died with 32 bruises and 30 abrasions. The cause of death was severe head injuries, likely to be the result of several accidental falls. The defendant parents were sentenced to two years of imprisonment.

The deceased child had been suffering from congenital heart disease and chronic lung problems, and had had difficulty in swallowing food since birth. The defendant parents admitted that they had beaten the deceased when he was "naughty" (*Ibid.*, para. 66). These beatings consisted of slapping him with their hands or hitting him with a wooden ruler. From the parents' perspective, they had applied only "no more than ordinary force" (*Ibid.*). The defendant mother had squeezed the cheeks of the deceased when he refused to open his mouth to allow the defendant to brush his teeth, leaving bruise marks on his face. Although the Court condemned the defendants' behaviour, it was also clear that the Court was sympathetic to the defendant mother. The Court made it explicit that it was not "overlooking or making light of the difficulties" (*Ibid.*, para. 93) faced by the defendant mother in caring for all the young triplets when her husband was away most of the time. It noted that the deceased was more difficult to raise than an average child. In the sentencing stage, the Court pointed out that the "most serious aspect of this particular case on the evidence was the wilful neglect rather than the wilful ill-treatment" of the child (*HKSAR v Lam Lui Yin and Yim Ching-ting;* transcript of the reasons for sentence, unreported, DCCC850/2005, 4 May 2006, para. 22). In spite of the finding of excessive beating and physical chastisement, the Court ruled that it was not a very serious case of ill-treatment, falling on the "less serious side of the scale of such contraventions" (*Ibid.*, 4 May 2006, para. 17). To the court, the major crimes committed by the defendants were their defaulting on all the follow-up medical appointments which had been arranged for the deceased child due to his inborn heart and lung problems since his discharge from the hospital, and their failing to take the deceased to attend medical care after his accidental falls, causing the brain injury and eventually his death.

Although both defendants were charged and convicted of wilful ill-treatment and neglect of the deceased causing him unnecessary suffering or injury to his health, the Hong Kong Court only elaborated on the legal meaning and application of wilful neglect but not ill-treatment. Adopting the ratio of the English case *R v Sheppard & Anor,* the Court took the meaning of "wilful" to refer to the subjective mind of the defendants. The facts of *Sheppard* were that two parents failed repeatedly to take their malnourished infant child for follow-up medical appointments, which eventually led to the child's death. The House of Lords ruled that the legal test for constituting the culpable mind for

wilful neglect is that the defendants must have either intentionally and deliberately, or recklessly disregarded the child's health ([1981] AC 394; discussed
and adopted in *Lam and Yim,* 6 April 2006, para. 82). Applying the *Sheppard's*
test to *Lam and Yim,* one finds that, indisputably, not taking the victim child
who had existing medical problems and who was in poor health condition to
the doctor was a grave mistake and constituted wilful neglect.

However, in contrast to "wilful neglect", the legal test for "wilful ill-treatment" is far from clear. Precedents from the United Kingdom will have far
less value because the English legal standard under the Children and Young
Persons Act of 1933 only uses the mere term "ill-treatment" without the adjec-
tive of "wilful". This may have reflected a wiser legal approach, for in reality,
it is difficult to envisage a factual scenario where ill-treatment does not involve
some deliberate or reckless abuse or cruelty. In *Lam and Yim,* the Hong Kong
Court did not elaborate on the legal meaning of wilful ill-treatment, but ruled
that the defendants had employed excessive force in their physical chastise-
ments to the deceased, and convicted the defendants for wilful ill-treatment.
While this was a justified conviction, the focus of the legal reasoning, with
regrets, was not on the "wilful" mind of the defendants. Rather, it was on the
frequency of the punishment and the degree of force inflicted on the victim.

Recalling that the deceased had more than 30 bruise marks and abrasions
on his small body, and he was beaten with a wooden ruler, leaving two parallel purplish bruise marks respectively on his left and right lower thighs, the
Court concluded that those two last occasions by themselves would not be
sufficient to constitute wilful ill-treatment unless this was routinely or regularly done (*Ibid.,* para. 116). It is puzzling to understand why the two purplish
bruise marks on the thighs of a two-year-old boy caused by beating with a
wooden ruler would not constitute "willful" ill-treatment under *Sheppard's* test
of deliberately or recklessly causing or likely to cause unnecessary suffering
or injury to a child's health, especially given the victim's tender age and his
poor health condition. The reasoning of the court only reflects heavily a result-
oriented approach, focusing largely on the final stage of the child's death and
thinking narrowly that timely medical treatment might have been the most
useful method of intervention. This has sadly downplayed the unnecessary
suffering caused to the child in the name of discipline, which in essence is
upholding the parents' wish to enforce compliance. Moreover, the measurement of what constitutes excessive standard and wilful ill-treatment adopted
by the Court is not only worrying and alarming, but also exposes the difficulty

and arbitrariness of asking the law to "regulate" corporal punishment by quantifying it, a task that is doomed to fail.

Case 3. HKSAR v Lam Wai-Man

The third reported case during the period studied (1997–2007), *HKSAR v Lam Wai-Man* ([1999] 3 HKLRD 855), involves equally gruesome facts of child abuse. The deceased child was twenty-one months old at the time of his death. His parents had separated shortly after his birth. He was in the care of his father most of the time, but for a short period of about two months immediately preceding his death, he was in the care of his mother. It was also mentioned in the judgment that the mother had refused to return the child to the father despite repeated requests. The child suffered 36 external wounds on his body including to his head, face, inner lip, shoulders, chest, knees, buttocks, and burn marks to the soles of his feet. He died of a serious brain injury.

The defendant was his mother, who explained the child was "prone to rebelliousness" (*Ibid.*, para. 18) and admitted to caning him when he was naughty and tying him with nylon string to a bed or into a pushchair to restrain him for as long as two hours at a time when he was disobedient. She was charged with wilful ill-treatment to a child under section 27(1) of the OAPO and with manslaughter. Since the defendant had pleaded guilty to both charges, the only issue before the Court of Appeal was sentencing. The judge sentenced the defendant to nine years of imprisonment, which was affirmed by the Court of Appeal. In contrast to the other cases discussed before, the intention of the mother was not mentioned in this judgment. Instead, the Court condemned the behaviour to be a "classic case of child abuse" (*Ibid.*, para. 14), in which the injuries were not accidental. This firm judicial position and a relatively heavy sentence compared with the other cases may partly be explained by the fact that the victim child was a healthy one when he was in the care of his father. But in a short period of less than two months, when the child was under the sole custody of his mother, he went through much suffering, and eventually died under her care.

Case 4. HKSAR v Hu Ting Qing

The last recorded case on corporal punishment, *HKSAR v Hu Tung Qing* (transcript of the reasons for verdict, unreported, DCCC516/2006; 17 November

2006; transcript of the reasons for sentencing, unreported, 7 December 2006) involved an elder brother disciplining a younger sixteen-year-old half-sister. The defendant was charged with indecent assault under section 122(1) of the Crimes Ordinance (Cap. 200, Laws of Hong Kong) and common assault. He was acquitted of the first charge, and he pleaded guilty to the second one. It was found that the defendant had on various occasions tied up the victim and beat her with a rattan stick or with a duster, a rather common implement used to discipline children in Hong Kong society. The judge sentenced the defendant to one year of probation because he accepted the defence counsel's mitigation that the defendant was motivated with "good intention" rather than any malicious will to hurt his sister (Hu, *Ibid.*, 7 December 2006, para. 3). This was due to the fact that the sister was "naughty" (*Ibid.*, para. 3), often returning home late and hanging out with bad companions. Apparently, the mother had entrusted the defendant with the task of teaching the younger sister. Nowhere in the judgment or in the sentencing statement did the court condemn the form of punishment as excessive and inappropriate. The welfare of the victim sister—that she was beaten to injury—was never mentioned in the reasoning of the case.

This adult-centred or parent-centred perspective in cases of corporal punishment shows itself to be a dominant and recurring theme when we also take into account the approach followed by the magistrate courts. As judgments are not available, here we only highlight two cases from the magistrate courts which were widely covered in the media.

Case 5. HKSAR v Chan

In 2005, in the case of *HKSAR v Chan*, a father forced his nine-year-old son to go naked on the streets because he had failed to finish his homework (FLCC1110/06, unreported, *Ming Pao News*, 2007). It turned out that it was the third time that the defendant had punished his son by this method of extreme shaming. In fact, at the time of hearing, the defendant had been convicted of assaulting his other eleven-year-old son and was sentenced to be bound over. On the current case being discussed, the defendant was charged with ill-treatment of his son, and was sentenced to two weeks of imprisonment, with a suspended sentence of twelve months. Despite the aforementioned history of child abuse, the magistrate gave the defendant a light sentence because he believed the defendant had good intentions and loved his son even as he was hot-tempered and used the wrong method to teach him.

Case 6. HKSAR v Ho

In 2007, a father demanded his fourteen-year-old son to do rope skipping 1300 times, to run 50 laps, and to stretch his leg muscles 1600 times a day. On one evening, he found that his son had not done so, and had even lied with his sister, feigning that he had done his daily exercise. In his anger, the father caned the son severely with a wooden ruler, causing numerous bruises on his shoulders, back and arms. The incident was later discovered by a school social worker, who reported it to the police. The father admitted to committing the offence of common assault. He was sentenced to one year of probation because the magistrate found that the father acted out of good intention, since the son had been suffering from poor health. In the magistrate's opinion, the father simply lost his temper when he found that the son had been dishonest. He had apologized to the son and had been remorseful. The magistrate also reminded the victim child that the father was motivated by good intention, and it was important for a child not to lie and to study diligently. He stressed that everyone in the family had the responsibility to maintain family harmony (*HKSAR v Ho,* TMCC68/07, unreported, *Sing Tao News, 2007*). The magistrate's reasoning could be most confusing to a child, for the magistrate was effectively blaming the child victim partly for the abusive behaviour of his father and for disrupting the "harmony" of the family, without reaffirming the child's rights and interests.

Case 7: Outside the legal terrain: a case where no sanction was imposed

In the name of goodwill and discipline, parents have committed acts of violence against their own children. More troubling is that society has been distinctly sympathetic to this group of parents and child caretakers. Not only have some judges failed to protect children's interests, but other institutions have also, as we will see in the following case, at times failed to impose any sanctions on the perpetrator. The case, which happened in 1997, concerned a four-year-old boy in Hong Kong who suffered a penetrating injury to his palm by a lead pencil (Lee, So, Wong, & Lau, 1989). The boy was brought to a hospital's accident and emergency department. The mother explained that the boy was holding a newly sharpened pencil in his right hand as he was rushing to the toilet, and had an accidental fall which caused the graphite end to pierce into the boy's palm. Later, it was revealed that the mother had inflicted the injury because the victim did not perform well at school. Despite the fact that the boy was suffering from developmental speech delay, the mother remained demanding when it came to his academic performance. She believed that physical punishment would push him to do his homework. The victim was also found to have multiple nonpatterned bruises over his back and scratch marks on his hands and face. The doctor in charge reported the case to the Social Welfare Department. Eventually, the mother admitted that she had caused the injury. But the Social Welfare Department only arranged counselling for the family and a neurodevelopment session for the child victim. The handling of this case illustrates the lack of recognition and awareness of the seriousness of corporal punishment and child abuse in Hong Kong. There is no clear direction and guidance on how such cases should be handled. By the time fatal tragedies happen, it may be far too late to intervene.

Conclusion

The cases discussed above bespeak an approach in tackling the issues of corporal punishment and children's protection which hinges on the severity of injury outcomes. In doing so, they have exposed the inadequacies and fallacy of such an approach. Because corporal punishment by parents is not defined in Hong Kong, the authorities only intervene where the injury suffered by the child victim is serious. Not only are preventive measures not adopted, cases are often framed as "tragedies", absolving parent perpetrators of their legal responsibility to a large extent.

What is evident from the court decisions analysed is the recurring theme of parents' intentions. Instead of focusing on the welfare of children or their best interests, the Court and Hong Kong society have adopted a parent-centric approach. The presumption is that as long as parents have acted in good faith, they have the undisputed right to discipline their children. But the review of cases in Hong Kong confirms that such discipline has resulted in much abuse when parents and caretakers unwittingly cause more harm than they had intended, or when they lost self-control. We should not forget that pain, inflicted even in the name of corrective discipline, is uncalled for in promoting healthy child growth, and in fact, any use of violence should be condemned. A long-term solution is to ban corporal punishment by parents in Hong Kong.

References

Bainham, A. (2005). *Children—The Modern Law*. Bristol, England: Jordan Publications.

Chan, K. L. (2005). *Study on Child Abuse and Spouse Battering: Report on Findings of Household Survey*. (A consultancy study commissioned by the SWD of the HKSAR). Retrieved from the Department of Social Work and Social Administration, the University of Hong Kong website: http://www.swd.gov.hk/doc/family/Report%20on%20findings%20of%20Household%20Survey.pdf

Chan, K. L. (2008). *Study on Child-Friendly Families: Immunity from Domestic Violence*. (A consultancy study commissioned by the UNICEF). Hong Kong: the University of Hong Kong.

Donnelly, M., & Straus M. A. (2005). *Corporal Punishment of Children in Theoretical Perspective*. New Haven, CT: Yale University Press.

End Physical Punishment of Children. (2010). *Corporal Punishment, Countdown to Universal Prohibition*. Retrieved from End Physical Punishment of Children website: http://www.endcorporalpunishment.org/pages/frame.html?http%3A//www.endcorporalpunishment.org/pages/progress/countdown.html

Fortin, J. (2003). *Children's Rights and the Developing Law*. London, England: Butterworths.

Freeman, M. D. A. (1983). *The Rights and Wrongs of Children*. London, England: Pinter.

Freeman, M. D. A. (2007). Article 3, The best interests of the child. In A. Alen, J. Vande Lanotte, E. Verhellen, F. Ang, E. Berghmans, & M. Verheyde (Eds.), *A Commentary on the United Nations Convention on the Rights of the Child* (pp. 1–75). Leiden, South Holland: Martinus Nijhoff Publishers.

Hong Kong SAR Government Secretariat (2008, 7 April). Letter to Mr. Fernando Cheung, Legislative Councilor on the Statistics on Domestic Violence in Hong Kong.

Hui, P. (2006, September 27). Activists seek law on corporal punishment. *South China Morning Post*, p. City 1.

Lau, J. T. F., & Liu J. L. Y. (1999). Conceptualization, reporting and underreporting of child abuse in Hong Kong. *Child Abuse & Neglect, 23*, 1159–1174. doi: 10.1016/S0145-2134(99)00075-7

Lee, A. C. W., So, K. T., Wong, H. L., & Lau, S. (1989). Penetrating pencil injury: an unusual case of child abuse. *Child Abuse & Neglect, 22*, 749–752. doi: 10.1016/S0145-2134(98)00050-7

Lieh-Mak, F., Chung, S. Y., & Liu, Y. W. (1983). Characteristics of child battering in Hong Kong: a controlled study. *British Journal of Psychiatry, 142*, 89–94.

McGillivray, A. (2004). Child physical assault: law, equality and intervention. *Manitoba Law Journal, 30*, 133–170.

Pinheiro, P. S. (2006). *World Report on Violence Against Children: Violence Against Children in the Home and Family.* Retrieved from United Nations Secretary-General, Geneva website: http://www.unicef.org/violencestudy/3.%20 World%20Report%20on%20Violence%20against%20Children.pdf

Pollard, D. (2003). Banning child corporal punishment. *Tulane Law Review, 77,* 575–657.

Samuda, G. M. (1988). Child discipline and abuse in Hong Kong. *Child Abuse & Neglect, 12,* 283–7. doi: 10.1016/0145-2134(88)90036-1

Two unusual fathers ended in court for extreme method of disciplining their children (in Chinese). (2007, January 18). *Ming Pao News,* A6.

United Nations. (2010). Declaration of the rights of the child: adopted by UN General Assembly Resolution 1386 (XIV) of 10 December 1959. Retrieved from the United Nations Cyberschoolbus website: http://www.un.org/cyberschoolbus/ humanrights/resources/child.asp

United Nations Committee on the Rights of the Child. (2006). *United Nations Committee on the Rights of the Child, 42nd session, General Comment no. 8.* Retrieved from the United Nations website: http://www.unhchr.ch/tbs/doc.nsf/ 898586b1dc7b4043c1256a450044f331/6545c032cb57bff5c12571fc002e834d/$ FILE/G0740771.pdf

United Nations. (2006). *Note by the Secretary General on the Rights of the Child to the General Assembly,* 61st session of the General Assembly, item 62(a), 29 August 2006. Retrieved from the United Nations website: http://www.unicef. org/violencestudy/reports/SG_violencestudy_en.pdf

United Nations. (1989). *Convention on the Rights of the Child.* Adopted and opened for signature, ratification and accession by General Assembly resolution 44/25 of 20 November 1989. Retrieved from the United Nations website: http://www2. ohchr.org/english/law/crc.htm.

"Unusual father" sentenced to probation for applying corporal punishment to his son (in Chinese). (2007, August 2). *Sing Tao News,* A21.

Part 3

Health Perspective

8
Multidisciplinary Collaboration

Ten Years of Research on Domestic Violence in Chinese Pregnant Women

Wing-Cheong Leung

Chapter summary

1. Domestic violence is an important public health issue, and pregnancy (by itself also a risk factor) provides a good window of opportunity for screening and intervention.
2. Emotional abuse could well be the precursor stage to physical abuse or even a major family tragedy such as suicide or homicide.
3. Multidisciplinary collaboration is necessary for research, screening and intervention.
4. The ultimate goal of our Domestic Harmony Research Team is to put forward routine domestic violence screening in pregnancy together with an effective intervention programme in Hong Kong.

How did we begin?

Our research journey on domestic violence in Chinese pregnant women began in 1997. At that time, I had just completed my Obstetrics & Gynaecology (O&G) specialist training in Queen Mary Hospital (QMH) and Tsan Yuk Hospital. My interest in research was still minimal. One afternoon, I met Professor H. K. Ma, who had come back from London to visit us in QMH. Professor Ma had been Head of the Department of O&G at the University of Hong Kong before her retirement in 1995. She inspired us with a research idea when she told us domestic violence in pregnant women had become an important research area internationally, but that as yet, there was no such data available for Chinese pregnant women. She and Professor P. C. Ho (Department Head at that time) asked me to start working on this research idea. I immediately accepted the task without a second thought.

The first prevalence study of domestic violence in Chinese pregnant women

Although I had accepted the task to perform a prevalence study of domestic violence among Chinese pregnant women, I doubted very much whether domestic violence was really a problem among the pregnant population of Hong Kong. Nevertheless, I did a literature review and found that there was indeed, as Professor Ma had suggested, no such previous study. Ours was going to be the first one on Chinese pregnant women.

In our clinical practice, we do not routinely ask pregnant women for any history of domestic violence unless there is reason for strong suspicion, such as multiple injuries, which are rare. As a result, even if domestic violence is a problem among the pregnant women who use our services, it is often overlooked.

We published the first prevalence study in 1999 (W. C. Leung, Leung, Lam, & Ho, 1999). Six hundred and thirty-one pregnant women attending their first antenatal clinic in Tsan Yuk Hospital, a maternity hospital in Hong Kong, were interviewed by a designated research nurse, Joyce Lam. Joyce later obtained her master's degree in counselling and became a professional counsellor as well as an important team member in our later projects. The interviews took place in a private setting with the husband or male partner absent. The questionnaire was derived from the Abuse Assessment Screen (AAS). This screen assessed past and recent history of domestic violence using four structured and directed questions:

1.   Have you been physically abused by your partner or someone important to you?
2.   Within the last year, have you been hit, slapped, kicked or otherwise physically hurt by someone?
3.   Since you have been pregnant, have you been hit, slapped, kicked or otherwise physically hurt by someone?
4.   Within the past year, has anyone forced you to have sexual activities?

The questions looked simple and straightforward, so I just translated them into Chinese for use in our study. At that time, due to my limited experience in research, I did not realize that we needed to validate the translated Chinese questionnaire against a standard Chinese assessment tool. This later became one major criticism of our study.

Nevertheless, the findings were impressive. Out of the 631 pregnant women, 131 (17.9%) had a history of abuse, 99 (15.7%) had been abused in the preceding year, 27 (4.3%) had been abused during their current pregnancy, and 59 (9.4%) had been sexually abused in the preceding year. The husband was the perpetrator in the majority of cases. The nature of abuse during pregnancy was mainly psychological—in the form of threats of abuse without causing any physical injury. Risk factors for domestic violence in pregnancy included unplanned pregnancy and women with husbands or partners who were unemployed or manual workers. Unexpectedly, domestic violence occurred more commonly among permanent local residents than new immigrants from mainland China.

The prevalence of domestic violence towards Chinese pregnant women from our study was comparable to those in Caucasian studies. On the other hand, the nature of abuse was very much different. There was not a single case of physical injury in our abused group. When I presented the findings of this study on different occasions, there were frequent criticisms from the audience on whether there was any significance at all of "verbal abuse" towards Chinese pregnant women. Was verbal abuse just part of our Chinese culture? It must be noted, by the way, that the AAS which we were using in this study was designed mainly for detecting physical abuse. It was only because Joyce, our research nurse, was so sensitive in picking up the occurrence of verbal or emotional abuse from the interviewed pregnant women that we arrived at our results.

Pregnancy outcome following domestic violence towards Chinese women

In order to answer the question of whether verbal or emotional abuse had any significant influence on women's health for the Chinese pregnant women we interviewed, we studied the pregnancy outcome of the cohort in our first prevalence study (W. C. Leung et al., 1999). No difference was found between the abused and nonabused groups in terms of antenatal complications, preterm delivery, mode of delivery, birth weight, birth asphyxia and admission to neonatal intensive care unit. This finding was in contrast to those of Caucasian studies in which domestic violence was associated with increased risk of miscarriages, preterm labour, fetal distress and low birth weight. However, a strong element of physical abuse was present in the Caucasian studies.

Is verbal or emotional abuse really not significant? If that is true, there will not be any point to pursue further studies in this area. We did have a strong belief that this was not the case. We hypothesized that domestic violence against these Chinese pregnant women, of which the nature was almost entirely verbal, might mainly affect their psychological well-being. In other words, the real impact of domestic violence in pregnancy in Chinese women might not be reflected by the usual physical pregnancy outcome parameters, but by mental health outcome measures such as postnatal depression. We continued our studies along this line.

Domestic violence and postnatal depression

In 2001, we confirmed this hypothesis by performing another domestic violence study on 838 women after delivery (W. C. Leung, Kung, J. Lam, Leung, & Ho, 2002). There was already a screening programme for postnatal depression in Queen Mary Hospital which started in 2000. It was a three-stage screening. Women after delivery were asked to complete the Stein's Daily Scoring System (SDSS) and Edinburgh Postnatal Depression Scale (EPDS) questionnaires on Day Two or Three postdelivery (Stage 1). They were then asked to complete another set of EPDS one to two days after they went home (Stage 2). At six weeks postdelivery, they would complete the third set of EPDS (Stage 3). SDSS was developed specifically to measure maternity blues in the puerperium, while EPDS is a useful screening tool for postnatal depression. It was reported that 11% to 17% of Chinese women scored highly on the EPDS six weeks to six months postpartum (Pen et al., 1994).

In our sample, 143 women (17.1%) had a history of abuse, and 139 (16.6%) had been abused in the preceding year. Abuse occurred during the current pregnancy in 87 women (10.4%). There were 14 women (1.7%) who had been sexually abused in the year preceding the study. Husband/boyfriend (27.9%), mother-in-law (26.7%) and employer/colleague (20.9%) were the three most common types of perpetrator of abuse. The nature of abuse was verbal and/or sexual in all the cases. The only risk factor that reached statistical significance was unplanned pregnancy ($p = 0.002$). The incidence of abuse was also found to be higher in permanent residents (those who have lived in Hong Kong for more than seven years), single/divorced women, smokers, drinkers and women with low income (< HK\$5000, or roughly < US\$640, per month), although the difference was not statistically significant. The abused group had significantly higher SDSS and EPDS scores at all stages of screening ($p = 0.003$, $p = 0.000$, $p = 0.010$ and $p = 0.001$ respectively). As the pregnancy advanced into the puerperium, the mother-in-law and employer/colleague became as important in perpetrating abuse as the husband, who was identified as the major perpetrator in our previous study. There are some possible explanations. Nowadays in Hong Kong, most couples do not live with their parents or parents-in-law. However, during pregnancy and especially after delivery, the parents and in-laws would usually give a lot of advice and comments. Some of these comments or traditional taboos may not be compatible with the knowledge that the pregnant women had obtained from their own reading, antenatal talks and information from the obstetricians and midwives. Conflicts might arise as a result, and it is therefore not surprising that the mother-in-law came into the scene with regards to domestic violence. Furthermore, the majority of those pregnant women were working (only 35% were housewives from our data). As the pregnancy advanced, the working pregnant women would have had to take more time off work to attend antenatal clinics and sometimes for hospital admissions. This might have resulted in conflicts with employers and colleagues.

There are a few possible explanations for the association between domestic violence and postnatal blues/depression. Firstly, domestic violence might lead to psychological trauma and then postnatal depression. Secondly, certain psychological traits or personality problems might lead to relationship problems and domestic violence. These psychological traits or personality problems might also predispose one to postnatal depression. Thirdly, the women who subsequently developed postnatal depression might share the commonality of greater sensitivity, and they might be prone to interpret innocuous comments retrospectively as verbal abuse.

Quality of life of victims of intimate partner violence

After establishing the significant relationship between domestic violence and postnatal depression, we knew that we should concentrate on the mental health consequences of domestic violence or intimate partner violence, which had become the more used term by that time. We published a paper in 2005 on the quality of life of victims of intimate partner violence (Leung, W. C. Leung, Ng,

& Ho, 2005). This study was led by Dr T. W. Leung, who was also working in QMH at that time.

A total of 1,614 O&G patients were classified into four groups (Group 1: requesting termination of pregnancy, $n = 300$; Group 2: subfertility patients, $n = 500$; Group 3: other general gynaecological patients, $n = 300$; Group 4: obstetric patients, $n = 514$). They were successfully interviewed in the absence of their male partners using a structured questionnaire modified from the AAS questionnaire. Those who reported ever having been abused, together with an equal number of nonabused women as controls, were asked to complete the World Health Organization Quality of Life Measure—Abbreviated Version (Hong Kong) Questionnaire. The overall lifetime prevalence of intimate partner violence was 7.2%, with the lifetime prevalence being 12.7%, 1.8%, 4.7%, and 10.9% respectively in Groups 1–4. The mean quality-of-life domain scores among the abused victims were significantly lower in the physical health, social relationship, environment and psychological health domains. We confirmed that the baseline quality of life of the victims of intimate partner violence was significantly impaired compared with that of nonabused controls.

Are we going to continue the journey?

On completing these background studies, we became convinced that domestic violence, or intimate partner violence, existed among Hong Kong Chinese pregnant women and was an important health issue—and in particular—a mental health issue. The question was whether obstetricians and gynaecologists should be involved. Our training in O&G had been focused traditionally on physical diseases, medical and surgical treatments. Antenatal screening had not included domestic violence. We had the impression that domestic violence should be within social workers' scope of practice. On the other hand, obstetricians and gynaecologists are equally committed to women's health. Our relationship with patients has many a time gone beyond the disease model. In other words, there was no reason why we should not be involved in this battle against domestic violence. The most difficult step in this battle was to organize opportunities for victims to speak out about their experience. This difficulty was further aggravated by our traditional Chinese cultural views which do not encourage women, if any family member at all, to expose family affairs to nonfamily members. But in view of this, pregnancy thus becomes an excellent or even the only opportunity for women to seek help.

Therefore, we decided to continue the journey—not alone, but through multidisciplinary collaboration.

Formation of a Domestic Harmony Research Team

Our collaboration first started with Professor A. Tiwari and her team from the Department of Nursing Studies of the University of Hong Kong. Our first project was to conduct a randomized controlled trial of empowerment training for abused pregnant Chinese women in Hong Kong. We also invited Professor J. Humphreys (Department of Family Health Care Nursing, University of California) and Professor B. Parker (School of Nursing, University of Virginia), who were experienced in domestic violence studies, to be our advisers and co-investigators.

The first randomized controlled trial of empowerment training for abused Chinese pregnant women in Hong Kong

The study was led by Professor A. Tiwari. It was undertaken between May 2002 and July 2003. I am most indebted to Professor Tiwari because I was away from Hong Kong during this study period to pursue my subspecialty training in Maternal Fetal Medicine in London. The notorious outbreak of SARS also occurred in 2003, and further complicated the logistics of our study. Nevertheless, the study was completed and the paper was able to be published in 2005 (Tiwari et al., 2005).

The objective was to evaluate the effectiveness of an empowerment intervention in reducing intimate partner violence and improving health status. A total of 110 Chinese pregnant women with a history of abuse by their intimate partners were randomized to the experimental or control group. Experimental group women received empowerment training specially designed for abused Chinese pregnant women while the control group women received standard care for abused women.

The intervention was based on an empowerment protocol developed by Professor B. Parker (Parker et al., 1999), designed to enhance abused women's independence and control. It consisted of advice in the areas of safety, choice making and problem solving. For example, as domestic violence is seen as a shame to the family, and one would not normally disclose it to someone outside the family, the protocol suggests that a pregnant woman might wish to establish a code as a safety precaution with trusted friends and neighbours. In addition, as gambling is popular in Hong Kong and heavy losses at the races or similar activities could be an excuse for the abuser to take out his anger on his partner and/or children, we included "heavy loss in gambling" as a risk factor. A component of empathic understanding, derived from Roger's client-centred therapy (Rogers, 1951), was also added to the empowerment protocol. Empathic understanding emphasizes the need to take in and accept the woman's perceptions and feelings. It was designed to help women value themselves and their own feelings positively. This is important because abusive experiences are likely to be ignored by others, particularly if the abuse was psychological and if the deleterious effects of partner violence on self-esteem went unrecognized.

The intervention was administered to each woman in the experimental group at entry into the study by Joyce Lam. The one-to-one interview lasted about 30 minutes. At the conclusion of the intervention, each woman was given a brochure reinforcing the information provided. Standard care for abused women was provided to the control group women. This consisted of a wallet-sized card with information on community resources for abused women, including information on shelter hotlines, law enforcement, social services and non-governmental organizations.

Data were collected at study entry and six weeks postnatal. The main outcome measures were: intimate partner violence [on the Conflict Tactics Scale (CTS)], health-related quality of life (SF-36) and postnatal depression [Edinburgh Postnatal Depression Scale (EPDS)]. Following the training, the experimental group had significantly higher physical functioning and had significantly improved role limitation due to physical problems and emotional problems. They also reported less psychological (but not sexual) abuse and fewer incidents of minor (but not severe) physical violence, and had significantly lower postnatal depression scores. However, they reported more bodily pain. We have shown that an empowerment intervention specially designed for abused Chinese pregnant women was effective in reducing intimate partner violence and improving the health status of the women.

We were very excited with the findings from this randomized controlled trial. We decided that the long-term goal was to put forward routine screening of domestic violence in pregnancy and to establish an effective intervention model. To achieve this ultimate goal, we realized that we needed to convince health policymakers and the public to accept this approach of screening and intervention. More research and thus further collaboration with various disciplines were necessary.

Expansion of our Domestic Harmony Research Team

Our Domestic Harmony Research Team further expanded through collaboration with Professor K. L. Chan and his team from the Department of Social Work and Social Administration, the University of Hong Kong. It was very interesting that I got to know Professor Chan because I was the obstetrician looking after Professor Chan's wife during her first pregnancy and indeed also her second pregnancy. We had also built up an experienced team of research nurses, led by Joyce Lam, who had helped us from the very beginning in our first prevalence study of domestic violence among Chinese pregnant women.

The expanded team also included Dr A. Cheung from the Faculty of Law, the University of Hong Kong; Mr H. K. Yip from Policy 21 Limited which provides evidence-based research services to the community; Dr Daniel Fong (principal statistician) from the Department of Nursing Studies, the University of Hong Kong; Dr D. Brownridge from the University of Manitoba; and other professionals.

With strong support from this multidisciplinary team, we were confident about continuing the journey.

The new Chinese Abuse Assessment Screen (C-AAS)

In response to the criticism that we had not formally validated the Chinese version of AAS, we performed a validation study on the instrument in 2007 (Tiwari et al., 2007).

The new C-AAS included six questions:
1. Within the <u>last year</u>, have you been <u>emotionally</u> hurt by someone?
2. Within the <u>last year</u>, have you been <u>physically</u> hurt by someone?
3. Within the <u>last year</u>, has anyone forced you to have <u>sexual</u> activities?
4. Since you've been <u>pregnant</u>, have you been <u>emotionally</u> hurt by someone?
5. Since you've been <u>pregnant</u>, have you been <u>physically</u> hurt by someone?
6. Since you've been <u>pregnant</u>, has anyone forced you to have <u>sexual</u> activities?

In our new C-AAS, emotional and physical violence were separately addressed in all time periods. This was because emotional or verbal abuse was the dominant form of abuse among Chinese pregnant women. Examples of emotional and physical abusive behaviours were listed to help respondents assess whether those behaviours were present in their intimate relationships. The examples were obtained from abused pregnant women who took part in our previous studies.

To assess the accuracy and the utility of the new C-AAS, a cross-sectional study was performed in an antenatal clinic of a public hospital and a community centre in Hong Kong. A total of 257 Chinese women, consisting of 100 pregnant women and 157 nonpregnant women, were recruited. The C-AAS was administered first, followed by the Chinese Revised Conflict Tactics Scales (CTS2) (Straus et al., 1996). This was performed in the same setting, and each participant was interviewed once either at an antenatal clinic (for the pregnant women sample) or at a community centre (for the nonpregnant women sample). The main outcome measures were: estimates of the sensitivity, specificity, positive and negative predictive values, and positive and negative likelihood ratios. Using the Chinese CTS2 as the standard, we found that the specificity estimates of the Chinese AAS for emotional, physical and sexual abuse were > or = 89%, while the sensitivity estimates varied from 36.3% to 65.8%. The sensitivity improved in the screening for more severe cases (66.7%). The positive predictive values were > or = 80%, and the negative predictive values varied from 66% to 93%. Factors such as the age difference between the couple and the woman's need for financial assistance were found to be associated with intimate partner violence. We demonstrated that the C-AAS has satisfactory measurement accuracy and utility for identifying intimate partner violence when the Chinese CTS2 is used as the standard.

From then on, the C-AAS became the screening tool whenever we had the chance to put forward routine domestic violence screening in pregnancy.

The first territory-wide survey on intimate partner violence among pregnant women in Hong Kong

So far, our studies were performed in a single university hospital. In our journey to put forward routine domestic violence screening in pregnancy, we anticipated criticisms on whether our findings would be reproducible in other hospitals throughout the territory. It was therefore essential to perform a territory-wide study on domestic violence in pregnant woman. This study was led by Professor A. Tiwari and Professor K. L. Chan (Tiwari et al., 2007, 2008). It would not have been possible to perform this study without the help from all the chiefs of service and collaborators in each of the participating hospitals.

The objective of this first population-based study in Hong Kong was to assess the impact of psychological abuse by an intimate partner on the mental health of pregnant women. The study involved the antenatal clinics in seven public hospitals in Hong Kong. A total of 3,245 pregnant women were recruited. The C-AAS and demographic questionnaires were administered face-to-face at 32–36 weeks of gestation. At one week postpartum, the C-AAS, EPDS and SF-12 Health Survey were administered by telephone. The main outcome measures were: intimate partner violence, postnatal depression and health-related quality of life. Of all participants, 296 (9.1%) reported abuse by an intimate partner in the past year. Of those abused, 216 (73%) reported psychological abuse only, 80 (27%) reported physical and/or sexual abuse, and 46 (57.5%) in the physical and/or sexual abuse group also reported psychological abuse. Women in the psychological abuse only group had a higher risk of postnatal depression compared with nonabused women (adjusted *OR*: 1.84, 95% *CI*: 1.12–3.02). They were also at a higher risk of thinking about harming themselves (adjusted *OR*: 3.50, 95% *CI*: 1.49–8.20), and had significantly poorer mental health-related quality of life ($p < 0.001$). The higher risks of postnatal depression and thinking of harming themselves were not observed in the physical and/or sexual abuse group, although significantly poorer mental health-related quality of life ($p < 0.001$) was observed. Psychological abuse by intimate partners towards pregnant women had a negative impact on their mental health postdelivery. Furthermore, psychological abuse in the absence of physical and/or sexual abuse could have a detrimental effect on the mental health of abused women. The findings underscored the importance of screening pregnant women for abuse by an intimate partner and the need to develop, implement and evaluate interventions to address psychological abuse.

Risk factors for domestic violence in Chinese pregnant women

Regarding the 3,245 pregnant women recruited in the territory-wide survey (Tiwari et al., 2007), the mean age was 30.8 (standard deviation, 4.8) years. Most of them were married (97.3%). Just over one-third (36.3%) had a monthly household income of less than $15,000, and approximately half (44.4%) were in need of financial assistance. Unplanned pregnancy was reported by 35.3% of the women and about 7% had had conflicts with their in-laws in the previous

12 months. Before adjusting for the effects of sociodemographic factors, the risk of being abused by an intimate partner varied among the hospitals ($p <$ 0.01). However, after controlling for the sociodemographic factors of being in debt, being in need of financial assistance, having an unplanned pregnancy and having conflict with in-laws, differences across the hospitals were not observed ($p = 0.07$).

Regarding the various social risk factors, Professor K. L. Chan performed an additional analysis and found that in-law conflict was the characteristic most significantly associated with intimate partner violence against pregnant women, after controlling for covariates (Chan et al., 2009). This underscored the need to obtain information on in-law conflict as a risk factor for intimate partner violence. In-law conflict should be included in risk assessments. For the prevention of intimate partner violence, family-based intervention working with victims as well as in-laws would be needed.

Pregnancy as a risk factor for domestic violence in Chinese pregnant women

One basic interesting question we had not answered was whether pregnancy, in addition to its function as a window for screening for domestic violence, was itself a risk factor for domestic violence. The answer was "yes" from Professor K. L. Chan's latest study (Chan et al., 2011).

A large, representative sample was studied containing detailed information on partner violence including physical and sexual abuse as well as perpetrator-related risk factors. Data from a representative sample of 2,225 men were analysed. The self-reported prevalence of men's violence against their female partners was computed and compared in terms of demographic, behavioural, and relationship characteristics. The preceding-year prevalence of physical assault, sexual violence, and "any violence or injury" among the group whose partners were pregnant were 11.9%, 9.1%, and 18.8%, respectively. This was significantly higher than the nonpregnant group. Pregnancy was significantly associated with increased odds of violence, including physical assault, sexual violence, and "any violence or injury" (ORs = 2.42, 2.42, and 2.60, respectively). Having controlled for relationship characteristics including social desirability, social support, in-law conflict, dominance, and jealousy of male perpetrators, pregnancy was significantly associated with "any violence or injury".

Conclusion

The way forward

Family-based intervention is probably the way forward. We have not included the husband or partner in our previous empowerment intervention. In a prevalence study on domestic violence against male partners of pregnant women, 13% of men reported that they had been abused by their female partners (W. C. Leung, Lam, Leung, & Ho). This bidirectional concept of domestic violence would be built into our new family-based intervention. A current study led by Professor A. Tiwari on "positive fathering" would further support the involvement of the male partner in the intervention.

We are going to perform another territory-wide randomized controlled trial to test the effectiveness of our new family-based intervention model for domestic violence in Chinese pregnant women. If the results from this trial are also encouraging, perhaps it signals it is time to proceed with routine domestic violence screening in pregnancy in Hong Kong.

Up to now, we have come to involve a large cohort of women with a history of abuse in our research. This will give us a good opportunity to study the longitudinal lifetime profile of domestic violence in these women. Emotional abuse could well be the precursor stage of physical abuse or even a major family tragedy such as suicide or homicide. If this hypothesis is confirmed, routine domestic violence screening in pregnancy will be even more invaluable.

References

Chan, K. L., Tiwari, A., Fong, D. Y., Leung, W. C., Brownridge, D. A., & Ho, P. C. (2009). Correlates of in-law conflict and intimate partner violence against Chinese pregnant women in Hong Kong. *Journal of Interpersonal Violence*, *24*, 97–110. doi: 10.1177/0886260508315780

Chan, K. L., Brownridge, D. A., Tiwari, A., Fong, D. Y., Leung, W. C., & Ho, P. C. (2011). Associating pregnancy with partner violence against Chinese women. *Journal of Interpersonal Violence*, *26*, 1478–1500. doi: 10.1177/0886260510369134

Leung, T. W., Leung, W. C., Ng, E. H., & Ho, P. C. (2005). Quality of life of victims of intimate partner violence. *International Journal of Gynaecology and Obstetrics*, *90*, 258–262. doi: 10.1016/j.ijgo.2005.05.010

Leung, W. C., Kung, F., Lam, J., Leung, T. W., & Ho, P. C. (2002). Domestic violence and postnatal depression in a Chinese community. *International Journal of Gynaecology and Obstetrics*, *79*, 159–166.

Leung, W. C., Lam, Y. H, Leung, T. W., & Ho, P. C. (2007). A pilot study on the prevalence of domestic violence against male partners of pregnant women in Hong Kong. *The Hong Kong Medical Diary, 12,* 25–27.

Leung, W. C., Leung, T. W., Lam, Y. Y., & Ho, P. C. (1999). The prevalence of domestic violence against pregnant women in a Chinese community. *International Journal of Gynaecology and Obstetrics, 66,* 23–30.

Leung, W. C., Wong, Y. Y., Leung, T. W., & Ho, P. C. (2001). Pregnancy outcome following domestic violence in a Chinese community. *International Journal of Gynaecology and Obstetrics, 72,* 79–80.

Parker, B., McFarlane, J., Soeken, K., Silva, C., Reel, S. (1999). Testing an intervention to prevent further abuse to pregnant women. *Res Nurs Health, 22,* 59–66.

Pen, T., Wang, L., Jin, J. (1994). The evaluation and application of the Edinburgh Postnatal Depression Scale. *Chin Mental Health J, 8,* 18–19.

Rogers, C. (1951). *Client-Centered Therapy, Its Current Practice, Implications and Theory.* Boston, MA: Houghton Mifflin.

Straus, M. A., Hamby, S. L., Boney-McCoy, S., Sugarman, D. B. (1996). The revised conflict tactics scales (CTS2): development and preliminary psychometric data. *J Fam Issues, 17,* 283–316.

Tiwari, A., Chan, K. L., Fong, D., Leung, W. C., Brownridge, D. A., Lam, H., Wong, B., Lam, C. M., Chau, F., Chan, A., Cheung, K. B., & Ho, P. C. (2007). A territory wide survey on intimate partner violence among pregnant women in Hong Kong. *Hong Kong Journal of Gynaecology, Obstetrics and Midwifery, 7,* 7–15.

Tiwari, A., Chan, K. L., Fong, D., Leung, W. C., Brownridge, D. A., Lam, H., Wong, B., Lam, C. M., Chau, F., Chan, A., Cheung, K. B., & Ho, P. C. (2008). The impact of psychological abuse by an intimate partner on the mental health of pregnant women. *BJOG, 115,* 377–384. doi: 10.1111/j.1471-0528.2007.01593.x

Tiwari, A., Fong, D. Y., Chan, K. L., Leung, W. C., Parker, B., & Ho, P. C. (2007). Identifying intimate partner violence: comparing the Chinese Abuse Assessment Screen with the Chinese Revised Conflict Tactics Scales. *BJOG, 114,* 1065–1071. doi: 10.1111/j.1471-0528.2007.01441.x.

Tiwari, A., Leung, W. C., Leung, T. W., Humphreys, J., Parker, B., & Ho, P. C. (2005). A randomised controlled trial of empowerment training for Chinese abused pregnant women in Hong Kong. *BJOG, 112,* 1249–1256. doi: 10.1111/j.1471-0528.2005.00709.x

9
Domestic Violence from a Health Perspective

Impact and Intervention

Agnes Tiwari

Chapter summary

1. Intimate partner violence (IPV) is linked with a range of physical, mental and reproductive health problems.
2. While some of the health consequences of IPV may be obvious (e.g., injury), others may be less obvious (e.g., some functional disorders).
3. The impact on health can persist long after IPV has ended.
4. Interventions for IPV survivors are available; however, evidence of their effectiveness is equivocal.

There is overwhelming evidence that intimate partner violence (IPV) is linked with a range of health problems (e.g., Bonomi, Anderson, Rivara, & Thompson, 2007; Campbell, 2002; Humphreys, Cooper, & Miaskowski, 2010; Krug, Dahlberg, Mercy, Zwi, & Lozano, 2002; Wuest et al., 2009). Given the association of IPV with significant morbidity, it is not surprising that much effort has gone into designing interventions to prevent IPV and address its related health consequences. This chapter describes the impact of IPV on health, and discusses the effects of interventions on preventing/reducing IPV and promoting the health of IPV survivors.

Impact of IPV on health

The impact of IPV on health may be short- or long-term with physical, mental and/or reproductive health effects.

Impact on physical health

Injury is the most obvious physical health consequence of IPV, and ranges from minor (e.g., scratches, cuts, bruises) to more serious injury (e.g., broken bones, internal bleeding, head trauma), and even death. In the United States, about three women are killed by their intimate partners each day (Catalano, 2007), with women being nine times more likely to be killed by an intimate partner than by a stranger (Campbell, Glass, Sharps, Laughon, & Bloom, 2007). In less industrialized countries, the rates of intimate partner homicide of females (femicide) may be even higher, although such global data are lacking (Campbell, 2002). Specifically, IPV is likely to account for a substantial but largely unrecognized proportion of maternal mortality during pregnancy (Fauveau, Koenig, Chakraborty, & Chowdhury,1988; Ganatra, Coyaji, & Rao, 1998).

Although abused women are more likely to be long-term users of health services, they generally do not present with obvious trauma, even in accident and emergency departments. For example, Dearwater and colleagues (1998) found that a higher proportion of women who had been battered in the past year (12–17%) presented at accident and emergency departments than women with acute traumas from abuse (2–3%). This indicates the need for universal rather than incident-based screening for IPV in accident and emergency care settings (Campbell, 2002).

While injury is an obvious outcome of IPV, it is not the most common physical outcome. A number of functional disorders, many of which have no identifiable medical cause, have been shown to be consistently linked with a history of intimate partner physical violence or sexual abuse (Leserman, 1996; Walker et al., 1997). Examples include irritable bowel syndrome, fibromyalgia, chronic pain, and gastrointestinal disorders. In addition, not only do abused women experience reduced physical functioning, more physical symptoms of illness, and a greater number of days in bed than nonabused women (Golding, 1996; McCauley et al., 1997; Sutherland, Bybee, & Sullivan, 1998), they often have physical health problems that are "above and beyond the effects of direct physical injury" (Kendall-Tackett, 2009, p. 215) and persist long after the abuse itself has stopped (Kibler, Johi, & Hughes, in press).

The link between IPV and physical health problems is complex. Some have used psychoneuroimmunology (PNI) as a framework for understanding how IPV impacts health (e.g., Kendall-Tackett, 2008; Kiecolt-Glaser et al., 2007;

Wilson, Finch, & Cohen, 2002). Briefly, severe or overwhelming stress (such as that associated with IPV) can alter and dysregulate the immune system, resulting in the release of too many proinflammatory cytokines (messenger molecules released by the immune system to fight infection and help heal wounds) and leading to excessive inflammation, which is related to such health problems as Type 2 diabetes, cardiovascular disease, chronic pain and neuro-degenerative disease (Kiecolt-Glaser et al., 2007; Wilson et al., 2002). Rather than accepting IPV survivors' decline into poor health, PNI research suggests that interventions can be provided to help counter the physiological changes, downregulate stress responses, and lower survivors' risk of health problems (Kiecolt-Glaser et al., 2007). Specifically, omega-3 supplements (e.g., fish oil supplements) and exercise have shown to be effective in reducing heightened stress response and may be used to increase IPV survivors' resilience to stress (Kendall-Tackett, 2009).

More recently, research has begun to explore the link between IPV exposure, chronic stress and poor overall health at the cellular level. Telomeres, protective components that stabilize the ends of chromosomes and modulate cellular aging, are hypothesized to be shorter in length among women with IPV exposure. In an exploratory study involving 61 formerly abused women and 41 nonabused women, mean leukocyte telomere length was measured by a quantitative polymerase chain reaction assay. Telomere length was found to be significantly shorter in the women who had formerly been abused, with length of time in the abusive relationship being associated with telomere length (Humphreys et al., in press). The findings have provided important new insight into the link between IPV exposure, duration of IPV-related stress, and telomere length molecular mechanisms regulating cellular aging. In addition, the long-held presumption that the stress of IPV may cause greater morbidity can now be fully investigated in finding out if IPV-related stress causes cellular aging.

Impact on mental health

Not all injuries from IPV are physical. Depression and post-traumatic stress disorder (PTSD) are the two most prevalent mental health sequelae of IPV. A meta-analysis of 18 studies has found a weighted mean prevalence of depression of 47.6% among abused women (Golding, 1999), which is much higher than the lifetime rates of between 10.2% and 21.3% found in general female populations (Kessler et al., 1994; Weissman, Bruce, Leaf, Florio, & Holzer, 1991). In the same meta-analysis, the weighted mean prevalence of post-traumatic stress disorder (PTSD) was 63.8%, which is also higher than the lifetime rates of between 1.3% and 12.3% in general populations of women (Davidson, Hughes, Blazer, & George, 1991; Kessler, Sonnega, Bromet, Hughes, & Nelson, 1995). A dose-response relationship has been suggested since severity or duration of IPV has been found to be associated with the prevalence or severity of both depression and PTSD (Golding, 1999). Furthermore, as PTSD and depression often overlap (Friedman & Schnurr, 1995; Hammarberg, 1992), it is important to recognize that depression detected in some IPV survivors may represent symptoms of PTSD (Golding, 1999).

Depression can act as a chronic stressor for survivors of IPV, causing a profound effect on their health (Kendall-Tackett, 2007) and contributing significantly to increased healthcare costs for abused women (Wisner, Gilmer, Saltzman, & Zink, 1999). In addition, depression has been shown to have an adverse impact on abused women's functioning (Heifrich, Fujiura, & Rutkowski-Kmitta, 2008) as it reduces their ability to establish and maintain relationships or to access social support (Carlson, McNutt, Choi, & Rose, 2002). It also impairs their capacity to perform self-care (Constantino, Sekula, Rabin, & Stone, 2000) or meet work requirements (Brush, 2000), and diminishes their motivation to make decisions and maintain independence (O'Brien, 2002).

PTSD, an anxiety disorder that develops after exposure to trauma, is characterized by distressing memories or emotions about the trauma, avoidance of trauma reminders and elevated arousal (Green & Kimerling, 2004). The PTSD symptoms (including flashbacks, intrusive images, exaggerated startle response, nightmares, and avoidance of triggers that are associated with the abuse) may still be experienced by IPV survivors long after they have left the dangerous situations. It has been suggested that the PTSD symptoms experienced by IPV survivors should be interpreted as responses to extreme traumatic stressors. In so doing, it would help to depathologize survivors and facilitate healing (Golding, 1999).

It has been suggested that PTSD and chronic pain co-occur at a high rate and may interact to negatively impact the course of either disorder (Kulich, Mencher, Bertrand, & Maciewicz, 2000; Sharp & Harvey, 2001). In a review of the literature on the prevalence and development of chronic pain and PTSD,

Otis, Keane, and Kerns (2003) concluded that chronic pain associated with PTSD is more intense and results in more distress and disability than chronic pain that is not associated with PTSD. None of the above studies, however, focused specifically on IPV survivors. In the context of IPV, Wuest and colleagues (2009) conducted the first study to examine the multivariate relationships among chronic pain, IPV, and PTSD. The findings indicated that PTSD symptoms were a significant mediator of the relationships between IPV severity and chronic pain severity. Not only did the study provide evidence linking PTSD, chronic pain, and IPV, it also highlighted the importance of paying attention to symptoms of PTSD when managing chronic pain in IPV survivors.

PTSD may also have negative impacts on IPV survivors' physical health through health risk behaviours. It has been suggested that the traumatic effect of IPV can be so stressful and crippling that it can impact survivors' perceptions about health and health risk behaviours (Rheingold, Acierno, & Resnick, 2004). Studies have also found that both trauma (such as IPV) and PTSD are associated with health risk behaviours such as smoking, alcohol abuse, drug abuse, sexual risk behaviours, and physical inactivity (Felitti et al., 1998; Walker et al., 1999).

Other mental health problems have also been found to be associated with IPV, for example, suicidal tendencies (Golding, 1999), anxiety, insomnia, and social dysfunction (Ratner, 1993). In studies that explored the occurrence of mental health problems in IPV survivors, important precursors have been identified, including frequency and severity of IPV, previous trauma, and partner dominance (Campbell, Sullivan, & Davidson, 1995; Silva, McFarlane, Soeken, Parker, & Reel, 1997). Conversely, self-care agency—a woman's ability to care for herself—was found to be a protective factor against depression (Campbell, Kub, Belknap, & Templin, 1997). Knowing the moderators and mediators of the association between IPV and survivors' mental health is important for designing appropriate interventions. For example, a recent study found that power within a sexual relationship mediated the relationship between IPV and depression: women who felt powerless also reported higher rates of IPV and higher levels of depression. For these women, an empowerment approach has been suggested to decrease their likelihood of experiencing violence victimization and the subsequent risk of depression (Filson, Ulloa, Runfola, & Hokoda, 2010).

Impact on reproductive health

Women survivors of IPV are more likely to report gynaecological problems
than nonabused women (M. P. Koss, Koss, & Woodruff, 1991). Common
gynaecological problems reported by abused women include sexually transmitted diseases, vaginal bleeding, genital irritation, chronic pelvic pain, urinary
tract infection, and vaginal infection (Campbell, 2002). Forced sex might
partly explain the link between IPV and gynaecological problems (Campbell
& Soeken, 1999). It is possible that trauma from forced sex (vaginal, anal or
urethral) may lead to increased direct transmission of micro-organisms into
the bloodstream or back flow of bacteria into the urethra. In addition, shame
and stress from forced sex may depress the survivor's immune system, while
abusers having unprotected sex with other partners may also be responsible for
the higher prevalence of gynaecological problems among those experiencing
IPV (Campbell, 2002). In addition, IPV can lead to human immunodeficiency
virus (HIV) infection and acquired immunodeficiency syndrome (AIDS)
through coerced sex or abusers interfering with their partner's use of condoms
(Maman, Campbell, Sweat, & Gielen, 2000).

Unwanted pregnancy is another reproductive health problem experienced
by women survivors of IPV. In many cases, IPV continues when a woman
becomes pregnant and may even escalate (Gazmararian et al., 2000; Mezey,
1997). Four categories of IPV in pregnancy have been proposed: (1) jealousy towards the unborn child; (2) anger towards the unborn child; (3) preg-
nancy-specific violence, not directed at the child; and (4) "business as usual"
(Campbell, Oliver, & Bullock, 1993).

IPV during pregnancy represents a serious threat to health and the risk of
death of the mother, fetus, or both. A number of studies have investigated
the associations between IPV, pregnancy complications and infant outcomes
including miscarriage, premature birth, low birth weight, fetal injury, fetal
death, maternal infections, poor weight gain, and depression (e.g., Bacchus,
Mezey, & Bewley, 2004; Boy & Salihu, 2004; Gazmararian et al., 2000;
Martin, Kilgallen, Dee, Dawson, & Campbell, 1998; Mezey, 1997; Parker,
McFarlane, & Soeken, 1994; Parsons & Harper, 1999; Taft, Broom, & Legge,
2004). Findings across the studies, however, were inconsistent. An exception
was the evidence for IPV being a risk factor for low birth weight. A meta-
analysis of 14 published studies has found a weak but significant association
between abuse during pregnancy and low birth weight (Murphy, Schei, Myhr,

& Du Mont, 2001). The reasons for low birth weight are likely to be complex, with premature delivery resulting from IPV, low maternal weight gain, lack of/delayed entry into prenatal care, and maternal smoking all playing a possible role (Berenson, Wiemann, Wilkinson, Jones, & Anderson, 1994; Curry & Harvey, 1998; Dietz et al., 1997; Lipsky, Holt, Easterling, & Critchlow, 2003).

To summarize, IPV is associated with adverse physical, mental, and reproductive health outcomes among survivors. Interventions are needed to reduce or eliminate violence and promote the health of those who have experienced IPV. In the next section, interventions for IPV survivors will be discussed.

Interventions for IPV survivors

There are numerous interventions for IPV survivors designed to prevent abuse or re-abuse and/or to improve the health consequences for survivors. Interventions may be primary, secondary, or tertiary. Primary interventions seek to prevent the onset of abuse, and include campaigns that mobilize communities against abuse (e.g., Ellsberg, Liljestrand, & Winkvist, 1997; Mehrotra, Burde, Banerjee, & Pardiwala, 2000) and school programmes on preventing violence (e.g., Foshee et al., 2000; Krajewski, Rybarik, Dosch, & Gilmore, 1996). Secondary interventions aim to prevent further abuse (e.g., McFarlane, Groff, O'Brien, & Watson, 2006; Tiwari et al., 2005), while tertiary interventions are designed to address the consequences of IPV (e.g., Champion et al., 2007; Constantino, Kim, & Crane, 2005).

Classification of interventions

Secondary and tertiary IPV interventions have been classified in a number of ways. For example, in a systematic review of advocacy interventions, Ramsay et al. (2009) classified them as (a) those that aim at directly helping survivors (through the provision of advocacy or therapy), and (b) those that aim at indirectly helping survivors (by improving the responses of professionals who work with survivors). In the *World Report on Violence and Health*, Krug et al. (2002) classified interventions for abused women under health service interventions (e.g., Leye, Githaniga, & Temmerman, 1999; Parker, McFarlane, Soeken, Silva, & Reel, 1999) or coordinated community interventions (e.g., Gamache, Edleson, & Schock, 1988; Littel, Malefyt, & Walker, 1998).

Effects of interventions

More recently, the effects of interventions for women who have experienced IPV were assessed in a systematic review conducted by Ramsay et al. (2009). A total of 10 trials involving 1,527 participants were included. Highlights of the trials in relation to preventing IPV and/or promoting the health of IPV survivors are presented as follows.

Psychological distress

In a clinical trial involving 30 abused women who were first-time residents of a domestic violence shelter (Constantino et al., 2005), a structured social support group intervention (with information on resources and an environment in which to chat with counsellor and friends) was provided to those in the intervention group over eight weekly sessions. Both the intervention and control groups received usual shelter care. Among the outcome measures, psychological distress was assessed immediately post-intervention using the Brief Symptom Inventory. Following the intervention, a statistically significant reduction in psychological distress was found.

Reduced psychological distress was also reported in a trial conducted by Hyman (2001) in an accident and emergency department. A total of 102 abused women were recruited to Hyman's study. Fifty-one were assigned to an intervention group and 51 to a control group. An Emergency Department Victim Advocacy programme based on empowerment counselling (empathic support, education, safety planning, linkage with community resources, and the pledge to follow up within 48 hours) was provided to those in the intervention group. The programme, which lasted 1.5 hours, was designed to enable the woman to assess her situation, help her identify signs of danger, and to establish "back-up" if the violence escalated. Women in the control group received standard social services care. Psychological distress was assessed three to four months post-intervention using the Symptom Checklist-90-Revised and Global Severity Index.

Two other studies were conducted involving the use of intensive interventions (more than 12 hours); however, no reduction in psychological distress or anxiety was found post-intervention (Jouriles et al., 2001; Sullivan, Tan, Basta, Rumptz, & Davidson, 1992). In Jouriles et al.'s trial, 36 mothers who had been physically abused by their male partners in the last 12 months were recruited and randomly assigned to an intervention or control group. An intervention, known as Project SUPPORT, provided the mothers and their children with social, emotional, and instrumental support. Specifically, the mothers were taught child management skills while support was provided to help them during the transition from the shelter. They also received help in obtaining physical resources and social support in order to become self-supporting. The intervention, in the form of weekly sessions, lasted 1–1.5 hours each over 8 months. Mothers in the control group received monthly contact, either in person or by phone, and were encouraged to use existing community or shelter services. Psychological distress was assessed using the Symptoms Checklist-90-Revised (as in Hyman's study) at the midway point of the intervention, immediately post-intervention, and also 4, 8, 12, and 24 months post-intervention, but no reduction was found.

Anxiety

In the trial conducted by Sullivan et al. (1992), 146 abused women were recruited from a shelter and assigned to an intervention ($n = 76$) or control ($n = 70$) group. Intensive one-on-one services with an advocate, who assisted the women to devise a safety plan and access community services, were provided to those in the intervention group. The 10-week, post-shelter intervention provided contact for the women for an average of seven hours per week. The Rape Aftermath Symptom Test was used to measure long-term fear and anxiety immediately post-intervention and at 6, 12, 18, 24, and 36 months after the intervention. No significant reduction in anxiety was found at the different time-points.

Depressive symptoms

The effect of the intervention on depressive symptoms was also assessed in Sullivan et al.'s (1992) trial using the Centre for Epidemiological Studies Depression Scale at 12 months follow-up. A significant reduction effect was found based on a multivariate analysis. In another study, postnatal depressive symptoms were used as the outcome measure to evaluate the effectiveness of a brief advocacy intervention for abused pregnant Chinese women in the antenatal clinic of a public hospital (Tiwari et al., 2005). Of the 110 women identified as abused by an intimate partner within the last 12 months, half were randomly assigned to an intervention group and half to a control group. An empowerment intervention was provided to women in the intervention group to enhance their independence and control (including advice on safety, choice making, and problem solving). In addition, empathic understanding was added to validate the women's feelings and to help them value themselves positively. The intervention, which lasted about 30 minutes, was provided on an individual basis by a midwife with a degree in counselling. An information brochure was also provided. Women in the control group received standard care in the form of a wallet-sized card with information on community resources for abused women (including shelter hotlines, law enforcement, social services, and nongovernmental organizations). The Edinburgh Postnatal Depression Scale (Chinese version) was used to assess postnatal depression at 6 weeks post-delivery (which, depending on gestation age at recruitment, was 16–34 weeks post-intervention). The results showed that significantly fewer women in the intervention group developed postnatal depression compared with the control group.

As a whole, results from the five studies (Constantino et al., 2005; Hyman, 1991; Jouriles et al., 2001; Sullivan et al., 1992; Tiwari et al., 2005) suggest that the evidence for positive effects of interventions on mental health (psychological distress, anxiety, depressive symptoms, and postnatal depression) is equivocal. Also, none of the five trials reported on the effects of the interventions on physical health including physiological functioning, physical injuries, and chronic health disorders.

IPV victimization: physical abuse

Several trials have assessed the effects of interventions for abused women on IPV victimization. In a trial involving 360 women recruited from primary care clinics or women, infants, and children clinics who had been identified as having been physically or sexually abused by an intimate partner within the last 12 months, nurse case management was provided to 180 women who were randomly assigned to the intervention group (McFarlane et al., 2006). The intervention aimed to empower abused women by increasing their independence (with a focus on protection, safety, enhanced choice making and problem solving). The nurse who facilitated the intervention gave anticipatory guidance and guided referrals tailored to the participants' individual needs. The sessions lasted for 20 minutes on average and were provided at baseline and at 6-monthly intervals for two years. The control group received a referral card listing a safety plan and sources for IPV services. Physical abuse was assessed using the Severity of Violence Against Women Scale at 6, 12, 18, and 24 months follow-ups. There was no evidence that the intervention led to a reduction in severe physical abuse either at 12 months or 24 months follow-up. Similarly, in Tiwari et al.'s (2005) study, a brief 30-minute intervention was also not associated with any reduction in severe physical abuse as measured at 6 weeks post-delivery using the Conflict Tactics Scale. Studies by Jouriles et al. (2001) and Sullivan et al. (1992), however, suggested that women who received the interventions experienced significantly less physical abuse than women in the control group, as measured by the Conflict Tactics Scale. Given the mixed results from the studies cited, there is insufficient evidence to confirm the benefits of interventions for abused women in terms of reducing physical abuse.

IPV victimization: emotional and sexual abuse

Emotional abuse as an outcome measure of the effectiveness of interventions for abused women has been reported by McFarlane et al. (2006), Sullivan et al. (1992), and Tiwari et al. (2005). Emotional abuse was measured using the Severity of Violence Against Women Scale (McFarlane et al., 2006), the Index of Psychological Abuse (Sullivan et al., 1992), and the Conflict Tactics Scale (Tiwari et al., 2005). A statistically significant reduction in emotional abuse at 16–34 weeks after receiving a brief, one-off intervention for abused women was reported by Tiwari and colleagues; however, neither the McFarlane et al. trial nor the Sullivan et al. trial found reduced emotional abuse post-intervention. Thus, there is equivocal evidence on whether interventions for abused women had a positive impact on emotional abuse. In addition, only the trial by Tiwari and colleagues reported on the effect of the intervention on sexual abuse (as measured by an extra item on sexual abuse in the Conflict Tactics Scale). No significant mean change differences in the level of sexual abuse between the intervention and control groups were found.

To summarize, despite efforts to provide interventions for abused women, there is insufficient evidence to determine if they have beneficial effects on reducing IPV and/or promoting health. As recommended in previous systematic reviews (Ramsay et al., 2002, 2009; Wathen & MacMillan, 2003), additional research using rigorous designs to test the effectiveness of IPV interventions on important abuse and/or health outcomes is needed.

Conclusion

There is ample evidence that IPV is associated with mortality and morbidity and that its impact on health can persist long after the abuse has ended. Interventions to prevent IPV and to reduce its impact on the health of survivors are therefore needed. However, in light of the lack of unequivocal evidence of the benefits of interventions, efforts on evidence-based approaches in IPV interventions remain a priority.

References

Bacchus, L., Mezey, G., & Bewley, S. (2004). Domestic violence: prevalence in pregnant women and associations with physical and psychological health. *European Journal of Obstetrics & Gynecology, 113*, 6–11. doi: 10.1016/S0301-2115(03)00326-9

Berenson, A. B., Wiemann, C. M., Wilkinson, G. S., Jones, W. A., & Anderson, G. A. (1994). Perinatal morbidity associated with violence experienced by pregnant women. *American Journal of Obstetrics and Gynecology, 170*, 1760–1769. doi: 10.1016/S0002-9378(94)70352-3

Bonomi, A. E., Anderson, M. L., Rivara, F. P., & Thompson, R. S. (2007). Health outcomes in women with physical and sexual intimate partner violence exposure. *Journal of Women's Health, 16*, 987–997. doi: 10.1089/jwh.2006.0239

Boy, A., & Salihu, H. M. (2004). Intimate partner violence and birth outcomes: a systematic review. *International Journal of Fertility, 49*, 159–163.

Brush, L. D. (2000). Battering, traumatic stress, and welfare-to-work transition. *Violence Against Women, 6*, 1039–1065. doi: 10.1177/10778010022183514

Campbell, J. C. (2002). Health consequences of intimate partner violence. *Lancet, 359*, 1331–1335. Retrieved from http://www.nnvawi.org/pdfs/alo/Campbell_1.pdf

Campbell, J. C., Oliver, C., & Bullock, L. (1993). Why battering during pregnancy? *AWHONNS Clinical Issues in Perinatal & Women's Health Nursing, 4*, 343–349.

Campbell, J. C., Sullivan, C. M., & Davidson, W. S. (1995). Women who use domestic violence shelters: changes in depression over time. *Women's Studies Quarterly, 19*, 237–255. doi: 10.1111/j.1471-6402.1995.tb00290.x

Campbell, J. C., Kub, J., Belknap, R. A., & Templin, T. N. (1997). Predictors of depression in battered women. *Violence Against Women, 3*, 271–293. doi: 10.1177/1077801297003003004

Campbell, J. C., & Soeken, K. (1999). Forced sex and intimate partner violence: effects on women's health. *Violence Against Women, 5*, 1017–1035. doi: 10.1177/1077801299005009003

Campbell, J. C., Glass, N., Sharps, P. W., Laughon, K., & Bloom, T. (2007). Intimate partner homicide. Review and implications of research and policy. *Trauma, Violence, & Abuse, 8*, 246–269. doi: 10.1177/1524838007303505

Carlson, B. E., McNutt, L., Choi, D. Y., & Rose, I. M. (2002). Intimate partner abuse and mental health: the role of social support and other protective factors. *Violence Against Women, 8*, 720–745. doi: 10.1177/10778010222183251

Catalano, S. (2007). *Intimate Partner Violence in the United States.* Retrieved from US Department of Justice, Bureau of Justice Statistics website: http://bjs.ojp.usdoj.gov/content/pub/pdf/ipvus.pdf

Champion, J. D., Shain, R. N., Korte, J. E., Holden, A. E. C., Piper, J. M., Perdue, S. T., & Guerra, F. A. (2007). Behavioural interventions and abuse: secondary analysis of reinfection in minority women. *International Journal of STD & AIDS, 18*, 748–753. doi: 10.1258/095646207782212180

Constantino, R. E., Sekula, L. E., Rabin, B., & Stone, C. (2000). Negative life experiences, depression, and immune function in abused and nonabused women. *Biological Research for Nursing, 1*, 190–198. doi: 10.1177/109980040000100304

Constantino, R., Kim, Y., & Crane, P. A. (2005). Effects of a social support intervention on health outcomes in residents of a domestic violence shelter: a pilot study. *Issues in Mental Health Nursing, 26*, 575–590. doi: 10.1080/01612840590959416

Curry, M. A., & Harvey, S. M. (1998). Stress related to domestic violence during pregnancy and infant birthweight. In J. Campbell (Ed.), *Empowering Survivors of Abuse: Health Care for Battered Women and Their Children.* Thousand Oaks, CA: Sage.

Davidson, J. R., Hughes, D., Blazer, D. G., & George, L. K. (1991). Post-traumatic stress disorder in the community: an epidemiological study. *Psychological Medicine, 21*, 713–721. doi: 10.1017/S0033291700022352

Dearwater, S. R., Coben, J. H., Campbell, J. C., Nah, G., Glass, N., McLoughlin, E., & Bekemeier, B. (1998). Prevalence of intimate partner violence in women treated at community hospital emergency departments. *JAMA, 280*, 433–438.

Dietz, P. M., Gazmararian, J. A., Goodwin, M. M., Bruce, C., Johnson, C. H., & Rochat, R. W. (1997). Delayed entry into prenatal care: effect of physical violence. *Obstetrics and Gynecology, 90*, 221–224. doi: 10.1016/S0029-7844(97)00252-4

Ellsberg, M., Liljestrand, J., & Winkvist, A. (1997). The Nicaraguan Network of Women Against Violence: using research and action for change. *Reproductive Health Matters, 5*, 82–92. doi: 10.1016/S0968-8080(97)90088-4

Fauveau V., Koenig, M. A., Chakraborty, J., & Chowdhury, A. I. (1998). Causes of maternal mortality in rural Bangladesh, 1976–85. *Bulletin of the World Health Organization, 66*, 643–651. Retrieved from http://www.ncbi.nlm.nih.gov/pmc/articles/PMC2491193/pdf/bullwho00070-0108.pdf

Felitti, V. J., Anda, R. F., Nordenberg, D., Williamson, D. F., Spitz, A. M., Edwards, V., Koss, M. P., & Marks, J. S. (1998). Relationship of childhood abuse and household dysfunction to many of the leading causes of death in adults: the Adverse Childhood Experiences (ACE) study. *American Journal of Preventive Medicine, 14*, 245–258. Retrieved from http://download.journals.elsevierhealth.com/pdfs/journals/0749-3797/PIIS0749379798000178.pdf

Filson, J., Ulloa, E., Runfola, C., & Hokoda, A. (2010). Does powerlessness explain the relationship between intimate partner violence and depression? *Journal of Interpersonal Violence, 25*, 400–415. doi: 10.1177/0886260509334401

Forshee, V.A., Bauman, K. E., Breene, W. F., Koch, G. G., Linder, G. F., & MacDougall, J. E. (2000). The Safe Dates program: one-year follow-up results. *American Journal of Public Health, 90*, 1619–1622. Retrieved from http://ajph.aphapublications.org/cgi/reprint/90/10/1619.pdf

Friedman, M. J., & Schnurr, P. P. (1995). The relationship between trauma, post-traumatic stress disorder, and physical health. In M. J. Friedman, D. S. Charney, & A. Y. Deutch (Eds.), *Neurobiological and Clinical Consequences of Stress: From Normal Adaptation to PTSD* (pp. 507–524). Philadelphia, PA: Lippincott-Raven.

Gamache, D. J., Edleson, J. S., & Schock, M. D. (1988). Coordinated police, judicial, and social service response to woman battering: a multiple baseline evaluation across three communities. In G. T. Hotaling, D. Finkelhor, J. T. Kirkpatrick, & M. A. Straus (Eds.), *Coping with Family Violence: Research and Policy Perspectives* (pp. 193–209). Thousand Oaks, CA: Sage.

Ganatra, B. R., Coyaji, K. J., & Rao, V. N. (1998). Too far, too little, too late: a community-based case-control study of maternal mortality in rural west Maharashtra, India. *Bulletin of the World Health Organization, 76*, 591–598. Retrieved from http://www.ncbi.nlm.nih.gov/pmc/articles/PMC2312494/pdf/bullwho00389-0066.pdf

Gazmararian, J. A., Petersen, R., Spitz, A. M., Goodwin, M. M., Saltzman, L. E., & Marks, J. S. (2000). Violence and reproductive health: current knowledge and future research directions. *Maternal & Child Health Journal, 4*, 79–84. doi: 10.1023/A:1009514119423

Golding, J. M. (1996). Sexual assault history and limitations in physical functioning in two general population samples. *Research in Nursing and Health, 19*, 33–44. doi: 10.1002/(SICI)1098-240X(199602)19:1<33::AID-NUR4>3.0.CO;2-M

Golding, J. M. (1999). Intimate partner violence as a risk factor for mental disorders: a meta-analysis. *Journal of Family Violence, 14*, 99–132. doi: 10.1023/A:1022079418229

Green, B. L., & Kimerling, R. (2004). Trauma, posttraumatic-stress disorder, and health status. In P. P. Schnurr & B. L. Green (Eds.), *Trauma and Health: Physical Health Consequences of Exposure to Extreme Stress* (pp. 13–42). Washington, DC: American Psychological Association.

Hammarberg, M. (1992). Penn Inventory for posttraumatic stress disorder: psychometric properties. *Psychological Assessment, 4*, 67–76.

Helfrich, C. A., Fujiura, G. T., & Rutkowski-Kmitta, V. (2008). Mental health disorders and functioning of women in domestic violence shelters. *Journal of Interpersonal Violence, 23*, 437–453. doi: 10.1177/0886260507312942

Humphreys, J., Cooper, B. A., & Miaskowski, C. (2010). Differences in depression, posttraumatic stress disorder, and lifetime trauma exposure in formerly abused women with mild versus moderate to severe chronic pain. *Journal of Interpersonal Violence*. Advance online publication. doi: 10.1177/0886260509354882.

Humphreys, J., Epel, E. S., Cooper, B. A., Lin, J., Blackburn, E. H., & Lee, K. A. (in press). Telomere shortening in formerly abused and never abused women. *Biological Research for Nursing*.

Hyman, K. (2001). *Impact of Emergency Department Intimate Partner Violence (IPV) Advocacy: A Longitudinal, Randomized Trial* (Doctoral dissertation). Pittsburgh, PA: University of Pittsburgh.

Jouriles, E. N., McDonald, R., Spiller, L., Norwood, W. D., Swank, P. R., Stephens, N., Ware, H., & Buzy, W. M. (2001). Reducing conduct problems among children of battered women. *Journal of Counseling & Clinical Psychology, 69*, 774–785. doi: 10.1037/0022-006X.69.5.774

Kendall-Tackett, K. (2007). Inflammation, cardiovascular disease, and metabolic syndrome as sequelae of violence against women: the role of depression, hostility, and sleep disturbance. *Trauma, Violence, & Abuse, 8*, 117–126. doi: 10.1177/1524838007301161

Kendall-Tackett, K. (2008). The psychoneuroimmunology of traumatic stress on heart disease and diabetes. *Family & Intimate Partner Violence Quarterly, 1*, 45–59.

Kendall-Tackett, K. (2009). Improving the health of adult survivors of family violence. *Family & Intimate Partner Violence Quarterly, 1*, 215–222.

Kessler, R. C., McGonagle, K. A., Zhao, S., Nelson, C. B., Hughes, M., Eshleman, S., Wittchen, H. U., & Kendler, K. S. (1994). Lifetime and 12-month prevalence of DSM-III-R psychiatric disorders in the United States: results from the National Comorbidity Survey. *Archives of General Psychiatry, 51*, 8–19. Retrieved from http://apsychoserver.psych.arizona.edu/JJBAReprints/PSYC621/Kessler%20 et%20al_Lifetime%20and%2012%20months%20prevalence_Archives%20 of%20Gen%20Psychiatry_%60994.pdf

Kessler, R. C., Sonnega, A., Bromet, E., Hughes, M., & Nelson, C. B. (1995). Posttraumatic stress disorder in the national comorbidity survey. *Archives of General Psychiatry, 52*, 1048–1060.

Kibler, J. L., Joshi, K., & Hughes, E. E. (in press). Cognitive and behavioral reactions to stress among adults with PTSD: implications for immunity and health. In K. A. Kendall-Tackett (Ed.), *The Psychoneuroimmunology of Chronic Disease: Exploring the Links Between Inflammation, Stress, and Illness*. Washington, DC: American Psychological Association.

Kiecolt-Glaser, J. K., Belury, M. A., Porter, K., Beversdoft, D., Lemeshow, S., Dickinson, S. L., & Glaser, R. (2007). Depressive symptoms, omega-6: omega-3 fatty acids, and inflammation in older adults. *Psychsomatic Medicine, 69*, 217–224. doi: 10.1097/PSY.0b013e3180313a45

Koss, M. P., Koss, P. G., & Woodruff, W. J. (1991). Deleterious effects of criminal victimization on women's health and medical utilization. *Archives of Internal Medicine, 151*, 342–347.

Krajewski, S. S., Rybarik, M. F., Dosch, M. F., & Gilmore, G. D. (1996). Results of a curriculum intervention with seventh graders regarding violence in relationships. *Journal of Family Violence, 11*, 93–112. doi: 10.1007/BF02336664

Krug, E. T., Dahlberg, L. L., Mercy, J. A., Zwi, A. B., & Lozano, R. (2002). *World Report on Violence and Health*. Geneva: World Health Organization.

Kulich, R. J., Mencher, P., Bertrand, C., & Maciewicz, R. (2000). Comorbidity of post-traumatic stress disorder and chronic pain: implications for clinical and forensic assessment. *Current Review of Pain, 4*, 36–48. doi: 10.1007/s11916-000-0008-4

Leserman J., Drossman, D. A., Li, Z., Toomey, T. C., Nachman, G., & Glogau, L. (1996). Sexual and physical abuse history in gastroenterology practice: how types of abuse impact health status. *Psychosomatic Medicine, 58*, 4–15. Retrieved from http://www.psychosomaticmedicine.org/cgi/reprint/58/1/4.pdf

Leye, E., Githaniga, A., & Temmerman, M. (1999). *Health Care Strategies for Combating Violence Against Women in Developing Countries*. Ghent, Belgium: International Centre for Reproductive Health.

Lipsky, S., Holt, V. L., Easterling, T. R., & Critchlow, C. W. (2003). The impact of police reported intimate partner violence during pregnancy on birth outcomes. *Obstetrics and Gynecology, 102*, 557–564. Retrieved from http://journals.lww.com/greenjournal/Fulltext/2003/09000/Impact_of_Police_Reported_Intimate_Partner.25.aspx

Little, K., Malefyt, M. B., & Walker, A. H. (1998). *Assessing the Justice System Response to Violence Against Women: A Tool for Communities to Develop Coordinated Responses*. Retrieved from Minnesota Center against Violence and Abuse website: http://www.mincava.umn.edu/documents/promise/pp3/pp3.html

Maman, S., Campbell, J. C., Sweat, M., & Gielen, A. C. (2000). The intersection of HIV and violence: directions for future research and interventions. *Social Science Medicine, 50*, 459–478.

Martin, S. L., Kilgallen, B., Dee, D. L., Dawson, S., & Campbell, J. C. (1998). Women in a prenatal care/substance abuse treatment program: links between domestic violence and mental health. *Maternal Child Health Journal, 2*, 85–94. doi: 10.1023/A:1022988722277

McCauley, J. Kern, D. E., Kolodner, K., Dill, L., Schroeder, A. F., DeChant, H. K., Ryden, J., Derogatis, L. R., & Bass, E. B. (1997). Clinical characteristics of women with a history of childhood abuse: unhealed wounds. *Journal of the American Medical Association, 277*, 1362–1368. Retrieved from http://jama.ama-assn.org/cgi/reprint/277/17/1362

McFarlane, J., Groff, J. Y., O'Brien, J. A., & Watson, K. (2006). Secondary prevention of intimate partner violence. A randomized controlled trial. *Nursing Research, 55*, 52–61.

Mehrotra, A., Burde, D., Banerjee, R., & Pardiwala, T. (2000). *A Life Free of Violence: It's Our Right*. New York, NY: United Nations Development Fund for Women.

Mezey, G. C. (1997). Domestic violence in pregnancy. In S. Bewley, S., J. Friend, & G. Mezey (Eds.), *Violence Against Women*. London, England: Royal College of Obstetricians and Gynaecologists (RCOG).

Murphy, C. C., Schei, B., Myhr, T. L., & Du Mont, J. (2001). Abuse: a risk factor for low birth weight? A systematic review and meta-analysis. *Canadian Medical*

Association Journal, 164, 1567–1572. Retrieved from http://www.cmaj.ca/cgi/reprint/164/11/1567

O'Brien, S. M. (2002). Staying alive: a client with chronic mental illness in an environment of domestic violence. *Holistic Nursing Practice, 16*, 16–23.

Otis, J., Keane, T., & Kerns, R. (2003). An examination of the relationship between chronic pain and post-traumatic stress disorder. *Journal of Rehabilitation Research and* Development, *40*, 397–406. Retrieved from http://www.rehab.research.va.gov/jour/03/40/5/pdf/Otis.pdf

Parker, B., McFarlane, J., & Soeken, K. (1994). Abuse during pregnancy: effects on maternal complications and birth weight in adult and teenage women. *Obstetrics and Gynecology, 84*, 323–328.

Parker, B., McFarlane, J., Soeken, K., Silva, C., & Reel, S. (1999). Testing an intervention to prevent further abuse to pregnant women. *Research in Nursing and Health, 22*, 59–66.

Parsons, L. H., & Harper, M. A. (1999). Violent maternal deaths in North Carolina. *Obstetrics & Gynecology, 94*, 990–993. Retrieved from: http://journals.lww.com/greenjournal/Fulltext/1999/12000/Violent_Maternal_Deaths_in_North_Carolina.16.aspx

Ramsay, J., Carter, Y., Davidson, L., Dunne, D., Eldridge, S., Feder, G., Hegarty, K., Rivas, C., Taft, A., & Warburton, A. (2009). Advocacy interventions to reduce or eliminate violence and promote the physical and psychological well-being of women who experience intimate partner abuse. *Campbell Systematic Reviews, 5*. doi: 10.4073/csr.2009.5

Ratner, P. A. (1993). The incidence of wife abuse and mental health status in abused wives in Edmonton, Alberta. *Canadian Journal of Public Health, 84*, 246–249.

Rheingold, A. A., Acierno, R., & Resnick, H. S. (2004). Trauma, posttraumatic stress disorder, and health risk behaviors. In P. P. Schnurr & B. L. Green (Eds.), *Trauma and Health. Physical Health Consequences of Exposure to Extreme Stress* (pp. 217–244). Washington, DC: American Psychological Association.

Sharp, T. J., & Harvey, A. G. (2001). Chronic pain and posttraumatic stress disorder: mutual maintenance? *Clinical Psychological Review, 21*, 857–877. doi: 10.1016/S0272-7358(00)00071-4

Silva, C., McFarlane, J., Soeken, K., Parker, B., & Reel, S. (1997). Symptoms of posttraumatic stress disorder in abused women in a primary care setting. *Journal of Women's Health, 6*, 543–552.

Sullivan, C. M., Tan, C., Basta, J., Rumptz, M., & Davidson, W. S. (1992). An advocacy intervention program for women with abusive partners: initial evaluation. *American Journal of Community Psychology, 20*, 309–332. doi: 10.1007/BF00937912

Sutherland, C., Bybee, D., & Sullivan, C. (1998). The long-term effects of battering on women's health. *Women's Health, 4*, 41–70.

Taft, A., Broom, D. H., & Legge, D. (2004). General practitioner management of intimate partner violence and the whole family: a qualitative study. *BMJ, 328*, 618–621. doi: 10.1136/bmj.38014.627535.0B

Tiwari, A., Leung, W. C., Leung, T. W., Humphreys, J., Parker, B., & Ho, P. C. (2005). A randomised controlled trial of empowerment training for Chinese abused pregnant women in Hong Kong. *BJOG, 112*, 1249–1256. doi: 10.1111/j.1471-0528.2005.00709.x

Walker, E. A., Keegan, D., Gardner, G., Sullivan, M., Katon, W. J., & Bernstein, D. (1997). Psychosocial factors in fibromyalgia compared with rheumatoid arthritis: II. Sexual, physical, and emotional abuse and neglect. *Psychosomatic Medicine, 59*, 572–577. Retrieved from http://www.psychosomaticmedicine. org/cgi/reprint/59/6/565

Walker, E. A., Gelfand, A., Katon, W. J., Koss, M. P., Von Korff, M., Bernstein, D. & Russo, J. (1999). Adult health status of women with histories of childhood abuse and neglect. *American Journal of Medicine, 107*, 332–339.

Wathen, C. N., & MacMillan, H. L. (2003). Interventions for violence against women. Scientific review. *JAMA, 289*, 589–600. Retrieved from http://jama.ama-assn. org/cgi/reprint/289/5/589.pdf

Weissman, M. M., Bruce, M. L., Leaf, P. J., Florio, L. P., & Holzer, C. I. (1991). Affective disorders. In L. N. Robins & D. A. Regier, D.A. (Eds.), *Psychiatric Disorders in America: The Epidemiologic Catchment Area Study* (pp. 53–80). New York, NY: The Free Press.

Wilson, C. J., Finch, C. E., & Cohen, H. J. (2002). Cytokines and cognition–the case for a head-to-toe inflammatory paradigm. *Journal of the American Geriatrics Society, 50*, 2041–2056. doi: 10.1046/j.1532-5415.2002.50619.x

Wisner, C. L., Gilmer, T. P., Saltzman, L. E., & Zink, T. M. (1999). Intimate partner violence against women: do victims cost health plans more? *Journal of Family Practice, 48*, 439–43.

Wuest, J., Ford-Gilboe, M., Merritt-Gray, M., Varcoe, C., Lent, B., Wilk, P., & Campbell, J. C. (2009). Abuse-related injury and symptoms of posttraumatic stress disorder as mechanisms of chronic pain in survivors of intimate partner violence. *Pain Medicine, 10*, 739–747. doi: 10.1111/j.1526-4637.2009.00624.x

10
Treatment and Screening of Intimate Partner Violence at a Hospital's Emergency Department

Chak-Wah Kam, Terry Chu-Leung Lau, and Fung-Ling So

Chapter summary

1. Intimate partner violence (IPV) has a high incidence in the community. It has substantial impact on the lives of victims, their children and other family members. It also places a significant demand on resources in the society.

2. The interdepartmental Clinical Practice Guide (CPG) sets out a multidisciplinary approach which enables clinicians (doctors and nurses) of a busy emergency department (ED) to provide holistic care for IPV patients, while taking up only a very minute proportion of their daily work.

3. IPV screening is very labour intensive in an ED with high patient census (attendance), and is of controversial value in the improvement of health outcome of victims.

Victims of intimate partner violence (IPV) are often sent to the emergency department and emergency clinicians can be main players in breaking cycles of violence to prevent devastating consequences for victims, children and families. A multidisciplinary approach with one-stop management in ED is vital for efficient and holistic care for IPV patients. IPV should have a greater weight in the undergraduate curricula of medicine and nursing, as well as more resources to strengthen postgraduate expertise development in this field. Ongoing territory-wide studies are highly recommended to monitor trends, and to investigate the problem's complex nature and the controversial effects of IPV screening. Special groups like male victims, ethnic minorities and same-sex partners also deserve more in-depth evaluation. Harmony restoration may yield greater gains than forced maintenance of the conventional configuration of having both parents in the family, if it is not feasible to resume shared living arrangements.

Emergency department management of intimate partner violence

Key issue

Violence against women by an intimate partner is a major contributor to ill health, and also jeopardizes women's mental well-being (World Health Organization, 2010). Intimate partner violence (IPV) has a high prevalence, causing tremendous harm not only to victims, but also to their children and other family members, with consequential impairment to their work performance and social life.

Definition of intimate partner violence

Intimate partner violence has been defined by the World Health Organization (WHO) as "any behaviour within an intimate relationship that causes physical, psychological or sexual harm to those in the relationship" (Krug, Dahlberg, Mercy, Zwi, & Lozano, 2002). Threat and harm can happen between current or former spouses and dating couples in a heterosexual, homosexual or bisexual relationship. Hence, these problems extend beyond the physical boundaries of home or family. Consequently, it has become more pertinent for IPV to encompass these complex situations, which have led to a change in the more conventional notion of "domestic violence".

Types of intimate partner violence

Abuse manifests in many forms (Virginia & Fisher, 2001), which include, but are not limited to:

<u>Physical abuse.</u> Physical abuse is a common injury mode which includes pushing, slapping, punching, kicking, beating and throwing objects, resulting in tenderness, bruises, abrasions, lacerations and occasionally, bone fracture. This is the major cause for emergency department (ED) consultations.

<u>Sexual abuse.</u> Sexual abuse usually involves forced, coerced or unwanted sex with partner, and may uncommonly present to the ED as rape by the ex-husband or boyfriend.

<u>Emotional abuse.</u> It is commonly inflicted in combination with physical abuse. If the victims are in isolation, they may seek help from social services rather than attend the ED. However, some mental cases received by the ED, such as persons with depression, may turn out to be the result of IPV.

<u>Economic abuse.</u> Economic abuse is to deprive the victim of money of his/ her own, money for emergency use, and/or the victim's earning capacity.

<u>Spiritual abuse.</u> It is the destruction of one's cultural or religious belief system.

The latter two types are presented to social workers more frequently than to emergency physicians.

Incidence and impact of IPV

In Hong Kong, the annual incidence as reported to the Central Registry of the Social Welfare Department (SWD) has been substantial, indicating IPV as a social malady constituting a tremendous community burden. The incidence ranged from 3,598 to 6,843 in the years 2005 to 2009 with a peak in 2008 (Social Welfare Department, 2010b) (Table 10.1). The annual number of cases presenting to the ED of Tuen Mun Hospital (TMH) followed a comparable trend until September 2007, when the ED of Pok Oi Hospital (POH) was reopened to cover catchment areas of the Tin Shui Wai and Yuen Long districts. The very low proportion of IPV cases received by hospital EDs—less than one case per 600 patient attendances daily, coupled with IPV's noncore topic status in the undergraduate curriculum of medicine, presents difficulties to its management within hospital EDs (Kam, 2004) and impedes expertise growth of ED clinicians in this area. Consequently, a very concise IPV management checklist (Appendix A) together with risk assessment is particularly helpful for busy ED doctors whose bulk of work consists of treating patients with medical or surgical illnesses.

For the common ailments of upper respiratory tract diseases (e.g., sore throat, cough, running nose), diarrhoea or minor accidental trauma of a similar Triage Priority Category as IPV cases (i.e., four, or semi-urgent), the consultation and prescription—or treatment—can be completed in about 10 to 20 minutes in just one session. In the ED Triage System, Category One comprises

Table 10.1 The annual incidence of IPV reported to the Central Registry of the Social Welfare Department and the Emergency Departments of Tuen Mun Hospital and Pok Oi Hospital for the years 2005–2009

	Annual incidence				
Unit	2005	2006	2007	2008	2009
SWD (Central Registry)	3598	4424	6404	6843	4807
TMH	343	404	335	286	237
POH	nil	nil	34[*]	132	170
TMH + POH	nil	nil	369	418	407

Note: * Data included after reopening of POH in September 2007.

SWD = Social Welfare Department. TMH = Tuen Mun Hospital. POH = Pok Oi Hospital.

critical or dying patients who require immediate treatment. Category Two includes emergency patients with rapidly deteriorating conditions, who should be managed within 15 minutes. Category Three refers to patients with urgent acute medical conditions requiring treatment within 30 minutes. Category Four (semi-urgent) encompasses patients with acute but non-life-threatening conditions requiring treatment within the next few hours, whereas Category Five (non-urgent) patients are those with very minor medical conditions and very low risk of acute deterioration, in whom delayed medical treatment after several hours will not affect the outcome. However, medical consultation and social worker assessment in IPV patient management take at least two to several hours to complete, and this kind of cases pose great challenges to ED clinicians since they may encounter the added difficulty and time-consuming task of communicating with a crying, depressed or distressed patient. Moreover, review after the social worker assessment is needed to reach consensus over a joint management plan.

Epidemiology of IPV and the characteristics of injury

Among 1,695 victims presented to the ED of TMH during the years 1999 to 2004, the annual incidence ranged from 183 to 338 (Lau et al., 2008). The average age was 39 years (range: 18 to 84) with a female predominance of 87%. Most female victims were in the age group of 31 to 40 years while the majority of male victims had an older age of 41 to 50 years. Around two-thirds (65%) of the victims were presented to the ED outside the office hours of medical social workers (MSW). About 10% had been abused once before, and 40% had suffered two or more recurrent episodes.

The head (39%), face (30%), upper limbs (37%) and lower limbs (17%) were commonly injured body regions, owing to slapping and punching to the former two regions, while the upper limbs were often injured in the course of self-defence by the abused. The great majority (73%) suffered mild injuries, and severe injuries were less common. Severe types encompassed lacerations or cuts (6.6%), nasal bone fractures (0.3%), limb fractures (0.8%), and ruptured tympanic membranes (0.9%). The majority (90%) of trauma were inflicted by hands or legs of the abusers, and the remaining 10% involved weapon use such as chair, telephone set, water bottles, sweeping brooms and knives. In-patient management was required for 8% of the patients owing to physical injury (68% of admitted patients) and mental trauma (the remaining 32%). The hospital admission rate decreased from 12% in 2001 to 4% in 2004 with the establishment of the short-stay unit of the ED to provide medium-term care.

A monthly variation analysis showed higher incidence during the summer season. This may be related to the school holiday break—as children stay at home for longer periods, it may more easily bring up situations of tension and conflict in the family and between the parents. The high summer temperatures in Hong Kong may also play a role, e.g., in causing greater irritability. The incidence was lower in January and February (Kam, Ng, & Ching, 2002), the time of the year which, besides having cooler temperatures, also coincide with the Chinese New Year, a traditional Chinese festival during which family and harmonious relationships are widely celebrated. It would take further investigation to confirm whether temperatures or festive seasons have an effect on the incidence of IPV.

Risk factors for IPV

Subsequent research in TMH among female victims presenting to the ED used a case control design to examine the risk factors for injury to married women (aged 18–60) from domestic violence (Tsui, Chan, So, & Kam, 2006). With the use of separate univariate analyses, the study revealed eight significantly predictive variables: woman being a new immigrant ($p = .003$), woman with no job ($p = .019$), husband with low educational level ($p < .001$), presence of extramarital affairs ($p < .001$), husband being unemployed ($p < .001$), husband with alcohol abuse issues ($p < .001$), husband being an illicit drug abuser ($p < .001$), and husband having mental illness ($p < .001$).

Five factors were identified to be significant in a logistic regression analysis: husband of low educational level (nil to primary) (adjusted $OR = 2.78$, $p = 0.023$, 95% CI [1.15, 6.73]), husband unemployed (adjusted $OR = 9.03$, [5.16, 15.80]), presence of extramarital affairs (adjusted $OR = 5.22$, [2.90, 9.40]), husband with alcohol abuse issues (adjusted $OR = 6.09$, [3.46, 10.72]), husband having mental illness (adjusted $OR = 9.44$, [2.35, 37.93]).

From the information conveyed by the women victims, risk factors for being a male abuser were:

1. Having mental illness (OR 9.44, [2.351–37.926], $p = 0.002$)
2. Being unemployed (OR 9.03, [5.163–15.796], $p < 0.001$)
3. Being alcoholic (OR 6.09, [3.460–10.716], $p < 0.001$)
4. Having an extramarital affair (OR 5.22, [2.899–9.395]; $p < 0.001$), and
5. Having a low education level [nil to primary level] (OR 2.78, [1.149–6.727], $p = 0.023$)

Associated risk factors for female victims were:

1. Woman has no paid job ($p = 0.019$)
2. Woman is a new immigrant ($p = 0.003$), and
3. Husband is an illicit drug abuser ($p = 0.032$)

Preventive strategies can thus be focussed on these identified issues. However, this study was conducted in one regional public hospital serving a population of over one million living in the New Territories in Hong Kong. It may only reflect the unique local socioeconomic status, and generalization to the wider city population may not be applicable (K. L. Chan, 2006). Extension of the study to all major public and private hospital EDs may overcome the limitation, but this may give rise to other constraints, such as limited study resources.

The core philosophy of IPV management

The essential management principles of IPV in the ED (American College of Emergency Physicians, 2010; Harmony House, 2006; Social Welfare

Department, 2010a; Wong, 2003; Working Group on Combating Violence, 2004; Virginia & Fisher, 2001) are listed below: —

(a)   To identify and treat the life-threatening physical injuries as the first priority;

(b)   To provide a prompt, nonjudgmental and holistic assessment for the victim (starting from the physical and psychological aspects);

(c)   To provide treatment of the physical trauma;

(d)   Non-mandatory report to the police;

(e)   To provide early or timely consultation or referral to the social services;

(f)   To provide risk evaluation and assessment for the need of safe shelter with stress on protection and prevention;

(g)   To identify any associated child abuse and provide the suitable services; and

(h)   To provide appropriate patient disposition to continue the necessary medical therapy through social worker follow-up management.

Advanced life support is the universal algorithm adopted in ED in the management of critical patients, including those in the trauma category. Life-threatening injury takes the top priority as the logical working sequence, which means saving the patient's life first and addressing mental issues subsequently.

Mandatory reporting of IPV to the criminal justice system or police can deter help-seeking in some patients who are contemplating reconciliation or harbouring worries of revenge by the abusers. In the ED in TMH, half of the IPV cases were reported to the police prior to medical consultation. The remaining clients were advised to report to the police on a voluntary basis or to make their own decision after counselling by social workers.

For major or life-threatening IPV injuries amounting to severe crimes, the clinicians may report to the police in good faith and should be immune from liability for noncompliance with the personal data (privacy) ordinance, similar to the case of reporting gazetted notifiable infectious diseases to the Department of Health in the absence of the patient's consent. Certainly, the clinician should try his/her best to obtain the patient's agreement as far as possible while balancing the benefits and risks of reporting to the police and the community. Police intervention can prevent the violence in many cases, but may also aggravate the abuser's anger towards the victim.

Information and advice on a variety of topics are to be imparted to victims, in order to empower them to address acute episodes and possible future incidents. These include information and advice on home safety assessment (knowing the location of sharp objects such as the scissors and cutting knives in the kitchen, and the escape route); emergency services telephone numbers in addition to the emergency "999" call to the police; having a handy "exodus" bag containing important identity documents, money and essential daily items; as well as the need for mental preparedness for immediate contingency response. Readers may refer to the Empowerment Information Sheet provided in Appendix B.

In the American College of Emergency Physicians (ACEP) Position Statement, it indicates that:

> Emergency medical services, medical schools, and emergency medicine residency curricula should include education and training in recognition, assessment and interventions in intimate partner violence, child and elder maltreatment and neglect. Hospitals and emergency departments (EDs) encourage clinical and epidemiologic research regarding the incidence and prevalence of family violence as well as best practice approaches to detection, assessment and intervention for victims of family violence" (American College of Emergency Physicians, 2010, The Position Statement).

Difficulties in identifying risk factors in IPV victims by ED clinicians

Owing to time and manpower constraints, early involvement of social workers is very instrumental. ED clinicians may encounter many difficulties in IPV evaluation and danger assessment (Kam, 2004) due to the following factors: —

(a)   A lack of undergraduate teaching in the medical and nursing curricula,

(b)   A relatively low number of battered spouse cases and hence aggregation of experience is difficult,

(c)   Few in-service training courses,

(d)   Insufficient clinical time to perform in-depth evaluation,

(e)   Unavailability of MSW during the peak attendance of such patients,

(f)   Non-severe injuries in the majority raise the clinical threshold for caution, and

(g)   Incomplete information from the victims concerning the aggressiveness of the abusers.

One of the useful available risk scoring systems for femicide in violent intimate relationship was devised by Campbell in 1995. It is a 20-point system for risk stratification.

The tragic fatal incident in Tin Shui Wai in the year 2004

Death from IPV is not frequent in Hong Kong. Episodic events have been noted since the incident in Tin Shui Wai (TSW), which has become a haunting memory for Hong Kong society. The tragedy occurred on 11 April 2004 in TSW when three members of a family (a mother and two young twin girls) who were recipients of the Comprehensive Social Security Assistance were stabbed to death. The alleged assailant, the father, was transferred to the regional hospital with critical injuries, and subsequently died on 23 April 2004 (Review Panel on Family Services in Tin Shui Wai, 2004).

The conflict and abuse were reported to be related to the divorce of the parents. The children's custody was granted to the mother, resulting in morbid grievance in the father. The mother was a new immigrant from mainland China, and she had sought help from social workers, shelters for women, and the police prior to the tragedy. Tremendous public attention and concern were consequently aroused, particularly focussing on TSW as a new community of underdeveloped social services with a disproportionately high incidence of families-in-conflict.

The IPV patient treatment process in the ED

The ED workflow for IPV victim management is summarized as below: —

1. Registration by the victim unless the injury is very severe or the victim is emotionally very unstable—in which case, victims will usually be under the escort of the police or ambulance crew, who will assist in the registration.

2. The triage nurse performs the initial assessment and wound treatment, followed by allocation of the victim to a more private or quieter area to settle down to await consultation. About 80% of admittances belong to Category 4 (out of 5), meaning a semi-urgent status; 20% belong to Category 3 (urgent); and less than 1% are classified as Categories 1 or 2 (critical or emergency). This signifies the great majority are of stable medical conditions despite occasional fatal cases.

3. Despite the low priority given to physical injuries, ED doctors will try to quicken treatment when possible to shorten the waiting time. The reason is that concomitant psychological trauma may cause the victim's premature departure from the ED without seeing the doctor, out of feelings

of helplessness or of an urgent need to return home to take care of any unattended children.

4.　Most of the physical examinations can be completed within 10 to 15 minutes. Afterwards, the victim will undergo the necessary imaging, wound treatment and social worker assessment coupled with counselling.

5.　Around 95% can be discharged after ED management. Less than 5% require in-patient treatment in the Emergency Medicine Ward (EMW) or other specialty wards owing to severe psychological problems (e.g., potential self-harm, acute stress reaction) requiring psychiatric intervention or physical trauma requiring surgery.

6.　During office hours, the MSW of the SWD can provide assessment, counselling and necessary referral for the victim to safe shelters or Integrated Family Services Centres (IFSC). After office hours and before midnight, the Crisis Intervention Team (CIT) of Harmony House (HH) provides on-site services in the EDs of TMH and POH for most days of the week. After midnight, hotline services of the HH or other nongovernmental organizations (NGOs) (Appendix C) will be utilized.

7.　The social worker assessment usually takes 30 minutes to over an hour to complete, covering risk stratification, counselling on disposal options, and the initial empowerment intervention to deal with the potential risk of recurrent conflict.

8.　If the victim is unwilling to stay for the social worker assessment, written referral to the MSW will be provided to have the assessment on the next working day. If the victim consents to disclose his/her personal data, the referral form will also be sent by fax to the MSW so that the latter can actively contact the victim if the victim does not turn up.

9.　In the Medical Examination Form of the Hong Kong Police Force, the front page written by the policeman stationed at the ED records the medical problem from the police's perspective and the back page is a short reply from the case doctor on the medical disease or injuries and the disposal including admission, discharge or death. Based on the above information, the incident is subsequently classified as assault, common assault or assault occasioning actual body injury (AOABI) by the policeman, and domestic violence is seldom indicated. This signifies insufficient knowledge about IPV or DV with the inherent risk of recurrent injury compared with a single and probable nonrecurrent assault by a stranger or an assailant not living together with the abuser.

10. ED nurses play an important role not only in wound and pain management, but also in the provision of psychological support throughout the patient's stay as well as of interim counselling and initial empowerment, especially when social workers are not forthcoming. The patient will be given an IPV victim Empowerment Information Sheet with a brief on the important principles and safety issues (Appendix B).

11. Effective management is highly dependent on the interdisciplinary cooperation among doctors, nurses, the MSW and the police.

12. Since an IPV patient generally presents to the ED because of physical injuries, the doctor in charge will be requested by the police or legal counsel to provide a medical report for the subsequent court trial.

13. In the medical report, the nature of the injuries (most commonly tenderness, meaning pain on touch; bruises and abrasions; followed by cut injuries and bone fractures), the site and colour which indicate their onset time, the mode of trauma (by blunt force, pointed or sharp object) and the likelihood of permanent disability are included. Occasionally, strangulation marks on the neck are encountered.

14. In the case where the defendant or the legal counsel disagrees with the assessment made in the medical report, the case doctor will be summoned to the court to give evidence as a professional witness, and to clarify the characteristics of the injuries in an impartial manner.

15. Case conference to identify the perpetrator and to decide if family reunion is appropriate generally does not apply to an adult IPV victim (who can explicitly identify the abuser and is mentally competent to make a choice), contrary to child abuse in which the perpetrator may be unidentified and the child victim not mature enough to exercise an independent choice for his/her own well-being.

16. After the completion of clinical management, most of the aftercare services are coordinated by social workers.

Recognition of covert IPV patients in the ED

For covert (concealed) cases in which IPV victims do not self-report the abuse, clinicians need to apply vigilance to recognize repeated ED attendance for so-called accidental trauma, e.g., by noting injuries on multiple parts of the body, of multiple ages or during pregnancy, which are more compatible with nonaccidental or intentional trauma. At times, depression, anxiety and self-harm can be the presenting problems. Direct enquiry made with great tact and sensitivity and with reference to screening tools such as the Hurt, Insult, Threaten, and Scream (HITS) screening tool and the Partner Violence Screen (PVS) (which will be discussed later in this chapter) may be able to elucidate the hidden diagnosis of IPV.

The dilemma of IPV victims

Victims who choose to tolerate abuse without seeking help are typically those who have strong cultural beliefs about maintaining an intact family with two parents and their children (if any) living together; are financially dependent on the perpetrator; have weak social networks. Evidently, victims with a low education level may not be aware of the social services available. Some even have the very traditional belief that women are subordinate to men, and should be obedient and loyal without protest even under maltreatment, owing to their so-called "fate". Some victims are unwilling to leave the matrimonial home for fear that leaving would mean allowing the woman with whom the husband is having an extramarital affair to unofficially replace them as the wife. Even worse, women from these extramarital relationships may move into the home to physically substitute the victims' previous role as wife.

The clinicians, together with social workers in the follow-up stages, need to provide impartial and nonjudgmental counselling to help the clients recognize their rights to equality, well-being (physical, psychological and others) and family harmony. This may enable a client's consequent decision of whether to maintain the status of a couple living in constant abusive conflict and with recurrent threat to the client and children, or to pursue living peacefully with the children as a single parent.

ED as the hub of multidisciplinary IPV support services

The ED acts as a safety net. It can serve as a one-stop service hub to provide timely, multidisciplinary and comprehensive support to address IPV victims' physical, psychological and social problems at an early and acute phase. The Emergency Short-Stay Unit (subsequently coined as Emergency Medicine Ward) plays an instrumental role in providing not only a safe shelter, but also an ideal venue to fulfil these needs if they are not accomplished in the ED with its high flow and heavy workload.

Future research is required to study different subgroups including abused males and repeat victims, different injury severity levels, mortality, health and social outcomes, the effectiveness of different interventions for victims as well as the treatment programmes for abusers, so as to better restore harmony between partners and prevent abuse.

It is envisaged that heightened vigilance of clinicians towards IPV coupled with polished skills in the management process can help mitigate the harm to IPV victims and other family members, especially to children who were witnesses or secondary victims of abuse. This will go a long way towards restoring family harmony—be it in a single-parent family or one with both parents—so that victims and children can live and thrive in an environment without threats as to their basic human rights.

Screening for IPV in ED

The controversies of IPV screening

IPV screening is a very controversial subject in contrast to cancer screening and immunizations against infectious diseases. Cancers that warrant screening are those of high prevalence and which can be detected at an early stage amenable to curative therapy (surgery with/without other adjuvant radiation therapy), using an affordable and non-invasive investigation with cost-effectiveness. As for immunization, the vaccine ought to be inexpensive enough to cover a mass population with high vulnerability to the infection without causing an inappropriately high rate of side effects. Certainly, the exact point of demarcation for providing such preventive procedures varies with different socioeconomic standards.

As underreporting is a common phenomenon in IPV, nowadays, ED physicians aim for a more active role in the management of IPV. Early identification to prevent its occurrence is of utmost importance, and IPV screening can help. However, Wong (2010) suggested some essential points to consider before adopting IPV screening:
(a)   What screening tool is to be used (which is the most concise and robust)?
(b)   Is the screening process acceptable to the staff?
(c)   Is the screening process acceptable to patients?
(d)   What services and support are to be provided to identified victims?

(e)   Does universal screening decrease further exposure and improve outcome (e.g., reducing the severity of abuse/injuries or preventing fatality) without inadvertent harm to the victims (e.g., reviving psychological trauma in settled victims or provoking the perpetrators)?

(f)   What are the implications of existing ED services on resources (e.g., manpower and time)?

The standard reference instruments for IPV screening

One of the standard reference instruments to diagnose and assess spousal abuse is the Revised Conflict Tactics Scale (CTS2) (Straus, Hamby, Boney-McCoy, & Sugarman, 1996) which has a Chinese version available (K. L. Chan, 2005; Tiwari et al., 2007). The original Conflict Tactics Scale (CTS) (Straus, 1979) not only measures the psychological and physical attacks on a partner in a dating, cohabiting or marital relationship, but also the usage of negotiation. Additional items have been included in the CTS2 to improve the validity and reliability as compared with the first version. There is stronger stratification in the severity levels of each subscale. New subscales have been introduced for sexual coercion and physical injuries, as a result of which, the CTS2 currently comprises 39 items covering five domains of interpersonal conflict tactics: physical assault, psychological aggression, injury, sexual coercion and negotiation. However, it is a very detailed assessment tool and is not suitable for screening within one to a few minutes; rather, it is most pertinent as a reference. Three other reference instruments are the Index of Spouse Abuse (ISA), the Composite Abuse Scale (CAS) and the Abuse Behaviour Inventory (ABI). Readers are encouraged to refer to the pertinent references for more details. Screening tools are assessed for their accuracy, validity and reliability by correlation with the reference instruments.

The common IPV screening tools

There are four common IPV screening tools, namely: the Hurt, Insult, Threaten, and Scream (HITS), the Partner Violence Screen (PVS), the Abuse Assessment Screen (AAS), and the Woman Abuse Screening Tool (WAST).

HITS (Hurt, Insult, Threaten, and Scream). The HITS screening tool (Sherin, Sinacore, Li, Zitter, & Shakil, 1998) was validated for female patients in family practice settings. It is more detailed and hence more time-consuming than the PVS outlined below. It covers verbal and physical aggression by one's spouse, and is rated on a five-point Likert scale (never, rarely, sometimes, fairly often and frequently) of severity. Its correlation with CTS is high (Cronbach's alpha = .85) and the score values range from 4 to a maximum of 20. The cut-off point for abuse is 10.5. Neither does it cover sexual violence, nor has it been validated for ED practice despite its high accuracy in family practice settings. It has been tested in American women and men as well as Hispanic and African-American women. Appendix D summarizes the content and format of HITS.

PVS (Partner Violence Screen). (Feldhaus et al., 1997). Domestic violence screening tools to be applied in the ED must be very precise, brief and accurate in view of the high work demand and rapid workflow. One of these tools is the PVS. It consists of three "yes or no" questions validated in the ED setting against two standard instruments—the Index of Spouse Abuse (ISA) and the CTS. It takes only 20 seconds for a patient to complete, but is only available in English. Any positive response signifies abuse. The sensitivity and specificity of the PVS are high. The positive predictive values range from 51.3% to 63.4%, and negative predictive values range from 87.6% to 88.7%. It has been tested in both sexes from a wide range of ethnicities and socioeconomic statuses. Below are the question items of the PVS:

(a) Have you been hit, kicked, punched, or otherwise hurt by someone within the past year? If so, by whom?

(b) Do you feel safe in your current relationship?

(c) Is there a partner from a previous relationship who is making you feel unsafe now?

The first item concerning physical abuse is believed to be more sensitive, specific and simple than the latter two regarding safety. In fact, the question on physical abuse identifies almost as many abused patients as the overall PVS and with better specificity.

AAS (Abuse Assessment Screen). (Parker & McFarlane, 1991; Weiss, Ernst, Cham, & Nick, 2003). It is a five-item tool developed by the Nursing Research Consortium on Violence and Abuse. It is primarily used for screening in pregnant women. It enquires into abuse (physical and sexual) in the past 12 months and any previous psychological abuse. It also covers physical injury during pregnancy. The body regions and the severity of injuries as well as the relationship with the perpetrators are also recorded. Any positive response indicates an abuse. It has been used as a main tool in the obstetrics and gynaecology outpatient setting, and can be applied to a wide range of ethnicities and demographics, but most commonly to low-income and uninsured women.

A Chinese version (Chinese AAS) has been tested against a Chinese version of the CTS2 among pregnant patients at obstetrical antenatal clinics and non-pregnant women at community centres in Hong Kong (Tiwari et al., 2007). The sensitivity estimates ranged from 36.3% to 65.8% and its value increased in the screening for more severe cases (66.7%). The specificity estimates for emotional, physical and sexual abuse were equal to or greater than 89%. The PPV (positive predictive values) were higher than 80%, and the NPV (negative predictive values) ranged from 66% to 93%. A handout of the Chinese AAS is shown in Appendix E.

WAST (Woman Abuse Screening Tool). (Fisher, 2001). This is an eight-question tool. Its two main disadvantages are its lengthy nature and the lack of a cut-off score for what amounts to abuse. It was developed for screening in female patients in family practice settings, and was later extended to use within EDs. It was tested in Caucasian, African-American and Latina women. The eight questions of WAST are as shown in Appendix F.

Findings of a systematic review of IPV screening tools

Rabin and colleagues have conducted a systematic review of the four common IPV tools (Rabin, Jennings, Campbell, & Bair-Merritt, 2009). Table 10.2 shows a summary of the findings and conclusion.

Screenings on the various forms of abuse (physical, psychological, sexual, economic and others) are related for many reasons. Emotional abuse often precedes physical abuse, so detection of the former can allow for early intervention and potential prevention of physical attack (Coker et al., 2007). Besides, sexual abuse in women carries a higher risk for adverse health outcomes than physical or emotional abuse (Bonomi, Anderson, Rivara, & Thompson, 2007). Healthcare providers need to balance between brevity and comprehensiveness in choosing screening tools to achieve their goals.

However, there is no common gold standard for comparison of the four frequently used IPV screening tools owing to the complex nature of IPV. Different periods of abuse (from ever, past 12 months to current) are used. Hence, comparison among the four tools is very difficult. Rabin et al. (2009) also argued that no single IPV screening tool has well-established psychometric properties

Table 10.2 Review of four common IPV screening tools

IPV screening tool	No. of items	Time frame	Clinical Setting	Population	Performance			
					Sensitivity	Specificity	Range	Remarks
HITS	4	Past 12 months	Both sexes in family practices	Caucasian women & men, Hispanic & African-American women	30–100	86–99	Very wide for sensitivity	Items with 5 severity levels
PVS	3	Past 12 months	Emergency departments	Women & men of a wide range of ethnicities and socioeconomic statuses	35–71	80–94	Very wide for sensitivity	--
AAS	5	Past 12 months & current pregnancy	Pregnant women	O&G OPD with wide ethnicity range but mostly low-income & uninsured groups	93–94	55–99	Very wide for specificity	Chinese version available
WAST	8	Ever	Women from family to ED practices	Caucasian, African-American and Latina women	47	96	Low sensitivity	Longest in length

Note: AAS = Abuse Assessment Screen.

HITS = Hurt, Insult, Threaten, and Scream.

IPV = Intimate Partner Violence.

PVS = Partner Violence Screen.

WAST = Woman Abuse Screening Tool.

and that there have been wide variations in accuracy among true positive and true negative cases.

The consequent recommendations by Rabin et al. (2009) were:

(a)   There was insufficient evidence to recommend for or against screening; and

(b)   Further testing and validation were critically needed.

Rabin (2009) actually echoed and reconfirmed the findings and recommendation of the US Preventive Services Task Force (USPSTF) in 2004. The latter identified that there was insufficient evidence to recommend for or against routine screening of women for IPV (US Preventive Services Task Force, 2004).

There is limited empirical data about the potential harms of screening and about effective interventions that decrease IPV. Rigorous studies are indicated to assess the potential harms of screening and to develop useful management and preventive measures before aggravation of abuse. IPV screening tools with relevant psychometrical properties are required. Regardless of the USPSTF recommendation in 2004, many leading medical organizations (including the American Medical Association [AMA], the American Academy of Pediatrics [AAP], the American Academy of Family Physicians [AAFP], the American College of Obstetricians and Gynecologists [ACO&G], and the American College of Emergency Physicians [ACEP]) recommend routine IPV screening as a part of regular patient care (Nelson & Johnston, 2004). Although the AMA and the AAP recognized that the expertise for quantifying behavioural-health outcomes was suboptimal, they expressed the concern that awaiting empirical evidence of improved outcomes could endanger the health of millions of victims (Nelson & Johnston, 2004). In fact, the debate on IPV screening is still ongoing.

E-HITS screening tool in Hong Kong emergency departments

When manpower is available for screening in the ED, the Extended HITS (E-HITS; see Appendix G) validated by C. C. Chan, Chan, Au, and Cheung (2010) for local Chinese can be a handy and concise tool. E-HITS is an extended screening tool based on Sherin's four-point HITS with an additional enquiry on sexual violence. It comprises five items, and takes about one minute to complete by trained ED triage nurses. It is easily comprehended by healthcare professionals, but implementation is compounded by time constraint since the usual ED triage duration is only about three to five minutes.

The addition of one more minute for each of the hundreds of patients a day in a typical Hong Kong ED would require much more labour. The face validity of the E-HITS (Chinese version) was evaluated and ascertained to be useful and pertinent in recognizing IPV by a panel of Chinese experts including a social worker, a psychologist, a senior emergency physician, a senior nurse, a trauma nurse and a nurse specialist. All had ample experience in the management of IPV patients. The CTS2—Revised Chinese Version (K. L. Chan, 2005)—was used as the reference standard. One hundred and ten IPV female victims and 116 non-IPV women (the control) were recruited in the EDs of TMH and POH in the year 2008 for validation and derivation of the demarcation point for IPV cases.

The respondents' scores on the E-HITS showed statistically significant positive correlations with those on injury, psychological aggression, physical assault and sexual coercion scales, and negative correlation with the negotiation scale of the revised Conflict Tactics Scale. Receiver Operating Characteristic (ROC) curve analysis identified that the E-HITS respectively attained a sensitivity and a specificity of 98.2% and 94.8% at a cut-off of 8.5 respectively. The overall accuracy was 99.1% as shown by the area under curve (AUC) in the ROC curve. All the parameters were in the high end. Consequently, the E-HITS can be a useful IPV screening tool for Hong Kong Chinese in EDs. However, the study has a number of limitations in terms of its generalization. These included testing at only two out of 15 public EDs, having only a short period of recruitment, using only convenience sampling, adopting a case-control design instead of a randomized control trial, and having a higher proportion of lower socioeconomic classes and new immigrants in the catchment areas of the NTW public EDs without participation from other regional or private hospital EDs. Further studies are required for the second stage of validation for generalization.

DV screening results in Hong Kong and overseas

In population-based surveys around the world, 10% to 69% of women reported physical assault by their intimate male partner at some point in their lives. The percentage of women reporting assault in the previous 12 months varied from 3% or less in Australia, Canada and the United States to 38% in Korea, and up to 52% among Palestinians in the West Bank and Gaza Strip (Krug et al., 2002).

The prevalence rates of DV identified by K. L. Chan's Household Survey (2005) were 10% for physical injury by a spouse ever and 4.5% in the preceding twelve months. In Chung's ED survey (1997), the prevalence was 5.3% ($N = 112$; 95% *CI* [1.1, 9.5]) for female patients presenting to a regional ED in HK with physical battery by their spouses within the preceding six months.

With reference to the PVS, the workers of an NGO (Harmony House) modified the scale by including an item for sexual abuse, and performed a DV screening in the ED of TMH in 2008 with a one-question tool in Chinese as follows:

> The issue of domestic violence in Hong Kong is worsening! Domestic violence means any behaviour causing harm by intimate partner or family members and it includes physical abuse (e.g., kicking, pushing, slapping, etc.) or spiritual abuse (e.g., intimidation, threats, insults, etc.) or sexual abuse (e.g., forced sex). Did you have experience of domestic violence in any way in the past one year?

However, the introductory part of the screening might be considered to be a leading question causing a higher positive response rate, even though its aim was to offer background information to the interviewees (see Appendix H).

In the survey, 60 males and 69 females were recruited in the evening periods of ten consecutive days. There was no male reporting having IPV, but eight female victims were identified, with an overall prevalence of 6% and 12% for females. All eight victims were provided with counselling and supporting services for the following three months by the same NGO. Evidently, the study requires an extension to a city-wide or multiregional whole-day survey before one can generalize the results to other populations.

Table 10.3 summarizes DV prevalence in Hong Kong and some overseas regions at various settings as found by past research. Results revealed that the reported rates are higher overseas than locally, and also greater among same-sex partners than heterosexual couples.

Future research of DV screening

Although it is arguable that screening at the ED can be useful for identifying victims for early intervention, this is often deterred by the heavy workload of the department, which places their main service focus on physical illnesses and trauma. Consequently, IPV screening is placed at a low level of priority. Besides, staff has also found investigation of IPV to be difficult and time-consuming in the busy triage station with low privacy settings. The majority

Table 10.3 IPV prevalence in Hong Kong and overseas regions of various settings

Study	Sample	Prevalence		
		Past 6 months	**Past 12 months**	**Any abuse in lifetime**
Chung et al. (1997)	Female A&E patients	5.3%, (1.1–9.5%)		
K. L. Chan (2005)	Households		4.5%	10% (physical), 7% (sexual) & 61.6% (psychological)
K. L. Chan et al. (2009)	Chinese pregnant women		9%	
da Silva et al. (2010)	Brazilian women (Outpatient clinic)		27.5%	
Leung et al. (1999)	Chinese pregnant women		15.7% (4.3% during the current pregnancy)	
Mak et al. (2010)	Same-sex partners			40% (physical), 20% (sexual) & 79.5% (psychological)
Rietveld et al. (2010)	O&G OPD in the Netherlands		9%	23%
Tang (1999)	Chinese wives		10%	67.2%
TMH (2008)— Project with Harmony House	Male & female A&E patients		0 (male), 12% (female), 6 % (overall)	
Zahnd et al. (2010)	Californian adults in the USA		27.9% (same-sex), 40.6% (bisexual) & 16.7% (heterosexual)	

of the ED triage process for stable cases takes only three to five minutes, and the addition of one minute for each IPV screening substantially increases the working time by 20% to 33%. Ramsden and Bonner (2002) reported that the screening rate was only 10% in an Australian ED despite training provided to the staff regarding the usage of an easy tool. Ramsay et al. (2002) found that the acceptability of screening by staff was low, with over 60% of doctors and about 50% of nurses unsupportive of screening.

The traditional Chinese convention of not bothering with others' family affairs and modern privacy issues were the important factors deterring ED staff from enquiring into DV (Chung, Wong, & Yiu, 1996; Wong, Chung, & Yiu, 1997). Ramsay et al. (2002) found that 43% to 85% of females accepted screening in England, but one-third of patients in Hong Kong declined an interview to estimate DV prevalence (Chung et al., 1996). Besides, the worry about inadvertent harm by screening (e.g., causing psychological trauma and family conflict) is another concern, though unsubstantiated in North American studies; and yet, to date, no outcome benefit (e.g., violence reduction) has been shown (MacMillan et al., 2009).

Not only did the systematic review of ED studies fail to find evidence for the efficacy of screening in reducing DV-related mortality or morbidity (Anglin & Sachs, 2003), but the USPSTF also failed to identify sufficient evidence to recommend for or against universal screening of women for IPV, as mentioned in the previous section (US Preventive Services Task Force, 2004). As to referral services for positive cases, there is another worry about the adequacy of the supply of social services. Identification without active and appropriate therapy might also be harmful, leading clients to develop a sense of helplessness.

Screening of high-risk women in other settings such as at social services provided as part of public assistance (CSSA), psychological counselling and family conflict will likely produce better results as well as reduce the work demand on EDs. On the other hand, automated computerized systems for self-administered assessment and provision of information on social services can be considered as an alternative option.

Without doubt, further research is needed to bridge the knowledge gaps, in order to identify effective screening tools to improve the health outcomes of victims, and to achieve the best multidisciplinary collaboration to overcome the tremendous complexities in the problem of IPV.

Conclusion

According to the incidence as noted by the Central Registry of the Social Welfare Department, IPV is a substantial social malady in Hong Kong. However, the very low proportion of IPV victims presenting to EDs and a lack of teaching on the subject within the undergraduate curricula hamper expertise development in ED clinicians. Development in this respect would require augmentation in both areas, through a concise management checklist which ensures quality assurance on the safety assessment for IPV victims, and through therapy on a multidisciplinary basis.

IPV screening at EDs is highly labour-intensive and has not been shown to improve the health outcomes of victims, not to mention creating potential harms. Where resources are available, the E-HITS screening tool validated in two regional EDs (TMH & POH) may be applied, to be followed with prompt access to sociopsychological support for the identified victims.

Enrichment of knowledge on abuse, risk perception, safety issues, crisis management and prevention is essential for victims. Brief education on self-empowerment and nonjudgmental counselling can be provided by ED clinicians when in-depth social worker services are not immediately available.

Harmony restoration, if not attainable in a co-parent family which continues to be fraught with perpetual conflict or violence, may possibly be accomplished in a single-parent family arrangement. This may have to be accompanied by a change in the cultural perception of what makes a family "complete".

References

American College of Emergency Physicians. (2010). *ACEP Policy Statements: Domestic Family Violence*. Retrieved from American College of Emergency Physicians website: http://www.acep.org/practres.aspx?id=29184

Anglin, D., & Sachs, C. (2003). Preventive care in the emergency department: screening for domestic violence in the emergency department. *Academic Emergency Medicine, 10*, 1118–1127. doi: 10.1197/S1069-6563(03)00371-3

Bonomi, A. E., Anderson, M. L., Rivara, F. P., & Thompson, R. S. (2007). Health outcomes in women with physical and sexual intimate partner violence exposure. *Journal of Women's Health, 16*, 987–997. doi: 10.1089/jwh.2006.0239

Campbell, J. C. (1995). *Identifying Risk Factors for Femicide in Violent Intimate Relationships*. Retrieved from The Johns Hopkins University School of Nursing website: http://www.son.jhmi.edu/research/CNR/homicide/Danger.htm

Chan, C. C., Chan, Y. C., Au, A., & Cheung, G. O. C. (2010). Reliability and validity of the "Extended-Hurt, Insult, Threaten, Scream (E-HITS)" screening tool in detecting intimate partner violence in hospital emergency departments in Hong Kong. *Hong Kong Journal of Emergency Medicine, 17*, 109–117.

Chan, K. L. (2005). *Study on Child Abuse & Spouse Battering: Report on Findings of Household Survey*. Retrieved from Department of Social Work and Social Administration, the University of Hong Kong website: http://www.swd.gov.hk/doc/family/Report%20on%20findings%20of%20Household%20Survey.pdf

Chan, K. L. (2006). Commentary: Screening for intimate partner violence in emergency departments. *Hong Kong Medical Journal, 12*, 322–323. Retrieved from http://www.hkmj.org/article_pdfs/hkm0608p322.pdf

Chan, K. L., Tiwari, A., Fong, Y. T., Leung, W. C., Brownridge, D. A., & Ho, P. C. (2009). Correlates of in-law conflict and intimate partner violence against Chinese pregnant women in Hong Kong. *Journal of Interpersonal Violence, 24,* 97–110. doi: 10.1177/0886260508315780

Chung, M. Y., Wong, T. W., Chan, R. T. F., & Lau, C. C. (1997). A study on the prevalence of domestic violence among female patients in an emergency department. *Hong Kong Journal of Emergency Medicine, 4,* 82–84.

Chung, M. Y., Wong, T. W., & Yiu, J. J. (1996). Wife battering in Hong Kong: accident and emergency nurses' attitudes and beliefs. *Accident and Emergency Nurses, 4,* 152–155. doi: 10.1016/S0965-2302(96)90063-6

Coker, A. L., Flerx, V. C., Smith, P. H., Whitaker, D. J., Fadden, M. K., & Williams, M. (2007). Intimate partner violence incidence and continuation in a primary care screening program. *American Journal of Epidemiology, 165,* 821–827. doi: 10.1093/aje/kwk074

DaSilva, M. A., Falbo Neto, G. H., Figueiroa, J. N., & Cabral, Filho, J. E. (2010). Violence against women: prevalence and associated factors in patients attending a public healthcare service in the northeast of Brazil. *Cadernos de Saúde Pública, 26,* 264–272. doi: 10.1590/S0102-311X2010000200006

Feldhaus, K. M., Koziol-McLain, J., Amsbury, H. L., Norton, I. M., Lowenstein, S. R., & Abbott, J. T. (1997). Accuracy of 3 brief screening questions for detecting partner violence in the emergency department. *JAMA, 277,* 1357–1361. Retrieved from http://jama.ama-assn.org/cgi/reprint/277/17/1357.pdf

Fisher, V. M. (2001). *Working with Battered Women: A Handbook for Health Care Professionals.* Retrived from Hotpeachpage website: http://www.hotpeach-pages.net/canada/air/medbook/index.html

Harmony House. (2006). *Crisis Intervention Services.* Retrieved from Harmony House website: http://www.harmonyhousehk.org/eng/serviceimage/service4_eng.htm

Kam, C. W. (2004). Letter to editor: difficulties in danger assessment of battered spouse in domestic violence. *Hong Kong Journal of Emergency Medicine, 11,* 173–177. Retrieved from http://www.hkcem.com/html/publications/Journal/2004-4/p248-p252.pdf

Kam, C. W., Ng, P., & Ching, W. M. (2002). *The Injury Severity of 183 Cases of Battered Spouse.* Abstract presented at the National Congress on Emergency Medicine, China.

Krug, E. G., Dahlberg, L. L., Mercy, J. A., Zwi, A. B., & Lozano, R. (Eds.). (2002). *World Report on Violence and Health* (pp. 87–113). Retrieved from World Health Organization website: http://libdoc.who.int/hq/2002/9241545615.pdf

Lau, C. L., Ching, W. M., Tong, W. L., Chan, K. L., Tsui, K. L., & Kam, C. W. (2008). 1700 victims of intimate partner violence: characteristics and clinical outcomes. *Hong Kong Medical Journal, 14,* 451–457. Retrieved from http://www.hkmj.org/article_pdfs/hkm0812p451.pdf

Leung, W. C., Leung, T. W., Lam, Y. Y., & Ho, P. C. (1999). The prevalence of domestic violence against pregnant women in a Chinese community. *International Journal of Gynecology & Obstetrics, 66,* 23–30. doi: 10.1016/S0020-7292(99)00053-3

MacMillan, H. L., Wathen, C. N., Jamieson, E., Boylr, M. H., Shannon, H. S., Ford-Gilboe, M., Worster, A., Lent, B., Coben, J. H., Campbell, J. C., McNutt, L. A., & McMaster Violence Against Women Research Group. (2009). Screening for intimate partner violence in health care settings: a randomized trial. *JAMA, 302*, 493–501. doi: 10.1001/jama.2009.1089

Mak, W. W. S., Chong, E. S. K., & Kwong, M. M. F. (2010). Prevalence of same-sex intimate partner violence in Hong Kong. *Public Health, 124*, 149–152. doi: 10.1016/j.puhe.2010.02.002

Nelson, J., & Johnson, C. (2004). Screening for family and intimate partner violence. *Annals of Internal Medicine, 141*, 81. Retrieved from http://www.annals.org/content/141/1/81.2.full.pdf

Norton, L. B., Peipert, J. F., Zierler, S., Lima, B., Hume, L. (1995). Battering in pregnancy: an assessment of two screening methods. *Obstetrics & Gynecology, 85*, 321–325.

Parker, B., & McFarlane, J. (1991). Identifying and helping battered pregnant women. *The American Journal of Maternal/Child Nursing, 16*, 161–164.

Rabin, R. F., Jennings, J. M., Campbell, J. C., & Bair-Merritt, M. H. (2009). Intimate partner violence screening tools: a systematic review. *American Journal of Preventive Medicine, 36*, 439–445. doi: 10.1016/j.amepre.2009.01.024

Ramsay, J., Richardson, J., Carter, Y. H., Davidson, L. L., & Feder, G. (2002). Should health professionals screen women for domestic violence? Systematic review. *British Medical Journal, 325*, 314–317. doi: 10.1136/bmj.325.7359.314

Ramsden, C., & Bonner, M. (2002). A realistic view of domestic violence screening in an emergency department. *Accident and Emergency Nurses, 10*, 31–319. doi: 10.1054/aaen.2001.0312

Review Panel on Family Services in Tin Shui Wai. (2004). *Report of Review Panel on Family Services in Tin Shui Wai (TSW)*. Hong Kong: Social Work Department.

Rietveld, L., Lagro-Janssen, T., Vierhout, M., & Wong, S. L. F. (2010). Prevalence of intimate partner violence at an out-patient clinic obstetrics-gynecology in the Netherlands. *Journal of Psychosomatic Obstetrics & Gynaecology, 31*, 3–9. doi: 10.3109/01674820903556388

Sherin, K. M., Sinacore, J. M., Li, X. Q., Zitter, R. E., & Shakil, A. (1998). HITS: A short domestic violence screening tool for use in a family practice setting. *Family Medicine, 30*, 508–512. Retrieved from http://www.orchd.com/violence/documents/HITS_eng.pdf

Social Welfare Department. (2010a). *Information Kit on Support Services to Victims of Spouse Battering*. Retrieved from Social Welfare Department, Hong Kong website: http://www.swd.gov.hk/vs/english/promote_new.html

Social Welfare Department. (2010b). *Statistics on Cases Involving Child Abuse, Spouse Battering and Sexual Violence*. Retrieved from Social Welfare Department, Hong Kong website: http://www.swd.gov.hk/vs/english/stat.html

Straus, M. A. (1979). Measuring intra family conflict and violence: the Conflict Tactics Scale. *Journal of Marriage and the Family, 41*, 75–88.

Straus, M. A., Hamby, S. L., Boney-McCoy, S., & Sugarman, D. B. (1996). The Revised
    Conflict Tactics Scales (CTS2): development and preliminary psychometric data.
    Journal of Family Issues, *17*, 283–316. doi: 10.1177/019251396017003001

Tang, C. S. K. (1999). Wife abuse in Hong Kong Chinese families: a community survey.
    Journal of Family Violence, *14*, 173–191. doi: 10.1023/A:1022028803208

Tiwari, A., Fong, D. Y. T., Chan, K. L., Leung, W. C., Parker, B., Ho, P. C. (2007).
    Identifying intimate partner violence: comparing the Chinese Abuse Assessment
    Screen with the Chinese Revised Conflict Tactics Scale. *British Journal of
    Obstetrics & Gynaecology*, *114*(9), 1065–1071.

Tsui, K. L., Chan, A. Y., So, F. L., & Kam, C. W. (2006). Risk factors for injury to
    married women from domestic violence in Hong Kong. *Hong Kong Medical
    Journal*, *12*, 289–293. Retrieved from http://www.hkmj.org/article_pdfs/
    hkm0608p289.pdf

US Preventive Services Task Force. (2004). Screening for family and intimate partner
    violence. *Annals of Internal Medicine*, *140*, 382–386.

Weiss, S. J., Ernst, A. A., Cham, E., & Nick, T. G. (2003). Development of a screen for
    ongoing intimate partner violence. *Violence and Victims*, *18*, 131–141.

Wong, T. W. (2003). *A&E Clinical Guideline No. 4 Management of Wife Battering*.
    Retrieved from http://aeis.home/

Wong, T. W., Chung, M. Y., & Yiu, J. J. K. (1997). Attitudes and beliefs of emer-
    gency doctors towards domestic violence in Hong Kong. *Journal of Emergency
    Medicine*, *9*, 113–116. doi: 10.1111/j.1442-2026.1997.tb00366.x.

Wong, T. W. (2010). Editorial: Domestic violence in the emergency department: to screen
    or not to screen? *Hong Kong Journal of Emergency Medicine*, *17*, 107–108.

Working Group on Combating Violence. (2004). *Procedural Guidelines for Handling
    Battered Spouse Cases*. Retrieved from Social Welfare Department, Hong
    Kong website: http://www.swd.gov.hk/en/index/site_pubsvc/page_family/sub_
    fcwprocedure/id_batteredspouse/

World Health Organization. (2010). Multi-country study on women's health and domes-
    tic violence against women. Retrieved from World Health Organization website:
    http://www.who.int/gender/violence/who_multicountry_study/summary_report/
    chapter1/en/index.html

Zahnd, E., Grant, D., Aydin, M., Chia, Y. J., & Padilla-Frausto, D. I. (2010). Nearly
    four million California adults are victims of intimate partner violence. Retrieved
    from University of California, Los Angeles website: http://www.healthpolicy.
    ucla.edu/pubs/files/IPV_PB_031810.pdf

Appendix A

Management Checklist of Domestic Violence, TMH AED

<table>
<tr><td>Checklist of Domestic Violence
(Spousal Abuse/ Non-accidental Injury / Elder Abuse)
TMH AED
(Please attach this completed form to the A&E Notes)</td><td>IPAS Label</td></tr>
</table>

A. GENERAL INFORMATION

Type of abuse	1. [ ] Physical (battery) 3. [ ] Psychological 5. [ ] Financial 2. [ ] Sexual 4. [ ] Neglect 6. [ ] Others:
Physical assault	Pls tick (can be more than one) 1. [ ] Threw things that could hurt 撻嘢掟,而可能整傷你 6.[ ] Punched or hit that could hurt 用拳頭 / 撻嘢打傷你 2.[ ] Twisted arm or hair 扭手臂 / 扯頭髮 7.[ ] Choked, beat up, kicked 勒住你頸 / 毆打你/ 踢傷你 3.[ ] Pushed or shoved or grabbed 推撞/ 推開/抓住你 8.[ ] Slammed against a wall 大力把你撞向牆壁 4.[ ] Slapped 掌摑你 9.[ ] Burned or scalded on purpose 故意燒傷 / 燙傷你 5.[ ] Use knife or gun 用刀/利器指向你 10.[ ] Others (pls specify)_________ 其他
Abuser (perpetrator)	1. [ ] Married spouse 4. [ ] Guardian 7. [ ] Domestic Helper 2. [ ] Cohabitant 5. [ ] Son / Daughter 8. [ ] Institution Staff 3. [ ] Parents 6. [ ] Boyfriend / girlfriend of parent 9. [ ] Others:
Weapon used	1. [ ] No 2. [ ] Yes: __________
Verbal threats to harm	1. [ ] No 2. [ ] Yes: __________
Episode of abuse	1. [ ] 1st 2. [ ] 2nd 3. [ ] Multiple: ______ times
Other domestic abuse involved	1. [ ] No 2. [ ] Yes (if NAI follow guideline for Mx)

<table>
<tr><td colspan="2">Victim – social factors</td></tr>
<tr><td>New immigrant to HK</td><td>1. [ ] No (Residency in HK >7 years)
2. [ ] Yes (Residency in HK <7 years)   From: a. [ ] Mainland China   b. [ ] others (pls specify) :</td></tr>
<tr><td>Family Monthly Income</td><td>1. [ ]$10000 below   2. [ ]$10000-$19999   3. [ ]$20000-$29999   4. [ ]above $30000</td></tr>
<tr><td>Years of residence in HK</td><td>Years   Months</td></tr>
<tr><td>Education level</td><td>[ ] Nil to primary   3. [ ] Secondary (S4-5)   5. [ ] Tertiary
[ ] Lower secondary (S1-3)   4. [ ] Matriculation</td></tr>
<tr><td>Occupation</td><td>1. [ ] Not at work   CSSA:[ ] Yes [ ] No   5. [ ] Employee (please select)
☐ Professional / managerial   ☐ Clerical
2. [ ] Retired   CSSA:[ ] Yes [ ] No   ☐ Services and sales operator   ☐ Mechanical / Machine
3. [ ] Student   ☐ Craft   ☐ Unskilled
4. [ ] Housewife   CSSA:[ ] Yes [ ] No   ☐ Others: __________</td></tr>
<tr><td>Alcohol abuse</td><td>Q1. Have you ever felt you should cut down your drinking?   [ ] Yes   [ ] No
你曾否覺得應該減少飲酒?
Q2. Have people annoyed you by criticizing your drinking?   [ ] Yes   [ ] No
你曾否因飲酒被人批評而感到煩惱?
Q3. Have you ever felt bad or guilty about your drinking?   [ ] Yes [ ] No
你曾否因飲酒而產生內疚?
Q4. Have you had an eye opener first thing in the morning to steady nerves or get rid of a hangover?   [ ] Yes [ ] No
你曾否需要在早上喝酒來鎮定神經才能展開一日之工作?</td></tr>
<tr><td>Illicit drug abuse</td><td>Use of illicit drug: 1. [ ] in last week   3. [ ] in last 12 months   5. [ ] never
2. [ ] in last 30 days   4. [ ] in lifetime</td></tr>
<tr><td>Mental illness</td><td>[ ] On medication and follow up by psychiatric institution   4. [ ] In remission and no follow up required
[ ] Follow up by psychiatric institution only   5. [ ] No
3. [ ] Default follow up</td></tr>
<tr><td>Chronic illness</td><td>1. [ ] Yes Pls specify the illness:__________   Debilitation at home: Yes / No
Debilitation at work: Yes / No
2. [ ] No</td></tr>
</table>

<table>
<tr><td colspan="2">Abuser – social factors</td></tr>
<tr><td>New immigrant to HK</td><td>1. [ ] No (Residency in HK >7 years)
2. [ ] Yes – (Residency in HK <7 years) From: a. [ ] Mainland China   b. [ ] others (pls specify) :</td></tr>
</table>

Years of residence in HK	Years Months		
Extramarital affairs	1. [ ] No	2. [ ] Yes	
Education level	[ ] Nil to primary [ ] Lower secondary (S1-3)	3. [ ] Secondary (S4-5) 4. [ ] Matriculation	5. [ ] Tertiary
Occupation	1. [ ] Not at work CSSA:[ ] Yes [ ] No 2. [ ] Retired CSSA:[ ] Yes [ ] No 3. [ ] Student 4. [ ] Housewife CSSA:[ ] Yes [ ] No	5. [ ] Employee (please select) ☐ Professional / managerial ☐ Clerical ☐ Services and sales ☐ Mechanical / Machine operator ☐ Craft ☐ Unskilled ☐ Others: __________	
Alcohol abuse	Q1. Has he ever felt he should **cut** down his drinking? [ ] Yes [ ] No 　　他曾否覺得應該減少飲酒? Q2. Have people **annoyed** him by criticizing his drinking? [ ] Yes [ ] No 　　他曾否因飲酒被人批評而感到煩惱? Q3. Has he ever felt bad or **guilty** about his drinking? [ ] Yes [ ] No 　　他曾否因飲酒而產生內疚? Q4. Has he had an **eye opener** first thing in the morning to steady nerves or get rid of a hangover? 　　他曾否需要在早上喝酒來鎮定神經才能展開一日之工作? [ ] Yes [ ] No		
Illicit drug abuse	Use of illicit drug: 1. [ ] in last week 3. [ ] in last 12 months 5. [ ] never 2. [ ] in last 30 days 4. [ ] in lifetime		
Mental illness	[ ] On medication and follow up by psychiatric institution 4. [ ] In remission and no follow up required [ ] Follow up by psychiatric institution only 5. [ ] No 3. [ ] Default follow up		
Chronic illness	1. [ ] Yes Pls specify the illness:__________ Debilitation at home: Yes / No Debilitation at work: Yes / No 2. [ ] No		

B. Principles of Management

1. NAI/ Child abuse

    a) Do not confront the suspected abuser. (b) Report to police is not mandatory in the initial Mx.(c) Admission to Pediatric is the main Mx to sort out the problem & provide treatment. **(d) Consider consult MCCA via operator during office hour to arrange early Paed FU in case of low risk cases. DAMA can carry high risk to the child.**

2. Elder   abuse

    a) Ensure safety at home before discharge; otherwise consider admission or placement by MSW as appropriate.

    b) Suitable MSS- MSW of XXX or CIT for Harmony House.

C. Interim management (Spousal Abuse/ Elder Abuse)

Patient is kept in Obs Ward f or :

1. [ ] immediate assessment by TMH MSW 9am – 5pm. (Tel 2468 @@@@)
2. [ ] telephone consultation to the Harmony House at any time. [HH] (Tel 2522 0434)- not for Elder Abuse cases.
3. [ ] telephone consultation to the Harmony House by CIT if service a/v- including Elder Abuse cases.
4. [ ] telephone consultation to the SWD Hotline Service. (Tel 2343 2255)
5. [ ] Others (to specify) : __________

*Please take **clinical photos** of injuries (after explanation).[ ] Yes   [ ] No

D. Pre-disposal factors of evaluation for Spousal/ Elder Abuse only

	Factors	Yes	No	Remarks
1.	Physical injury treated			Severe injuries may require in-pat Mx.
2.	Psychologically stable			Unstable cases may require in-pat Mx.
3.	Low risk on returning home			High risk cases would require a safe shelter (via MSW, Harmony House or relatives).
4.	MSW assessment done in AED			Assessment in AED is preferred to prevent default.
5.	MSW referral arranged			
6.	Contingency plan for escape a/v			
7.	Police informed			
8.	Discussed with supervisor			Especially when doubt occurs
9.	Child abuse involved			Apply NAI Mx protocol
10.	Others -			

E. Disposal

1. Patient is discharged (Spousal/ Elder Abuse):

    a. [ ] after MSW assessment in AED.

    b. [ ] after telephone contact with the Harmony House, which will provide the immediate comprehensive socio-psychological support and service.

    c. [ ] with MSW referral as the patient has a safe shelter, is psychologically stable but cannot wait for MSW assessment in AED (has also informed patient that MSW may later contact the victim).

    d. [ ] with MSW referral as the risk of recurrent battering is low, there is no imminent risk to the patient's life on returning   home. Informed patient that MSW may later contact the victim.

2) Patient is admitted to the ward :-

    a. [ ] (TMH) for in-patient Rx because of   NAI cases.

    b. [ ] (TMH / CPH) for in-patient Rx because of the emotional instability and potential self-harm.

Appendix B

IPV Empowerment Information Sheet

<u>Information on the Management of Victims of Intimate Partner Violence (IPV) in the Emergency Department (ED) of Tuen Mun Hospital</u>

1. Attendance for IPV related issues will be triaged and brought to the designated consultation room for medical assessment.
2. Please wait patiently in the ED. Please notify staff if you need to leave the ED temporarily.
3. During office hours, attendance will be offered, including interview with a social worker and contact with Harmony House through the service hotline for counselling and shelter arrangement if required. From Tuesdays to Saturdays (19:00 to 00:00), interview with on-site social worker from the Crisis Intervention Team will be arranged.
4. Please read the instruction sheet on "Contingency plan for victims of IPV". It helps the attendant to have better preparation on the establishment of a contingency plan so as to protect the personal safety of the victim and their children.
5. If you encounter Intimate Partner Violence, your safety is the top priority, and you should seek help immediately from the following agents:

<u>Service hotlines for IPV victims:</u>
- Harmony House ☎ 25220434
- Wai On Home for Women, Po Leung Kuk ☎ 27930223
- Serene Court of Christian Family Service Centre ☎ 27876865
- Sunrise Court, Po Leung Kuk ☎ 28908330
- Caritas Family Crisis Support Centre ☎ 18288
- The Hong Kong Council of Social Service ☎ 1878668
- Harmony House (for men) ☎ 22951386
- Christian Family Service Centre (for men) ☎ 27871355
- Po Leung Kuk (for men) ☎ 28901830
- Social Welfare Department (24 hours) ☎ 23432255
- CEASE Crisis Centre ☎ 18281
- Dawn Court, Po Leung Kuk ☎ 22433210

(Please wait patiently as these hotlines may need to be redirected. To leave a message, remember to give your name, contact phone number and details of the safety of your current location. Call Police "☎999" if you encounter emergency situations.)

Appendix C

Nongovernmental Organization Services for IPV

<u>Information for Crisis Intervention Team (CIT) Services and Relevant
Hotlines for Intimate Partner Violence Cases in the Emergency Department
(ED) of Tuen Mun Hospital</u>

Service time: Every Tuesday to Saturday   19:00–00:00

How to contact CIT staff?

Choice 1. Direct to CIT counter in
designated room in ED

↓

Choice 2. Emergency Medicine Ward

↓

Choice 3. CIT pager to leave message

↓

Choice 4. Contact CIT hotline if out of service hours

<u>Relevant hotlines for Intimate Partner Violence:</u>
- Wai On Home for Women, Po Leung Kuk ☎ 27930223
- Serene Court of Christian Family Service Centre ☎ 27876865
- Sunrise Court, Po Leung Kuk ☎ 28908330
- Caritas Family Crisis Support Centre ☎ 18288
- The Hong Kong Council of Social Service ☎ 1878668
- Harmony House (for men) ☎ 22951386
- Christian Family Service Centre (for men) ☎ 27871355
- Po Leung Kuk (for men) ☎ 28901830
- Social Welfare Department (24 hours) ☎ 23432255
- CEASE Crisis Centre (also handles elder abuse) ☎ 18281
- Dawn Court, Po Leung Kuk ☎ 22433210

Appendix D

The Hurt, Insult, Threaten, and Scream (HITS) Screening Tool

How often does your partner:
(1)   Physically hurt you?
(2)   Insult you or talk down to you?
(3)   Threaten you with harm?
(4)   Scream or curse at you?

Scoring: five-point Likert scale
Never (1 point)
Rarely (2 points)
Sometimes (3 points)
Fairly often (4 points)
Frequently (5 points)

Note: Scores > 10.5 are positive; for Spanish version, cut-off score is 5.5 (Norton, Peipert, Zierler, Lima, & Hume, 1995). HITS (Copyright 2003) reprinted with permission from Kevin Sherin, MD, MPH (Kevin_Sherin@doh.state.fl.us).

Appendix E

Handout of the Chinese Abuse Assessment Screen (English version)

<u>Instructions for administration</u>:
1.   The woman should be provided with a private space for the completion of the AAS.
2.   The woman should <u>not</u> complete the AAS in the presence of her partner.
3.   The woman may take as long as she requires to complete the AAS.

1 (a)	Within the last year, have you been <u>emotionally</u> hurt by someone?
	
	<u>Examples</u> of emotional hurt:
	The *partner:*
	  • yells at you
	  • is hypercritical towards you
	  • shames you in front of friends/family/strangers
	  • ridicules you (e.g. about your appearance or behaviour)
	  • monitors you
	  • isolates you from friends/family
	  • threatens to hit you
	  • threatens to throw something at you
	  • accuses you (e.g. of doing something wrong)
	  • destroys something belonging to you
	
	If <u>yes</u>, by whom (check all that apply)
	☐ Husband
	☐ Ex-husband
	☐ Cohabiter
	☐ Boyfriend
	☐ Other (specify) ______________
		YES	NO

1 (b)	Within the last year, have you been <u>physically</u> hurt by someone?	YES	NO

Examples of physical hurt:

The *partner:*
- throws something at you
- pushes or shoves you
- slaps you
- grabs you
- drags your hair
- threatens you with a weapon
- hits you
- beats you up
- kicks you
- chokes you
- burns or scalds you

If yes, by whom (check all that apply)
- ☐ Husband
- ☐ Ex-husband
- ☐ Cohabiter
- ☐ Boyfriend
- ☐ Other (specify) ______________________

1 (c)	Within the last year, has anyone forced you to have <u>sexual</u> activities?	YES	NO

Examples of forced sexual activities:

The *partner:*
- insists on having sex with you against your wish (he may or may not use force)
- ignores your request to use condom when you have sex
- insists on having oral or anal sex (he may or may not use force)

If yes, by whom (check all that apply)
- ☐ Husband
- ☐ Ex-husband
- ☐ Cohabiter
- ☐ Boyfriend
- ☐ Other (specify) ______________________

2 (a)	Since you've been pregnant, have you been <u>emotionally</u> hurt by someone? If <u>yes</u>, by whom (check all that apply) ☐ Husband ☐ Ex-husband ☐ Cohabiter ☐ Boyfriend ☐ Other (specify) _________________	YES	NO
2 (b)	Since you've been pregnant, have you been <u>physically</u> hurt by someone? If <u>yes</u>, by whom (check all that apply) ☐ Husband ☐ Ex-husband ☐ Cohabiter ☐ Boyfriend ☐ Other (specify) _________________	YES	NO
2 (c)	Since you've been pregnant, has anyone forced you to have <u>sexual</u> activities? If <u>yes</u>, by whom (check all that apply) ☐ Husband ☐ Ex-husband ☐ Cohabiter ☐ Boyfriend ☐ Other (specify) _________________	YES	NO
3.	Are you afraid of your partner or anyone you listed above?	YES	NO

Appendix F

The Woman Abuse Screening Tool (WAST)

1. In general, how would you describe your relationship?
   * A lot of tension
   * Some tension
   * No tension
2. Do you and your partner work out arguments with:
   * Great difficulty
   * Some difficulty
   * No difficulty
3. Do arguments ever result in you feeling down or bad about yourself?
   * Often
   * Sometimes
   * Never
4. Do arguments ever result in hitting, kicking, or pushing?
   * Often
   * Sometimes
   * Never
5. Do you ever feel frightened by what your partner says or does?
   * Often
   * Sometimes
   * Never
6. Has your partner ever abused you physically?
   * Often
   * Sometimes
   * Never
7. Has your partner ever abused you emotionally?
   * Often
   * Sometimes
   * Never
8. Has your partner ever abused you sexually?
   * Often
   * Sometimes
   * Never

Note: WAST reprinted with permission from the Society of Teachers of Family Medicine. Copyright 1996.

Appendix G

The Extended Hurt, Injury, Threaten, and Scream Screening (E-HITS) Tool

Please circle how often your partner did each of these things in the past 12 months?

1. Has your partner ever physically hurt you in the past 12 months?
    1. Never
    2. Rarely
    3. Sometimes
    4. Often
    5. Frequently
2. Has your partner ever insulted you in the past 12 months?
    1. Never
    2. Rarely
    3. Sometimes
    4. Often
    5. Frequently
3. Has your partner ever threatened to harm you in the past 12 months?
    1. Never
    2. Rarely
    3. Sometimes
    4. Often
    5. Frequently
4. Has your partner ever screamed or cursed at you in the past 12 months?
    1. Never
    2. Rarely
    3. Sometimes
    4. Often
    5. Frequently
5. Has your partner ever forced you to have sexual activities in the past 12 months?
    1. Never
    2. Rarely
    3. Sometimes
    4. Often
    5. Frequently

Appendix H

Data Sheet used in the Study in Tuen Mun Hospital

Sex: ☐ Male   ☐ Female   Time:___________________

Age: ☐ 18–30   ☐ 31–40   ☐ 41–50   ☐ 51–60   ☐ 61 or above

(A) Introduction

I am a social worker of Harmony House/voluntary worker, and my name is ________________. Domestic violence has great impacts on personal health! Harmony House is carrying out a collaborative study with the ED of Tuen Mun Hospital. This study is to survey domestic violence incidence of the recruited patients, and your identity will be kept anonymous. All the information is confidential and will only be used for group analysis and subsequent reporting.

(B) Survey question

"The issue of domestic violence in Hong Kong is worsening! Domestic violence means any behaviour causing harm by intimate partner or family members, and it includes physical abuse (e.g., kicking, pushing, slapping, etc.) or spiritual abuse (e.g., intimidation, threats, insults, etc.) or sexual abuse (e.g., forced sex). Did you have experience of domestic violence in any way in the past one year?

YES   /   NO

(C) Follow-up measure (only for domestic violence case)

☐ Need to follow up (With patient consent for follow-up)

Name:_________________________   Contact Phone No.:__________________

☐ No follow-up

Reason: ☐ Had social worker follow up   ☐ Patient refused

☐ Information sheet on social services given to patient

Remark:____

Name of social worker/voluntary worker:_______________________

Date:______________________

For official use by social worker:

Social worker to follow up:______________________________

Date of interview :____________________

Part 4

Multidisciplinary Approach to Prevention

11
Child Maltreatment

Child Policy from a Child's Right Perspective

Chun-Bong Chow and Patrick P. K. Ip

> **Chapter summary**
>
> 1. Child maltreatment and domestic violence are very prevalent. According to self-reported studies, about half of our children have been maltreated either physically, sexually, psychologically, or have been neglected; yet only a small percentage of cases are being reported and are amenable to child protection services.
> 2. Impact of child maltreatment on physical, mental, social, sexual and scholastic functioning is profound, long-term and often lifelong with huge economic cost to society.
> 3. Effective intervention programmes are now available, but their effect can be marginal depending on service availability and quality, staff competence and cross-sectoral collaboration:
>   i. Screening and early detection—no conclusive evidence of their efficacy.
>   ii. Remedial services—available but expensive, labour-intensive and with inconsistent results.
>   iii. Prevention is hence the key, yet investment is grossly inadequate.
>   iv. Having an explicit policy on child safety and child welfare is important, but there is lack of a child policy in Hong Kong, and services are fragmented and poorly organized.
> 4. The child protection approach in past decades has produced improvement in outcomes, but child maltreatment still persists and is increasing in Hong Kong. A public health approach is very much needed.

> 5.   A rights-based approach based on the United Nations Convention
>   on the Rights of the Child (UNCRC) as legal framework will
>   further enhance effectiveness of child protection services. A child
>   policy as well as a child commission is very much needed to make
>   Hong Kong a most livable city for our future generations.

Child policy review through case studies

Children in Hong Kong are often viewed as enjoying excellent health as indicated by their good vital statistics. However, the child welfare policy and
service delivery model in Hong Kong have long been criticized as being short-
sighted, and as lacking the vision to plan for primary prevention especially on
child protection and to address forthcoming problems in advance.

On the service level, the current manpower allocation and funding system
demonstrate a typical failure to address the long-term needs of children and
underprivileged families. The social work workforce and administrative
system in Hong Kong are still following the traditional government administrative practice dating from the colonial years. A front-line social worker in the
Social Welfare Department needs to be rotated to another post within a couple
of years (usually every three years). This arrangement is contradictory to the
principle of providing most effective social service through continuity of care
and building of rapport, trust and relationship with time and mutual understanding. Any reasonable child policy must give due consideration to the nature
and the difficulty of supporting children in underprivileged and high-risk families, and therefore, should secure a stable working team instead of allowing
frequent staff rotations. A field of expertise like child protection is demanding and is highly dependent on experience, taking years and even decades to
build up the necessary skills and, equally important, trust and rapport with
working partners and the most high-risk families. Any sensible policymaker
should be aware of the consequences of frequent and routine rotation of social
workers, which leads to abrupt changes of the key case manager (case social
worker) working with a family at risk. There are many examples in which loss

of contact and trust due to the current rotation system resulted in avoidable tragedies and deteriorated care and relationship.

On the policy level, while the government claims there is central coordination, after years of lobbying by professionals and calls from the United Nations Committee on the Rights of the Child, still no child policy nor a children's commission has materialized. As a result, services are fragmented, and vulnerable children are suffering from this lack of leadership. The following two tragic case studies illustrate some of the problems in Hong Kong.

Case study 1. A three-month-old baby girl born to parents identified as at risk to social welfare service found dead from starvation in 2010:

Wing Yee, a three-month-old baby girl, was found comatose at home by her parents one day. She died later from starvation.

The parents of Wing Yee are a couple with poor parenting skills. The elder son of the couple had been found to be physically abused by the parents two and a half years ago. The son and the family were being supported and followed up by a key case worker in the Family and Child Protective Services Unit since then. In the subsequent year, the son was being cared for by his maternal grandmother. The initial case social worker who had close contact with the family was rotated to another post within the Social Welfare Department during the mother's late stage of pregnancy. The case was closed soon after it was handed over to the new case social worker, as the risk of child abuse was considered as minimal with the son now being cared for by his maternal grandmother. However, no particular attention was paid to the new pregnancy and the possibly more challenging situation posed by the delivery of the new baby.

The baby girl, Wing Yee, enjoyed an uneventful delivery and was born at term with a birth weight of 2.9 kg. She was discharged from hospital soon after delivery. Wing Yee's mother was receiving Comprehensive Social Security Assistance (CSSA) all along. Her father had lost his job a few months earlier during the pregnancy. They did not have any savings and did not apply for CSSA for either the father or Wing Yee, despite the fact that they faced great financial difficulty soon after Wing Yee's discharge from hospital. The CSSA payment Wing Yee's mother received was not sufficient to cover the expenses of the whole family, including the expensive cigarette consumption of both parents. Soon after returning home, Wing Yee's parents started to dilute her milk with water whenever they used up their money. When Wing Yee was two months old, her parents contacted the Family and Child Protective Services Unit for assistance, but were advised to seek help from the Integrated Family Service Centre instead because their previous case file was closed. No further assistance was sought from Wing Yee's parents since then.

When Wing Yee was found dead at three months old, the police visited the home and found poor hygiene conditions, with soiled nappies scattered on the floor, dirty and unchanged milk teats, a wet and filthy bathroom, and a foul-smelling baby crib without any proper bed sheets. The forensic pathologist found severe muscle atrophy, sunken eyeballs, loss of visceral fat, and even atrophy of internal organs in the victim. Wing Yee's body weight at three months old was only 2.6 kg, even much less than her birth weight of 2.9 kg. Both parents were charged with child abuse and were imprisoned. The coroner challenged the effectiveness of the social welfare system in protecting young children in at-risk families, and questioned whether a single home visitation after delivery could have already saved the baby girl's life.

This potentially avoidable tragedy demonstrates the shortsightedness of the child protection system and its structural defect, as well as the lack of a child policy that safeguards children in underprivileged families. The unnecessary routine rotation of an experienced social worker led to the breakdown of rapport between the family and the social support system and, as a result, a loss of the opportunity to pick up early risks facing a young and growing child. The current social support system failed to be proactive, and failed to serve its function of safeguarding a child's rights and needs.

The social welfare and social work system in Hong Kong should take a more proactive role, in particular, in the handling of high-risk families with young children. The current system adopts the approach of providing "on-demand" service only to those who seek assistance. As we know it, as children at risk would rarely seek assistance as clients themselves, their needs are usually neglected or ignored. In order to address the gap, social workers should take a more proactive role in following up at-risk children born to parents struggling with family problems, starting at birth. They are also strongly advised to attend community clinics, maternal and child health centres, and even to provide regular home visitations in order to preempt unmet needs of young children, instead of relying on crisis management after a tragedy has already happened.

Case study 2. Siblings found neglected and exhibiting developmental delay—do a child's rights or a parent's rights come first?

A thirty-eight-year-old mother who is an abuser of heroin and psychotropic substances was found to be leaving the care of her four young children to their eighty-three-year-old grandmother. Behaviour of the mother was erratic and unpredictable, often bursting with violence. The causing of a scald injury to the two-year-old brother, Chi Fung, during preparation of a cup of instant noodles by the six-year-old elder brother, Chi Kei, led to exposure of child neglect. Chi Fung was found to suffer first-degree burns on his neck, chest and part of his lower limbs. The subsequent recovery was satisfactory except for the complication of skin scarring. Chi Kei, the elder brother, was found to have attention deficit hyperactivity disorder and oppositional deviant disorder. He easily got angry and behaved violently in the same way as his mother did. The four-year-old sister was found to have mild developmental delay while the one-year-old youngest brother was developmentally normal.

The four children were found to be at risk of suffering further damage to their health and development under the current situations of care and nurture. However, the initial consideration of removing the children to foster care was objected to by their mother, who thought that the care for the children was already good enough and that it was no different from her own childhood experience. In addition, the multidisciplinary team of the Multidisciplinary Case Conference (MDCC) had lately been challenged by the mass media on their decision to break up a family, and had become wary of missteps. This case study highlights how in planning long-term welfare for children at risk and formulating policy to safeguard their rights and welfare, we need to strike a balance between advocating as child care professionals on behalf of children's rights and following the principle of upholding family unity and respecting the rights of the parent.

In the innovative model of the integrated early childhood programme under the Comprehensive Child Development Service (CCDS), infants and young children born to mothers abusing heroin and psychotropic drugs are identified during pregnancy or early childhood, and followed up longitudinally through collaboration of the medical, social work and educational sectors. Almost 20% of children born to these mothers have been found to be at risk of child abuse. These children require intensive support and close collaboration of social workers from the Family and Child Protective Services Unit (FCPSU), the Integrated Family Service Centre (IFSC) and the Society for the Aid and Rehabilitation of Drug Abusers (SARDA), the police, school teachers and medical professionals for the formulation of welfare plans, provision of support and placement.

Summary and reflection

From the above two cases, one can see that one of the major problems in Hong Kong is a lack of coherent policy to guide and integrate the provision of child protection services to better minimize and even close gaps. Child policy forms the cornerstone and the core component of government policies in many developed countries. Safeguarding the rights and welfare of children has been regarded as the cardinal objective of family policy and as a prominent campaign issue in most Western countries at the time of democratic elections. In Asian and traditional Chinese culture, children have long been regarded as a lesser component of the family. The rights and welfare of young children are frequently ignored as they cannot voice out their needs, and cannot make open complaints.

To the surprise of many overseas professionals, there has not been any implementation of a well-defined child policy in Hong Kong, and the child protection system is far from satisfactory. As children are usually regarded as being owned by their parents, the rights of an individual child are not properly respected in many families in Hong Kong. There is a lack of continuity in social care and long-term planning in both service delivery and the design of child protection intervention models.

Introduction

Child maltreatment is a serious problem in Hong Kong. The recent tragedy of a three-month-old baby starving to death in case study 1 is just the tip of the iceberg. The incidence of child maltreatment has increased significantly over the past decade, accompanied with its inherent complexities, which often compound the damage caused to our children. Traditional ways of tackling child maltreatment in terms of provision of welfare supplements and protection against immediate dangers through intervention by a single social service agency are no longer sufficient to stem this rising tide. We need to adopt a new and holistic approach towards child maltreatment—one that is a rights-based, community-oriented, child participatory public health approach, rather than the former model which is limited to welfare dispensation at specified centres, primarily family-driven and solely focused on child protection.

Prevalence of child maltreatment in Hong Kong

Child maltreatment has long been recognized as a major public health and social problem. In Hong Kong, based on mortality statistics, each year, about 50 to 90 children under 18 years of age die of external causes, 1 to 20 of which are due to "assaults". Findings of the Child Fatality Review conducted by the Social Welfare Department in the year 2006 revealed that 46 children under 18 years of age died of unnatural causes, 20 in accidents (11 traffic, 5 from accidental fall from height and 4 at home), 14 of suicide, and 13 from jumping from height. In a review of 494 suspected child abuse cases reported by Medical Coordinators on Child Abuse of the Hospital Authority during the period June 1997 to August 1999, 58% were substantiated to be child abuse and 5 had died (1%) of serious head injuries (Hong Kong Medical Coordinators on Child Abuse, 2003). Based on hospitalization statistics from the Hospital Authority for the years 2001 to 2008, we found that 5,093 (2,711 boys, 2,375 girls) were admitted with diagnosis of child maltreatment, of which 62 were treated in a paediatric intensive care unit, and 7 died (0.14%). The total bed days occupied were 46,668, costing about two million Hong Kong dollars each year in direct medical costs. The number of cases admitted for maltreatment also rose from 429 cases in 2001 to 760 in 2008. The number of child abuse cases under the Child Protection Registry kept by the Social Welfare Department rose from 622 cases in 2005 to 993 in 2009.

However, according to the findings of the household surveys conducted in Hong Kong (Chan, 2005), the self-reported incidence of violence was 6.1% for severe physical abuse, 57.6% for psychological abuse, 0.3% for sexual abuse, 27.4% for neglect by parents, and about 30% for having an experience of witnessing domestic violence. This amounted to around 70,000 children under 18 years of age being severely or very severely abused by their adult carers each year. But the yearly notification figure was around 600 in the year 2006, giving a notification rate of less than 1%. This finding was not at all surprising, and has been well reported worldwide (Gilbert, Widom et al., 2009).

Many studies have looked into the contributory or risk factors of child maltreatment. In general, they can be divided into individual, relationship, family and societal factors. Despite a better understanding of these factors and an increased awareness among the public and professionals, the gap between actual prevalence and notification is still widening, and interventions that are both preventive and remedial are not being delivered in time and to the targeted high-risk group.

The pattern of child maltreatment, including the socioecological contributing factors, has also evolved rapidly in the present society. There is a great need to set up a robust data collection system that will cut across social, health, education and judicial services (Al Eissa & Almuneef, 2010). The present Child Protection Registry collated by the Social Welfare Department provides only basic statistics on the number and types of abuse cases, perpetrator-child relationship, and little information on prevention. It needs to be revamped. The guidelines from the World Health Organization and Centre of Disease Control and Prevention may be useful references (German et al., 2001; Holder et al., 2001; Sethi & World Health Organization, 2004).

Despite the fact that domestic violence is common in Hong Kong, it is often unreported. In the 2005 population survey on spouse battering, about 10% of respondents reported having been physically assaulted or having physically assaulted their spouse, while 2% of respondents reported having physically injured their spouse or having been physically injured by their spouse during the twelve months prior to enumeration. However, about 12% and 5.5% of children have reported witnessing physical assault or injuries between their parents respectively (Chan, 2005). Domestic violence is common in Hong Kong and has been increasing rapidly in incidence. Compared to the prevalence rate obtained from the household survey, the number of reported cases of spouse battery of 4,807 in 2009 from the Social Welfare Department is a gross underestimate. The spouse battery rate of 7 per 1000 Accident and Emergency Department attendances is also very low (Wong et al., 1998). Violence is grossly underreported and data are scattered among social welfare, police and medical systems. Many children do witness violence among their parents. Child abuse occurs in 30–50% of cases of family violence, and about 30% of parents who assault their spouse also abuse their children (Krug, 2002). Thus children in families with spouse violence may be in effect experiencing a double, if not triple, tragedy.

Impact of child maltreatment

Recent studies have demonstrated serious long-term impacts of child maltreatment on physical, psychological, social and sexual, scholastic and cognitive functioning, as well as on aggression, violence and criminality. Table 11.1 shows a summary of the recent findings (Pinheiro, 2006). There are strong relationships between early childhood adverse experiences and medical and psychological complications that manifest throughout childhood as well as into adult life. Past research has also documented physiological abnormalities in the hypothalamic-pituitary axis response, as well as anatomical changes including smaller brain volumes and size differences in the limbic structure, in children with history of post-traumatic stress disorders (American Academy of Pediatrics et al., 2008). These observations indicate that the exaggerated behavioural responses and developmental problems seen in complex post-traumatic stress disorders have strong anatomical and physiological underpinnings that will last into later life. Even more important is the intergenerational effect of abuse. Recent researches on epigenetics have shown that adverse events during early childhood will alter the genetic composition of the victim child, which can be passed onto the next generation, posing a double impact.

The economic cost of interpersonal violence is enormous and was estimated to be 3.3% of the GDP in the US (Waters et al., 2004). For child abuse and neglect, the total estimated cost was 104 billion US dollars in 2007 (Wang & Holton, 2007). However, it was noted that such estimation was undermined by immense variations in measurement, data sources, samples and definitions, if not assumptions (Corso & Fertig, 2010). For Hong Kong, the hospitalization cost is around 2 million Hong Kong dollars a year, and if we assume the direct and indirect medical costs including subsequent delinquency and crime to be similar as in the US, the total cost will be 31.4 million a year!

The burden of child maltreatment on children and the society is thus substantial. The impact of neglect is not known, as it is even more likely to be underreported. There is mounting evidence that the consequences of child neglect can be more damaging than those of physical or sexual abuse (Dubowitz, 2009). More research is needed to better define what constitutes neglect, and to identify its effect on children.

The impact of domestic violence on children cannot be overestimated. Simply being exposed to domestic violence and not directly experiencing abuse may have detrimental effects on a child's emotional and social

Table 11.1 Consequences of child maltreatment (Gilbert, Widom et al., 2009; Pinherior, 2006)

Types of abuse / Consequences	Physical	Psychological	Sexual (Irish, Kobayashi, & Delahanty, 2010)
Physical			
Deaths	0.6% of all deaths		
Education and employment			
Low educational achievement	OR = 1.7		
Low skilled employment	OR = 1.4		
Mental health			
Behavioural problem	Strong	Strong	Strong
Post-traumatic stress disorder	OR = 1.9	OR = 1.7	OR = 2.3
Depression	OR = 1.3–2.4		
Attempted suicide	OR = 2–3		OR = 2–7
Self-injurious behaviour			
Alcohol problems	Esp. in girls		
Drug misuse/dependency			
Physical health	OR = 1.3–9.8		
General adult health			OR = 9.1
Chronic pain in adulthood			OR = 8.1
Obesity	OR = 1.3		OR = 10.2
Healthcare use/cost			OR = 1.35–2.21
Quality of life	No study done		
Irritable bowel syndrome			OR = 5.3
Liver diseases			
Ischemic heart disease			OR = 7.3
Sexual and reproductive health			
Prostitution/sex trading	OR = 2–3		OR = 2–3
Teenage pregnancy			
Sexually transmitted disease, HIV	OR = 2	OR = 2	
Aggression, violence, criminality			
Criminal behaviour	OR = 1.5		

OR = odds ratio

development. Immediate responses to traumatic experiences include shock, terror, guilt, anxiety, hostility, sense of vulnerability and depression. Such effects can also manifest as sleep disturbance, nightmares, exaggerated startle response and psychosomatic symptoms, and can affect cognitive functions in terms of impairment in concentration, lowered self-efficacy and intrusive thoughts. Children of abused caregivers are significantly more likely to demonstrate both internalizing behaviours, such as anxiety and depression, as well as externalizing behaviours, such as aggression and attentional issues (McFarlane, Froff, Obrien, & Watson, 2003; Thackeray, Hibbard et al. 2010). In addition, children exposed to violence are more likely to have difficulty relating to their peers and performing well academically (Stirling, 2008). Local studies also demonstrated similar findings—78.8% of children who had witnessed domestic violence demonstrated strong feelings of threat, helplessness, anxiety and fear; 42.3% experienced a very high level of stress for being in the conflict; 61.6% had low self-esteem. Boys tended to demonstrate disruptive behaviours to resolve conflict (40.6%) while girls tended to show withdrawal, a lack of confidence and a depressive mood (Chan, 2002). Domestic violence has also been called the leading precursor of child maltreatment for its intergenerational effect. Training of paediatricians regarding the prevalence and early recognition of domestic violence and its impact on children is thus of great importance. Also, a full child protection investigation which includes an assessment of mental health should be conducted for all children living in families with a documented history of domestic violence.

Screening and early recognition

The over 100-fold difference between self-reported incidence of child maltreatment and substantiated cases signifies the gross underrecognition and shortfall in response of professionals and the public. Factors for such underreporting are many, including inadequate training, restricted access to qualified social workers, concern that services available cannot meet demand for support, premature judgment that reporting may not bring benefits to the child or family, and fears about damaging professional-child relationships. One major concern of professionals is about the effectiveness of interventions on children's lives overall when resources are insufficient and services are uncoordinated. Hence, the development of effective intervention services with good feedback to referrers is important.

Having a set of good guidelines or referral protocols will facilitate recognition and response from professionals. Guidelines on handling child abuse should be developed locally to accommodate the wide variation in ecological factors contributing to child maltreatment in different societies. The 2007 procedural guideline was developed involving all stakeholders and based on local data and information (Social Welfare Department, 2007). However, the training on its usage is often sectoral, defeating the multidisciplinary nature of the guide. The model developed by the National Institute for Health and Clinical Excellence (NICE) is worth referencing. The guide, *When to Suspect Child Maltreatment* (2009), was developed after extensive literature review, again involving all stakeholders. It is accompanied with a quick reference guide, training plan, implementation guide, costing and audit templates, and requires local authorities to implement in full in accordance with a timeline.

Recently, the International Society on Prevention of Child Abuse and Neglect (ISPCAN) has piloted three ISPCAN child abuse screening tools (ICAST) in several countries for cross-cultural, multinational and multicultural research, which facilitates comparison regarding child maltreatment across time and nations. The three instruments are ICAST-C (the children version), ICAST-P (the parent version) and ICAST-R (the retrospective version) (Dunne et al., 2009; Runyan, Dunne, & Zolotor, 2009; Zolotor et al., 2009). Preliminary testing results were encouraging. The internal consistencies among scales were good to excellent, having an alpha coefficient of 0.72 to 0.86, but further validation is needed. However, such tools may be useful for international comparison, but not for the local situation. A risk assessment tool for spouse battering and child abuse has been developed by Chan (2007). The instrument comes with a training manual and may be a useful screening tool. However, the instrument requires appropriate professional qualification and sufficient training to administer, and will need further evaluation upon full introduction in the field. In a systemic review, none of the screening methods substantially improved the detection rate and, rather, carried the risk of overwhelming child protection workers with false positive referrals. The review concluded that experienced clinical assessment was likely to be more accurate than screening tests, and illustrated the importance of training and developing experienced clinicians (Woodman, 2008). A recent study conducted in Spain documented increased reporting of child maltreatment cases after a phased training programme of health, social services and school professionals (Cerezo

& Pons-Salvador, 2004). More intensive and multidisciplinary training using interactive training methodology is required if we are to improve early recognition of child maltreatment.

It has also been found that the rate of officially recognized child maltreatment and the types and quantity of services provided are partly affected by legislation and policies governing recognition of and response to child abuse. In a recent study by the Legislative Council Secretariat, the legislation and provision of services in Hong Kong performed poorly when compared with those in the UK, Australia and Canada (T. Wong, 2007). The recommendations from the consultancy study on social and legal measures for the prevention and intervention of domestic violence in Hong Kong should be implemented and reviewed for their implications for children (Chan, 2005). For policies governing responses to child maltreatment, in general, there are two broad but overlapping approaches, namely the child and family welfare approach and the child safety approach (Gilbert, Kemp et al., 2009). Hong Kong is practising a child safety approach and tends to concentrate on the investigation of maltreatment and the assessment of future risks, rather than on broader child and family welfare needs. When a child is suspected of being maltreated, a multidisciplinary case conference composed of social, healthcare, education and relevant professionals will be held to formulate a welfare plan for the child and family. The family will be referred to relevant agencies for follow-up action. However, the progress of the family and the child is seldom monitored and the outcome seldom evaluated. There is no data on the outcome of such families, e.g., on the revictimization rate. For this reason and others, the policy and service model in Hong Kong should be reviewed.

With the prevalence of family violence and its effects on a significant proportion of families, both the American Academy of Family Physicians (American Academy of Family Physicians, 2000) and the American College of Obstetricians and Gynecologists (ACOG) have called for measures to improve identification and facilitate disclosure of domestic violence. The US Preventive Services Task Force found that, although screening does increase identification of domestic violence, there is still insufficient evidence that universal domestic violence assessments reduce morbidity or mortality in the abused; on the contrary, there may be collateral harmful effects (US Preventive Services Task Force, 2004). The ACOG recommended the use of the following three questions for domestic violence screening: —

i.   Within the past year—or since you have been pregnant—have you been hit, slapped, kicked or otherwise physically hurt by someone?

ii. Are you in a relationship with a person who threatens or physically hurts you?

iii. Has anyone forced you to have sexual activities that made you feel uncomfortable?

The American Academy of Pediatrics has recommended paediatricians to identify abused women in paediatric settings as another form of child abuse prevention (Thackeray, Hibbard et al., 2010). Recommendations have also been made to consider different means of identifying domestic violence by universal screening or targeted screening of high-risk families. But it is equally important to have a plan in place to respond to positive screens.

Clinical assessment and treatment

As discussed above, children who have been maltreated are at high risk of experiencing mental and social health problems including post-traumatic stress, depression, dissociation, reactive attachment, low self-esteem, social problems, suicidal behaviours, aggression, conduct disorders, and problem behaviours (e.g., delinquency, risky sexual behaviour and substance abuse). Yet most of the existing welfare plans mainly concentrate on the prevention of further physical maltreatment without providing timely mental health assessment and services to children. Rarely are maltreated children in Hong Kong referred for mental health assessment. While family configuration and problems will be reviewed in the multidisciplinary case conference (MDCC), family dynamics, especially the views of the children, are seldom examined and considered in the welfare plan. The assessment matrix of the Hong Kong Procedural Guide for Handling Child Abuse Cases 2007 also focuses more on risk assessment of the child's safety rather than the child's well-being needs in a family context. A more structured family-child assessment should be developed. Child participation is crucial in the development of an effective welfare plan and for the management of chronic stress experienced by the child.

Evidence for effective interventions in the area of child maltreatment is very much lacking. However, recent research studies have documented several evidence-based interventions for child abuse and neglect (Shipman & Taussig, 2009). Examples include the Parent-Child Interaction Therapy (PCIT), a short-term behavioural intervention for children and their parents which focuses on enhancing the quality of the parent-child relationship and teaching positive approaches to child behaviour management; abuse-focused cognitive behavioural therapy (AF-CBT) which is a short-term intervention for physically abusive parents and their school-age children based on behavioural, cognitive-behavioural and family system theories; trauma-focused cognitive behavioural therapy (TF-CBT), which is a short-term cognitive behavioural intervention used to treat traumatized children ages 3 to 17; and child parent psychotherapy (CPP), an attachment-based intervention used to treat traumatized children from birth to 6 years of age. The involvement of parents or significant caregivers in the intervention, which is a main component of the family dynamic assessment, is crucial. For further information, readers can refer to the NCTSN website (www.nctsn.org) or to recently published literature and reviews (Barlow el al 2006; Shipman et al 2009). Service provision of these types of therapies in Hong Kong is grossly limited, and few research studies have been conducted. As these therapies have been shown to produce significant impact on enhancing the mental health of maltreated children and their families, they should be researched and introduced in Hong Kong. This will need commitment from the government to the multidisciplinary and cross-sectoral approach, as introduction of these therapies would require considerable collaboration among researchers and health agencies, especially those that specialize in mental health and child and family welfare.

Out-of-home care is one of the most widely used interventions for maltreated children. However, there are few studies looking into their effects, such as the effects of better training of foster parents on maximizing a child's welfare, and the effects of multidimensional treatment foster care (MTFC) on reducing long-term adverse impacts. At present, further research on this issue is needed in Hong Kong.

In light of its prevalence and both its short- and long-term impacts on children, domestic violence is also a paediatric issue. Plans for early identification, assessment and response should be part of the clinical practice for paediatricians (Thackeray, Hibbard et al., 2010). However, it is not a common practice to conduct domestic violence assessments in child advocacy centres (Thackeray, Scribano, & Rhoda, 2010). Guidelines should be promulgated to medical practitioners to guide their response where domestic violence is suspected.

Prevention

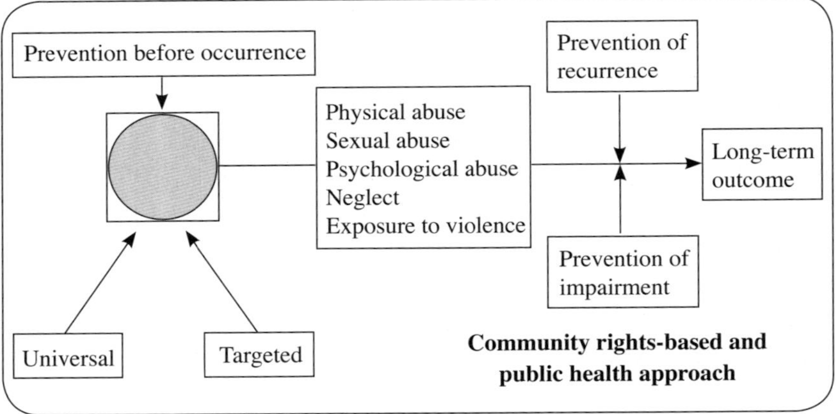

Figure 11.1　Framework for prevention of child maltreatment and associated impairment (adapted with modification from MacMillan, et al., 2009)

Given the high prevalence of and the huge impacts caused by child maltreatment, as well as the lack of effective early detection mechanisms, prevention is the most important means to combat the problem. There are three approaches at present: (a) universal and targeted prevention of maltreatment before it occurs; (b) prevention of recurrence and adverse outcomes associated with maltreatment; and (c) community approach of prevention by improving the social, economic and political environments in which children and their families live (MacMilan et al., 2009).

A public health approach involving a cycle of four steps may be useful. The approach works by: (a) defining and measuring the problem; (b) identifying the causal, risk and protective factors; (c) developing interventions and determining their effectiveness; (d) implementing interventions with ongoing monitoring of outcomes. Hence it is vital to have robust child maltreatment surveillance to monitor the frequency and causal factors of child maltreatment. Then there must also be a mechanism to analyse the available information to determine the most appropriate strategy and most effective intervention, and a cross-sectoral infrastructure to implement interventions with multidisciplinary training. Finally, a mechanism is needed to audit and monitor outcome measures, in order to evaluate implemented programmes.

There was previously a lack of evidence for effective intervention in the field of child maltreatment, but fortunately, there has been significant progress in the research on interventions in recent decades (Barlow, Simkiss, & Steward-Brown, 2006; Mikton & Butchart, 2009).

The intervention programmes can generally be grouped into three types. The first type is prevention before occurrence of maltreatment. Several programmes have been found to be effective. Home visitation—especially the nurse-family partnership developed by David Olds—is most promising in reducing physical abuse and neglect (Donelan-McCall, Eckenrode, & Olds, 2009). The early start programme has been found to reduce injuries and hospital admissions due to child abuse (Howard & Brooks-Gunn, 2009). The Triple P—Positive Parenting Programme—has demonstrated positive effects on substantiated child maltreatment, out-of-home placements and reports of injuries (Prinz, 2009; Prinz, Sanders, Shapiro, Whitaker, & Lutzker, 2009). However, enhanced paediatric care for families at risk produced positive but not significant effects (Dubowitz, Feigelman, Lane, & Kim, 2009).The second type of interventions attempts to prevent re-exposure to and adverse outcomes of child maltreatment. For details, please refer to the section on "Assessment and treatment".

The third type of intervention uses a community rights-based approach (Bennett, Hart, & Ann Svevo-Cianci, 2009; Doek, 2009). Child maltreatment is often considered a public health problem in medical literature, and a child protection or welfare issue in social work studies. Public health approaches use surveillance, prevention, and cost-effective and population (universal or targeted) strategies; protective approaches concentrate on the professional and legal response to cases of maltreatment; welfare approaches emphasize needs assessment and provision of support or services. These approaches have resulted in improved outcomes, yet the numbers for maltreatment have continued to increase, indicating they are still short of meeting the existing needs.

Protection, though necessary, is not sufficient to ensure that a child is not maltreated. Likewise, protection alone cannot result in optimal growth and development of a child. A rights-based approach in which rights to participation and provisions are as important as rights to protection will fill in the gap by ensuring that the physical, psychological, social, moral and spiritual needs of children are met for their development to the best of their potential. A rights-based approach based on the guidelines by the UNCRC will also provide a legal framework for implementing policy, accountability and social justice, all of which will enhance public health response as well as child protection and welfare services. With child maltreatment defined as a violation of rights, the government and policymakers will also be obliged to assume responsibility and accountability, and to intervene in accordance with international legal obligations.

Finally, child participation aims to promote in government agencies, parents, and professionals a greater respect for children's rights. It places greater attention on children's views towards maltreatment, suffering and intervention, and capitalizes on the young generation's present and potential contribution towards dealing with domestic violence issues. This will significantly increase the chances of success of protective measures against violence. In the UN study on violence against children, the Secretary-General states, "I recommend that States actively engage with children and respect their views in all aspects of prevention, response and monitoring of violence against them, taking into account article 12 of the Convention on the Rights of the Child" (Secretary General of United Nations, 2006, p. 27; Feinstein & O'Kane, 2008; Pinherior, 2006).

Child maltreatment results from a complex interplay of individual, family and community factors. Measures to combat violence must address the general circumstances in which children live. Community-level change is critical to alleviating individual and family stress that contributes to child maltreatment (McDonell & Melton, 2008). Children, who lack a voice in the community, are most vulnerable to such adversities. A holistic approach to developing a coherent policy agenda focusing on child well-being will be most useful in increasing visibility of existing services, steering focused policy changes and evaluation, and effecting community changes that are to the best interest of children. No single policy will be able to provide all the answers for reducing poverty, protecting children's rights, strengthening families and enhancing children's development and well-being. Having an explicit child policy may not be the only solution, but increasing the visibility of children's conditions within a family context and providing the means for assessing how the policies affect them will certainly help build Hong Kong into a more livable city for our future generations (Chow, 2009).

For the social and legal measures regarding the prevention and intervention of domestic violence in Hong Kong, a review has been conducted with

21 recommendations (Chan et al., 2005). For details, please refer to the report. Similar reviews should be conducted for child maltreatment in Hong Kong.

Conclusion

Despite the efforts that have been put into improving services for child maltreatment and domestic violence, the prevalence as well as the complexity of child abuse has continued to escalate. Literature reviews indicate that while there has been progress in the development of tools for early recognition of child maltreatment, the gaps between identification and true incidence have not yet been bridged. It is thus imperative to invest more on preventive measures. Recent studies have demonstrated many effective intervention measures. It is false economy not to invest on these measures, and the investment needs full commitment from the government and integrated efforts from all sectors, so as to develop a robust infrastructure. This infrastructure includes setting up a sound surveillance system, detecting child maltreatment at early stages, and providing prompt and appropriate remedial as well as effective prevention intervention. More effort should be paid to the long-term follow-up of child abuse victims and the rehabilitation of the child and family. A rights-based, public health and life-course approach of intervention with accountability in a community setting is needed to tackle this very problem which carries both huge short- and long-term costs to society.

The UNCRC should be the basis for the formulation of policies, strategies and services for children. The implementation of the UNCRC is based on three important assumptions. First, the family has the primary responsibility for the upbringing of the child. But such upbringing must be consistent with the rights stipulated in the UNCRC. Second, the government must work in partnership with the family in the fulfilment of the rights of the child and in their best interests. Third, both the government and society have the duty to monitor and to ensure the full implementation of the UNCRC to all children without discrimination. In case of a dispute within a family or an institution giving rise to potential harm to a child, the government and society must intervene to protect the child whose life or health is at stake. This can be achieved through close collaboration of families, professionals and the government, and together, we can build a happy, healthy and harmonious society in which our children will flourish and develop to their full potential.

References

Al Eissa, M., & Almuneef, M. (2010). Child abuse and neglect in Saudi Arabia: journey of recognition to implementation of national prevention strategies. *Child Abuse & Neglect, 34*, 28–33. doi: 10.1016/j.chiabu.2009.08.011

American Academy of Family Physicians. (2000). *Violence (position paper)*. Retrieved from the American Academy of Family Physicians website: http://www.aafp. org/online/en/home/policy/policies/v/violencepositionpaper.html

American Academy of Pediatrics, Stirling, J. Jr., Committee on Child Abuse and Neglect and Section on Adoption and Foster Care, American Academy of Child and Adolescent Psychiatry, Amaya-Jackson, L., National Center for Child Traumatic Stress, & Amaya-Jackson, L. (2008). Understanding the behavioral and emotional consequences of child abuse. *Pediatrics, 122*, 667–673. doi: 10.1542/peds.2008-1885

Barlow, J. S. D., Simkiss, D., & Steward-Brown, S. (2006). Interventions to prevent or ameliorate child physical abuse and neglect: findings from a systematic review of reviews. *Journal of Children's Services, 1*(3), 6–28.

Bennett, S., Hart, S. N., & Ann Svevo-Cianci, K. (2009). The need for a general comment for Article 19 of the UN Convention on the Rights of the Child: toward enlightenment and progress for child protection. *Child Abuse & Neglect, 33*, 783–790. doi: 10.1016/j.chiabu.2009.09.007

Cerezo, M. A., & Pons-Salvador, G. (2004). Improving child maltreatment detection systems: a large-scale study involving health, social services and school professionals. *Child Abuse & Neglect, 28*, 1153–1169. doi: 10.1016/j.chiabu. 2004.06.007

Chan, K. L. (2002). *Study of Children Who Witnessed Family Violence*. Hong Kong: Christian Family Service Centre and Department of Social Work & Social Administration, the University of Hong Kong.

Chan, K. L. (2005). *Peace at Home: Report on the Review of the Social and Legal Measures in the Prevention and Intervention of Domestic Violence in Hong Kong*. Retrieved from the Hong Kong Social Welfare Department website: http:// www.swd.gov.hk/doc/Report%20on%20the%20Review%20of%20the%20 Social%20and%20Legal%20Measures%20in%20the%20Prevention%20 and%20Intervention%20of%20Domestic%20Violence%20in%20Hong%20 Kong.pdf

Chan, K. L. (2005). *Study on Child Abuse and Spouse Battering: Findings of Household Survey* (Report No. CB(2)2158/04-05(02)). Retrieved from the Hong Kong Legislative Council website: http://www.legco.gov.hk/yr04-05/english/panels/ ws/ws_fvi/papers/ws_fvi0705cb2-2158-2e.pdf

Chan, K. L. (2007). *Training Manual of the Risk Assessment Tools for Spouse Battering and Child Abuse in Hong Kong Chinese Families*. Retrieved from the Department of Social Work and Social Administration, the University of Hong Kong website: http://www.socialwork.hku.hk/people/staff/files/attach-ment/20070828122730.pdf

Chow, C. B. (2009). Asia's world city deserves a child commission. *Hong Kong Journal of Paediatrics*, *14*, 70–73.

Corso, P. S., & Fertig, A. R. (2010). The economic impact of child maltreatment in the United States: are the estimates credible? *Child Abuse & Neglect*, *34*, 296–304. doi: 10.1016/j.chiabu.2009.09.014

Doek, J. E. (2009). The CRC 20 years: an overview of some of the major achievements and remaining challenges. *Child Abuse & Neglect*, *33*, 771–782. doi: 10.1016/j.chiabu.2009.08.006

Donelan-McCall, N., Eckenrode, J., & Olds, D. L. (2009). Home visiting for the prevention of child maltreatment: lessons learned during the past 20 years. *Pediatric Clinics of North America*, *56*, 389–403. doi: 10.1016/j.pcl.2009.01.002

Dubowitz, H. (2009). Tackling child neglect: a role for pediatricians. *Pediatric Clinic of North America*, *56*, 363–378. doi: 10.1016/j.pcl.2009.01.003

Dubowitz, H., Feigelman, S., Lam, W., & Kim, J. (2009). Pediatric primary care to help prevent child maltreatment: the safe environment for every kid (SEEK) model. *Pediatrics*, *123*, 858–864. doi: 10.1542/peds.2008-1376

Dunne, M. P., Zolotor, A. J., Runyan, D. K., Andreva-Miller, I., Choo, W. Y., Dunne, S. K., Gerbaka, B., Isaeva, O., Jain, D., Kasim, M. D., Macfarlane, B., Mamyrova, N., Ramirez, C., Volkova, E., & Youssef, R. (2009). ISPCAN Child Abuse Screening Tools Retrospective version (ICAST-R): Delphi study and field testing in seven countries. *Child Abuse & Neglect*, *33*, 815–825. doi: 10.1016/j.chiabu.2009.09.005

Feinstein, C., & O'Kane, C. (2008). *Children's and Adolescent's Participation and Protection from Sexual Abuse and Exploitation*. Retrieved from the UNICEF Innocenti Research Centre website: http://www.unicef-irc.org/publications/pdf/iwp_2009_09.pdf

German, R. R., Lee, L. M., Horan, J. M., Milstein, R. L., Pertowski, C. A., Waller, M. N., & Guidelines Working Group Centers for Disease Control and Prevention (CDC). (2001). Updated guidelines for evaluating public health surveillance systems. *MMWR*, *50*(RR13), 1–35.

Gilbert, R., Kemp, A., Thoburn, J., Sidebotham, P., Radford, L., Glaser, D., & MacMillan, H. L. (2009). Recognising and responding to child maltreatment. *The Lancet*, *373*(9658), 167–180. doi: 10.1016/S0140-6736(08)61707-9

Gilbert, R., Widom, C. S., Browne, K., Fergusson, D., Webb, E., & Janson, S. (2009). Burden and consequences of child maltreatment in high-income countries. *The Lancet*, *373*(9657), 68–81. doi: 10.1016/S0140-6736(08)61706-7

Holder, Y., Peden, M., Krug, E., Lund, J., Gururaj, G., & Kobusingye, O. (Eds). (2001). *Injury Surveillance Guidelines*. Retrieved from the World Health Organization, Geneva website: http://whqlibdoc.who.int/publications/2001/9241591331.pdf

Hong Kong Medical Coordinators on Child Abuse. (2003). Management of child abuse in Hong Kong: results of a territory-wide interhospital perspective surveillance study. *Hong Kong Medical Journal*, *9*, 6–9.

Howard, K. S., & Brooks-Gunn, J. (2009). The role of home-visiting programs in preventing child abuse and neglect. *The Future of Children*, *19*, 119–146.

Irish, L., Kobayashi, I., & Delahanty, D. L. (2010). Long-term physical health consequences of childhood sexual abuse: a meta-analytic review. *Journal of Pediatric
Psychology*, *35*, 450–461. doi: 10.1093/jpepsy/jsp118

Krug, E. G., et al. (Eds). (2002). *World Report on Violence and Health* (p. 68). Geneva,
World Health Organization.

MacMillan, H. L., Wathen, C. N., Barlow, J., Fergusson, D. M., Leventhal, J. M.,
& Taussig, H. N. (2009). Interventions to prevent child maltreatment and
associated impairment. *The Lancet*, *373*(9659), 250–266. doi: 10.1016/
S0140-6736(08)61708-0

McDonell, J. R., & Melton, G. B. (2008). Toward a science community intervention.
Family & Community Health, *31*, 113–125. doi: 10.1097/01.FCH.0000314572.
66528.fe

McFarlane, J., Froff, J., Obrien, J., & Watson, K. (2003). Behaviors of children who are
exposed and not exposed to intimate partner violence: an analysis of 330 black,
white and Hispanic children. *Pediatrics*, *112*, e202–e207.

Mikton, C., & Butchart, A. (2009). Child maltreatment prevention: a systematic
review of reviews. Bulletin of the World Health Organization, *87*, 353–361. doi:
10.1590/S0042-96862009000500012

National Institute for Health and Clinical Excellence. (2009). *When to Suspect
Child Maltreatment: Full Guideline*. Retrieved from the National Institute for
Health and Clinical Excellence website: http://www.nice.org.uk/nicemedia/
live/12183/44954/44954.pdf

Pinheiro, P. S. (2006). *Report of the Independent Expert for the United Nations Study
on Violence Against Children* (p. 65). Retrieved from the UNICEF website:
http://www.unicef.org/violencestudy/reports/SG_violencestudy_en.pdf

Prinz, R. J. (2009). Dissemination of a multilevel evidence-based system of parenting
interventions with broad application to child welfare populations. *Child Welfare*,
88, 127–132.

Prinz, R. J., Sanders, M. R., Shapiro, C. J., Whitaker, D. J., & Lutzker, J. R. (2009).
Population-based prevention of child maltreatment: the US Triple P System
Population Trial. *Prevention Science*, *10*, 1–12. doi: 10.1007/s11121-009-0123-3

Runyan, D. K., Dunne, M. P., & Zolotor, A. J. (2009). Introduction to the development of the ISPCAN child abuse screening tools. *Child Abuse & Neglect*, *33*,
842–845. doi: 10.1016/j.chiabu.2009.08.003

Secretary General of the United Nations. Report of the independent expert for the
United Nations study on violence against children. Presented to United Nations
General Assembly, 29 August 2006.

Sethi, D., & World Health Organization. (2004). *Guidelines for Conducting Community
Surveys on Injuries and Violence*. Geneva, Switzerland: World Health
Organization.

Shipman, K., & Taussig, H. (2009). Mental health treatment of child abuse and neglect:
the promise of evidence-based practice. *Pediatric Clinic of North America*, *56*,
417–428. doi: 10.1016/j.pcl.2009.02.002

Social Welfare Department. (2007). *Procedural Guide for Handling Child Abuse Cases.* Retrieved from the Hong Kong Social Welfare Department website: http://www. swd.gov.hk/doc/fcw/proc_guidelines/childabuse/Acrobat%20Document%20 (revised%20on%20280510).pdf

Thackeray, J. D., Hibbard, R., Dowd, M. D., Committee on Child Abuse and Neglect, & Committee on Injury, Violence, and Poison Prevention. (2010). Intimate partner violence: the role of the pediatrician. *Pediatrics*, *125*, 1094–1100. doi: 10.1542/peds.2010-0451

Thackeray, J. D., Scribano, P. V., & Rhoda, D. (2010). Domestic violence assessments in the child advocacy center. *Child Abuse & Neglect*, *34*, 172–182. doi: 10.1016/j.chiabu.2009.10.002

US Preventive Services Task Force. (2004). Screening for family and intimate partner violence: recommendation statement. *Annals of Family Medicine*, *2*, 156–160.

Wang, C. T., & Holton, J. (2007). *Total Estimated Cost of Child Abuse and Neglect in the United States.* Economic Impact Study, September 2007. Retrieved from the Prevent Child Abuse America website: http://www.preventchildabuse.org/ about_us/media_releases/pcaa_pew_economic_impact_study_final.pdf

Waters, H., Hyder, A., Rajkotia, Y., Basu, S., Rehwinkel, J. A., & Butchart, A. (2004). *The Economic Dimension of Interpersonal Violence.* Retrieved from the World Health Organization website: http://whqlibdoc.who.int/publications/2004/9241591609.pdf

Wong, T. (2007). Child protection in selected overseas places. Retrieved from the Research and Library Services Division, Legislative Council Secretariat, Hong Kong website: http://www.legco.gov.hk/yr06-07/english/sec/library/0607rp03-e.pdf

Wong, T. W., Chung, M., Lau, C. C., Ng, P., Wong, W. Y., & Ngan, J. (1998). Victims of domestic violence presenting to an accident and emergency department. *Hong Kong Practitioners*, *20*, 107–112.

Woodman, J., Pitt, M., Wentz, R., Taylor, B., Hodes, D., & Gilbert, R. E. (2008). Performance of screening tests for child physical abuse in accident and emergency departments. *Health Technology Assessment*, *12*(33), 1–118.

Zolotor, A. J., Runyan, D. K., Dunne, M. P., Jain, D., Péturs, H. R., Ramirez, C., Volkova, E., Deb, S., Lidchi, V., Muhammad, T., & Isaeva, O. (2009). ISPCAN Child Abuse Screening Tool Children's version (ICAST-C): instrument development and multi-national pilot testing. *Child Abuse & Neglect*, *33*, 833–841. doi: 10.1016/j.chiabu.2009.09.004

12 Multidisciplinary Case Conference for Child Abuse and Battered Spouse Cases

Anna Wai-Man Choi

Chapter summary

1. The Multidisciplinary Case Conference (MDCC) is a mechanism which assembles a team of professionals from health, legal and social services disciplines in Hong Kong to assess and handle family violence cases.
2. The procedures on conducting an MDCC can be found in the procedural guides for handling child abuse cases and battered spouse cases (Social Welfare Department, 2004, 2007).
3. This chapter examines the handling procedures for an MDCC and the functions it serves in tackling child and spouse abuse cases.
4. Development and improvement of the MDCC to further promote and protect the welfare of victims and their families are also explored.

Introduction

MDCC for child abuse cases

Child protection is a team effort involving different professionals, such as social workers, teachers, police, and health professionals. Child health and welfare professionals in Hong Kong have worked closely in handling child maltreatment because of increased awareness of child abuse and neglect in the community since 1990 (Mulvey, 1997). Multidisciplinary collaboration is a common and critical work approach in dealing with child maltreatment.

According to the Procedural Guides for Handling Child Abuse Cases Revised 2007 (PG-CAC) issued by the Social Welfare Department, "The MDCC is a forum by which professionals having a major role in the handling and investigation of a suspected child abuse case can share their professional knowledge, information and concern on the child health, development, functioning and his/her parents'/carers' ability to ensure safety of the child" (Social Welfare Department, 2007, p. 83).

In order to facilitate the operation of the MDCC, a case manager will be assigned to take up the major tasks of coordination and management. The social worker or caseworker from a social service agency who is in immediate charge of handling the suspected child abuse case would be the case manager in most situations. In practice, this caseworker is most likely the first to have known of the case, and is often a social worker from the Integration Family Service Centre (IFSC), the Family and Child Protective Services Units (FCPSU) or the Medical Social Services Units (MSSU). If it is an unknown case, which means a new case that has not been assigned to anyone, the FCPSU will properly take up the case management work. The case managers play a very important role in initiating and preparing the MDCC for suspected child abuse cases. They are also the key person to supervise the implementation of, or to implement, the welfare plan of the cases—including interventions and remedies agreed upon—following MDCC meetings.

Another key person of the MDCC is the chairperson. In most situations, this position will be taken up by the officer in charge or the supervisor of the key caseworker for the suspected child abuse case. The social workers or officer in charge of the FCPSUs will provide support or assume the role of chairperson if necessary. The chairperson facilitates and monitors the involvement of professionals as well as the overall progress of the MDCC. He/she should have adequate knowledge and skills in handling family violence, and must also wield sufficient experience in collaborating across disciplines. Thorough understanding of the roles and functions of different professionals is essential when holding the MDCC meeting, owing to the diverse constitution of the group's membership. In addition, the child and his/her parents of the case under review may be fully or partially involved in the proceedings, upon careful consideration and consensus among the members of an MDCC.

A clear time frame concerning the conducting of MDCCs for suspected child abuse cases can be found in the PG-CAC. The guide recommends that the MDCC be conducted within ten working days after the receipt of referral to allow for prompt discussion and formulating of an appropriate welfare plan, which is crafted in a holistic manner and presented to the child and his/her family by a multidisciplinary platform. The roles and tasks of participants and the chairperson are also outlined in the PG-CAC. For example, each member is to prepare a written report/memo on the case for the MDCC's reference as far as possible, and should openly share their professional views during the meetings. The chairperson ensures that the focus and objective of the MDCC remain centred on the child's welfare and protection at all times. The PG-CAC also contains other material, including a sample invitation letter for convening an MDCC, sample minutes, a sample letter to parents on the outcome and decisions of the conference, making it a useful reference kit for facilitating the smooth running of MDCCs.

MDCC for spouse abuse cases

The Procedural Guidelines for Handling Battered Spouse Cases (PG-BSC) (Social Welfare Department, 2004) issued by the Social Welfare Department first and foremost recommends multidisciplinary cooperation in the handling of complicated cases. The guidelines are designed with reference to the procedures of MDCC for child abuse cases, and thus, the role of case managers and the operational features outlined resemble those discussed in the previous section.

In most circumstances, the spouse abuse cases are handled by social workers of IFSC and FCPSU, who become the key workers and case managers. When evaluating the need for convening an MDCC, the PG-BSC will also consider whether the case involves suspected child abuse, whether the welfare plan would involve three or more service units, and whether the case is complicated in nature and likely to elicit different and even opposing views among concerned parties in the formulating of the welfare plan (Social Welfare Department, 2004, pp. 12–13).

The victims of battered spouse cases are often adults who come with their own concerns and views regarding their situations. It is therefore not uncommon for them to be involved in the MDCC to make their opinions known. For cases involving mentally incapacitated persons (MIPs), the guidelines have also highlighted the consideration of the relevant provision in the Mental Health Ordinance, such as involvement of the guardian (if any), in order to safeguard the safety and welfare of such persons. In general, the PG-BSC provides an outline for related professionals on conducting MDCCs.

Concerns and difficulties in practice

The procedural guidelines serve as practical frameworks for MDCCs in handling suspected child abuse cases and complicated spouse abuse cases. In order to conduct an effective and constructive MDCC, several major issues such as family participation, the nature of MDCCs, the case assessment, and staff provision should be considered.

Involvement of victims and families: empowerment versus blaming

The MDCC is not only a forum for professional exchange, but also an opportunity for the family involved to gain a better understanding of the crisis and the welfare plan devised for them and the victim(s). Family participation in MDCCs for child abuse cases started in around 1996, and has had a very empowering effect on the families (Ip, 2000). More effort should be put into enhancing empowerment of victims and their families, so as to avoid retraumatization of the victim-survivors. It would do well to encourage both families and professionals to be more receptive to family participation in MDCCs. In practice, depending on the nature of the cases (e.g., whether the parent/carer is a suspected abuser), the parent(s) and child(ren) would participate either throughout the entire conference proceedings, or only in the prescribing and explanation of the finalized welfare plan.

An example of family participation in the MDCC can be observed in a case in which a young boy, aged four, was evaluated and suspected for having been sexually abused. The boy reported that his father had kissed his penis in the sitting room at home, and this was witnessed by his sister, who was aged ten. The mother found out about the incident from her daughter, but viewed it as just a game between the father and the son. Following disclosure by the son, both parents attended the MDCC. During the MDCC, the definition of sexual abuse, the concerns of the professionals (e.g., well-being of the child victim), the decision of the case nature (i.e., an at-risk case) and welfare plan were all explained to the parents. The focus of the discussion was placed on protecting the child rather than blaming the parents/abusers. The awareness and understanding of the risks of child abuse were enhanced in both parents.

For battered spouse cases, participation of the victims is highly recommended. In this circumstance, victims and their families would have the chance to express their concerns, and their views should be given due respect. During the MDCC, they can discuss openly with professionals about the nature of the case as well as the welfare plan, in order to reach a mutual and considered understanding and to conduct a suitable welfare plan. Support provided for victims and their families is of paramount importance—during the MDCC as well as after—in the form of giving a general introduction to the purpose and procedures of the conference, clarifying and addressing the families' concerns, and following up for feedback after the case conferences.

Safety issues must be considered before allowing an abuser/suspected abuser to participate in an MDCC. Oftentimes, the (suspected) abuser is also a family member of the victim, e.g., a spouse or a parent, who may live in the same household or have regular close contact with the victim. Sensitive issues covered in the discussion may provoke the abuser/suspected abuser, and may lead him/her to take it out on the victim and/or other family members after the MDCC has ended. This would defeat the purpose the MDCC has set out to accomplish, by putting the victim and others in risk of danger. Medical practitioners have also pointed out that the presence of the (suspected) abuser may inhibit genuine and balanced discussion, and a child victim's interests may be overwhelmed by eloquent expressions of parental demands (Lee, Li, & So, 2005; Medical Coordinators on Child Abuse, 2003). Therefore, protection for the victims should be of first priority in deciding whether or not to include certain family members in an MDCC; and regardless of which parties end up attending the MDCC—the victim alone, or together with the (suspected) abuser—it is recommended that risk assessment be conducted in all cases regarding the possible recurrence of violence. Victim support and safety plans for the cases must be carefully managed to avoid introducing further harm. Pre-meeting coaching and post-meeting follow-up can also serve to enhance the effectiveness of family participation in MDCCs.

The nature of MDCCs: a regular mechanism versus one of many viable options

Comparing the two procedural guidelines on MDCCs, the information given for child abuse cases is more detailed than that for battered spouse cases. The PG-CAC contains a guide for participants, as well as a reference kit for the chairperson, and sample letters and minutes. A concrete time frame for the conference proceedings and the guidelines for preparation and follow-up are also given to the parties concerned. These materials facilitate the operation of MDCCs and cooperation between the different parties.

A study by Lee, Li and So (2006) reported that, among the 109 and 320 patients admitted for evaluation of child abuse in Tuen Mun Hospital (one of the public hospitals in Hong Kong) for the periods 1994–1995 and 2002–2003, 93% and 90% of respondents were involved in an MDCC respectively. According to Lee et al.'s findings, a very high proportion of suspected child abuse cases in hospitals are managed by the MDCCs. In Hong Kong, there is no community clinical or one-stop centre for child protection. Therefore, hospitals become a common temporary shelter for children who are suspected during the initial investigation and management of having been abused, especially of having been physically abused (Lee et al., 2006). It is therefore seen that the MDCCs are a common and routine practice for multidisciplinary cooperation in handling child abuse cases.

On the other hand, the PG-BSC mainly consists of an enumeration of points to consider when deciding whether or not to hold an MDCC, some notes for the conference convenor, information on handling personal data, and a brief guide on conducting the MDCC for battered spouse cases. Operational and practical manuals are compact in description as well. In the guidelines, multidisciplinary collaboration is emphasized (Social Welfare Department, 2004, p. 15). Referring to the PG-BSC, the MDCC is presented as just one of the viable options to facilitate multidisciplinary cooperation, rather than a preferred or customary mechanism for handling battered spouse cases. The nature of the MDCCs for child abuse cases and battered spouse cases is therefore different.

One example is of a ten-year-old boy who suffered an injury to his limbs because his father had beaten him with a stick. The boy was admitted into hospital, and arrangements were made for his mother and young sister to stay at a shelter for battered women. The MDCC for suspected child abuse cases was conducted to assess the case and devise a welfare plan for the two children. The situation of the mother was also discussed because she also suffered abuse at the hands of her husband. In this case, the MDCC for child abuse cases was able to extend its advantageous effects to the adult victim.

In another case where a forty-year-old woman was abused by her husband and admitted into shelter with her eight-year-old daughter, the outcomes were different. The woman became worried about the care of her four-year-old son, who was living with his father at home. However, this case was not considered for an MDCC since there was no report of any obvious injury on the boy. Following that, the mother would pay regular visits to the son to ensure his safety, and sometimes had serious conflicts with her husband when they met. From these two cases, we can see that the deciding factor for convening an MDCC is mainly whether children are at risk, or if the case involves any child physical abuse causing obvious injury. Unfortunately, protection for adult victims of spouse abuse and children who do not exhibit obvious injury, e.g., in child neglect cases, is regrettably ignored.

Based on the PG-CAC and the PG-BSC, the foci of MDCCs for child abuse cases and for battered spouse cases are slightly different. The MDCCs for child abuse cases aim to determine the nature of an incident, conduct relevant risk assessment and devise a welfare plan for the child and the family. Determining the case nature—e.g., whether the case is a child abuse or at-risk case (Social Welfare Department, 2007, p. 106)—is the first and main item on the meeting agenda because it is not often easy to obtain the whole picture of the case. The causes of harm/injury to the child and the identification of the abuser require in-depth investigation by different sources. The MDCC often collects views from different disciplines, inviting discussion between the parties involved, in order to make a collective decision on the nature of the case which subsequently informs the welfare plan's design. The case nature as determined by the MDCC has no binding effect on the prosecution of the abuser. The parents would also be involved in the process of deliberation, and/or would be informed of the final decision of the case nature.

In contrast, according to the PG-BSC, the MDCCs for battered spouse cases are to be conducted for known and complicated cases, rather than for purely suspected ones. Therefore, the main agenda is not determining the case nature, but rather, to address the risk level of the cases and the eventual welfare plan for the victim and family.

Case definition and assessment: common understanding versus varied opinions among professionals

Multidisciplinary collaboration is frequently recognized as a strategy to curtail family violence, and the MDCC is a platform for different professionals to capitalize on this multidisciplinary effort to reach desirable results. However, working together is inherently paradoxical because conflicts may arise from the different views of different parties working towards a common goal (Rappaport, 1981). As power dynamics and conflicts are inevitable in collaborative work, knowing how to transform conflicts into shared trust and a common vision is vital (Chan, Lam, & Cheng, 2009).

In fact, a common understanding of the concerned matter is imperative in order to facilitate multidisciplinary collaboration. However, the definition of child abuse and spouse battering as well as the assessment methods for family violence may differ among professionals, one example being the degree at which physical punishment should be considered abuse. Some professionals still view physical abuse as an "inappropriate, harsh and excessive physical punishment" not including corporal punishment, even though corporal punishment has been abolished in the penal system and in schools since 1990 and 1992 respectively (Ip, 1997).

In a study on the admission of suspected child abuse cases in a hospital, the most common reason for admission was suspected physical abuse (87%) followed by suspected sexual abuse (10%) (Lee et al., 2006). Abandoned children and children left unattended at home are often excluded from being considered for an MDCC, because some front-line workers do not consider this as a kind of child neglect (Lee & So, 2005). Although the definition, indicators/checklist, characteristics and the guide to risk assessment for child abuse are built-in in Chapter Two of the PG-CAC Revised 2007, defining child abuse in practice is mostly dependent on the views of the professionals involved. The practice may vary among professionals of different disciplines, and even among individuals within the same profession. In a multi-hospital study, the proportion of reaching an established case of child abuse varied from 13% to 78% among different public hospitals (Medical Coordinators on Child Abuse, 2003).

On the other hand, the definition of spouse battering is also inconsistent both inter- and intra-professionally (i.e., among different professionals and within the same profession). Referring to the PG-BSC, the problem of battered spouses is framed in gender-neutral terms rather than as a gender-related issue (Chan & Lam, 2005). Under this gender-neutral account, spouse battering is viewed as a kind of family problem and is grouped under the services for family and children. The conception of policies as well as service provision and development is therefore in line with the perceived interests of a family, such as rebuilding family harmony and cohesion. In understanding the nature of spouse battering, the focus may be put on the problem or dysfunction of the family. The rights of the women victims may as a result be overlooked.

However, according to the Declaration on Elimination of Violence Against Women adopted by the United Nations General Assembly on 20 December 1993, "the term 'violence against women' means any act of gender-based violence that results in, or is likely to result in, physical, sexual or psychological harm or suffering to women, including threats of such acts, coercion or arbitrary deprivation of liberty, whether occurring in public or in private life" (United Nations, 2000, p. 3). Violence against women is an issue of widespread concern, and is recognized as a serious infraction of human rights on the international platform (Choi, Chan, & Brownridge, 2010). In addition, violence against women cannot be fully understood without considering the entrenched inequality of women in Chinese families under the heavy influence of traditional Chinese cultural and Confucian values. For these reasons, applying a gender-neutral view on spouse battering in the PG-BSC fails to fully reflect the situation of violence against women. Without an appropriate and agreed stance on violence against women, different values and attitudes among professionals may limit and even affect the progress of discussion and decision on a welfare plan for victims. In fact, the MDCC for battered spouse cases was not developed until the occurrence of the Tin Shui Wai tragedy in 2004, which prompted the development of relevant guidelines. Up to now, MDCCs for battered spouse cases have rarely been conducted, and are still far from a common practice.

Moreover, the assessment tools for family violence are diverse. In the MDCCs, varying assessment results generated by different tools would often be presented by the professionals. This lack of a common "language" in the MDCCs may not only impede work progress, but may also bring about misunderstandings and miscommunication regarding the nature and risk level of the cases. Lee and So (2005) have pointed out that uniform understanding and a consistent method for handling domestic violence are lacking among professionals; both a clearer direction and a universal risk assessment are needed. The report of a review panel on family services in Tin Shui Wai (Review Panel on Family Services in Tin Shui Wai, 2004) and a review on the implementation of the Integrated Family Service Centre service mode (Department of Social Work and Social Administration, 2010) also recommended the development of more indicators and locally validated tools for risk assessment, so as to minimize inconsistent interpretations and analyses of cases.

Nevertheless, the association between spouse abuse and child abuse has been confirmed in a local study (Chan, 2005). The assessment of spouse abuse should be made more comprehensive by including other possible forms of family violence (Choi et al., 2010). Similarly, an MDCC ought to take into account the correlation of different forms of violence in a family for any thorough case discussion.

Staff provision: expert versus generic staff development

Family violence cases are complex in nature, and the professionals involved require relevant skills and knowledge to handle them. They must equip themselves with practical techniques and communication skills for multidisciplinary collaboration, especially for case managers/key workers who need to take up the role of a coordinator. Working skills and relationships with different professionals need time to develop; however, the requirement of job rotations in some disciplines, such as for social workers, police officers and also medical professionals, would limit the development of an expert/specialized worker in this area (Ip, 2000). When existing members of the MDCC leave, training for a new batch of workers will be needed, and the former practice of multidisciplinary collaboration will have to be redeveloped. This could potentially mean a misemployment of time when the rotations are frequent. Since the participation of professionals is the core element for the functioning and operation of MDCCs, case progress will be affected if job rotations and staff training/handover are arranged without thoughtful planning. In light of this, a stable membership of expert/specialized workers in family violence is essential for continual effective practice in multidisciplinary collaboration and MDCCs.

Ill-defined delegation of work among different service units may also impede the progress of MDCCs. The case allocations between FCPSU and other caseworker service units (e.g., IFSC) are frequently fraught with ambiguity, and more than often, cause disputes over case referrals (Review Panel on Family Services in Tin Shui Wai, 2004). One example of poor delegation of work can be observed in the Child Abuse Investigation Unit (CAIU) and the Criminal Investigative Department (CID) of the police. Perhaps surprisingly, the CAIU handles only a small proportion of child abuse cases, with the majority being handled by the CID (Lee & So, 2005). As the latter is not a specific unit for handling child abuse cases, its officers may not possess adequate training in the area. Indeed, the operation of MDCCs is highly reliant on participation and professional knowledge from different disciplines. The limited building up of expertise in disciplines under the job rotation system, beyond dispute, has adverse effects on the operation of MDCCs.

Conclusion

The system of the multidisciplinary case conference (MDCC) for child abuse, which was developed as a routine mechanism of intervention, has been in place for many years. The MDCC for complicated battered spouse cases has been recommended for use since 2004, after a number of family tragedies occurred in the community. When conducted with proper management, the MDCC is very helpful for handling family violence cases and providing the necessary support for the professionals and families involved. However, if undertaken only for the sake of fulfilling a procedural requirement, or to shift responsibility, then it would be a waste of valuable professional time (Ip, 2000). When dealing with the complicated case natures of family violence, multidisciplinary collaboration is required in order to make a thoughtful assessment and well-informed welfare plan. The MDCC may not be the only means of multidisciplinary communication and decision making on welfare plan for victims (Lee, Li, & So, 2005), but it does provide a satisfactory and much-needed platform for different professionals to share opinions formulated from their areas of expertise, and which, operated effectively, can save time by avoiding misunderstandings and overlapping efforts.

References

Chan, K. L. (2005). *Study on Child Abuse & Spouse Battering: Report on Findings of Household Survey*. Retrieved from Department of Social Work and Social Administration, the University of Hong Kong website: http://www.swd.gov.hk/doc/family/Report%20on%20findings%20of%20Household%20Survey.pdf

Chan, Y. C., Lam, L. T. G., & Cheng, C. H. H. (2009). Community capacity building as a strategy of family violence prevention in a problem-stricken community: a theoretical formulation. *Journal of Family Violence, 24*, 559–568. doi: 10.1007/s10896-009-9254-3

Chan, Y. C., & Lam, L. T. G. (2005). Unraveling the rationale for a one-stop service under the Family and Child Protection Services Units in Hong Kong. *International Social Work, 48*, 419–428. doi: 10.1177/0020872805053466

Choi, W. M. A., Chan, K. L., & Brownridge, D. A. (2010). Unraveling in-law conflict and its association with intimate partner violence in Chinese culture: narrative accounts of Chinese battered women. *Women's Health and Urban Life—An International and Interdisciplinary Journal, 9*, 72–92. Retrieved from https://tspace.library.utoronto.ca/bitstream/1807/24425/1/9.1_choi_etal.pdf

Department of Social Work and Social Administration. (2010). *Building Effective Family Services: Review on the Implementation of the Integrated Family Service Centre Service Mode Hong Kong*. Hong Kong: Department of Social Work and Social Administration, the University of Hong Kong.

Ip, P. (1997). Multidisciplinary decision-making. In C. O'Brian, C. Y. L. Cheung, & N. Rhind (Eds.), *Responding to Child Abuse: Procedures and Practice for Child Protection in Hong Kong* (pp. 47–62). Hong Kong: Hong Kong University Press.

Ip, P. (2000). Child abuse and neglect in Hong Kong. *Hong Kong Journal Paediatrices*, 5, 61–64. Retrieved from http://hkjpaed.org/pdf/2000;5;61-64.pdf

Lee, C. W. A., & So, K. T. (2005). Responding to domestic violence in Yuen Long District. *Hong Kong Journal of Paediatrics*, 10, 96–100. Retrieved from http://hkjpaed.org/pdf/2005;10;96-100.pdf

Lee, C. W. A., Li, C. H., & So, K. T. (2006). The impact of a management protocol on the outcomes of child abuse in hospitalized children in Hong Kong. *Child Abuse & Neglect*, 30, 909–917. doi: 10.1016/j.chiabu.2006.03.003

Medical Coordinators on Child Abuse. (2003). *Child Abuse Surveillance Report 2000–2002: A Report by the Medical Coordinators on Child Abuse to the Coordinating Committee (Paediatrics)*. Hong Kong, China: Medical Coordinators on Child Abuse.

Mulvey, T. (1997). Historical overview: developments in child protection services and procedures. In C. O' Brian, C. Y. Cheng, & N. Rhind (Eds.), *Responding to Child Abuse: Procedures and Practice for Child Protection in Hong Kong* (pp. 3–15). Hong Kong: Hong Kong University Press.

United Nations. (2000). *Declaration on the Elimination of Violence Against Women*. Retrieved from United Nations website: http://www.un.org/documents/ga/res/48/a48r104.htm

Review Panel on Family Services in Tin Shui Wai. (2004). *Report of Review Panel on Family Services in Tin Shui Wai*. Paper submitted to the Subcommittee on Strategy and Measures to Tackle Family Violence of the Legislative Council Panel on Welfare Services. CB(2)2610/04-05(01).

Rappaport, J. (1981). In praise of paradox: a social policy of empowerment over prevention. *American Journal of Community Psychology*, 9, 1–25. doi: 10.1007/BF00896357

Social Welfare Department. (2004). *Procedural Guidelines for Handling Battered Spouse Cases*. Retrieved from Social Welfare Department, Hong Kong website: http://www.swd.gov.hk/en/index/site_pubsvc/page_family/sub_fcwprocedure/id_batteredspouse/

Social Welfare Department. (2007). *Procedural Guidelines for Handling Child Abuse Cases Revised 2007*. Retrieved from Social Welfare Department, Hong Kong website: http://www.swd.gov.hk/en/index/site_pubsvc/page_family/sub_fcwprocedure/id_childabuse1998/

13
Multidisciplinary Response in Domestic Violence

How We Started and Where We Are Heading

Margaret Fung-Yee Wong

Chapter summary

1. Domestic violence is a complicated interpersonal, social, legal, safety and health issue. The author stresses the importance of adopting a multidisciplinary model and approach in addressing this very complex and traumatic issue, with particular reference to intimate partner abuse.
2. The development of such a model and collaborative effort is outlined from 1985–2010.
3. The first decade (1985–1995) was characterized by the setting up of the first women and children's shelter in Hong Kong, and the beginning of public educational programmes and training programmes on spousal abuse for professionals.
4. The second decade (1995–2005) witnessed substantial service development in shelters, crisis intervention, batterers' treatment, screening, and a proliferation of research studies. The expansion prompted close collaboration among different professions.
5. The future challenges for professionals, advocates, service providers and the government in combating domestic violence are examined. Recommendations are made in terms of building up a coordinated community approach, identifying possible gaps and focusing on gender equality education.

Introduction

Violence inflicted by one person onto another, be it onto a loved one or a stranger, has never been a one-dimensional issue. The causes of family violence—as well as its conflict, trauma and impact—are intermingled with the complex dynamics of relationships, emotions, gender roles, cultural and societal values, traditional beliefs, as well as perpetuation of power and control (Adams, 2007; R. E. Dobash & Dobash, 1979; Hamberger & Hastings, 1986; Pence, 1993). Nor is family violence and sexual violence merely a "Hong Kong issue", although this book focuses mainly on the situation in Hong Kong. Violence occurs in all corners of the world and transcends all races and creeds (Seager, 2003).

Because of the complexities embedded in violence, no single profession, agency or government department can address domestic violence, sexual violence or any kind of intimate-relationship violence alone (Shepard & Pence, 1999). Indeed, domestic violence victim support services in Hong Kong began from a shared compassion and conviction among different professions, all committed to helping abused women live a life of dignity, promoting mutual respect in relationships, and advocating for gender equality and a violence-free community.

This chapter focuses on domestic violence, in particular, intimate partner abuse, bearing in mind that domestic violence includes violence against any member of the household or in any relationship extending from a marriage. While noting that victims may be men as well as women, attention will be focused on women victims, who constitute 83.5% of the total number of reported spouse battering cases in Hong Kong in 2009 (Social Welfare Department, 2010). We shall take a look at when and how multidisciplinary collaboration first began, and how it has evolved and expanded in the past two decades. The challenges ahead and future aspirations for the different professions will also be examined.

When it all began—1985–1995: first signs of multidisciplinary collaboration

Prior to 1985, spousal abuse was a taboo subject and something that was silenced. Victims of spousal abuse, a majority of whom were women, had nowhere to turn to. Many of their stories were being told but not heard.

Entangled in a mesh of issues including rigid gender roles, financial dependency, family relationships, emotional ties, parental considerations, and a host of other tangible and intangible socioeconomic factors, violence against women was not only tacitly tolerated by the individual, but, in many ways, condoned by the community.

Community awareness of domestic violence, in particular spousal abuse, only began in 1985 with the setting up of the first shelter for women and children in Hong Kong. The need for a shelter to provide refuge to victims of domestic violence was revealed by the findings of a survey conducted by a medical doctor at United Christian Hospital. The call for victim protection was eventually translated into reality through the collaborative advocacy efforts of a medical doctor, a social worker from the Family Welfare Society and a lawyer. With the sponsorship of the Hong Kong Council of Women, Harmony House went into operation in April 1985 to provide a safe haven for victims of spousal abuse (Women's Commission, 2006). The colonial government granted permission for the use of a vacant barrack as the shelter premises. For four years, volunteers were recruited to support the shelter financially and operationally. It was not until 1989 that the government recognized the work of the refuge, and began to provide regular subvention.

The number of women victims admitted to the first shelter in 1985 was 156 (Harmony House, 2001, 2002). In 2008, there were 476 battered spouse cases admitted to the four shelters in Hong Kong (Social Welfare Department, 2010), representing an increase of 200 fold. The first hotline for women victims in 1986 received 365 calls. In 2008, the same hotline handled 4,710 calls (Harmony House, 2008). The number of newly reported battered spouse and child abuse cases has been steadily rising since 1998 as shown in the following Table 13.1.

The road to recovery for abused women starts when they enter the refuge. Yet to many others, their plight seems never-ending, with the cycle of violence spiraling faster and the violence becoming more and more severe. The majority of abused women often tolerate abuse for five years or more before they finally seek help (see Figure 13.1). The reasons for not seeking help early on are understandable. Many of the women are financially dependent on their partners. Unfamiliarity with community resources and confinement by the rigid interpretations of gender roles also prohibit these women from leaving the abusive relationship.

Table 13.1 Total number of newly reported battered spouse and child abuse cases

Year	Newly reported battered spouse cases	Newly reported child abuse cases
2009	4,807	993
2008	6,843	882
2007	6,404	944
2006	4,424	806
2005	3,598	763
2004	3,371	622
2003	3,298	481
2002	3,034	520
2001	2,433	535
2000	2,321	500
1999	1,679	575
1998	1,009	409

(Source: Central Information System on Battered Spouse and Sexual Violence Cases, SWD, 1998–2010)

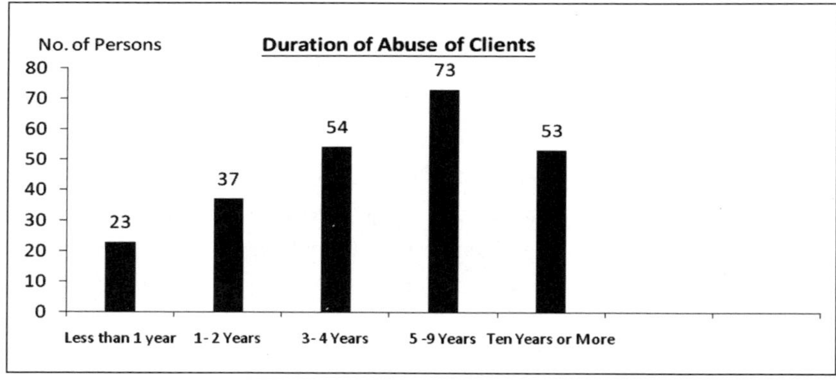

(Source: Harmony House Annual Report 2004–05)

Figure 13.1 Duration of abuse

In the course of the cycle of violence, many of them may have attempted to break their silence by approaching healthcare professionals and seeking help from the law enforcement system. Unfortunately, the knowledge about and the sensitivity towards spousal violence a quarter of a century ago was still at an embryonic stage. The community at large and the helping professions were not fully conversant with the needs of victims, and often interpreted abuse differently on the basis of their own subjective beliefs, values and understanding of what constituted violence.

In 1993, the United Nations General Assembly offered a formal definition on violence against women:

> An act of gender-based violence that results in or is likely to result in, physical, sexual or psychological harm or suffering to women, including threats of such acts, coercion or arbitrary deprivations of liberty, whether occurring in public or private life (United Nations, 1993).

Similarly, the World Health Organization (WHO) considers family and intimate partner abuse as any form of interpersonal violence which causes physical, psychological or sexual harm. Acts of abusive behaviour include (Women's Commission, 2006):

(a) Physical aggression—hitting, kicking, beating;

(b) Psychological abuse—intimidation, belittling and humiliating;

(c) Sexual abuse—forced intercourse and sexual coercion; and

(d) Controlling—isolation, restriction of movements and access to family, friends, information or support.

Defining domestic violence in the context of gender by the United Nations and the identification of various forms of abuse by the WHO marked a direct acknowledgement of gender inequalities in the society, and provided a platform for common understanding of domestic violence. Worth mentioning are the community education and public awareness programmes, as well as the training workshops for healthcare professionals and law enforcement officers, organized by various mutual support groups and nongovernmental organizations between the mid-1980s and 90s.

Kwan Fook, a self-help group set up in 1990 consisting of survivors of domestic violence, also played a prominent role in advocacy. One example of their advocacy efforts was their urging the government to introduce the Public Housing Conditional Tenancy Scheme for abused women who were going through divorce proceedings.

If knowledge and understanding are prerequisites for positive change, the years between 1985 and 1995, during which the publicity programmes and professional training programmes were developed, certainly laid down the foundation for change and paved way for further partnership between the advocates, nongovernmental organizations, and healthcare and law enforcement professionals.

The heyday of service development and multidisciplinary response—1995–2005

The decade from 1995 to 2005 witnessed substantial development of a wide spectrum of services for domestic violence (Harmony House, 2006). Multidisciplinary responses were expanded from the health and law enforcement sectors to other professions, including the legal arena. A number of statutory infrastructures were set up by the government as well to address issues related to domestic violence and gender equality.

Between 1995 and 2005, three major advances in the field of domestic violence were made:

1.   Pioneering of new services for domestic violence which reflected an ever-strong linkage and close collaboration between medical healthcare professionals, law enforcement officers, teachers and social workers.
2.   Evidence-based information was generated from a number of researches, which threw light on service and policy gaps in domestic violence.
3.   Active involvement from the legal profession which paved way for the review of legislation on domestic violence.

We shall take a look at these developments in greater detail below.

New services and multidisciplinary response

The public education programmes and professional training conducted from 1995 to 2005 enhanced public and professional awareness of domestic violence and its ramifications in the community. Front-line social workers and advocates who had often been scrambling for community resources to support victims saw the need for more collaboration with other systems and expertise. A number of new services piloted in this period demonstrated this collaboration:

Rain Lily—Sexual Violence Concern Group

The Rain Lily was part of an initiative of a nongovernmental organization: the Concern Group on Sexual Violence. The initiative was launched in 1997 to provide outreach and crisis support for victims of sexual assault. Close liaison was established with the medical profession in victims' referral. Crisis counselling, ongoing support and escort services were provided to rape victims who were going through an extremely difficult stage in their lives.

Seeds of Hope—Crisis Intervention Team (CIT)

The CIT was a medical-social multidisciplinary model designed to support victims of domestic violence. In 2001, Harmony House piloted the CIT and stationed social workers beyond office hours in the accident and emergency departments of three local hospitals. According to front-line experience, victim support was insufficient beyond regular office hours. Statistics from the Hospital Authority in 2004 showed that 1,251 battered spouse cases were identified by medical healthcare professionals (Harmony House, 2005). Unfortunately, not all of them were followed up in a timely manner (Sullivan, 2008). The multidisciplinary approach proved to be effective as over 60% of the cases identified were unknown to any service agencies prior to connecting with the CIT (Harmony House, 2005). The CIT therefore fulfilled the dual purposes of crisis support as well as early identification.

Batterer Intervention Programmes

About one-third of the abused women return to their spouses upon discharge from a shelter (See Figure 13.2).

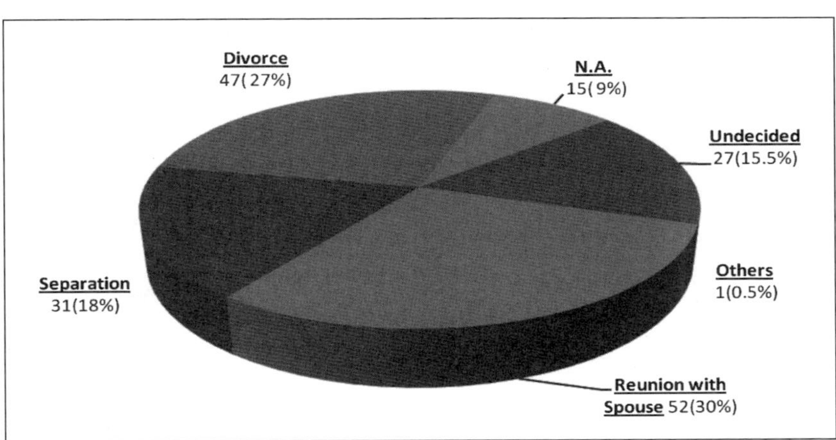

(Source: Harmony House Annual Report 2007–08)

Figure 13.2   Marital status upon discharge from shelter

Some of these women victims are later readmitted to the shelter, since the abusers have not actually changed their cognitive thinking and their controlling behaviour. To ensure the safety of these women, advocates and social workers began to look into programmes specifically designed for male batterers. Since 2000, a number of services including Man Hotline, batterer intervention groups and parenting groups designed especially for men were introduced (Harmony House, 2003, 2004, 2005). These initiatives were undertaken by NGOs and women shelters, as well as by the Family and Children Protective Service Units under the Social Welfare Department.

One of the most challenging aspects in working with batterers was the difficulty in engaging them in the treatment process, given their tendency to strong denial and rigid gender role beliefs (Adams, 2007; Adams, Cayonette, & Robinson, 2000; Y. C. Chan, 2005; Pence, 1993). In one of the batterers programmes, the number of batterers who underwent case and group counselling was 62, while that of women victims admitted to the shelter run by the same agency was 179 (Harmony House, 2008). Difficulty in reaching out to male batterers was an important issue to be addressed.

The introduction of various batterer intervention programmes (BIP) since 2000 had both micro- and macro-implications. At a micro and service development level, BIPs were addressing intimate partner abuse or domestic violence at the core of the problem, with a primary objective of safeguarding victims and stopping violence. At a macro level, the difficulties of reaching out to batterers prompted social workers, legal professionals and academics to examine existing policies and legislation, and to advocate for changes in order to further pursue the goal of curtailing domestic violence.

Screening of domestic violence in hospitals and schools

Another milestone in domestic violence service development between 1995 and 2005 was the introduction of screening in hospitals. In the early 1990s, the Joint Commission on Accreditation of Healthcare Organizations (JCAHO) in the United States had already set up standards requiring all accredited hospitals to implement policies and procedures to identify, screen and refer victims of abuse and neglect. The procedures were since updated regularly (Joint Commission on Accreditation of Healthcare Organizations, 2010).

In 2004, domestic violence screening was piloted in United Christian Hospital in Hong Kong by the CIT (Harmony House, 2005; Sullivan, 2008). In

2007–08, screening was conducted for 342 patients, with 4% being screened as domestic violence cases (Harmony House, 2008). Although there was still a long way to go before universal screening of all patients was achieved, progress was certainly made at that time in diagnostic assessment and identification of domestic violence in the healthcare setting (Sullivan, 2008).

Similar initiatives were conducted in collaboration with schools and teachers. Using a mobile educational vehicle, "Harmony Express", screening was conducted on 1,551 Primary Three and Four students between September 2007 and March 2008. A total of 41% of the students indicated that they were either sometimes or often physically or verbally abused by their parents (Harmony House, 2008). Child witnesses to domestic violence were also identified through screening and joint effort between social workers and teachers.

Other pioneering services

Following the CIT pilot initiative, the need for support beyond office hours and for 24-hour outreach and crisis intervention gradually gained recognition, resulting in the setting up of the Family Crisis Support Centre by Caritas Hong Kong in 2002.

Involvement of evidence-based researches and implications for service development

Research on mandatory counselling

Parallel to the initiative on batterers treatment and intervention mentioned earlier, a research on *Controlling Domestic Violence and Wife Abuse: A Plea for Mandatory Counselling for Wife Abusers* was conducted by Dr M. C. Chiu in collaboration with Harmony House in 2000 (Chiu, 2001). One of the recommendations made in the research report was to advocate for mandatory counselling for batterers through the court system.

The initiation of batterers treatment programmes and the research studies came to have significant implications, in terms of expanding the multidisciplinary network to include academics and the legal profession in the subsequent advocacy work regarding the review of the Domestic Violence Ordinance cap. 189.

Research on child witness to domestic violence

A qualitative study which collected stories about children who had witnessed domestic violence pinpointed to the trauma experienced by these "silent victims" of abuse (Yeung-Chan, 2002). The publication of a storybook and of the research studies was an example of collaboration between service, practice and research. The concern about intergenerational violence prompted the development of support and intervention programmes for children who had witnessed domestic violence.

Study on child abuse and spouse battering

Another major research study released in 2005 — the *Study on Child Abuse and Spouse Battering* (Chan, Chiu, & Chiu, 2005; Legislative Council Secretariat, 2005) was commissioned by the Hong Kong government. The study identified a host of risk factors for domestic violence and, based on the findings of a household survey, showed that

(a)   one in every ten couples experienced spouse abuse,

(b)   an estimate of 160,000 couples were affected by domestic violence, and

(c)   about 13.9% of respondents were ever battered by their spouses.

Figures generated from the same research study also indicated that

(a)   about 45% of child respondents in the study encountered physical assault by their parents, and

(b)   an estimate of 70,000 children under 18 suffered from severe violence by their parents within a year.

Apart from the above findings on the prevalence and risk factors of domestic violence, the study brought out an important message which had long been voiced by front-line professionals: the number of domestic violence cases known to service providers was only the tip of the iceberg.

Other research studies

According to the *Bibliography of Gender Studies in Hong Kong 1998–2003* compiled by the Gender Research Centre of the Chinese University of Hong Kong, there were 43 local researches/studies/articles related to violence (Tam

& Leahy, 2004). The same bibliographical study for the period of 2004–2009 showed over 100 entries on domestic violence (Tam, Lee, Wong, & Lo, 2010). The development in clinical practices, services and policies on domestic violence could partly be accounted for by these vigorous quests for empirical evidence.

Clearly, domestic violence could not be waved away with a magic wand. To reduce harm and achieve prevention, all sectors of the community and different professionals, academics and practitioners alike had to collaborate and address the problem collectively.

The legal profession as part of the multidisciplinary response

Domestic violence is much more than an interpersonal relationship issue; it is also a social, safety, and health issue. It is a violation of human rights and an act which contravenes law and justice. Involvement of the legal profession is crucial to communicate the fact that domestic violence is not a private but a public and legal matter.

Between 1995 to 2005, the legal profession had already been playing an important role in advocating the protection of victims of domestic violence. The amendments in legislation made in 2002 which made marital rape a criminal offence were a case in point.

Beginning in 2002, the NGO sector called for review of the Domestic Violence Ordinance (DVO) cap. 189. A coalition formed by 19 organizations and community groups recommended comprehensive amendments to the ordinance (Alliance for the Reform of Domestic Violence Ordinance, 2007; Harmony House Proposed Amendments 2002; Hong Kong Council of Social Service, 2007; Law Society of HK, 2005; Legislative Council Secretariat, 2007; Legislative Council Secretariat, 2006; Legislative Council Brief, 2007; Ming Pao, 2005). The Law Society, the umbrella group of the legal profession, also submitted recommendations to the government.

Triggered by the Tin Shui Wai homicide and suicide tragedy (Review Panel on Family Services in Tin Shui Wai, 2004) in which an abused woman together with her two children were killed by her husband, concerted efforts were made by different professions to call for amendments to the DVO 189. Finally in 2008, twenty-two years after its enactment in 1986, amendment to the DVO 189 were introduced by the government. The revised Ordinance cap. 189 Domestic and Cohabitation Relationships enacted in 2010 included provisions to cover intimate partner abuse victims from same-sex relationships

(Hong Kong Government, 2010). This was a significant change compared with the previous ordinance.

The amendments to the legislation no doubt enhanced the protection of victims, and further, conveyed a strong message to the community that violence would not be tolerated. However, it had to be noted that, very often, domestic violence cases were not brought to the courts at all. The total number of prosecuted cases, as shown in Table 13.2, represented only a small percentage of reported cases. For those of us who have worked with victims and survivors of domestic violence, it is not difficult to understand that it is an extremely excruciating process for victims to openly point fingers at the abuser in front of the court. The majority of domestic violence cases were sentenced with bail, fine, bind-over, probation or suspended sentences (see Table 13.3).

Nonetheless, in 2005, twenty years after the setting up of the first shelter for women and children, community awareness of domestic violence had increased, so had the collaboration among different professions. A summary of the sources of referral is shown in Table 13.4. Without the sensitivity, linkage and joint efforts of various professions, a lot of the cases would not have been identified, and victims would have remained in silence.

Table 13.2 Number of prosecutions of battered spouse and child abuse cases

	Battered Spouse			Child Abuse		
Case	2001	2002	2003[a]	2001	2002	2003[a]
Convicted	80	83	62	243	225	134
Not convicted	39	52	30	70	53	32
Total no. of prosecution	119	135	92[b]	313	278	166[c]
Total no. of newly reported cases	2,433	3,034	3,298	535	520	481

Note: [a] till November 2003

[b] 9 cases prosecuted in 2003 have not been concluded. Results are pending.

[c] 14 cases prosecuted in 2003 have not been concluded. Results are pending.

(Source: Central Information System on Battered Spouse and Sexual Violence Cases, SWD, 1998–2010. Available from http://www.info.gov.hk/gia/general/200402/18/q10c.htm)

Table 13.3   Sentencing of convicted cases

	Battered Spouse			Child Abuse		
Sentencing	2001	2002	2003[a]	2001	2002	2003[a]
Life imprisonment	1	1	0	1	1	0
Jail	28	28	17	70	66	21
Suspended sentence	15	13	9	8	5	3
Fine	12	16	20	16	17	8
Probation	7	9	7	88	94	77
Community Services Order	7	11	5	33	23	11
Bail/Conditional release	4	2	3	4	4	1
Others	6	3	1	23	15	13
Total	80	83	62	243	225	134

Note: [a] Till November 2003

(Source: http://www.info.gov.hk/gia/general/200402/18/q10c.htm)

Table 13.4   Sources of referral based on total reported cases in the Central Information System

	n (%)	
Reporting agency	2008 (Jan to Dec)	2009 (Jan to Dec)
Social Welfare Department	1,159 (16.9%)	1,409 (29.3%)
Nongovernmental organizations	128 (1.9%)	235 (4.9%)
Hospital Authority	825 (12.1%)	912 (19.0%)
Legal Aid Department	2 (0.0%)	0 (0.0%)
Hong Kong Police Force	4,729 (69.1%)	2,250 (46.8%)
Department of Health	0 (0.0%)	1 (0.0%)
Others	0 (0.0%)	0 (0.0%)
Total	6,843 (100%)	4,807 (100%)

(Source: Central Information System on Battered Spouse and Sexual Violence, Social Welfare Department, 2010)

Multidisciplinary infrastructures

Working group on combating violence

Recognizing the complexities of domestic violence and the need for coordination between different departments and professions, the government set up the Working Group on Battered Spouses in April 1995. The Working Group was later renamed as the Working Group on Combating Violence (WGCV) to address both domestic violence and sexual violence issues. The WGCV was considered as a central coordinating and multidisciplinary mechanism to facilitate the collaboration between the government, its departments, and non-governmental organizations (Women's Commission, 2006).

Members of the WGCV included representatives from a number of government bureaus and departments: the Labour and Welfare Bureau, the Security Bureau, the Education and Manpower Bureau, the Home Affairs Bureau, the Social Welfare Department, the Housing Department, the Department of Justice, Police and Law Enforcement, the Legal Aid Department, the Health Department, and the Hospital Authority. Service providers from the NGO sector were also members of the WGCV. Under the WGCV, several multidisciplinary guidelines on assessment, intervention and cross-sector referral for domestic violence and abuse cases were compiled, including the Procedural Guidelines for Handling Battered Spouse Cases (2004) and the Procedural Guidelines for Handling Adult Sexual Violence Cases (2010).

Two other central coordinating bodies—the Committee on Child Abuse and the Working Group on Elder Abuse—were also set up. The Procedural Guidelines for Handling Child Abuse Cases 2007 was also compiled under the Committee on Child Abuse.

These central mechanisms served to enhance multidisciplinary collaboration, and to provide a platform for various disciplines to address issues related to domestic violence identification, treatment and prevention.

District Committees

At the frontline, the District Coordinating Committees on Family and Child Welfare Services provided a forum to coordinate multidisciplinary efforts at a district level. In March 2005, fourteen district liaison groups on family violence were established to facilitate collaboration between front-line social workers and police officers in handling domestic violence cases.

Equal Opportunities Commission (EOC)

The EOC was set up in 1996 as a statutory body to implement three ordinances: the Sex Discrimination Ordinance, the Disability Discrimination Ordinance and the Family Status Discrimination Ordinance. The EOC played an important role in promoting equal opportunities for both men and women, and was mandated to eliminate discrimination on the grounds of sex, marital status, pregnancy, disability and family status.

Women's Commission (WoC)

The WoC was set up in January 2001 as part of the pledge of the Hong Kong government to implement the Convention on the Elimination of All Forms of Discrimination Against Women (CEDAW). The primary objective of the WoC was to enable women to fully realize their due status, rights and opportunities in all aspects of life. The commission assumed an important role in advising the government on policies, legislation and initiatives which had an impact on women. Its members included representatives from women organizations, community groups, academia, the Social Welfare Department, and the Labour and Welfare Bureau (Women's Commission, 2001–2003).

One of the major achievements of the WoC relating to domestic violence was their report titled *Women's Safety in Hong Kong: Eliminating Domestic Violence*, released in January 2006. The report outlined a number of recommendations and strategies to address domestic violence. In the preparation of the report and recommendations, the WoC strategically linked up with various key governmental departments throughout the discussion and performed the role of a facilitator in enhancing multidisciplinary collaboration.

2005–2010 and beyond—challenges and future development

Between 2005 and 2010, in terms of services for domestic violence, the government set up a second crisis centre in 2007, which was called the CEASE Crisis Centre, operating under the Tung Wah Group of Hospitals. The CEASE was designed to provide round-the-clock integrated one-stop support for victims of domestic violence and adult victims of sexual abuse. From 2007 to 2010, the CEASE provided support to close to 350 sexual violence victims, sheltered over 1,000 victims and families, and undertook some 300 outreach efforts. An integrated approach was adopted, involving: regular training and sharing with front-line police officers, social workers, and medical professionals; the establishment of referral procedures and a common understanding of case handling; and the provision of a seamless continuum of supporting services for domestic violence victims irrespective of their gender, ethnicity and age.

A new victim support programme to provide support and escort services for legal and court attendance, police statement taking and medical treatment was also introduced by the government in 2010.

Together with the five refuges for victims of domestic violence, the specialized Family and Child Protective Services Units under the government, and the Integrated Family Service Centres in the various districts, these new developments are a powerful testimony that awareness, support and intervention, advocacy, cross-sectoral and multidisciplinary collaboration against domestic violence have come a long way.

What lies ahead then? What are the challenges? Is the multidisciplinary approach here to stay? What more can the different professions contribute towards stopping domestic violence?

Let us examine these questions under the following perspectives:

(a)   the approach,

(b)   the gaps,

(c)   the focus, and

(d)   the strategy.

The approach

The multidisciplinary approach practised in Hong Kong for addressing domestic violence has definitely accomplished positive outcomes. Looking ahead, multidisciplinary responses can be further consolidated by undertaking the following activities outlined in the coordinated community response model first developed by Ellen Pence (Shepard & Pence, 1999):

(a) Reiterating a common philosophical understanding of victim protection, accountability and deterrence;

(b) Developing the "best practice" policies and protocols;

(c) Reducing fragmentation in infrastructures and systems;

    (d) Regular monitoring of the system and policies;

    (e) Building a supportive community-based infrastructure;

    (f) Developing direct interventions with abusers;

    (g) Reducing harm for victims and children; and

    (h) Evaluating policies and services from the victims' perspectives.

Particularly important is the regular review of the existing understanding of domestic violence and victims needs. Sharing a common philosophical understanding is essential among different professionals and the community at large.

More than a decade ago, when I first started working with victims of domestic violence, I had a vision and a dream, that shelters for women would not be hidden somewhere out in the bush. Nor should shelter addresses be kept confidential. Why? Was I out of my mind? How can we protect women and children if the abusers are able to find out where the victim spouse or partner is staying?

It would be an infeasible dream if protection of victims of domestic violence, women and children were the responsibilities of a few. However, it is not at all a far-fetched dream if the community as a whole—police officers, social workers, healthcare professionals, members of the general public—is engaged in securing protection for the abused. As such, the whole community will partake in condemning violence in all its forms and against all persons. Each individual in the community will look out for one another, including upholding each other's freedom from fear of physical, emotional and sexual harm. There will be little cause for fear of rights being violated in public or in private with a community watch system in place.

A multidisciplinary approach is an important means to moving closer to realizing the above dreams. Within each profession, we can also mobilize as many experts as possible. The social work profession can reach out to fellow social workers and provide them with training to enhance their sensitivity to issues of abuse, as well as their assessment and intervention skills. By the same token, the healthcare profession can reach out to medical doctors, nurses and paramedical personnel, and use a healthcare approach to advocate on behalf of victims. Legal professionals can take on a legal approach and pursue further advancement in victim protection through legislative reform. Academics can strive to incorporate knowledge about domestic violence into their teaching curriculum.

As much as these various approaches show divergences, they are linked by a common conviction: to bring an end to violence against women. Their paths will converge eventually.

The gaps

In terms of overall support for victims, Hong Kong has been doing a good job in providing a host of services through refuges, 24-hour crisis intervention and support, counselling, aftercare and follow-up, and victim support services.

However, there are specific groups in our community that may have difficulties accessing all these services due to personal as well as cultural barriers. These groups include ethnic minorities, people from the lesbian, gay, bisexual and transgender (LGBT) community as well as male victims from heterosexual relationships. Reaching out to the above special groups will be a challenge for all professionals.

Second, in terms of addressing intergenerational violence, we have not done enough for our children. Child witness to domestic violence has long been recognized as a form of child abuse in the international scene. Properly defining child witness to domestic violence as child abuse will open up a new frontier and paradigm in domestic violence prevention and harm reduction, allowing the design of specific and targeted interventions.

Third, along the line of prevention, diagnostic screening, if not universal screening, is one of the most effective means of early identification and intervention. Screening can be implemented in the healthcare setting as well as the school setting. Pilot initiatives have been undertaken, and the government should take an active role in promulgating and supporting this concept and its associated practices.

In terms of legal initiatives, the recent amendments to the DVO 189 reflect a commendable joint effort by the legal and social professions. Continued attention has to be paid to examine the outcome of some of the recommendations, including the number of batterers who were ordered by court to attend an anti-violence programme (AVP) as attached to the injunction order. Continuous monitoring has to be made to explore possibilities of reaching out to batterers and finding ways of engaging them in positive change. This will mean generating and evaluating alternatives to the injunction order, e.g., ordering batterers to attend an AVP when being bound over, or using AVP as an alternative sentencing.

The focus

In the past twenty-five years, specific services developed have been primarily related to tertiary prevention. Considerable resources have also been devoted to public awareness programmes and publicity through the media. To stop the cycle of violence, we also need to invest more into educating our children early on.

How do we incorporate knowledge on gender equality, emotion management and positive interpersonal relationship building skills into our school curriculum? How can teachers play a role in teaching students about gender roles and stereotyping? How do we prepare our younger generation to learn about mutual respect in intimate relationships? How can we help adolescents address dating violence? How can we involve parents in the process? These are just a few of the questions that need answering.

Prevention and education targeted towards our children are to be our future focus. After all, it is our children who will inherit what we impart to them now.

The strategy

I have a second vision, a second dream—that shelters will be managed and led by male staff. Domestic violence is not a woman's issue. I know of shelters in North America which are administered and supported by men. *The call for stopping violence against women should best come from men.* Men who are holding high positions in various professions, men who are leaders in the community, men who themselves have been affected by domestic violence, and men who have the courage and audacity to say "NO" to violence against women have a definite advocacy role to play.

Gender equality is not about pitting one gender against another. It is about helping all genders to break away from stereotypes and the boundaries imposed by culture, and to realize their unique potential and capacities. To support and safeguard women, we have to involve men in the process.

Concluding remarks

When I was asked to contribute a chapter to this book, I decided to do a bit of stocktaking, beginning with the inception of the first shelter in Hong Kong in 1985. We have come a long way a quarter of a century since. I am grateful to Dr Chan, who kindly gave me this opportunity to document my experience.

My last words are a tribute to the thousands of faces which I have had the privilege of meeting and knowing over the years—faces of women and children whom I have come across seeking refuge in shelters. Their immense courage and perseverance have been the veritable driving force behind all the work done in the last twenty-five years. Their stamina will continue to spur us on.

References

Adams, D. (2007). *Why Do They Kill? Men Who Murder Their Intimate Partners.* Nashville, TN: Vanderbilt University Press.

Adams, D., Cayonette, S., & Robinson, E. (2000). *Emerge Batterer Intervention Program.* Cambridge, MA: Emerge.

Alliance for the Reform of Domestic Violence Ordinance. (2007). *For Justice, Equality and Harmony: Proposal on Reform of the Domestic Violence Ordinance.* Hong Kong: The Alliance.

Chan, K. L., Chiu, M. C., & Chiu, L. S. (2005). *Peace at Home: Report on the Review of the Social and Legal Measures in the Prevention and Intervention of Domestic Violence in Hong Kong.* Hong Kong: the University of Hong Kong.

Chan, Y. C. (2005). *An Evaluation Report on Third Path Man Services: Batterers Treatment Program* (2nd ed.). Hong Kong: Harmony House.

Chiu, M. C. (2001). *Mandatory Counseling Reconstruction of Harmonic Relationship: A Plea for Mandatory Counseling for Wife Abusers.* Hong Kong: Harmony House.

Dobash, R. E., & Dobash, R. (1979). *Violence Against Wives: A Case Against the Patriarchy.* New York, NY: Free Press.

Hamberger, L. K., & Hastings, J. E. (1986). Characteristics of spouse abusers: predictors of treatment acceptance. *Journal of Interpersonal Violence, 1,* 363–373. doi: 10.1177/088626086001003008

Harmony House. (2001). *Annual Report 2000–01.* Hong Kong, China: Harmony House.

Harmony House. (2002). *Annual Report 2001–02.* Hong Kong, China: Harmony House.

Harmony House. (2002). *Harmony House Proposed Amendments to the Domestic Violence Ordinance (Cap. 189).* Legislative Council Paper No. CB(2)2539/01-02(01).

Harmony House. (2003). *Annual Report 2002–03.* Hong Kong, China: Harmony House.

Harmony House. (2004). *Annual Report 2003–04.* Hong Kong, China: Harmony House.

Harmony House. (2005). *Annual Report 2004–05.* Hong Kong, China: Harmony House.

Harmony House. (2006). *Annual Report 2005–06.* Hong Kong, China: Harmony House.

Harmony House. (2007). *Annual Report 2006–07.* Hong Kong, China: Harmony House.

Harmony House. (July 25, 2007). *Submission to the Legislative Council Welfare Panel: Prosecution of Batterers.* Hong Kong: Harmony House.

Harmony House. (2008). *Annual Report 2007–08.* Hong Kong, China: Harmony House.

Hong Kong Government. (2010). *Domestic Violence Ordinance, cap. 189.* Hong Kong, China: Hong Kong Government.

Hong Kong Council of Social Service. (2007). *Submission to the Legislative Council on Prosecution of Batterers and Handling of Domestic Violence Cases by the Law Enforcement and Social Welfare Department.* Hong Kong, China: Hong Kong Council of Social Service.

Joint Commission on Accreditation of Healthcare Organizations. *Behavioral Health Care Accreditation Program Standard CTS.02.02.05*. Retrieved from the JCAHO website: http://www.jointcommission.org/NR/rdonlyres/4DOF9019-E4E7-49FD8191-700688637BB3/0/July2010NPSGs_Scoring_BHC.pdf

Law Society of Hong Kong. (2005). *Report on Domestic Violence Ordinance*. Hong Kong, China: Law Society of Hong Kong.

Legislative Council Secretariat. (2005). *Report on the Findings of the Research on Spousal and Child Abuse*. Discussion paper number CB(2)2158/04-05(04). Hong Kong, China: Legislative Council.

Legislative Council Secretariat. (2006). *Supplementary Information on Law Enforcement Handling of Domestic Violence*. Discussion paper number CB(2)2389/05-06(01). Hong Kong, China: Legislative Council.

Legislative Council Secretariat. (2007a). *Review of the Domestic Violence Ordinance. Discussion Paper for the Legislative Council Welfare Panel*. CB(2)723/06-07(03). Hong Kong, China: Legislative Council.

Legislative Council Secretariat. (2007b). *Summary of Public Submissions on the Review of the Domestic Violence Ordinance*. Discussion paper number CB(2)330/07-08(01). Hong Kong, China: Legislative Council.

Legislative Council Brief. (2007). *Domestic Violence (Amendment) Bill 2007*. HWF/CR 1/328/01. Hong Kong, China: Legislative Council.

Ming Pao. (4 November 2005). Media report on the Hong Kong government's intention to review the Domestic Violence Ordinance. Hong Kong, China: Ming Pao.

Pence, E. (1993). *Education Groups for Men Who Batter: The Duluth Model*. New York, NY: Springer Publishing.

Review Panel on Family Services in Tin Shui Wai. (2004). *Report of Review Panel on Family Services in Tin Shui Wai*. Hong Kong, China: the Government of the Hong Kong SAR.

Seager, J. (2003). *The Penguin Atlas of Women in the World*. Middlesex, England: Penguin Books Ltd.

Shepard, M., & Pence, E. L. (1999). *Coordinating Community Response to Domestic Violence: Lessons from the Duluth and Beyond*. Thousand Oaks, CA: Sage Publications.

Social Welfare Department. (2010). *Central Information System on Battered Spouse and Sexual Violence Cases*. Hong Kong, China: Social Welfare Department.

Sullivan, P. L. (2008). *An Evaluation of the Seeds of Hope Crisis Intervention Team Project on Domestic Violence*. Hong Kong, China: Harmony House.

Tam, S. M., & Leahy, T. (Eds.) (2004). *A Bibliography of Gender Studies in Hong Kong 1998–2003*. Hong Kong, China: Gender Research Centre (CD-ROM), the Chinese University of Hong Kong.

Tam, S. M., Lee, C. K., Wong, F. Y., & Lo, K. W. (Eds.) (forthcoming). *A Bibliography of Gender Studies in Hong Kong 2004–2009*. Hong Kong, China: Gender Research Centre (CD-ROM), the Chinese University of Hong Kong.

United Nations General Assembly. (1993). *Declaration on the Elimination of Violence Against Women*. UN General Assembly resolution 48/104. Geneva, Switzerland: United Nations.

Women's Commission (2003). *Women's Commission Report*. Hong Kong, China: Woman's Commission.

Women's Commission. (2006). *Women's Safety in Hong Kong: Eliminating Domestic Violence*. Retrieved from Women's Commission website: http://www.women.gov.hk/download/report-full-version-10-jan-06.pdf

Yeung-Chan, S. (2002). 恐懼與困惑:暴力家庭兒童的真實個案故事 [Fear and confusion: real-life cases of children living with a violent family]. Hong Kong, China: Cosmos Books.

Index